BOULDERING COLORADO

More than 1,000 Premier Boulders throughout the State

Bob Horan

FALCONGUIDES ®

GUILFORD, CONNECTICUT
HELENA, MONTANA

AN IMPRINT OF THE GLOBE PEQUOT PRESS

FALCONGUIDES®

Copyright © 2008 Morris Book Publishing, LLC
Portions of this book previously published in *Best of Boulder Bouldering* in 2000 by
Falcon Publishing, Inc.

Photos by Bob Horan unless otherwise indicated
Text design by Casey Shain
Maps by Scott Lockheed © Morris Book Publishing, LLC

Library of Congress Cataloging-in-Publication Data
Horan, Bob.
  Bouldering Colorado: more than 1,000 premier boulders throughout the state/Bob
Horan.—1st ed.
    p. cm.
  ISBN 978-0-7627-3638-6
1. Rock climbing—Colorado—Guidebooks. 2. Colorado—Guidebooks. I. Title.
GV199.42.C62H67 2008
796.5'22309788—dc22

2008005975

Printed in China
10 9 8 7 6 5 4 3 2 1

WARNING:

Climbing is a sport where you may be seriously injured or die. Read this before you use this book.

This guidebook is a compilation of unverified information gathered from many different climbers. The author cannot assure the accuracy of any of the information in this book, including the topos and route descriptions, the difficulty ratings, and the protection ratings. These may be incorrect or misleading, as ratings of climbing difficulty and danger are always subjective and depend on the physical characteristics (for example, height), experience, technical ability, confidence, and physical fitness of the climber who supplied the rating. Additionally, climbers who achieve first ascents sometimes underrate the difficulty or danger of the climbing route. Therefore, be warned that you must exercise your own judgment on where a climbing route goes, its difficulty, and your ability to safely protect yourself from the risks of rock climbing. Examples of some of these risks are: falling due to technical difficulty or due to natural hazards such as holds breaking, falling rock, climbing equipment dropped by other climbers, hazards of weather and lightning, your own equipment failure, and failure or absence of fixed protection.

You should not depend on any information gleaned from this book for your personal safety; your safety depends on your own good judgment, based on experience and a realistic assessment of your climbing ability. If you have any doubt as to your ability to safely climb a route described in this book, do not attempt it.

The following are some ways to make your use of this book safer:

1. Consultation: You should consult with other climbers about the difficulty and danger of a particular climb prior to attempting it. Most local climbers are glad to give advice on routes in their area; we suggest that you contact locals to confirm ratings and safety of particular routes and to obtain firsthand information about a route chosen from this book.

2. Instruction: Most climbing areas have local climbing instructors and guides available. We recommend that you engage an instructor or guide to learn safety techniques and to become familiar with the routes and hazards of the areas described in this book. Even after you are proficient in climbing safely, occasional use of a guide is a safe way to raise your climbing standard and learn advanced techniques.

3. Fixed Protection: Some of the routes in this book may use bolts and pitons that are permanently placed in the rock. Because of variances in the manner of placement, weathering, metal fatigue, the quality of the metal used, and many other factors, these fixed protection pieces should always be considered suspect and should always be backed up by equipment that you place yourself. Never depend on a single piece of fixed protection for your safety, because you never can tell whether it will hold weight. In some cases, fixed protection may have been removed or is now missing. However, climbers should not always add new pieces of protection unless existing protection is faulty. Existing protection can be tested by an experienced climber and its strength determined. Climbers are strongly encouraged not to add bolts and drilled pitons to a route. They need to climb the route in the style of the first ascent party (or better) or choose a route within their ability—a route to which they do not have to add additional fixed anchors.

Be aware of the following specific potential hazards that could arise in using this book:

1. Incorrect Descriptions of Routes: If you climb a route and you have a doubt as to where it goes, you should not continue unless you are sure that you can go that way safely. Route descriptions and topos in this book could be inaccurate or misleading.

2. Incorrect Difficulty Rating: A route might be more difficult than the rating indicates. Do not be lulled into a false sense of security by the difficulty rating.

3. Incorrect Protection Rating: If you climb a route and you are unable to arrange adequate protection from the risk of falling through the use of fixed pitons or bolts and by placing your own protection devices, do not assume that there is adequate protection available higher just because the route protection rating indicates the route does not have an X or an R rating. Every route is potentially an X (a fall may be deadly) due to the inherent hazards of climbing—including, for example, failure or absence of fixed protection, your own equipment's failure, or improper use of climbing equipment.

There are no warranties, whether expressed or implied, that this guidebook is accurate or that the information contained in it is reliable. There are no warranties of fitness for a particular purpose or that this guide is merchantable. Your use of this book indicates your assumption of the risk that it may contain errors and is an acknowledgment of your own sole responsibility for your climbing safety.

CONTENTS

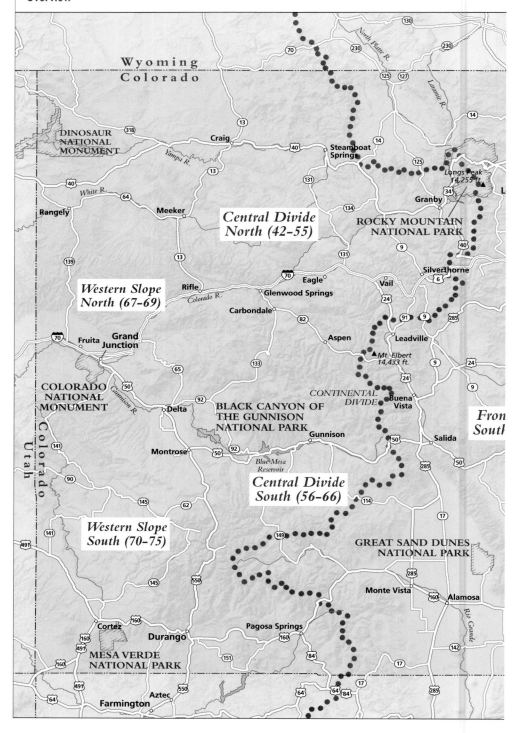

Wyoming
Colorado

DINOSAUR NATIONAL MONUMENT

Craig

Yampa R.

Steamboat Springs

North Platte R.

Laramie R.

Rangely

White R.

Meeker

Central Divide North (42–55)

Granby

ROCKY MOUNTAIN NATIONAL PARK

Longs Peak 14,255 ft.

Western Slope North (67–69)

Rifle

Eagle

Glenwood Springs

Carbondale

Colorado R.

Vail

Silverthorne

Fruita

Grand Junction

COLORADO NATIONAL MONUMENT

Delta

Gunnison R.

Aspen

Leadville

Mt. Elbert 14,433 ft.

Colorado
Utah

BLACK CANYON OF THE GUNNISON NATIONAL PARK

CONTINENTAL DIVIDE

Buena Vista

Montrose

Gunnison

Blue Mesa Reservoir

Central Divide South (56–66)

Salida

Western Slope South (70–75)

GREAT SAND DUNES NATIONAL PARK

Monte Vista

Alamosa

Rio Grande

Cortez

Durango

Pagosa Springs

MESA VERDE NATIONAL PARK

Farmington

Aztec

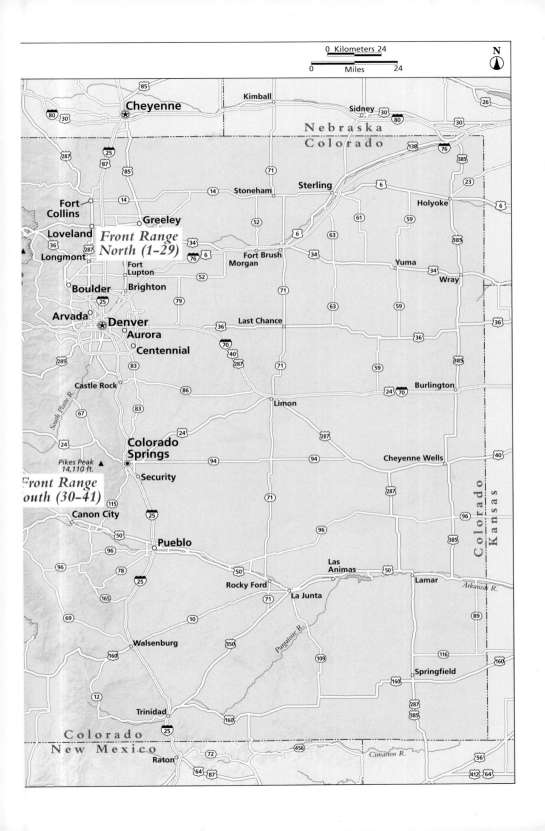

Mark Wilford bouldering at Horsetooth Reservoir.

INTRODUCTION

Bouldering is at the heart of all climbing. A boulderer must utilize gymnastic, acrobatic, and aerobatic techniques. The outcrops and boulders are the apparatuses, and each individual problem is a unique performance. Strength, dexterity, poise, grace, and balance all can be developed on the boulders. For the serious boulderer, difficulty and style are equal goals. Endurance and recovery also are greatly enhanced through bouldering, and it is on the short cliffs that the all-important mental parameters of the sport are honed.

Bouldering Colorado is a compilation of the best boulders the state of Colorado has to offer. (Of course there are other boulders that individuals have established and would classify as such—and my apologies if they have not appeared in this text.) Much of the knowledge I share in this book I gained from personal and shared experience over the last thirty years. With bouldering's growing popularity, many new problems are being established as we speak. In this book I reveal new bouldering areas for the first time.

The search for new boulders in Colorado began with the realization that there was still a lot of virgin rock that held the potential for new routes. Many fall lines on boulders that flow off the diverse Colorado terrain were, and still are, being explored. This exploration has turned into a desire to search out accessible areas for prime boulders within the magnificent Colorado landscape. In a sense, each new discovery has served as soul food, feeding the fire of the boulderer's quest. Traditionally, areas such as Horsetooth Reservoir, Carter Lake, Flagstaff Mountain, Eldorado Canyon, Castlewood Canyon, Colorado Springs, Red Cliff, Redstone, Independence Pass, Skyland of Crested Butte, Hartmann Rocks, Unaweep, Naturita, Telluride, and Durango have been the hot spots for the state's bouldering enthusiasts, and for good reason. These areas, however, are but a percentage of what Colorado has to offer. Thousands of virgin boulders exist throughout the state.

A serious boulderer's criteria, and the standard used to determine if a boulder and its routes are considered classic and able to qualify among the best in the state, are described below. Many of the problems included in this book required several visits to complete. The following standards were applied:

- The boulder must have a reasonably safe landing zone (and even if it meet this requirement, pads and spotters are recommended for all problems). With the development and use of multiple pads, landing zones that were once considered bad can be padded to create a safer, softer landing zone.
- The boulder should have moderate to difficult problems.
- The problems on the boulder should qualify as classic. Although relative, this involves solid holds and sequence. (All of the problems included in this book are considered classic.)

This book will give you all the information you need to access these natural treasures. The excellent rock quality and beauty of these boulders and their surroundings are experiences that you can enjoy and help preserve for generations to come. Colorado residents as well as visitors are fortunate to have one of the world's greatest concentrations of boulders for climbing and exploring. Variations in rock type, holds, steepness, and environment provide bouldering and training possibilities for climbers of all abilities. Good climbing and enjoy!

HOW TO USE THIS GUIDE

The bouldering areas described in this book are listed from north to south and are broken up into six main quadrants. First come the boulders of the **Front Range North,** which includes classic and new areas such as Poudre Canyon, Horsetooth Reservoir, Carter Lake, Estes Park, and Rocky Mountain National Park. The Front Range North also includes the wealth of bouldering found in the Boulder area, Clear Creek, Morrison, and Mount Evans. Second is the **Front Range South,** which includes areas such as Castlewood Canyon, Garden of the Gods, Woodland Park, Sheep Nose, Eleven Mile Canyon, and Shelf Road. Third is the bouldering of the **Central Divide North,** which includes areas such as Steamboat Springs, Frisco, Redcliff, Wolcott, Redstone, and Independence Pass. Fourth is the **Central Divide South,** which includes Buena Vista, San Luis Valley, Monte Vista, Hartman Rocks, Lost Canyon, and Skyland of Crested Butte. Fifth is the **Western Slope North,** which includes areas such as Unaweep. Finally we describe the **Western Slope South,** which includes Naturita, the awesome Long Park Road of Paradox Valley, Telluride, and Durango.

Area maps and the text describe the position of the boulders in relation to the roads, and trails are presented in an easy-to-use manner. Descriptive photos of the boulders and problems accompany the text. Almost all of the descriptive boulder photos include a climber for size scaling and perspective.

RATINGS

The V system is the core rating system used throughout this book. For problems that are "highball" (far off the ground), an (hb) will follow the rating. Those that are extremely dangerous and highball will be followed by an (xhb). On the (hb) problems a crash pad, spotter(s), or toprope are seriously recommended.

The V system rating has, without a doubt, become the universal bouldering language used by today's up-and-coming boulderers. It has broken down the range of difficulty into a useful language. Since the V system was established in the early 1990s at Hueco Tanks, Texas (soon after the first comprehensive bouldering guides such as *Colorado Front Range Bouldering* were published in the United States), many people have taken up bouldering as a favorite pastime, and the V system has become somewhat universal. To see how it compares to the classic Yosemite Decimal System and the old B system, check out the table below.

Although the V system is in vogue, in large part due to its higher numbers of comparison, boulderers must take a lighthearted approach to bouldering with each other. It is difficult to create a consistently accurate grade without an ascent consensus. Usually when a route is completed, the first person to ascend tacks on a grade based on his or her experience with the grading scale and the level at which he or she climbs within it.

This is more or less a suggested grade, and until other climbers repeat the problem and a general consensus is gathered, the original grade holds. After other people climb the route, the grade may be pushed up or down.

Exposure to a long fall is not reflected in a V grade. For the problems that are high-ball, an (hb) is given. If the problem is a highball with serious potential for danger, an (xhb) is given. Only a small percentage of the boulder problems in this book are given such ratings. Of course, injuries can happen on even the shortest boulder problems, so always be aware of your landing zone.

Some of the grades in this book are only tentative, as only a few people have climbed some of the problems. A problem may feel harder for some and easier for others, depending on one's height, arm span, leg span, and so on. Over time you should get a general feel for the grading scale and be able to make your own decisions; the grades are offered only to give you a general sense of difficulty. Keep in mind that grades can be used to classify, but they really shouldn't be taken too seriously. The heart of bouldering is in the exploration and personal challenge. The greatness of physical and mental strength is measured in its essence through compassion and vision. Do not be offended by whatever grading system a person chooses to use. As many of us have said, the best thing we can do to a rating system is not use it at all.

Have fun!

RELATIVE BOULDERING SCALES

Yosemite	V System	B System	Fontainebleau
	V0	B5.8	
	V0	B5.9	
5.10a/b	V0	B5.10	
5.10c/d	V1	B5.10+	5c
5.11a/b	V2	B1−	
5.11c/d	V3	B1	6a
5.12a	V4	B1	6b
5.12b	V5	B1+	6c
5.12c/d	V6	B2−	6c
5.13a	V7	B2	7a
5.13b	V8	B2	7b
5.13c/d	V9	B2+	7b+
5.14a	V10	B2+	7c
5.14b	V11	B2+	7c+
5.14c	V12	B2+	8a
5.14d	V13	B3	8b
5.15a	V14	B3	8b+

ACCESS

All the areas covered in this book are on public land and fall within the jurisdiction of city parks, state parks, national parks, or the federal Bureau of Land Management. All of these agencies have statutes and regulations regarding public access and activities. It is important to become familiar with these rules, because they vary somewhat from one area to the other. Some areas require an entrance fee.

Some areas described in this book have seasonal raptor closures. The closures are usually posted. It is the user's responsibility to become acquainted with each area's regulations. If there is any doubt about a given area, then find an alternative. Get updates from authorities, because the closures are sometimes lifted early. There are some areas on the Front Range that were relatively popular in the 1960s but have since become privately owned. As time goes on, areas may change and regulations may go into effect, and access may be halted all together or limited. Hopefully the areas in this book will forever remain public domain. In the meantime respect the environment and enjoy your access to it.

The areas in this book were set aside for the preservation and enjoyment of the natural environment. Already these areas are feeling the effects of their ever-growing popularity. As responsible outdoor participants, it is our duty to help preserve these beautiful areas by removing litter and staying on the trails or footpaths as much as possible. Many of the bouldering areas described in this book are used and treasured by a diverse public, most of whom do not boulder. Have some consideration and lend a helping hand by keeping these places at least as nice as you found them.

WEATHER

The weather in Colorado is good for the majority of the year, although the areas at higher alpine levels are usually completely covered in snow during winter and spring. Since most bouldering takes place at a fairly low elevation, as long as the sun is shining, the conditions are usually moderate enough for a good bouldering session. If it snows, just wait a few days. When the sun reappears, it is sure to dry the rocks. Colorado winters usually host at least one short period of extended cold or rain, which occurs in late winter to early spring. The fall and spring normally have the best bouldering weather, although on a nice winter day in Colorado, conditions could not be better.

SAFETY

Pulled tendons and twisted ankles are the most common injuries that result from bouldering. Concentrating on safety is the key to a long life of injury-free and fun bouldering.

Avoiding injury is very simple. If you feel there is any chance that you may hurt yourself if you fall, use a rope that is securely anchored. In addition, warm up and progress slowly to help prevent injury to the joints, tendons, and muscles.

Bouldering with a partner offers the reassurance of a good spot and provides incentive to push each other. The spotter should stand behind the boulderer and be prepared for a possible slip or miss. The role of the spotter is not to catch the falling climber; instead it is to properly realign the feet of the climber with the landing zone, perhaps also in some small way allowing a gentler landing. The spotter should pay particular attention to protecting the falling climber's head. When working together properly, a spotter and boulderer take off a little bit of the psychological edge.

EQUIPMENT

One of the true pleasures of bouldering is the simplicity of gear needed. A pair of shoes and a chalk bag are usually enough to please most boulderers. At times a toprope may be used for those problems that are too highball to be safe. Today many boulderers carry a crash pad along with them. This lightweight, backpacked unit is a good thing to have and will ultimately help prevent injury.

Legend

Interstate Highway	
Paved Road (major)	
Paved Road (minor)	
Unpaved Road	
Tunnel	
Trail	
Railroad	
Railroad Tunnel	
Forest/Park Boundary	
Gate	
River/Creek	
Lake	
Buildling	■ or □
Parking	Ⓟ
Steps	
Tension Wire	
Interstate Highway	70
U.S. Highway	6 287
State/County Roads	31 119
Forest Service Road	300
Bridge	
Picnic Area	
Campground	
Peak/Elevation	x
Crag/Boulder	
Cliff	cliff face
Talus	
Mine Site	
Tree	
Compass	N

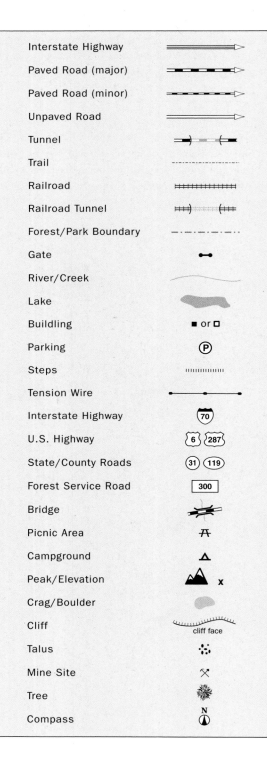

Hank Caylor on the second ascent of *Skyeye Arête Block* (V4), Eldorado West.

Fort Collins Area Overview

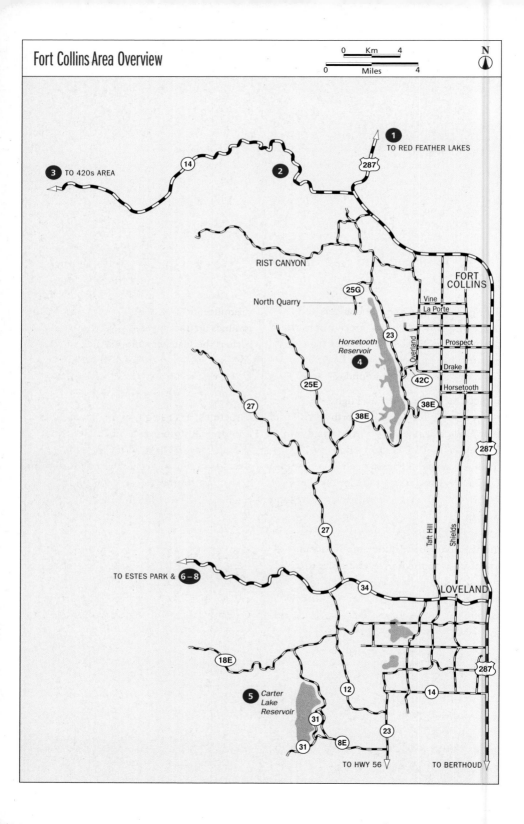

0   Km   4
0   Miles   4

N

3 TO 420s AREA

14

2

1 TO RED FEATHER LAKES
287

RIST CANYON

North Quarry

25G

FORT COLLINS

Vine
La Porte

Overland

23

Prospect

Horsetooth Reservoir
4

Drake

42C

Horsetooth

25E

27

38E

38E

287

Taft Hill

Shields

TO ESTES PARK & 6–8

34

LOVELAND

27

18E

12

14

5 Carter Lake Reservoir

31

287

31   8E   23

TO HWY 56   TO BERTHOUD

FORT COLLINS AREA

1 RED FEATHER LAKES

This granite area has many boulders and blocks throughout the evergreen forests that surround Red Feather Lakes. Most bouldering areas lie to the west of the lakes. Camping can be found around the lakes.

Directions: Head north on Highway 287 along the foothills from the northwest end of Fort Collins. Follow 287 north toward Laramie, Wyoming. Go past Highway 14 (Poudre Canyon) approximately 10 miles to Livermore. Head west onto County Road 74E (Red Feather Lakes Road) and take this west for about 20 miles to Red Feather Lakes. For the Boy Scout Area, turn right (north) onto Boy Scout Camp Road and follow this for approximately 3.2 miles to a right turn through the forest access to a point where you cannot drive any farther. Continue west on foot to the bouldering on the left.

2 POUDRE CANYON

There are more than 40 miles of boulders and blocks to explore along the Poudre River and its slopes. The Poudre River Canyon is a peaceful, scenic bouldering experience, and a refreshing river adds to its magnificence. Plenty of Forest Service campgrounds are located along the road. Areas such as the Hatchery Blocks, the Pull Out Area, and the Bog are reached before the popular 420s Area (see next section), and they are well worth a visit.

Directions: Take Highway 287 north along the foothills from Fort Collins. Head west onto Highway 14 (Poudre Canyon Road). Mileage to the select number of areas begins at the junction of Highway 287 and Highway 14. The bulk of the bouldering is found 35 miles west from Highway 287.

Gateway Mountain Park

From the intersection of Highway 14 and Highway 287, head west for 5.2 miles to Gateway Mountain Park. A parking fee is required.

Poudre Canyon/Red Feather Lakes/The 420s Area

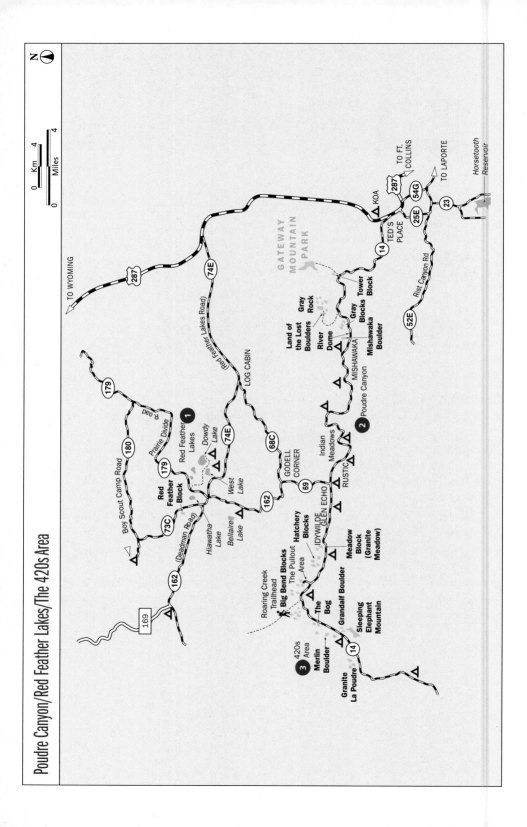

Tower Block ▲

From the parking lot, head south up the gravel road. This gray and black streaked block can be seen on the south side of the faint road. Four excellent problems are found on its north face.

1. The Bump V4 Climb up the left side via the arête and hand holds.

2. Thick Streak V4 Climb up the thicker black streak on the left.

3. The Streaker V5 Climb up the thinner black streak on the right.

4. Right Away V3 Climb up the right side of the block via the arête.

Lower Canyon

The following areas are spread out as you continue up the canyon west from Gateway Mountain Park.

Mishawaka Block

This nice block is approximately 13.5 miles from the junction of Highway 14 and Highway 287, down the road to the east of the old Mishawaka Inn and across the river to the north.

Granite Meadow

Approximately 36.2 miles from the junction of Highway 14 and Highway 287, these small granite warm-up blocks can be seen on the north side of the road.

Meadow Block ▲

This is the obvious granite block with a sheer west face.

1. Periodical V1 Climb up the center of the west face.

Hatchery Blocks

From the town of Rustic, drive approximately 7 miles farther west on Highway 14 (approximately 37.2 miles from the junction of Highway 14 and Highway 287). You will see these blocks on the north side of the road. These quality blocks are a mile east of the Roaring Creek trailhead, which is the starting point for the 420s bouldering area.

Bass Block ▲

This warm-up block is the first of the nice blocks that you will see in this area.

1. Bait V1 Climb up the center of the south face.

Hatchery Block ▼

This is the most intriguing and largest block in this area. Several problems have been done with many variations.

1. John's Face V3 Climb the southeast arête of the east wall.

2. Scott's Wall V5 Climb up the white crystals in the middle of the east face.

3. Warmer V1 Climb the right side.

4. Jug Ahoy V3 Climb up the large holds on the northeast arête.

5. Northern Classic V3 Climb good edges straight for the top.

6. Chris's Face V4 Climb the slopers left of the dihedral.

The Pull Out Area

This area is located another 0.8 mile up and west of the Hatchery Blocks, just before the Roaring Creek trailhead. In the distance you can see a dirt road on the right (north) side of the road with approximately five small granite blocks at its end. Park off road or take the dirt road to a parking area close to the first boulder in the trees. You will find good warm ups with problems ranging from V0 to V4.

Graytan Boulder ◄

You can see this gray and tan boulder just west of the end of the dirt road parking area. It is a great yet steep warm-up boulder.

1. Gray and Tan V0 Climb up the center of the south face.

Smashing Pumpkins Boulder ▼

This granite dud is found to the south of Graytan Boulder, about 50 feet to the south. Its back (west) side is surrounded by trees.

1. TP V0 Climb up the slightly left-leaning crack in the slab.

2. Shaving Cream V1 Climb the slab between the leaning crack and the prow.

3. Pumpkin Puss V4 Climb up the thin face, to the right of the round prow, left of the tree.

3 THE 420S AREA

See map on page 10.

This area has become infamous over the past few years due in large part to the push of very difficult bouldering lines by some of the most recent state-of-the-art boulderers. The area is approximately 40 miles west from the intersection of Highway 287 and Highway 14 (Ted's Place).

To get to the area, drive approximately 0.5 mile past the Roaring Creek trailhead (16 miles past Pingree Park Road) and park. Hike down the jeep trail for approximately ten minutes, until you reach the boulders. The first significant boulder is Hank's Boulder. It sits alone within the camp circle, next to a large gnarled pine tree. It is named for the infamous Tom Henry, a transient boulderer, like many of us, who has seen and climbed with the greats and at this moment (reflecting on the boulder) is immortalized as one of the greats himself.

Hank's Boulder ▼

Hank's Boulder is the first obvious lone boulder you encounter as you approach the rest of the boulders that lie slightly upslope to the west and north. Hank's Boulder sits in a camp circle up the road. You can access the rest of the boulders within reach of this land-mark boulder. Five problems have been done on this classic boulder.

1. Hanky Panky V9 Climb the arête on the left side of boulder's east face.

2. Natural Tattoo V8 Sit start, then climb up the right of the arête to sloper lip and right. Also known as *Scarface.*

3. Gnarled Oak V11 Climb up the blackened face with rail between *Natural Tatoo* and *Hank's Arête.*

4. Hank's Arête V4 Climb the arête to the right of *Gnarled Oak,* left of the lunge problem.

5. Hank's Lunge V5 Climb up the middle of north face utilizing side pull to the top.

Sandstoner Block ▲

To find this block hike upslope to the north-east. It is the first block you see upslope from Hank's Boulder.

1. Mind Set V8 Climb up the right arête of the west face.

2. Granite Sand V4 Climb the middle of the west face.

3. Wewillywinkle V4 Climb up the left arête of the west face.

Johnny and Hodgey Boulder ▶

From Hank's Boulder take a faint trail to the west, over the stream to the main 420s Area. This is the first boulder on your left after you cross the stream. It is shaped like a tooth and offers cool problems.

1. Johnny and Hodgey Arête V5 Climb the arête on left side of the east face.

Balance Boulder
(west face)

Chunky Boulder

This boulder is upslope and up the creek from the Johnny and Hodgey Boulder.

1. Southwest Arête V2 (hb) Sit start to the southwest arête of the boulder.

2. Chunky V5 Climb up small edges from the middle of the face.

Balance Boulder

This boulder is in the center of the 420s Area. Puffing Stone Boulder is adjacent to it. It has four good problems.

1. Can Opener V9 Climb steep-leaning corner out left.

2. Chubby Demon V6 Climb the southwest arête right of *Can Opener*.

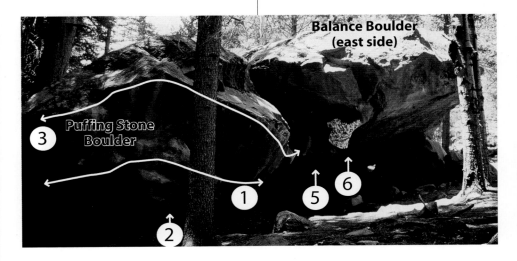

Balance Boulder
(east side)

Puffing Stone
Boulder

3. Bottle Opener V10 Climb up and to the right of *Chubby Demon*.

4. Cork V11 Climb up the steep face via dynos.

5. Circadian Rhythm V13 Climb to the right of the rock bowl, up the supersteep face using underclings to the slopers.

6. Its Ice V4 Climb the face to the right of *Circadian Rhythm* to the mantle shelf.

7. Stickman V4 Climb the north face, out of the cave via crimps and heel hooks.

8. Hickman Over Poudre Bridge V? Climb the north face to the left of *Stickman,* up and left utilizing slopers and crimpers.

Puffing Stone Boulder

This is the shorter boulder adjacent to Balance Boulder in the heart of the 420s Area. It has a sloper rail and a bowl-dish feature on its east face. See photo on page 17.

1. Puffing Stone Traverse V6 Traverse the east face of the boulder.

2. Puffing Stone Direct V2–V3 Sit start on east face to the top.

3. Fast V8 Traverse from *Circadian Rhythm* along the lip to *Puffing Stone Traverse*.

Toads Block ▼

Toads Block is south of Puffing Stone Boulder and Balance Boulder. It is characterized by some easy warm ups, with the down climb on the west side. There are several good problems to warm up on.

1. Tsunami V7–V8 Climb left of *The Perch* arête, up and right across the wavy face.

2.The Perch V6 Climb the arête.

3.The Warm Up V? Climb from the right of the northeast corner, starting down low, right of *The Perch,* and up and out the north overhang.

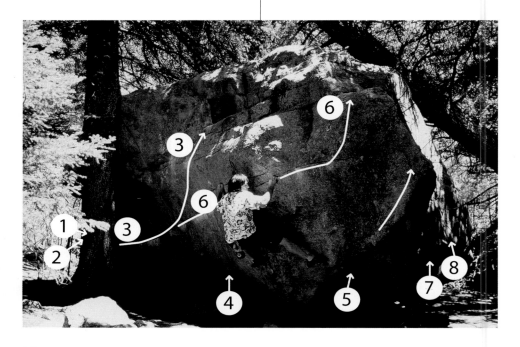

4. North Face V1 Climb up just right of the center of the face.

5. Northwest Arête V2 Climb the sheer northwest arête of the boulder.

6. Bisher Traverse V7–V8 Traverse across the seam on the face, left to right with a dynamic finish.

7. Southwest Face V3–V4 Climb up the southwest face starting with an undercling.

8. Southwest Mantle V? Climb the scooped face with a mantle.

Granite La Poudre Area

This area is located approximately 44.5 miles west of the junction of Highways 14 and 287. The blocks and boulders here are just upslope on the north side of the road. There is a house just east of Blunk's Block and close to Yard Boulder. Be cautious, courteous, and low key. A parking circle is found just below the fall line.

Blunk's Block ▼

1. The Classic V1 Climb up the shelved overhang on the southwest corner.

Yard Boulder ▲

This beautiful boulder is located to the east, below and in the meadow, from Blunk's Block. It borders a house fence line, so be courteous.

1. Longest Yard V3 Climb up just right of the center of the west face.

4 HORSETOOTH RESERVOIR

Thanks to the tectonic uplift that helped scatter the many Dakota sandstone blocks and boulders that lie on the slopes above Horsetooth Reservoir, this is truly a site to behold. Distinctive Dakota sandstone can be found from one end of the reservoir to the other. The blocks and boulders are then capped off with beautiful outcrops and mini-cliffs full of face, crack, and traverse problems. This area was John Gill and friends' outdoor gym, and many world-renowned problems were established here during that time. Since then boulders and climbers alike have traveled from all corners of the globe to set themselves on the many challenges this area has to offer. Such Gill legacies as *Right Eliminator* and *Left Eliminator,* Mental Block's *Pinch Overhang,* the *Torture Chamber* outcrop traverse, to name a few, are a must. Other routes such as Holloway's Meathook on Eliminator, or a variety of Steve Mammen, Mark Wilford, and Scott Blunk problems have continued the Horsetooth standard and tradition of difficulty on the boulders. Today many extreme boulderers have put up a variety of new variations and problems, such as *Moon Arête* at Rotary Park. The abundance and quality of rock and atmosphere make this a bouldering paradise for climbers of all abilities.

Directions: In Fort Collins locate College Avenue/Highway 287, which runs north-south through the center of town. Locate Drake Road, south of the center of town, and head west toward the foothills. There are two roads that will lead you to County Road 23, the reservoir's main road. One way is County Road 42C, which takes you to a more central location. The other is County Road 38E, which leads you to the south side of the reservoir. To reach CR 42C, follow Drake Road west to Overland Trail and go right for a short distance to a left on CR 42C. This will end at the main reservoir road, CR 23. To reach Torture Chamber, Duncan's Ridge, and Piano Boulder, you'll want to go toward the south end of the reservoir by heading left (south) on CR 23. To reach areas such as Rotary Park, the Scoop, Land of the Overhangs, and the North Quarry, head right (north) at the intersection of CR 42C and CR 23. To reach CR 38E, follow Drake Road west to a left on Taft Hill Road to a right on CR 38E. This will lead you to the Torture Chamber outcrop, where CR 38E intersects with CR 23.

Torture Chamber

Torture Chamber (V4) is an extensive traverse that follows the bucketed lip of the diagonal-ing, upper west end of this Dakota sandstone outcrop. This well-known Gill traverse is used as a natural apparatus to strengthen bouldering skills and endurance. Other infamous routes such as *Borgman's Bulge* (V5) and *Nemesis* (V6–V7) can be found by walking downslope to the lower east end of the outcrop. Many other classic (mostly toprope) problems consist of roofs, faces, and cracks and are well worthwhile.

Directions: From the intersection of Taft Hill Road and CR 38E, drive approximately 1.8 miles to a point where you meet CR 23. Park in the pull off on the right (east) side of the road. The top of Torture Chamber Ridge borders the east end of the pull off. Walk

Horsetooth Reservoir

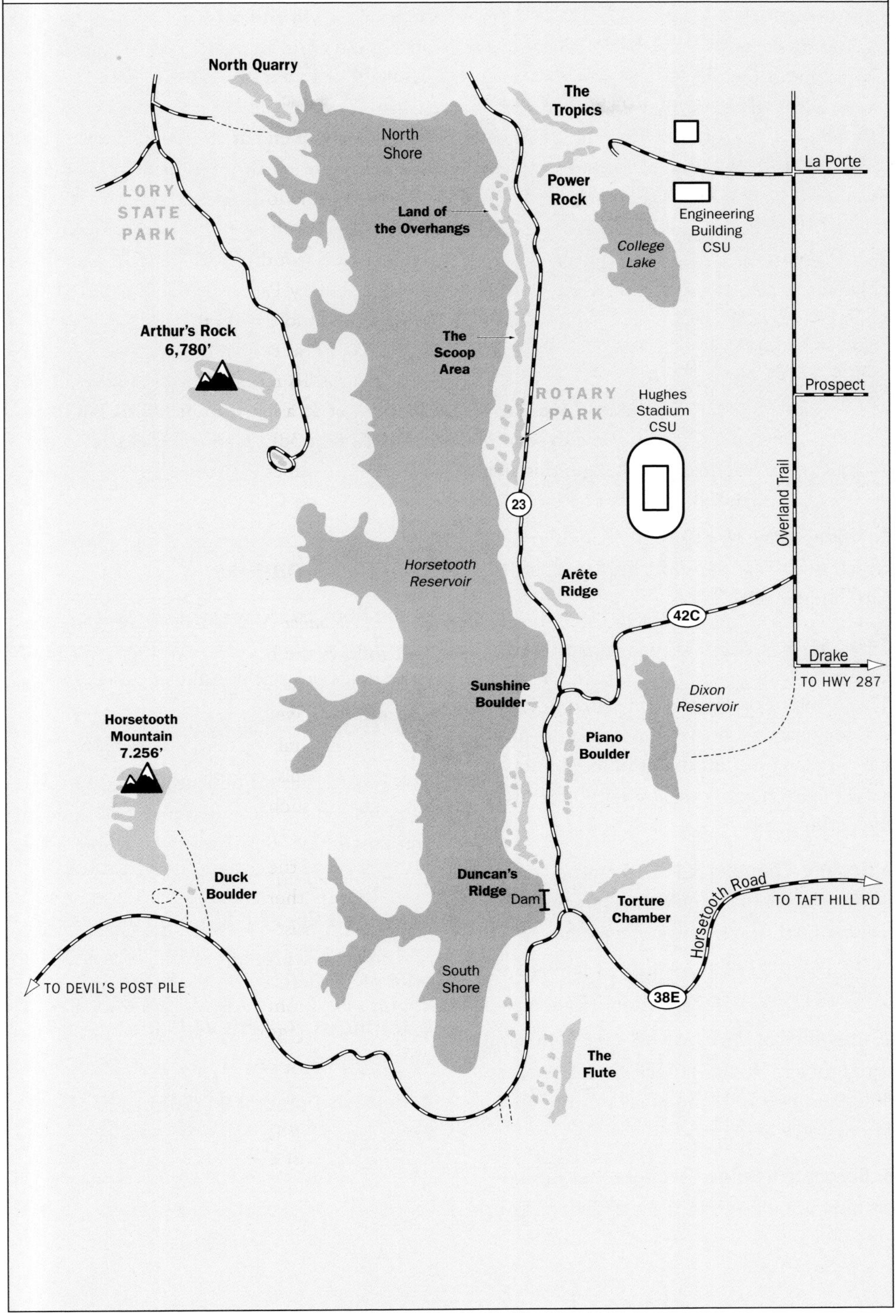

N
North Quarry
The Tropics
North Shore
La Porte
Lory State Park
Power Rock
Land of the Overhangs
Engineering Building CSU
College Lake
Arthur's Rock 6,780'
The Scoop Area
Rotary Park
Hughes Stadium CSU
Prospect
23
Overland Trail
Horsetooth Reservoir
Arête Ridge
42C
Drake
To Hwy 287
Sunshine Boulder
Dixon Reservoir
Horsetooth Mountain 7.256'
Piano Boulder
Duck Boulder
Duncan's Ridge
Dam
Torture Chamber
Horsetooth Road
To Taft Hill Rd
To Devil's Post Pile
South Shore
38E
The Flute

down the ridge to begin the lengthy traverse, which finishes at the short head wall at the parking pull off.

Torture Chamber Traverse

This is the upper part of the outcrop. There is somewhat of a bucket rail lining the lip of the overhang just off the ground. The traverse begins downslope about 100 feet from the parking area.

1. Torture Chamber V4 By the time you finish this endurance problem, your arms may feel tortured. Traverse upslope to the tail end of the parking pull off, finishing with a short head wall.

2. Chamber of Variation V8 This is an eliminate problem that avoids all the big bucket holds and uses only the smaller crimpers throughout the traverse.

3. Borgman's Bulge V5 Climb out of the prominent bulge arête right of the cracks in the corner. Located left of *Torture Chamber's* east-most starting point.

4. Big Roof V0 Downslope you will see a large roof sticking out of the trees. Climb the large holds out of the right side of the roof.

Nemesis Tower

You can see this prominent block is broken away from the main outcrop several hundred feet downslope from Torture Chamber. There are several toprope routes on Nemesis Tower.

1. Nemesis V6–V7 (TR) Climb the scooped face using small crimps, then climb up the arête on the left.

2. Northeast Nemesis V4 (TR) Climb up the northeast face.

3. Nemesis Dihedral V4 (TR) Climb the thin finger crack left of *Northeast Nemesis.*

Horsetooth Mountain

These soft sandstone boulders are found on the south meadows of Horsetooth Mountain. Drive around the south shore to the west and you will find a sandy road that leads off to the north.

Duck Boulder ▲

This duck–shaped boulder has a nice sandy landing below its challenging south face.

1. The Duck V4 Climb up the neck on the left side of the south face.

Mantle Block

This protruding piece of sandstone offers challenging mantle problems.

1. Willie's Mantle V4 Climb up and mantle the center of the north side.

Duncan's Ridge

Beach Area

Horsetooth Reservoir

To Road

Duncan's Ridge

This extensive outcrop arises from the north-west side of Spring Canyon Dam and continues to the north. The main blocks are just offshore on the far-south end of the outcrop just below the road. A number of great Gill problems are established. The northwestern uprising offers many toprope problems.

Directions: Drive another 0.4 mile from Torture Chamber to reach this block-laden outcrop. From the intersection of CR 38E and CR 23, head across the top of the dam to the north side and park. Walk downslope toward the waterfront to the classic blocks that you will see down and to the west.

Beach Area

These cubicles of rock arise just off the beach on the far-south end of Duncan's Ridge. They are the first and most classic of the extensive outcrop.

1. Thin Crack V5 (TR) Climb the obvious thin crack line at the far-south end of Duncan's Ridge.

2. Leaning Cling V4 Left of *Thin Crack* and down below on a prominent block bordering the beach level, climb the steep mini-corner to the undercling with a lengthy reach up top.

3. Layaway V5 Left of the *Leaning Cling* block is another intriguing wall block with a pocket halfway up its south face. Grab for a layback hold and reach to a good edge.

4. Regular Line V1 Where this section begins to head to the north, climb the small crack to a roof.

5. Direct Bulge V5 Climb *Regular Line* with a direct start.

Piano Area

From Duncan's Ridge parking area, drive farther north for approximately 0.2 mile and park. Upslope on the east side of the road is a spiny ridge of rock. You will see a prominent round-shaped boulder known as Piano Boulder detached from the ridge above.

Piano Boulder ▼

A crack around its top upper quarter characterizes Piano Boulder.

1. Piano Traverse V5 Traverse along the crack utilizing heel hooks, hand jams, and small crimpers. You can also do other straight-up problems.

Bulbous Boulder

This short boulder can be found just below Piano Boulder.

1. Low Traverse V5 Traverse right to left on the rounded holds.

Bootie Block

Hike about 40 feet farther south from Piano Boulder, to a ridge block with a slab and a crack splitting its west face.

1. Bootie V1 Climb the slab just left of the crack utilizing good edges.

Arrow Boulder

You will discover this short boulder another 75 feet farther south along the ridge. It is characterized by a Gill arrow. The arrow was painted on in the 1960s to mark the line.

1. Arrow Up V5 Climb to the top crimping the small edges. This is a one- or two-move problem.

Sunshine Boulder ▼

From Piano Boulder continue north another 0.6 mile. Sunshine Boulder is located downslope to the northwest from the road. This large single boulder block sits below the Marina Ridge. Many great problems can be done on its north face.

1. The Horn V0 Climb the southwest corner utilizing the horn.

2. Muscle Cling V5 Start with the undercling and reach up to small edges.

3. Standard Route V3–V4 Traverse the upper-diagonal ledge system from far right to far left.

4. Sunshine Traverse V4 Traverse from far lower left around right to the south face.

5. Lower Sunshine V7 Traverse from left to right utilizing small crimps.

Rotary Park

Whenever Horsetooth Reservoir boulders are mentioned, most people think of this world-renowned area. The boulders, blocks, and outcrops at Rotary Park offer some of the reservoir's best problems. Most of the John Gill classics such as *Pinch Overhang* and the *Eliminator* routes were done in the 1960s.

Rotary Park

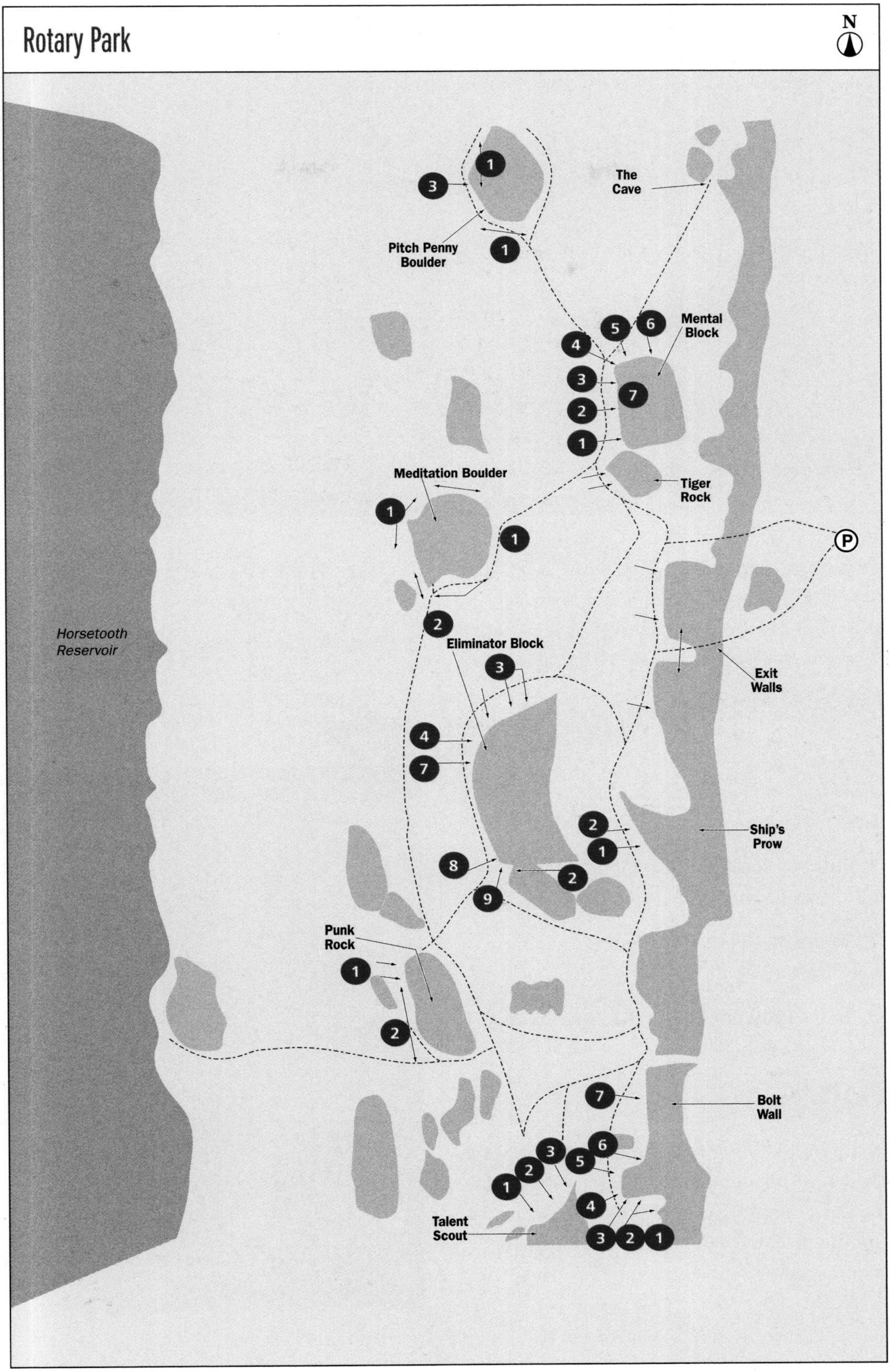

N

Horsetooth
Reservoir

Pitch Penny Boulder

3   1

1

The Cave

4   5   6   **Mental Block**

3

2   7

1

Meditation Boulder

1

1

Tiger Rock

2

Eliminator Block

3

4

7

Exit Walls

2

1

8

2

Ship's Prow

9

Punk Rock

1

2

7   **Bolt Wall**

6

3   5

2   3   4

1

3   2   1

Talent Scout

P

The Cave · Mental Block · Rotary Park · Ship's Prow · Bolt Wall · Meditation Boulder · Eliminator Block · Punk Rock · Talent Scout · To Pitch Penny Boulder

Directions: From the junction of CR 23 and CR 42C, continue north for approximately 1.3 miles to a large parking facility. Walk down to the west through a break in the ridge.

Ship's Prow

Walk south below the ridge to a pointy arête with a prominent southwest-facing jagged crack.

1. Curving Crack V0 (hb) Climb the crack on the southwest face.

2. Southwest Face V4 Climb the thin face left of the crack.

3. Ship's Prow V1 Climb the arête through the prow on the left.

Bolt Wall

From Ship's Prow head south below the ridge to a steep section that has a right-facing dihedral crack in it. Two old bolt holes characterize this wall and can be seen up on the face. Excellent face problems exist here. Many are highball.

1. Classic Flake V0 Climb the flake on the far-right side of the wall.

2. Corner Cling V0 Climb the corner system left of *Classic Flake*.

Ship's Prow · Bolt Wall

3. Cat's Eye V3 (hb) Climb up the middle of the face utilizing small edges.

4. West Bulge V0 Climb up the bulged face around the corner and to the left of *Cat's Eye*.

5. Finger Fighter V1 Climb the pin-scarred finger crack using face holds.

6. Another Mammen Traverse V7 From the crack, traverse left across the face.

7. Standard Faces V0–V2 (hb) Climb a variety of highball faces left of the crack.

Talent Scout ▼

From Bolt Wall head down a trail to the southwest. This small block has a distinctive slabby northwest face.

1. Standard Talent V1 Climb the steep slab on the right side of the northwest face.

2. Talent Scout Roof V6 Climb up the middle of the face.

3. Power Glide V7 Climb up the left side of the northwest face avoiding the left arête.

4. Left Arête V0 Climb up the arête on the left side.

Punk Rock

From Talent Scout head down a trail to the northwest. Punk Rock was unearthed in the 1980s and has since become a classic.

1. Punk Rock Traverse V5 Traverse the west face from left to right.

2. Kelly's Traverse V8 Traverse the west face from right to left, staying close to the ground.

Eliminator Block

This large rectangular-shaped block is located up to the northeast of Punk Rock, or just below Ship's Prow at the ridgetop. Classic problems abound.

1. Cave Crack V3 Climb the crack on the south face of the block. This route is located in a cove formed where the Eliminator's south side leans up against another block.

2. Mammen Traverse V9 Traverse from the far left across the edge system on the south face to a dyno finish and mantle on the far right.

3. North Slabs V0–V1 Climb a variety of slab routes on the north face.

4. Arête Crack V2 (hb) On the far-left side of the west face is a wide crack that diagonals up to the right.

5. Meathook V10 Climb directly up to the wide crack via small crimpy underclings.

6. Cheathook V8 Step in from the block onto clings then up.

7. Left Eliminator V4 (hb) This Gill problem ascends the left side of the west face right of Meathook, gaining the wide crack above with a crank from a small right-hand

edge and a long reach for the left hand to the shelf.

8. Right Eliminator V4 Another classic Gill problem on the far-right side of the west face. Crank up on two small crimps and reach for a good finger jug.

9. The Prow V4 Climb the classic arête right of *Right Eliminator*.

10. Moon's Arête V9 Climb the right wall from the arête up the south face via slopers and crimps.

Meditation Boulder

This isolated flat-topped boulder is located downslope and to the northwest of Eliminator Block.

1. Meditation Traverse V2 Traverse around the whole boulder.

2. Meditation Roof V2 Climb through the roof on the south face.

3. Meditation Low V4 Traverse down low across the boulder.

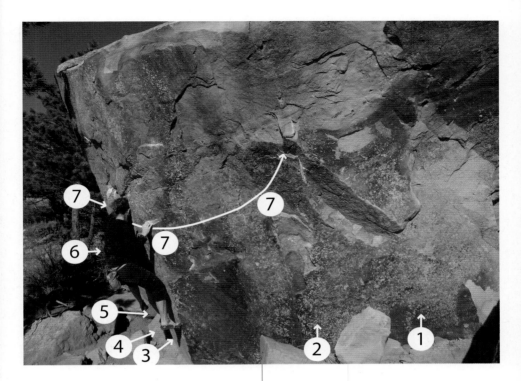

Mental Block ▲

The natural dimensions of this overhanging test block make this an extreme boulderer's delight. Many very strenuous and tenuous problems such as *Pinch Overhang* are found on its west and north faces.

1. Layback Overhang V3 Climb up and mantle the far-right side of the west face via a short foot-long corner.

2. Pinch Overhang V5 Pinch the four-by-four pinch hold with your right, slap for the sloping top, match the mantle.

3. Standard Route V4 Climb the overhanging northwest corner left of *Pinch Overhang* via secure edges to the top.

4. Corner Lock V4 Left of *Standard Route,* reach for the finger lock in the little corner and then reach for the top.

5. Willie's Lunge V3 Dyno off the two good holds for the top just left of *Corner Lock.*

6. North Roof V4 Start below the small roof, crank up left, then finish up the arête.

7. Mental Block Traverse V9 Traverse from the left side of the north face around to the right and finish up *Pinch Overhang.*

Pitch Penny Boulder ▲

This boulder is located downslope to the northwest from Mental Block.

1. Penny Traverse V3 Traverse the west face.

2. Silver Dollar V7 Traverse the west face utilizing the lower holds.

3. Southwest Dyno V1 On the left side of the southwest face, grab good holds and fire up for the top.

4. Southwest Traverse V3 From *Southwest Dyno*, traverse to the right.

The Tropics

This lengthy south-facing outcrop is located just east of Soldier Canyon Dam. It is best accessed by driving from the east, taking Overland Road to LaPorte Avenue and then heading west, past the CSU engineering research buildings, to its end. You will see the uplifting eastern slopes of the Tropics just below Soldier Canyon Dam. This is a great winter area for outdoor bouldering. It holds a large number of boulder challenges all along its outcrop.

1. Paradise Roof V1 Climb the large holds to the top of the lower roofed section of the outcrop.

2. Paradise Traverse V0 Traverse from far right to a resting corner.

3. The Steep V2 Climb the overhang up from the *Paradise Traverse* roof.

4. AAA V4 Utilize the arête across when traversing.

5. Mantle V1 Climb the mantle shelf in the bulge left of AAA.

6. Pocket Crank V2 Climb the finger pockets without the jugs.

7. Edgemeister V0 Climb the face to the right of *Pocket Crank*.

8. Arête V3 Climb the jug below the crack to the arête, then climb the crack.

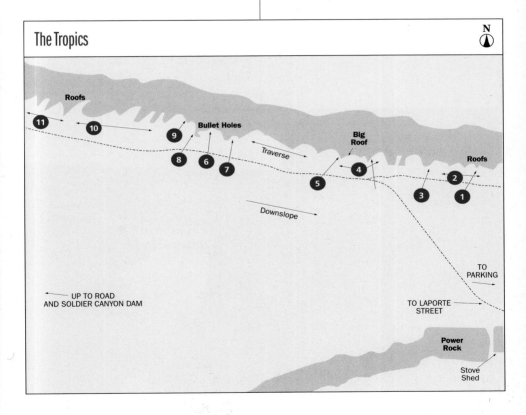

9. Gumby Roof V6 Left of *Arête* climb the slab.

10. Mega Traverse V7 Traverse the lip of the overhang approximately 120 feet upslope from arêtes.

11. Upper Traverse V3 Upslope from *Mega Traverse* is another traverse that utilizes unique holds and edges and finishes at the whitened face.

Power Rock

Across from the Tropics outcrop, at the very lower southeast ridge of the dam, there is a north-facing overhanging section of outcrop that is hidden behind the brush.

1. Circular Traverse V4 Traverse on good holds up and around for a great training pump.

North Quarry

The red square-cut sandstone walls of this area offer fun face routes that are well-worthwhile. Park on the west side of Horsetooth Dam and walk´ west along the northern shores of the reservoir until you reach the quarry. You can also drive farther north past the dam and follow the signs to Lory State Park. There is a good trail just before the parks entrance station. Walk east through the obvious gully; continue past a stabled house to the quarry.

1. Cinch V7 Located on the far-northeast section of the wall, this problem is left of a hanging cable. Mantle and lunge to a sloping hold, then grab and surmount the dihedral.

2. Physical Graffiti V6 (hb) Left of *Cinch* is a shallow corner. Climb this to the break.

3. Little Arête V1 Climb arête to the top break.

4. Leaning Dihedral V2 Climb the arête around the corner from *Little Arête.*

5. Desert Crack V3 Climb the crack to the break.

6. Magazine Face V4 (hb) Climb the sheer face on the south facing wall around the corner to the left of *Desert Crack.*

7. Magazine Arête V3 Climb the arête to the left.

8. Motion Picture Slab V3 Climb the thin slab on the short block 25 feet up left from *Magazine Face.*

9. Arête Motion V0 Climb the arête on the left side of the block.

10. Drill Markers V? Climb the drill groove left of *Motion Picture Slab.*

11. Sunshine Face V2 Climb the sheer face 20 feet left of *Motion Picture Slab.*

5 CARTER LAKE

The slopes and ridges that surround the Carter Lake reservoir offer a classic bouldering area with a wide variety of problems. The area is characterized by a mile stretch of sandstone outcroppings with boulders and blocks scattered below. A magnificent view of the east face of Long's Peak and the shimmering shoreline makes this a beautiful place for bouldering. Famous problems such as *Kahuna Roof* and *Super Chief* are found on the north end of this vast area. The other area, Biglandia, is in the northeast portion of the reservoir area and is characterized by east-facing, overhanging miniature Flatiron-like formations. Landings here are good.

Directions: Carter Lake is located west of the town of Berthoud just beyond the first tectonic wave, or foothill uplift. Locate Berthoud and Highway 287. Head due west on Highway 287/56. At a point where the road curves to the south, continue straight (west) on Highway 56. Soon it will curve once again to form another road, this time to the north on CR 23. Follow the road a short way to a left onto CR 8E. The CARTER LAKE sign points in the direction. Take CR 8E west to the entrance station. Follow the road up from the entrance station for 0.5 mile, where the road splits and becomes County Road 31. For the South Dam and Middle Dam Areas, head south (left) at the split and follow CR 31 around to the large parking lot on the right side of the road. The boulders and trail are visible from the lot. For the North Dam Area and Biglandia, as well as an alternative to the Middle Dam Area, take the split from CR 8E to the right (north) onto CR 31 and follow the road. Park on the south side of the dam, which is the right side of the road. The Fawn Hollow Trail is located across the road to the west. Follow the trail

Carter Lake

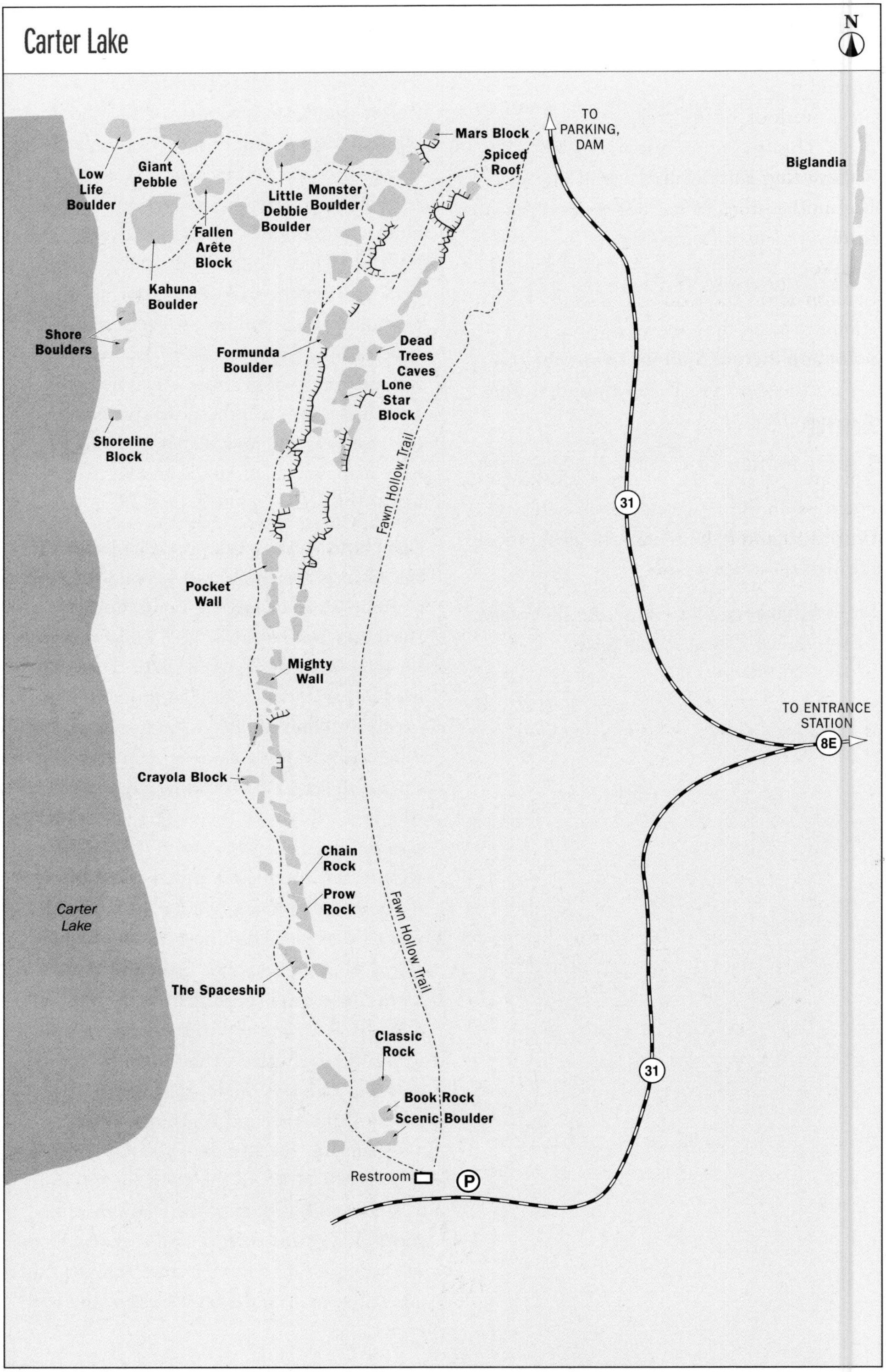

N

Biglandia

TO PARKING, DAM

Mars Block
Spiced Roof

Low Life Boulder

Giant Pebble

Little Debbie Boulder

Monster Boulder

Fallen Arête Block

Kahuna Boulder

Shore Boulders

Formunda Boulder

Dead Trees Caves

Lone Star Block

Shoreline Block

Pocket Wall

Mighty Wall

Crayola Block

Chain Rock

Prow Rock

The Spaceship

Classic Rock

Book Rock

Scenic Boulder

Restroom

P

Carter Lake

Fawn Hollow Trail

31

TO ENTRANCE STATION

8E

31

to the south for approximately 200 yards and cut out to the ridgetop. Descend down easy ground to the boulders trail. You will see a great overlook of the rocks at the ridge break. This is the quickest approach for *Kahuna Roof* and its surrounding blocks. For Biglandia, continue up the road for approximately 1.2 miles to the Carter Knolls picnic area. You can see the tops of the Biglandia outcrop across the road to the south. Follow a faint road on the west side of the ridge to a point and then skirt around to the east side.

South Dam Area

This area includes the boulders, blocks, and outcrops on the south end of the reservoir. Start at Fawn Hollow Trail and break out through the ridge gap to the boulders.

Scenic Boulder ▼

This is the first prominent boulder you reach as you head upslope out of the parking lot. It is characterized by smooth Dakota sandstone unlike the harder sandstone that follows. Its overhanging south side has classic bouldering.

1. Pocket Lunge V2 Lunge from the pocket on the right to the top.

2. Standard Scenic V3 Climb the pocket to the finger lock up the middle of the boulder.

3. Southline V4 Climb up and left to the sloper.

4. West Bulge V2 Start at the corner on the left and reach up and out right then to the top.

The Spaceship ▼

Follow the trail past several blocks (Book Rock, Classic Rock, Split Boulder, and Cave Boulder) until you see this pointy rock spire. This spire is characterized by a pointy, leaning, brown-tinted face with an arête leaning to the southeast.

1. Southern Arête V0 Climb up the spire utilizing the prominent arête.

Prow Rock ▲

Follow the trail farther to the north to a point where you meet the ridgeline again. This west-facing prow with a steep north face connects with an adjacent wall to form a corner.

1. North Pocket V1 Left of the prow climb the steep face via pockets.

2. Dishhut V5 (hb) Climb slopers up the black-streaked prow to the right of *North Pocket*.

3. Grumpy V1 Climb the corner right of *Dishhut* and finish up the prow.

Chain Rock ▶

This classic wall connects with Prow Rock and has a prominent cave and crack that goes out it.

1. West Face V1 Climb the small finger-pocketed seam on the right side of the wall.

2. Chain Reactor V2 Climb up the steep face just left of *West Face*.

3. Cavus Maximus V1 Climb the right side of the cave on large holds to the arête.

4. Chainman V4 Climb the small holds left of the cave.

5. North Face V0 Climb good holds left, around the corner from the cave.

Crayola Block

This rectangular multicolored rock is located across the trail to the north approximately 75 feet from Chain Rock. It has an overhanging northwest face. It is also the landmark for where the ridgeline breaks into a lower and upper tier. From this point on, the boulder problems are found on both upper and lower portions of the ridge.

1. Melting Traverse V2 Traverse the entire northwest face of the block.

Mighty Wall

This wall is located up just a few feet to the northeast of Crayola Block, or approximately 150 feet north of Chain Rock. It is characterized by an orange face that is split by a seam. It is on the start of the lower ridge split.

1. Regular Route V3 Climb the steep face starting on the right side.

2. Bob's Crimp V4 Right of the seam, climb out from the hueco onto small edges.

3. West Corner V3 Climb the overhanging corner up the middle of the face.

4. Dicey Prow V5 Climb the arête on the left end of the wall via good flakes. V5 sit start.

Middle Dam Area

You can access this portion of boulders, blocks, and outcroppings by continuing north along the ridge for 75 yards, or driving north from the junction of CR 8E and CR 31 to the North Dam Area parking lot, then hiking the Fawn Hollow Trail south to a point where you can access these boulders and outcrops.

Pocket Wall

Continue due north from Mighty Wall for approximately 50 yards to a prominent upper ridge top block that has a pocketed prow and a short corner.

1. Westward V3 Climb the pockets and small holds on the west face.

2. Northwest Pockets V2 Climb the pockets on the northwest corner to the corner with the single pocket.

3. The Gimp V8 Climb the contrived thin face right of the seam.

4. North Seam V3 Climb the thin seam on the north face.

Burnt Boulder

This orange boulder is located approximately 90 feet northwest of Pocket Wall. It is characterized by a small crack.

1. Clockwork Orange V6 Traverse across the west face.

Lone Star Block

Continue north along the ridge to a prominent block dislodged from the lower ridge's south end; a thin crack splits its southwest face. A large dead tree can be seen to the northwest.

1. Southwest Crack V1 Climb the thin crack splitting the block.

2. Arêteach V0 Climb the wall and arête left of the crack. V2 sit.

3. Lone Traverse V3 Traverse left to break from *Arêteach*.

4. Muscle Traverse V5 Traverse from left to right across to the crack.

5. Full Muscle V6 Traverse across the entire block.

Dead Trees Caves

This cave area is located just northeast of a rock characterized by the dead trees that lean up against it. Continue north from Lone Star Block, past the dead trees rock, to a prominent cave.

1. Roof Cave Crack V2 Climb the roof crack via hand jams.

2. Flaky Pull Roof V5 This is another roof problem located above *Roof Cave Crack*. Climb the steep huecoed roof.

3. Have Another V8 Climb the roof right of *Flaky Pull Roof*.

Formunda Boulder

This boulder is located down below and to the west of Dead Trees Caves.

1. Formunda V6 Climb up to the large pocket and then use the good edges.

Mini Bus Block

Located behind and to the west of Formunda Boulder.

1. Mini Me V4 Climb from down low to sloping holds gaining corner with pockets.

2. Short Bus V8 Move from the hueco to the corner and up.

3. Huecoed V5 Climb from the hueco to the arête out left.

Swiss Cheese Wall

Continue north from Dead Trees Caves for approximately 45 feet to this short pocket-filled wall.

1. Dihedral Games V5 Climb the dihedral to the top.

North Dam Area

This area is characterized by independent boulders and blocks with only a few outcrop problems. It has become a world-renowned destination. To get to this area, you may hike north from the South Dam Area through the Middle Dam Area, or follow the driving directions to the North Dam Area on page 39.

From the dam, hike south on the Fawn Hollow Trail for approximately 200 yards, then cut to the west toward the ridgetop. Descend through easy ground to the Spiced Roof area. The Mars Boulder is just to the north, below the lower ridge break. You can see the Monster Boulder straight ahead and below the lower tier. You can see the Kahuna Boulder farther downslope and to the west. Depending on the time of year and the amount of precipitation throughout any particular year, the lower blocks, including the Kahuna, may be partially submerged. If the lower boulders are exposed, many good problems are revealed.

Monster Boulder

This boulder lives up to its name. Its massive size makes this one of Carter Lake's largest boulders. Most problems are found on its west and northwest faces. From the ridgetop descent, continue southwest to the huge boulder.

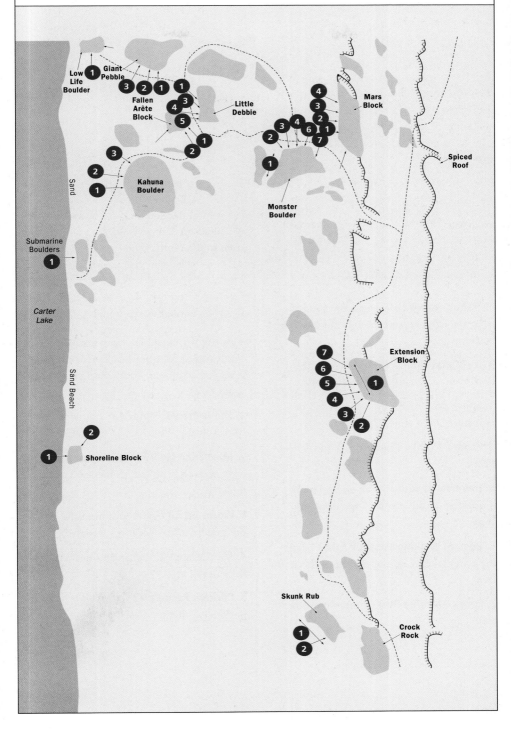

1. Train in Vain V10 Traverse the west face from the left, past and through the northwest corner.

2. Dispuntia Dudes V6 (hb) Start at the northwest arête and climb to the top.

3. Splick V5 Climb thin layaways left of *Dispuntia Dudes* arête.

4. Krum V4 (hb) Climb the face just left of *Splick*.

5. Traverse du Jour V7 Traverse from the northwest corner across to the northeast arête.

6. Days of Whining Posers V7 (hb) Climb the crimpy edges up the middle of the north face.

7. Pete's Arête V3 (hb) Climb the northeast arête.

Mars Block

This lengthy block lies approximately 90 feet northwest of Monster Boulder. Many moderate face climbs are located on its west and south faces.

1. The Arête V3 Climb the southwest arête of the block.

2. Mars Traverse V5 (hb) Traverse out of the cave, from right to left, to the left-facing dihedral.

3. Worm Up V0 Climb jugs from the lip up the middle of the boulder's west face.

4. Mantleope V2 Mantle up from the large flake to the top.

5. Pockets Pockets V2 (hb) Climb up to the pockets on the face.

Little Debbie Boulder ▲

This boulder is located down below Monster Boulder to the northwest. The classic west side has many good problems.

1. Crapulator V2 Climb up from the undercling on the right side of the west face.

2. Tension V8 Climb from under the roof right of *Crapulator* and extend up and left to the undercling-type hold, then to sloper lip.

3. Dynoman V8 Dyno up off the small edges to the side pull, then to a bucket.

4. Squeeze Job V4 Climb up to the sloper crack, then to a large lip.

5. Sloper Chief V5 Climb the wall right of the black water streak via slopers to the hole, then top out.

6. Round About Arête V7 Climb out from the hand pocket to the rounded arête.

7. Gaston's Face V5 Climb seam to the intricate layaways on the north face.

Giant Pebble Boulder

This boulder is located downslope to the northwest of Little Debbie Boulder.

1. South Face V0 Climb the right side of the south face.

2. Con Job V4 Climb the bulge left of *South Face,* with dyno topout.

3. Bob's Cornered V2 Climb the classic leaning corner up the middle of the south face.

4. The Weeping Crescent V6 Traverse the north wall of the boulder from the northwest arête, right to left.

Fallen Arête Block ▲

This block has recently slipped off its edge and has landed upright, creating a steep pillar.

1. Fallen Arête V? (hb) Climb the northeast arête.

2. Slip Sliden V3 Climb the southeastern arête and face.

This boulder is located downslope and to the west of Giant Pebble Boulder.

1. South Face Route V1 Climb the good edges to the cap.

2. Barbed Wire V3 Climb up the smooth holds to the top.

Kahuna Boulder ▼

From Giant Pebble Boulder head downslope to the southwest. This world–renown boulder hosts some of the best problems in the state. Depending on the time of year and amount of precipitation, this boulder may be very close to if not submerged by Carter Lake.

1. Kahuna Roof V5 One of the gem problems up the middle of the west face.

2. Super Chief V9 Climb crimpers and slopers on the left side of the west face. Dynos and swings are usually encountered on this awesome problem.

3. Beach Crack V3 Climb the northwest corner of the block to the good holds up and right.

Submarine Boulders ▲

Depending on the precipitation for any given year, these boulders can be fully submerged. But if they are exposed, they are excellent boulders with many good problems. Submarine Boulder itself is located down and southwest of Kahuna Boulder and sits just offshore if not submerged.

1. Up Periscope V1 Climb out the west leaning face.

Shoreline Block

Continue along the sandy shore to the south and you will see this block.

1. Shoreline V0 Climb the corner on the west face.

2. Shore Arête V1 Climb the northeast arête.

Biglandia

You can find this east-facing extended outcrop, reminiscent of a mini-Flatirons, by continuing north and then east from the North Dam Area and then around the bend to the Carter Knolls parking area. Hike out across the roadway to the south along a faint two-track grassy-dirt road that leads around the overhanging hogback's east side. The outcrop is described from north to south.

Big Betty Boulder ▲

Downslope to the east, lying in the meadow-covered valley, is a single erratic that has face and traverse problems.

1. Southeast Face V0 Climb the less-than-vertical face.

2. Betty's Traverse V5 Traverse around the entire block.

Redneck Wall

This crack-featured wall is perhaps the tallest formation of them all and overhangs gradually.

1. T-Neck V3 Climb the arête on left side of the wall left of the crack.

2. V-Neck V2 Climb the large holds left of the crack on the left side of the wall.

3. Redneck Traverse V7 Start right of *V-Neck* and traverse to the left to the arête.

4. Hot Bath V6 Climb the finger crack to the top.

5. Cream Filled V6 (hb) Climb the right hand crack of the three middle cracks.

Abdo Wall ▲

Located approximately 75 yards south of Redneck Wall and past a yellow wall that has two difficult cracks. This wall is characterized by a greenish brown east face that has criss-crossing seams.

1. Pinchaloaf V4 Climb up the left side of the wall utilizing a pinch.

2. Abdo Cave V8 Climb upslopers, up and left to the top.

3. Abdo Man V3 Climb out from jugs, out left to finish out right.

4. Vertical Lawn V7 Climb from *Abdo Man,* out right to the top.

Rotund Wall

Located just left (south) from Abdo Wall.

1. The Rotund V7 Traverse from the left side of the wall to the right side, staying up high.

2. Ponts De Lyon V4 Climb up the purplish holds to the top.

Reservoir Dogs ▲

Located another 200 feet south from the other walls, Reservoir Dogs is characterized by a sheer brownish east face with traversing chalk marks.

1. Reservoir Dogs V6 Traverse from right to left, with a diagonaling finish.

The Chump ▼

The Chump is a sheer welded tuff wall just left of Reservoir Dogs.

1. The Chump V6 Climb up the middle of the east face.

2. Old Nag V9 Climb the north side arête via pockets.

3. Charlie Horse V9 Traverse from right to left.

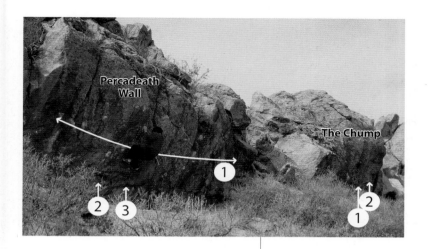

Percadeath Wall ▲

Percadeath Wall is just left of the Chump and has a fire pit ruin at its base. Traverse chalk is seen across its face.

1. Percadeath Traverse V8 Traverse from the left side to the right side.

2. Perci V4 Climb up the holds left of the pit.

3. Percadeath V4 Climb the holds straight above the pit.

Bob's Traverse Wall ▼

This wall is located on the south end of the outcrop just before the barbed wire fence. It is also characterized by traverse chalk on its east face.

1. Make You Fine V6 Traverse from right to left on jugs. This is Biglandia's longest traverse.

2. The Sloper V7 Traverse the wall, staying down low.

3. Sky Pilot V2 (hb) Climb the lichen-free section on the left end of the wall to the top.

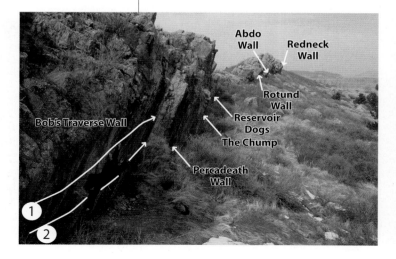

Estes Park Area Overview

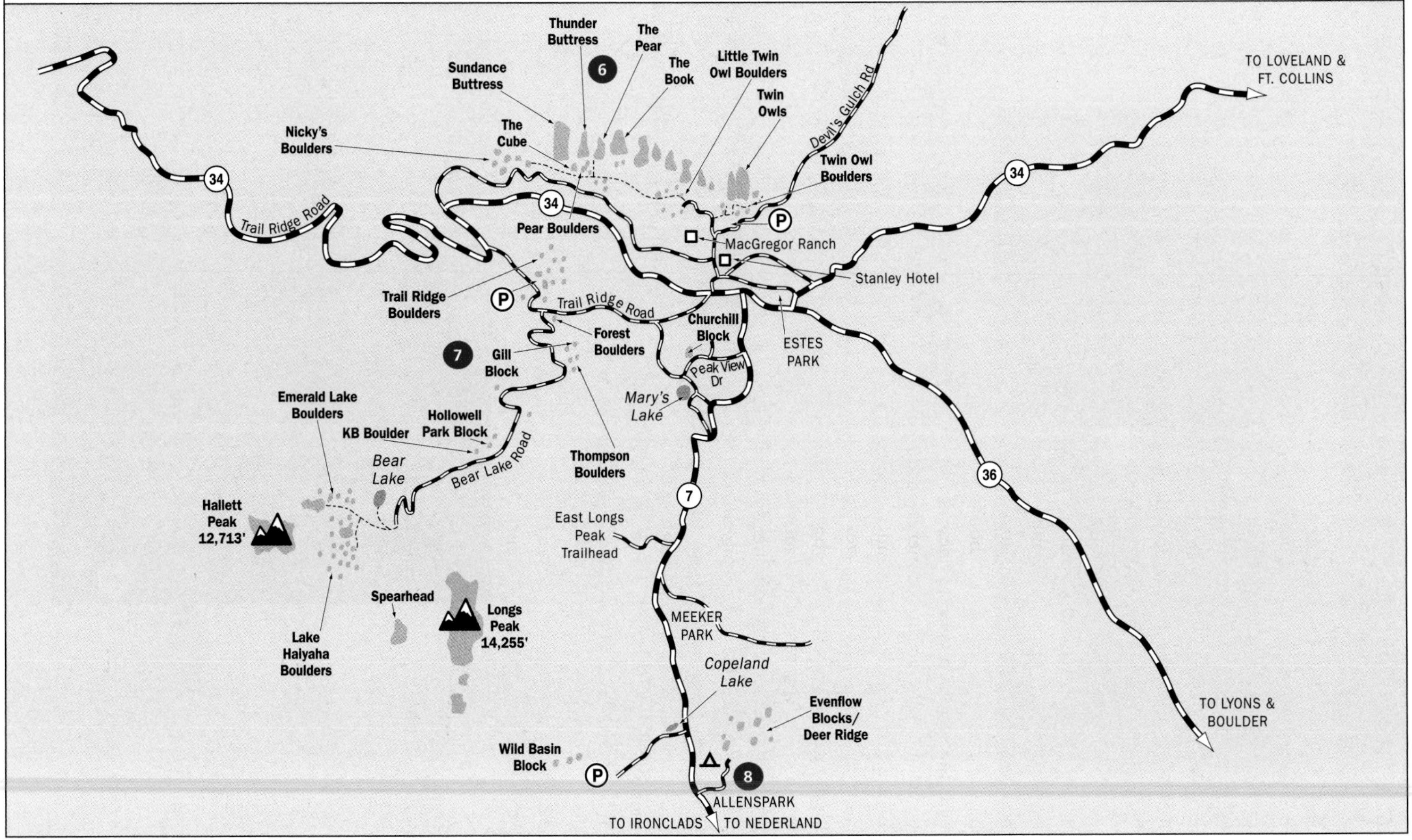

TO LOVELAND & FT. COLLINS

TO LYONS & BOULDER

34

36

Stanley Hotel

Deat's Gulch Rd

Twin Owl Boulders

Little Twin Owl Boulders

Twin Owls

MacGregor Ranch

The Book

The Pear

Thunder Buttress

6

Sundance Buttress

The Cube

Nicky's Boulders

Trail Ridge Road

34

ESTES PARK

Churchill Block

Peak View Dr

Mary's Lake

Pear Boulders

Trail Ridge Road

Forest Boulders

Thompson Boulders

7

East Longs Peak Trailhead

7

Gill Block

Trail Ridge Boulders

Hollowell Park Block

KB Boulder

Bear Lake

Bear Lake Road

MEEKER PARK

Copeland Lake

Evenflow Blocks / Deer Ridge

8

ALLENSPARK
TO NEDERLAND

TO IRONCLADS

Wild Basin Block

Emerald Lake Boulders

Longs Peak 14,255'

Spearhead

Lake Halyaha Boulders

Hallett Peak 12,713'

Trail Ridge Road

34

N

ESTES PARK

Bouldering in and around Estes Park can't be beat. The endless fall lines of boulders are mind-boggling. Every buttress and monolithic granite formation in this area is surrounded by boulderfields. Many of the boulders are found in grassy meadows or on gradual hillsides and are easily accessible.

For the more adventurous boulderer, longer hikes within Rocky Mountain National Park reveal an unlimited supply of boulders and blocks. Recent activity on higher ground has made the boulder-strewn talus the serious boulderer's destination, especially in the warm summer months. Because of its convenience and scenery, Lumpy Ridge is one of the area's prize bouldering locations. The higher grounds are also hard to beat for their beauty and serenity. Bouldering sessions often end up in peaceful meditative sightseeing adventures from atop the many boulders.

The erratic flow of the high peaks' monolithic granite will leave you awestruck. With the growing popularity of bouldering, many new boulders and problems have been discovered and established over the past ten or so years. Choose a direction and enjoy.

Directions: Estes Park is located at the threshold of the east entrance of Rocky Mountain National Park. If coming from the north, from Front Range cities such as Fort Collins and Loveland, take Highway 34 west to the town center. If coming from the south (Boulder and Denver), take Highway 36 to the town center. Estes Park has many modern conveniences such as restaurants, hotels, and shops.

6 LUMPY RIDGE

Lumpy Ridge, along with the majestic east face of Long's Peak, is perhaps the first thing that will catch your eye as you arrive in the Estes Park Valley. These towering white-granite formations are strewn across the landscape to the north. Many boulder fall lines appear as you walk along the east-west trail that skirts the front (south) side of these formations.

Note: Almost all bouldering on Lumpy Ridge is included within the boundaries of Rocky Mountain National Park, and all park rules apply, including but not limited to the following: Pets are not allowed; overnight camping requires a permit and is allowed only in

Lumpy Ridge

N

Thunder Buttress

The Pear

The Book

Batman Rock

Twin Owls

Tree Boulder **1**

Highly Horizontal Block **1**

Scrunch Block **1**

Horizontals Block **1**

The Cube **5**

4

The French Fry

Scoop Boulder

Pear Boulders

Best Boulder

1 **2** **2**

Pear Trail

Earthling Boulder

Trail Boulder

2

Two and Only Two Boulder

World's Greatest Boulder

1

Back Boulder

5

1

Book Boulders

2

Little Twin Owls

High and Mighty Boulder

2

2

Golden Shower Rock

Apex Boulder

Angry Man Boulder **2**

2

2

2

Golden Shower V6

Tooth

Clingon Boulder

1

1

2

Jaws Boulder

Little Twin Owl Boulders

Melancoly Whale

1 **1**

V2

1

Rocky Mountain National Park

Black Canyon Trail

High Boulder **1**

Twin Owl Boulders

Sap Boulder

1

Dihedral Block

2

Bolt Boulder **1**

Gem Lake Trail

To Gem Lake

Lumpy Ridge Trailhead

P

New Parking Area

Devil's Gulch Road

designated sites; fires are not allowed; and, of course, pack out all your trash. Be sensitive to vegetation and wildlife when hiking off-trail, and consider using eco-colored chalk. It helps minimize the visual impact of bouldering for other park visitors.

Directions: From Estes Park, head north on Highway 34 past the Stanley Hotel (made famous by Steven King's novel *The Shining*) to a right (north) turn on MacGregor Avenue. Drive past the MacGregor Ranch Museum turnoff and take a left on the new paved road toward the new Lumpy Ridge Trailhead parking area. This adds approximately 0.7 mile to the approach to areas west of the old parking area. It adds approximately 0.5 mile to the Twin Owl Boulders approach. Do not try to access bouldering through MacGregor Ranch—it is no longer allowed.

From the new parking area below the Twin Owls formation, hike northwest to the Gem Lake Trail, then go west on that trail (away from Gem Lake) to the Twin Owl Boulders, the Little Twin Owl Area, Book Boulders, Pear Boulders, and Spring Boulders.

Twin Owl Boulders

From the new parking area, head north and then west along the Gem Lake Trail. The trail will head downslope, and soon you will start to see the boulders on its sides. You will encounter the High Boulder and Dihedral Boulder followed by the Sap Boulder and huge Bolt Boulder on the right side of the trail.

High Boulder ▼

Located directly behind Dihedral Block just off the Gem Lake Trail, High Boulder is characterized by an overhang on the west face and lengthy slabs on its east face.

1. Slopes Away V2 Climb the sloping shelf out left to the top.

2. Pretty Slab V0 Climb the good edge of the slab of the east face.

3. Start Stoned V1 Climb the slab to the right of *Pretty Slab.*

4. Tame Traverse V0 Climb across the face to the right along break.

Dihedral Block ▶

Soon after heading west down the Gem Lake Trail you will encounter this nice block that has a left-facing dihedral.

1. Scary Out V4 Climb the face a few feet left of the dihedral.

2. Pop A Loose Nut V9 Climb the left-facing dihedral to the desperate topout.

3. Aren't Arête V4 Climb the arête on the south face.

Sap Boulder ▼

This caved boulder is located a short ways down the trail on the right.

1. Sap V9 Climb from inside the cave on the west face, out to the lip, then left.

2. Flaming Amigo V7 Climb out from the lower right side of the cave, up the arête to finish left.

3. Vevala V1 Climb up the large holds on the east face.

4. Veeks V3 Climb from the left and traverse right to the crack and up.

Bolt Boulder ▲

Hike farther west to this huge boulder on the right side of the trail. It is characterized by a large roof on its west face.

1. Pedophile V9 (hb) Right of the bolt line on the lower west face. Climb the thin, steep face via slopers and pinches.

2. Slabs Away V4 (hb) Climb the thin slab up the middle of the south-facing wall.

Little Twin Owls Area

From the Lumpy Ridge Trailhead parking area, hike north to the Gem Lake Trail and take it west toward the old parking area and the Twin Owls Trail. Take the Twin Owls Trail west and north and head toward the Little Twin Owls formation. The first big boulder you see is Jaws Boulder.

Jaws Boulder ▲

Located east of the Little Twin Owls formation, this huge boulder is characterized by a large roof on its southwest side and steep faces on its north and south sides. When looking at the boulder from the west, it resembles a large shark.

1. Harpoon V2 Climb northwest face to the top.

2. Hooked V? Traverse from left to right down low.

3. Jugs Away V2 Climb from the far-right end of the southwest corner and ascend the scoop.

4. Under Roof V4 Undercling out to the good edges on the south face then to the top.

5. The Plank V? Climb up slopers left of the seam on the north face.

6. Seamed V1 Climb from the seam on the north face and move left to the slab finish.

Melancholy Whale Boulder

This boulder is located southwest of Jaws Boulder.

1. Melancholy Whale V8 Climb the southwest arête.

Tooth Boulder ▲

Located just north of Jaws Boulder, Tooth Boulder is characterized by a pointy, tooth-shaped piece of quality granite that has a leaning arête.

1. Tweek Fest V2 Climb the thin, steep slab of the west face.

2. Leaning Arête V0 Climb the classic arête on the southwest corner.

3. Dentured Face V0 Climb the slab right of the arête.

Clingon Boulder ▲

This boulder is located just west of Tooth Boulder and is characterized by a diagonaling crack.

1. Clingon Crack V3 Climb the right-leaning crack on the east face.

2. Dilithium Crystal V3 Climb up the crack about 5 feet and then straight up the face to the top.

High and Mighty Boulder

This boulder is located upslope from Clingon Boulder, approximately 150 feet north.

1. Balls Wall V2 (hb) Climb up and along the roof on the southeast face.

2. High Arête V0 (hb) Climb the arête right of *Balls Wall*.

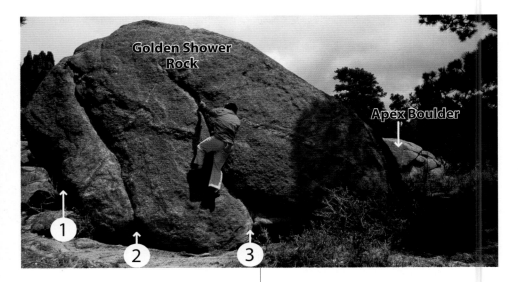

Golden Shower Rock ▲

This boulder is located southeast of High and Mighty Boulder, or up on the left side of the trail, approximately 85 feet northeast of Tooth Boulder.

1. Broken Arêteo V6 Climb up the overhanging arête to the crack, out left.

2. Seems Left V2 Climb up the seam on the left side of the south face.

3. Seems Right V1 Climb the seam on the right side of the south face.

Apex Boulder ▼

Continue up the trail to the northeast for approximately 75 feet to this roofed boulder.

1. Apex V2 Climb up and out the roof on the south face.

2. Northout V0 Climb up the north face.

To Twin Owls Formation

Angry Man Boulder ▲

Continue once again up the trail to the northeast, through an aspen grove that has a large boulder on the left. Continue past this boulder to Angry Man Boulder. Aspen trees sit behind it to the north.

1. Angry Man Left V7 Sit down low to grab slopers and bust out to the lip and left to topout.

2. Livid Man V10 Sit down low and bust out right to the lip and topout.

Book Boulders

Hike due west on the lower trail (Black Canyon Trail) from the old parking area, for approximately 20 minutes. Eventually you will be hiking alongside these boulders, which are located on the left side of the trail.

World's Greatest Boulder

This boulder sits trailside and is characterized by an overhanging crack in its north side.

1. Northwest Seam V1 Climb the seam on the northwest face.

2. Overcrack V2 Climb the crack in the overhang along the trail.

3. Flakeo V0 Climb the flake to the slab on the north point.

3. Excelslab V0 Climb the large holds up the slab on the far-left side of the east face.

4. Arêtete V2 Climb the arête on the southeast corner.

5. Cracklay V2 Climb the crack on the south face.

Back Boulder

Located just south of World's Greatest Boulder, Back Boulder is the easternmost of two boulders.

1. FinO V1 Climb the overhanging fin on the southern tip of the boulder.

Two and Only Two Boulder

This boulder is located next to and just west of Back Boulder.

1. Sit Arête V2 Start low and climb up the southwest arête.

2. Pepsi Mantle V0 Leap up the southwest face to the top and mantle.

Lower Pear Boulders

Continue west along the trail, through a gate, and past the sign for the Pear, a large rock formation up on the ridge. To reach the Lower Pear Boulders, continue left (west) for another 75 feet and look out to the right (north). You will see the first boulder off the trail.

Trail Boulder ▲

This is the first boulder you see off the trail to the north.

1. Southern Exposure V0 Climb up the middle of the south face.

Earthling Boulder ▼

Beyond Trail Boulder to the north, you will discover this awesome boulder that has a very welcoming south face. This is the center boulder of the three.

1. Rightaway V8 Climb from the right end of the shelf and throw left to the arête.

2. Middle Earth V4 Climb up to the top from the right end of the shelf.

3. Northeast Arête V1 Climb the right-leaning arête on the northeast face.

Best Boulder ▲

This awesome boulder is located just up and north from Earthling Boulder and offers excellent positioning.

1. Curvature V4 Climb up and left from the scoop.

2. Voluptuous V9 Climb the small edges and lay back right of the scoop.

Upper Pear Boulders

The Upper Pair Boulders are reached by hiking up the trail toward the Pear. The first boulder, Scoop, can be seen upslope to the north, 120 yards ahead.

Scoop Boulder ▲

This boulder is located approximately 120 yards due north of Earthling Boulder. You also may access this next set of boulders by hiking up the Pear Trail for approximately 150 yards and heading east. The beautifully rounded cube-shaped boulder has a concave east face, which has a seam splitting its right side.

1. The Seam V6 (hb) Climb the seam on the right side of the east face via some small edges and smears.

2. Achilles V1 Climb the northeast arête, with mantle finish.

3. Middle Smear V2 Climb the slab on the west face.

Tree V Boulder

Located just northwest of Scoop Boulder, Tree V Boulder has a pine tree at the base of the leaning crack.

1. Tree V Crack V2 Climb the right-leaning crack, which has a pine tree at its base.

Horizontals Block

This block is located a few feet northeast of Scoop Boulder and is characterized by horizontal breaks across its faces.

1. Zontals V1 Climb from left side of the northwest face over the roof.

2. Roofazontals V1 Climb the southwest arête from the roof to the slab.

Highly Horizontal Block

Continue upslope to the north for 60 feet to a block with cracks across its south face.

1. Up and Away V0 Climb the right side of the south face.

Scrunch Block

Scrunch Block is across to the right (east) of Highly Horizontal Block.

1. Bals V0 Climb the slab of the block.

Rolling Thunder Boulders

These gems—the Cube, Spring Boulders, and the French Fry—are located west of the Pear Boulders up in the dense wooded hillside below Thunder Buttress. Continue west past the Pear sign for approximately ten minutes. At a point where the trail heads upslope, look into the woods to the right (north) and you will see the Cube's south side through the trees, up toward Thunder Buttress. Head up through the woods, aiming for the lower huge roof on Thunder Buttress.

The Cube ▼

This cube-shaped block is located in the wooded slopes directly south of the large roof on Thunder Buttress. It has several high-ball problems in the moderate range with great landings.

1. Southern Sun V2 (hb) Climb the southwestern arête of the block's south face.

2. Southside Slim V2 (hb) Climb the steep face and seam right of the tree on the south face.

3. Eastern Draw V1 (hb) Climb from a side pull to the sloped holds below the roof to the finish around the roof to the left.

4. Northern Sun V2 Climb the northeast arête.

5. Northeast Throw V3 Climb the face and leaning arête right of the northeast corner.

6. North Face V1 (hb) Climb the big holds to the dihedral up the middle of the north face.

7. North Star V3 Climb the right side of the north face with a jump-start.

8. Golden Gate V0 Climb the golden-edged west face's left side.

9. Gold Card V4 Climb up the middle of the golden west face.

Spring Boulders

From the Cube continue west for approximately 200 yards. You can follow a faint deer trail to a spring. These boulders are located east and west of the spring and within view of each other.

Western Spring Boulder ▲

From the spring, hike due west 120 feet until you reach this white-toned boulder.

1. Whitehedral V1 (hb) Climb the right-facing corner on the west face.

2. Spring Traverse V3 Traverses the south face right to left.

3. Low Life V2 Climb the seam to the ramp on the east face.

4. Black and White V1 Climb through holds on the right side of the east face.

The French Fry

You can access this french fry–shaped block by hiking due east from the Cube approximately 250 yards or by hiking up the Pear

Trail approximately 200 yards and cutting out to the west through the woods about 150 yards. It is characterized by a golden south face and a gray and tan east face.

1. Golden Earth V1 (hb) Climb the left side of the golden south face.

2. Touch of Gray V5 (hb) Climb the east face's left side to the top.

3. Gray Stone V4 Climb the face to the right of *Touch of Gray*.

4. Ramp Route V2 Climb up the east face starting at the ramp.

5. Cryin' Out Loud V5 Climb the thin face right of latter.

6. West Face V1 (hb) Climb the right side of the west face up slab.

Nicky's Boulders

This boulder-filled meadow is located off the road just past Nicky's Resort on Highway 34. From Estes Park take Highway 34 approximately 1.8 miles to Nicky's Resort and park on the right side of the road. Hike upslope a short way until you intersect the main trail leading east-west. Go east to the Whale's Eye or west to the Monkey Hang Area. The boulders are located just off the trail. The Whale's Eye is located in close proximity to a new housing development. Please be courteous.

Trailside Boulder

This is a smaller boulder that sits just off the trail and in front of the larger Whale's Eye Boulder. Hike to the main trail from the parking area and head east.

1. South Face V1 Climb up the south face to the undercling, then out left.

Whale's Eye Boulder ▼

This whale-shaped block with its crystallized eye is located just off the trail to the north, behind the smaller Trailside Boulder.

1. Whale's Eye V3 Climb up the south face through crystallized eye.

2. Northeast Face V4 Climb from the flake on the northeast face.

3. North Face V3 Climb the pockets up the black and tan streak.

Unnamed Boulder

This boulder is located just up the trail to the northwest of the Trailside Boulder.

1. Uneasty V1 Climb the east face's left side

2. Unnorthy V2 Climb the northeast arête.

High Boulder

High Boulder is located due north of Unnamed Boulder. It is characterized by a seam on its southeast side.

1. Seams Good V1 Climb the seam on the southeast face.

2. Miscenter V2 (hb) Climb up the middle of the southeast face.

Bill McKee Boulder

Continue approximately 100 feet northwest of High Boulder to find this overhang boulder.

1. South Face V1 Climb the large holds out of the overhang on the south face.

2. North Face V1 Climb the northwest corner.

Upper Boulder ▼

Located 75 feet due north upslope from Bill McKee Boulder. A dead tree sits on this large boulder's west side.

1. South Face V2 (hb) Climb the south-facing slab.

2. Left Arête V3 (hb) Climb the southeastern arête.

3. Southeast Face V3 (hb) Climb the face just to the right of *Left Arête*.

4. Sunny Face V2 (hb) Climb the face left of the northeast arête.

5. Northeast Arête V0 Climb the northeast arête.

Monkey Hang Area

Continue up the trail approximately 100 yards due west of the east-most boulders. There is private land just beyond and to the west of these blocks.

Monkey Hang Boulder ▲

This boulder nearest the houses has a nice traversing face route.

1. Southwest Traverse V2–V8 Traverse up the top from left to right, or low for added difficulty on the northwest side.

2. Monkeyman V4 Climb up the center of the south face.

3. Monkeywoman V5 Climb the steep face on the right side of the south face.

4. Monkey Hang V4 Climb up to the large-hold arête on the northeast side.

Soup Boulder ▼

This boulder is immediately south of Monkey Hang Boulder. It has a scoop on the south face.

1. West Traverse V2 Traverse the west face to the north.

2. Scoop Left V3 Climb the face left of the scoop on the southeast side.

3. Scoop V0 Climb up through the middle of the scoop.

4. Southeast Corner V3 Climb the steep face on the right side of the southeast face.

Tomato Block

This sheer block is approximately 75 feet south of Soup Boulder.

1. Paste V3 Climb the face on the left side of the south face.

2. Ketchup V0 Climb up the right side of the south face.

3. Salsa V3 Climb the face right of southeast corner.

Mary's Lake

Continue on Peak View Drive for another mile, then take a left toward Mary's Lake. Drive up a short way to a pull off on the right. The rocks are across the road.

7 ROCKY MOUNTAIN NATIONAL PARK

See map on page 50.

The bouldering within this park is massive. Moraines and meadows, hillsides and valleys are full of boulderfields. Some of the bouldering is located close to the roadside, while other areas require a lengthier and involved alpine hike. Many of the monolithic, big-walled mountains have huge talus fields below them that are full of boulders and blocks. Many of these rocks are found in and around the big-wall base camps, which is how they were probably initially discovered and played upon. This is a great pastime for an overnight bivy site.

Note: An entrance fee is required to access the following areas, and all park rules apply, including but not limited to the following: Pets are not allowed; overnight camping requires a permit and is allowed only in designated sites; fires are not allowed; and, of course, pack out all your trash. Be sensitive to vegetation and wildlife when hiking off-trail, and consider using eco-colored chalk. It helps minimize the visual impact of bouldering for other park visitors.

Trail Ridge Boulders

Drive west on Highway 36 to the park's east entrance (Beaver Meadows). Continue west on Trail Ridge Road approximately 1.2 miles and park on the right side. The boulders can be seen due east and south from this pull off.

Suzuki Boulder ▼

On the north side of the road sits this tall boulder, which has a tree against its south face.

1. Overhang V2 Climb the crack in the overhang on the left side of the southwest face.

2. Arête V3 (hb) Climb the arête to the right of *Overhang*.

3. South Face Left V2 (hb) Climb the face to the left of the bush on the south face.

4. Traverse V5 Traverse the south face, right to left.

5. Southeast Arête V3 Climb through the overhang via the arête on the southeast side.

6. East Face V1 Climb the left side of the east face.

7. Middle East V5 Climb up the middle of the east face.

8. East Crack V3 Climb the layback crack on the east side.

Suzuki Satellite

This boulder is immediately south of big Suzuki Boulder.

1. Suzuki Arête V4 Climb the southeast arête of the block.

2. East O V2 Climb out the overhang on the east face.

Upper Slope Boulders

This is a vast area full of boulders and blocks. From Suzuki Boulder head upslope toward the large formation. You will see boulders in the trees upslope to the north in all directions.

Forest Block ▼

This block is located upslope in the trees on the way to the upper crag and talus field.

1. Forester Crack V1 Climb the crack on the east side of the block.

Twin Blocks ▲

These are located upslope on the flattened area within the forest.

1. Marching Face V3 Climb up the left side of the west face of the west block.

Trail Ridge Boulder

This boulder is located across the road to the south from Suzuki Boulder.

1. South Face V2 Climb the overhanging south face.

2. NE Arête V4 Climb the northeast arête.

3. North Slab V1 Climb the slab on the north face.

Bear Lake Road Boulders

You can reach these areas by hanging a left (south) off Highway 36 past the Beaver Meadows Entrance Station onto Bear Lake Road. Follow Bear Lake Road. The areas are found just off the roadway.

Forest Boulders

This area is approximately 0.5 mile from the intersection of Highway 36 and Bear Lake Road. Park at a small pull off just off the road. The boulders are up on the east side of the slope, a short way within the trees.

Spaceship Rock ▲

Spaceship Rock is an awesome boulder with several lines around its base. It is characterized by a thin seam/crack on its west side.

1. To the Moon V8 Climb the seam crack on the west side.

Gill Block

This block is located on the east side of the road approximately 3 miles from the junction of Highway 36 and Bear Lake Road.

Thompson Boulders

You can see this boulderfield on the left (east) side of Bear Lake Road, just past the Moraine Park turnoff. Many fun and challenging boulders and problems abound. Park just before the Thompson Creek Bridge. Hike a short way upslope to the north to the heart of the field, which stretches north-south.

Thom's Boulder ▼

This is the first prominent boulder you will encounter as you head upslope from the bridge.

1. Thom's Bulge V3 Climb the overhanging face on the south side of the boulder.

Yellow Boulder

This boulder is several yards north of Thom's Boulder and sits on top of a small platform rock.

1. Mellow Yellow V2 Climb up the middle of the west face.

Hollowell Park Boulders

From the east entrance station, take Trail Ridge Road west. Turn left (south) onto Bear Lake Road. Follow this for approximately 3.5 miles to the Hollowell Park parking lot. From the lot, hike east to the picnic area. Then head north uphill, until you reach a horse trail. Then hike east-northeast to the large block in the trees.

Hollowell Park Block ▶

This massive block is located just northeast of the parking area and offers great challenges on all sides. Some are highball and a toprope may be desired.

1. West Face V6 Climb the left side of the north face.

2. Western Pinch V4 Climb the right side of the north face via a reachy move.

3. Traversity V2 Traverse to the north face from the right side of the west face.

4. Western Highball V4 (hb) Climb the lengthy middle of the west face to the top.

5. High Arête V2 (hb) Climb the right side of the west face ending on the southwest arête.

6. South Face V0 Climb over the bulged south face utilizing the leaning corner.

7. Southeast Corner V2 Climb up to the top from a jug on the southeast end.

8. Eastern Dyno V2 Lunge for the top from down on the east face.

9. North Corner V0 Climb the right-facing corner on the north face. Best for down climb also.

KB Boulder

From the Hollowell parking lot, hike west for a few minutes, in the opposite direction of Hollowell Boulder, passing horse fencing and a boulder to the right. Hike a few more minutes through the woods, then down to a meadow. At the meadow head to the right, upslope, for about 150 feet. The big egg-shaped boulder can be seen in the trees. The rock's texture and landings are great.

1. Snizzle Sticks V7 Climb the corner on the far-left side of the boulder.

2. Thai Stick V5 (hb) Climb up the middle of the gray face.

3. KB V8 Climb up the finger crack to the scoop.

4. Crack V4 Climb the finger crack behind the tree to the top.

Emerald Lake

This area, along with Chaos Canyon/Lake Haiyaha, requires a more involved hike than the roadside bouldering areas. Take a shuttle from the Park and Ride area across from Glacier Basin Campground or drive to the Bear Lake trailhead located at the end of Bear Lake Road. The Emerald Lake boulders are found in a massive talus field that flows off Hallett Peak in the distance. It is full of boulders and blocks, some very large and others with perfect height and positioning. Awesome problems are found everywhere.

From the Bear Lake parking area, follow the signs up to Emerald Lake. The bouldering is found scattered in the talus field below the lake itself, to the right and left of the main trail. Cross the creek to the left for Kine Block and Whispers of Wisdom Boulder. Head upslope for Large Block and Tommy's Arête.

Kine Block ▲

This beautiful block of high country is found just off the trail, up and across the creek from the main Emerald Lake trail. You will find straight-up overhanging problems and an awesome traverse.

1. Kine V5 Climb over the roof on the right side of the east face, to small edges then up to the top.

2. Kine Traverse V11 Traverse across the east face of the boulder.

Whispers of Wisdom Boulder ▶

This massive boulder is found just east of Kine Block.

1. Whispers of Wisdom V9 (hb) Climb up the severely overhanging east side of the boulder.

High Places Block ▲

This large block is located out in the talus, 100 feet south of Kine Block.

1. High Places V2 Climb up the middle of the north face via good holds.

Top Boulder ▶

This nice boulder is found to the west of Kine Block, amid the talus maze.

1. Topper Arête V3 Climb up the southwest arête.

Platform Boulder ▲

This boulder is found amid the talus maze west of Kine Block.

1. Du Soeil V2 Climb up the south face.

Large Block ▶

This massive block is on the right side of the Emerald Lake trail, upslope and to the north of Kine Block. *Large Roof* and *Tommy's Arête* are located here.

1. Large Roof V10 Climb from down low on the overhanging west side of the block. Crimpers and levers abound.

2. Tommy's Arête V6 Climb the prominent arête on the north side of the block.

Hallett Boulder

Located on the way up to Hallett Peak, this boulder and block looks down valley and is found on a hidden ledge. It is characterized by a left-leaning edge system in the overhang.

1. Fireball V? Climb the left-leaning edge system in the overhang of the face.

2. Stranger in a Strange Land V? Climb up the left side of the overhang just right of the prow.

3. Dyno Problem V? Dyno up to the lip to the left of *Stranger in a Strange Land*.

Chaos Canyon/Lake Haiyaha

Chaos Canyon bouldering is located around and above Lake Haiyaha. Problems are scattered all around the lake and the massive talus field above. Many state-of-the-art problems can be found. Most are located on severely overhanging sides of the boulders, with crimpy, strenuous moves.

From the Emerald Lake trailhead, follow the trail up to the left (west) to the sign that points to Lake Haiyaha. The trail leads up and around to the lake's shores. The lower boulders are about a forty-five-minute hike on a nicely groomed trail; the upper boulders are reached by a more obscure trail.

Lake Boulder

This beauty of a boulder is found along the shores of Lake Haiyaha. It is the obvious boulder that dominates the eastern shoreline as you approach the lake off the main trail.

1. European Human Being V12 Climb the face left of the northwest arête.

2. Gang Bang V8 Climb the steep and difficult arête.

3. Nothing But Sunshine V14 Climb the holds between *Gang Bang* and *Handy Capps*.

4. Handy Capps V9 Utilize the undercling to a dead point move. Right of *Nothing But Sunshine*.

5. Centaur V13 Climb the overhanging brown yellow wall up and left to edges. Right of *Handy Capps*.

6. Skyscraper V5 Climb the overhanging brown face left of *Stars and Stripes*.

7. Stars and Stripes V11 (hb) Climb the sloper edgeways out the roof and up to the pocket.

Freaky Boulder

This boulder is located up within the talus several feet from the lake's south end.

1. **Freak of Nature V14** Climb the separate block out the underside, then hook your heel on the right side of the arête up and right through the bulge.

Marble Block ▼

This is another boulder amid the talus. Hike to the left (east) of the talus, and you will see this large block.

1. **The Marble V10** Climb the bulge on the left side of the west face.

2. **Sheer V4 (hb)** Climb up the left side of the west face.

Sunspot Boulder ▼

This leaning, somewhat perched boulder is up the talus on the left, just before a grassy flat.

1. **Sunspot V11** Climb out the severe overhang to the jugs.

2. **McFly V10** Traverse out the cave to the left of *Sunspot*.

Bivy Block

This block is to the northwest and across the grassy flat from Sunspot Boulder. It has a steep north face with good problems

1. Bivy Site V3 (hb) Climb up the middle of the north face.

Lakeview Boulder

This large boulder is upslope a short way and to the southeast of Bivy Block.

1. Lakeview Arête V3 Climb up the right-hand arête on the west face.

Tommy's Arête Block

This block is a big draw due to its awesome features. It can be found among the talus, characterized as a spiked block with arêtes.

1. Tommy's Arête V7 Climb out the over-hanging prow/arête.

2. The Automator V13 Climb the 15-foot overhanging arête just left of *Tommy's Arête.*

3. Triple Threat V10 Climb the big arête in the underbelly.

4. Another Tommy's Arête V8 Climb the arête right of the underbelly.

Deep Purple Block

This block is located just past Tommy's Arête Block.

1. Deep Purple Dynamics V9 (hb) Climb up the middle of the overhanging face.

Bush Block

This is another block amid the talus.

1. Bush Pilot V11 Climb from the dihedral to the crimp slaps to the arête.

Autobot Pit

This is a corridor-style pit with routes that climb out its wall. A fall off these faces might be strange for a landing, but definitely worthwhile.

1. Autobot V5 Climb out the 29-foot pit on the overhanging face.

2. Gobot V4 Climb the overhanging left-leaning face.

Wild Basin

These boulders, located in the Wild Basin area, offer good problems to form a decent alternative bouldering area close to the roadside.

To reach these boulders from the north via Estes Park, head south on Highway 7. Go about a mile past Meeker Park, and then take a right (west) at the Wild Basin turnoff. From the south, take Highway 7 approximately 2 miles past Allenspark. Take a left (west) at the Wild Basin turnoff. Continue west and take a right at the split in the road. Go approximately 1.5 miles past Copeland Lake to a parking area on the left side of the road.

Wild Basin Block

You can reach this boulder from the parking area by hiking up the road 120 feet to a NO PARKING sign. Then cut off to the right (west) through the aspens until you reach this large block.

1. West Meany V9 Climb the black streak, on the far-left side of the west face.

2. Dynoright V6 Climb the face via the corner to the right of *West Meany.*

3. White and Tan V2 Climb the face to the right of the white and tan bulge.

4. Goldie V6 Climb up to the shelf, starting low in the gold rock.

5. Straight Gold V3 Climb straight up from the gold rock.

6. Southwest Arête V4 Climb the arête on the southwest corner.

7. South Face V2 Climb up the left side of the south face. Best for down climb.

8. Slabs V0 Climb the easy route on the south face.

9. Wild Traverse V4 Traverse the south face from right to left. Other traverses exist.

8 ALLENSPARK

See map on page 88.

The Allenspark area offers good bouldering sites that are well worthwhile. The Ironclads, located south of Allenspark, have good boulders that surround the larger Clad Irons formations. To the east across the valley you will find the awesome Deer Ridge Blocks. These big blocks can be seen upslope to the northeast of Allenspark, peering out of the thinly forested slopes.

Ironclads

This area has many boulders that surround the Clad Iron formations.

Directions: From the town of Lyons, head west on Highway 7, through South St. Vrain Canyon, and continue toward the town of Allenspark. A short way past Highway 72, take a left on Forest Road 115 and follow it up to the heart of the Clad Irons. You will find plenty of bouldering to pick and choose from.

Even Flow Blocks/Deer Ridge

These large blocks offer some of the best bouldering found along the Peak to Peak Highway (Highway 72). Their tops can be seen peeking out of the forested slopes just northeast of Allenspark. Although there are four main blocks with many problems, you can find other boulders and blocks within the trees. The clean gray and white granite offers steep to overhanging faces with horizontal breaks. The landings are great.

Directions: From the town of Lyons, head west on Highway 7, through South St. Vrain Canyon, and continue toward the town of Allenspark. Approximately 1 mile past the town, take a right onto the dirt subdivision road. Stay to the right and follow the road around to the southeast and then back north (approximately 2 miles) to a parking circle at its end. You will see a fire ring within the circle. Park and head up to the northeast through the forest. The first block is not too far upslope, so stay low at first. It is a good idea to spot these blocks from Highway 7 (seen upslope to the northeast from Allenspark), so as to get oriented to their whereabouts. The first blocks are reached with a ten-minute hike.

Troy Blocks

These are the first blocks you will see on the lower end of the slope. The Trojan Horse is the large, tall granite block on the left. The smaller, cubed Gray Stone is pressed up against the southwest end of Trojan Horse. From the parking area, hike to the

northeast for ten minutes and you will see these gem blocks.

Trojan Horse

This is the large, towering block on the left with an overhanging west face.

1. The Ladder V2 Climb up good holds on the steep north face.

2. The Horse V8 Climb up the steep west overhang to the top.

3. Trojan V5 Climb up the leaning arête from down low on the southeast face.

Gray Stone ▲

This classic block is to the right of Trojan Horse and has a sheer west face with many classics.

1. Far Left V2 Climb up the far-left side of the west face.

2. Left V3 Climb up the right of *Far Left*.

3. Central Route V4 Climb up the middle of the west face.

4. Horizontal Hop V4 Climb the west face to the right of the center with semi-dynamic to the top.

5. Far Right V3 Climb up the far-right side of the west face.

House Block
(east face)

House Block ◄

This massive block is upslope about 50 yards to the northeast from Trojan Horse.

1. South Visor V5 (hb) Climb out the overhang to the slab above on the south side of the boulder.

2. Conquer Crack V3 Climb the finger/hand crack on the northeast side of the block.

Moby Boulder ▼

This large elongated boulder is found another 75 yards upslope to the northeast from House Block. Many steep face problems line its south face.

1. Harpooner V4 Climb the steep shield on the far left end of the south face.

2. Edge Ladder V7 Climb the horizontal breaks in the middle of the upper end of the south face.

LYONS AREA

This area encompasses Rabbit Mountain and the Pile Tor to the east, Button Rock Reservoir and Big Elk Meadows to the northwest, and Hall Ranch and South St. Vrain Canyon to the southwest.

9 BIG ELK MEADOWS

This area has had a recent wave of development. You can find many classic problems on conglomerate granite in the draws below Kenny Mountain or just up off the road.

Directions: From the town of Lyons, head west on Highway 36 toward Estes Park. After Pinewood Springs, approximately 10 miles from Lyons, turn left (west) onto County Road 47 and look for the BIG ELK MEADOWS sign. For Dragon's Den, follow the road approximately 2.2 miles to a dirt pullout on the north side of the road.

Gem Boulder

From the parking area at 2.2 miles, head up to the south side of the road into the trees a few feet and you will see this awesome boulder, which has a steep and pointy north face.

1. Left Arête V4 Climb up the left arête of the north face.

2. The Gem V5 Climb up the middle of the north face.

3. Right Away V3 Climb up the right side of the north face.

Double Trouble Block ▼

This block is located just east of Gem Boulder and is square cut.

1. Get Over It V10 Climb out the thin overhang.

2. Square Meal V1 Climb up the left side of the east face.

Lyons Area Overview

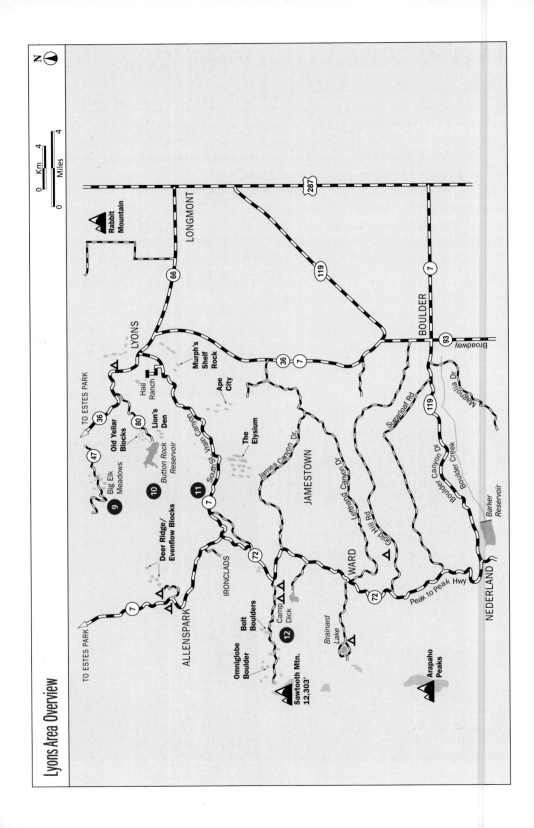

Dragon's Den

To find this area hike to the northwest, downslope to a gully, then up and over a small knoll, following it for a short distance. Cross over at a point where you see rebar sticking out of a rock in the creek. Continue along the trail approximately 300 feet to a rock pile. Scramble upslope for about five minutes. This will take you to the middle of the area.

The Matterhorn

This is the first spire you'll see as you enter Dragon's Den. Most of the problems are sit-down starts.

1. Dragon's Breath V4 Climb the slopers on the left arête to the top.

2. Dragon's Lair V5 Traverse across the face, right to left.

3. Drag On V4 Climb from the center to the left and up the arête.

The Cave

This is the obvious caved wall.

1. Whale V4 Climb from the undercling, out bulges to the lip.

2. Dungeon Bitch V5 Traverse from the right side of the cave to the corner, then up the underclings to the lip.

3. Dungeon V5 From the small undercling, fire for the lip.

4. Rockin' Bones V1 Climb the arching arête from the right side of the cave to the top.

Other boulders are scattered about, including Choss Roof Boulder, Dragon Fire Block, Gill Slab (easy), Highball Wall, Y-Boulder (easy), and Horsefly Block.

10 BUTTON ROCK RESERVOIR

This area is well worth a visit. The road and trails make this a convenient outing with a pleasant stream nearby, and many new areas have been developed. You should also check out the River Wall for some of Colorado's favorite single-pitch climbs concentrated in one area. Most recently, the Old Yellar Blocks and the Lion's Den have been favorite bouldering destinations. Although the hiking for the Lion's Den is more involved (forty to forty-five minutes), it is well worth the distance. The setting is serene and peaceful and there are lots of granite duds to play on.

Directions: From the town of Lyons, head northwest on Highway 36 toward Estes Park. Approximately 3.7 miles past the junction of Highway 36 and Highway 7, turn left at Shelly's Cottages onto County Road 80. Follow the dirt road about 3 miles, around, up, over, and down to the end, where it is gated off. Park in the large parking lot.

To reach Old Yellar Blocks, go through the gate and hike up the dirt road past a spillway. The River Wall is located across the stream to the right of the spillway. You can see Old Yellar Blocks across the stream and behind the upper part of the spillway that leads up to the Old Yellar formation.

For the Lion's Den, continue up the road for approximately fifteen minutes to a point where the telephone wires have crossed back from over the creek. At this point, take the faint switchback trail up to the left into the trees. A few more minutes up the road, and well marked with a sign, is the "new" Sleepy Lion Trail—this is not the trail you want; you've gone too far. For the Lion's Den, follow the faint Old Sleepy Lion Trail upslope via switchbacks. Along the way you pass Switchback Boulders, including Paulaner

Wall and the Prow. The trail eventually flattens as it heads through a meadow to the southwest, and soon takes you to an old road. Follow this road into a large clearing and then back around to the east. Look toward the eastern ridgeline close to the summit to see the boulders. This is the Lion's Den. You can find Lower Den by hiking down to the north through the forest.

Old Yellar Blocks

These fun blocks have really unique lip problems that are well worth checking out. Hike up the road from the parking lot. Just past the spillway, look upslope (north) to see this fall line of small blocks. Cross the creek wherever it is feasible.

Little Step Block ▲

This block is located just above Water Block, the middle of the three Old Yellar Blocks.

1. Welded Face V1 Climb up the left side of the south face.

2. Tuff V1 Climb up the middle of the south face.

3. Right On V1 Climb the edges on the right side of the south face.

4. Full On V5 Traverse from the left side of the south face around the corner to the lip of the east side and across to the right.

5. Lip Stick V2 Traverse from left to right across the lip of the east side.

Big Step Block

This block is located just upslope from Little Step.

1. Big Step V3 Traverse the lip of the block from far left to far right.

2. Sit Roof V2 Climb out the right side of the block from a sit start.

The Lion's Den

This area is located up Old Sleepy Lion Trail (see Directions). It offers nice walls, boulders, and blocks in an open, scenic setting. Although there is bouldering around the switchbacks, the best of the crop is found at the Den proper.

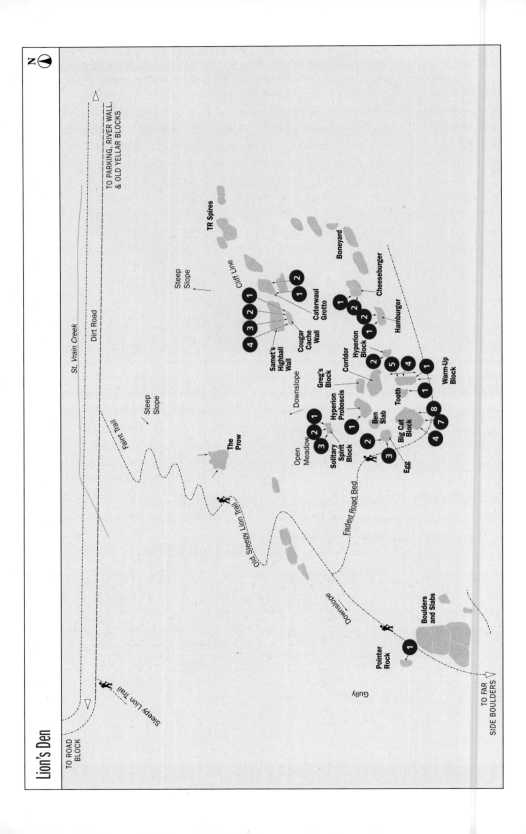

Lion's Den

Hyperion Proboscis ▲

As you approach the Lion's Den from the west, this obvious leaning pillar formation sits just off to the left of the faint trail roadbed behind some trees and on the edge of the meadow 100 feet downslope from the Egg.

1. Hyperion Proboscis V7 Climb out the overhanging pillar utilizing the arêtes on either side.

Solitary Spirit Block ▶

This block is located 150 feet to the northwest of Hyperion Proboscis. It's characterized by its tomato shape.

1. Solitary Confinement V2 Climb the east arête.

2. Solitary Spirit V3 Climb the scooped face with long reaches.

3. Seldom Seen V1 Climb the slab on the west face.

Greg's Block

This block is located to the northeast of Hyperion Proboscis and north of the large Big Cat Block. It is the northern block of a cluster.

1. Greg's Dada V2 Climb the finger seam of the west face.

The Egg

Appropriately named for its egg shape, this boulder is located just northwest of Big Cat Block. The egg shape makes for good bulge problems out good solid edges.

1. Egg Roof V7 Climb the finger seam out from the cave on the northeast face. Utilize the crystal and slap for the rounded top.

2. Over Easy V8 Climb the prow of the west face via crimpy edges and crystals.

3. Poached V4 Climb the west face from the prow across the horizontal, to white hold then good flakes.

4. Scrambled V4 Climb from the high platform to good holds up top.

Big Cat Block ▶

This large block is located just south of the Egg. Highball problems abound.

1. Scaredy Cat V3 (hb) Climb the finger seam on the left side of the west face.

2. The Big Cat V4 (hb) Climb the quality finger flake to the water groove on the west face.

3. Lion Bitch V6 (hb) Climb the arêtes and prow up the reddish brown, small-edged rock.

4. Knee Bar Pussy V6 (hb) Climb up the southwest prow.

5. Punch the Kitty V5 (hb) Climb up the scoop on the south face.

6. Alley Cat V0 (hb) Climb the dihedral and crack on the far-left side of the south face.

7. Tigger V0 Climb the flakes on the middle of the south face; a pine tree is above.

8. Catfish V0 Climb the east arête to the crack finish.

Corridor ▲

This highball, flat-surfaced wall offers solid rock with lots of good edges and flakes. It is located about 40 feet upslope to the east of the Egg.

1. Schwank V1 Climb out over the roof from the right side of the block.

2. Linoleum V2 Climb up the scoop in the center of the south face.

3. Hall Pass V1 Climb layback crack in the tannish rock to the ripple top.

4. Main Line V1 Climb layback on the block beyond *Hall Pass.*

The Tooth

This is a wall within the corridor just west of Warm-Up Block, east of Big Cat Block.

1. Rollerball V0 Climb the south-facing prow.

2. Canines V2 Climb the layaway to the prow with green-lichen face.

Warm-Up Block

This fin-shaped rock is a good warm-up for the area. It is located just east of the Tooth and Big Cat Block.

1. South Arête V0 Climb good holds up the south prow.

2. PW Traverse V4 Traverse from right to left across the block's east face.

3. Moss Boss V1 Climb from the horn to good flakes.

4. Choss Boss V1 Climb the hand crack on the east face.

5. Crack N Up V1 Climb the thin finger crack through the blackened rock.

6. Slab Master V1 Climb the layback seam through the pinkish rock.

Hyperion Block ▲

This smaller block protrudes from the ground and is located just east of Warm-Up Block.

1. Hyperion Lunge V0 A running-jump problem up the center of the north face.

2. Hyperion Arête V3 Climb the short arête to the right.

Lower Den

These boulders are located in the pine forest approximately 100 feet downslope east of the Lion's Den proper. The rock is good, but you have to explore. Hike due east downslope on the old road and then follow it north to the canyon's edge.

The Hamburger

This aptly named boulder/block is located due east about 100 feet from Hyperion Block. It has bulged ends.

1. Happy Meal V3 Climb horizontals on the northwest face, over the bulge and up.

2. Hamburger V5 Climb from horizontal out the crimpy bulge.

The Cheeseburger ▼

The Cheeseburger is located in a meadow setting about another 100 feet northeast of the Hamburger.

1. Supersize It V1 Climb the northwest face up breaks left of the tree.

2. Cheeseburger V3 Climb upslopers right of the tree.

3. Extra Cheese V3 Climb southwest face utilizing a pinkish hold.

Caterwaul Grotto

Continue downslope from the Cheeseburger to the rim of the canyon. Look for a break and a pine tree and go into the corridor. Caterwaul Grotto is located to the northeast of the Hamburger-Cheeseburger area.

1. The Howling V4 Climb the blackened face of the corridor, behind the pine tree.

2. Sweetness V0 Climb good holds to the hueco and up.

3. Right Now V4 (hb) Climb the black face above the ramp.

4. Steadman's Heffer V2 Climb the small buttress above the nice soft landing.

Cougar Cache Wall ▼

This pyramid-shaped rock is located 100 feet up and west of Caterwaul Grotto at the far-west end, just off the cliff line. It is also approximately 300 feet downslope to the northeast of the Egg.

1. Cougar Left V1 Climb the good holds on the far-left side of the north face.

2. Bathtubs V0 Climb jugs just right of *Cougar Left*.

3. Cougar's Crank V1 Climb the north face up to the right of *Bathtubs* to the horn.

4. Cougar n a Bing Bing Bling V3 Climb out from the undercling on the red face to the right of *Cougar's Crank*.

5. Cougar Cooze V1 Climb the face a few feet to the right of *Cougar n a Bing Bing Bling*.

6. Cougar Cache Traverse V3 Traverse in either direction across the north face.

The Catacombs

This collection of boulders and blocks is located downslope from Cougar Cache Wall. Walk around to the west and down from Highball Wall (aka Samet's Highball Wall), heading slightly to the north, and soon you cross into this cluster of rock.

Pumatron Block

This block is located just to the southwest of Highball Wall. It is capped with a unique rock formation.

1. Pumatron V4 Climb up the slab on the right, then out left to the summit.

2. KneeHigh V2 Climb the face on the right side to the arête, then to the summit.

Road Block ▼

This obvious roadside block is located up Button Rock Road another fifteen minutes past the Old Sleepy Lion Trail turnoff. It is seen on the right side of the road. Its south face has an appealing set of highball problems.

1. Humanoid Height V4 (hb) Climb the crack on the left side of the block's south face.

2. Genetic Control V5 (hb) Climb the seam and edge system on the right side of the south face.

11 SOUTH ST. VRAIN CANYON

See map on page 88.

This canyon extends from the town of Lyons in the east up toward the divide on the west. Many granite boulders, blocks, and walls extend rampantly through this stream-fed canyon. Eventually the canyon leads west to Camp Dick, another bouldering area full of excellent boulder problems.

Directions: From the intersection of Highway 36 and Highway 7 in Lyons, take Highway 7 west through this canyon (the mileages start at the intersection). The first area is the Hall Ranch Open Space Park on the north side of the highway (not described). At 3.1 miles Murph's Shelf Block is on the south side (not described), followed by Ape City at 5 miles and the Elysium at 7 miles, both found on the south side of the road.

Ape City

From the junction of Highway 36 and Highway 7, drive up South St. Vrain Canyon on Highway 7 toward Allenspark for approximately 5 miles. Park on the south side of the road at the pull off near mile marker 28.

Follow the faint trail downslope and left from the parking area. Cross the creek where it is safe and head up the trail beyond a boulder in the trees. Locate the fall line and hike up the draw for a few minutes and you will see the first significant rocks. Some of the problems are airy but reasonable.

Sexy Block

This block is a short way upslope across the stream on the south side. It has a sheer, somewhat blank south face with good problems on its northwest corner.

1. Silverback V7 Climb the thin northwest prow.

The Elysium

This fall line of granite boulders and blocks offers a huge amount of problems with great variety and challenge. The boulders here are of every shape and size and have bulges, overhangs, steep faces, and arêtes, as well as tricky slab climbing. This is often the case for the topouts. Take caution when crossing the

river during runoff season, which is usually late spring and summer. Also take note of the poison ivy that can be found throughout this area. This is one of St. Vrain's best bouldering areas and is still fresh and crisp. Only recently have people begun to visit the area.

Directions: From the intersection of Highway 7 and Highway 36 in Lyons, go west on Highway 7 for approximately 7 miles to a parking lot on the left (south) side of the road. This is a large lot for day use only. Up to the southeast, at the top of the slope, you will spot a small bulbous granite outcrop. Below you will see the fall line of granite that leads all the way to the stream. Park and cross the stream where it seems fit. Head upslope toward the obvious large boulders within the draw.

Jupiter Boulder

This is the first boulder you cross as you head up through the boulderfield.

1. Fat City V8 Climb the northwest prow of the boulder to the top.

2. Silly Warm Up V2 Climb the north face of the boulder.

Ragland Block

This block is located just south of Jupiter Boulder and has a pointy top.

1. Shorebreak Direct V6 (hb) Climb the northwest arête from down low to the bulge, out left and up.

2. Shorebreak V2 (hb) Climb up the center of north face, over a bulge to the slab, then to the top.

3. Like Glass V1 (hb) Climb the northeast slab right of the crack.

4. Flip Flop Slab V0 Climb the slab left of the crack.

Swell Block

This is the larger block located just to the south of Jupiter Boulder and Ragland Block.

1. Reef Rash V2 Climb the left side of the north face from down low.

2. Big Wednesday Traverse V7 Traverse from right to left and up.

3. Big Wednesday V4 Climb from under the overhang on the right side, up and out.

4. Bailing Out V2 Climb from the left side of the overhang around to the slab.

5. Miserlou V7 Climb from the left side of the overhang across to the right and up.

6. Charlie Don't Surf V8 Climb across the overhang, finish out its center.

7. Fear of Close Out V6 Climb out the center of the overhang via crimpy lip moves.

8. Charger V8 Climb from the far-right side of the overhang, across left to center, then up.

9. Lip Trick V5 Climb from the far-right side of the overhang, across left, then mantle up.

PJ Boulder ▼

This boulder is just east of Swell Block. It has a wide horizontal crack on its north face.

1. State of Love and Confusion V8 (hb) Climb the north face via the small edge to the wide crack, exit left.

2. Grievance V4 (hb) Climb the north face several feet left of *State of Love and Confusion* via small edges to flake.

3. Red Mosquito V7 Climb the face just right of the northeast corner.

4. Nothingman V4 Climb the northeast arête.

Lebowski Boulder ▲

This boulder is several yards east of the previous boulders.

1. The Dude Abides V4 Climb the thin southeast arête.

2. Over the Line V5 Climb the seam on the south face.

3. Mark It Zero V0 Climb up the west face.

4. No Frame of Reference V3 Climb the northwest corner of boulder.

Huxley Boulder ▼

This boulder is across to the southeast from Lebowski Boulder.

1. Doors of Perception V4 (hb) Climb up the west face left of the tree, then up and over the bulge to the top.

2. Island V3 Climb the seam to the left of *Doors of Perception* up and over the bulge.

12 CAMP DICK

This somewhat-alpine bouldering area offers lots of quality granite boulders spread throughout the valley floor. Some of the boulders sit along the stream, while others are within the forest of pine and aspen. At the tail end of the main boulders, you come to a meadowesque setting with awesome views of the Indian Peaks and Continental Divide. There is camping at the east end of the valley, with a convenient four-wheel road that runs several miles to the west. If you don't have a four-wheel drive vehicle, the hiking here is very pleasant. A nice trail is located on the north side of the stream, or you can simply walk along the road.

Directions: From Boulder, head west up Boulder Canyon (Highway 119) toward

Nederland. Once in Nederland, take the first traffic circle to the right onto Peak to Peak Highway (Highway 72) toward Ward. Continue north on Peak to Peak Highway approximately 6.5 miles and you will come to a hairpin in the road; look for the sign to Camp Dick. At the hairpin, go west off Highway 72 and take the paved road about 1.3 miles, past Peaceful Valley Campground and the Camp Dick Campground, until it dead ends at the Buchanan Pass trailhead. Park here or continue up the rugged four-wheel drive road. If you do not have the right vehicle, forget it; the hike is much better anyway.

Some of the boulders are located along the Buchanan Pass Trail. Others are located along the road. See the map.

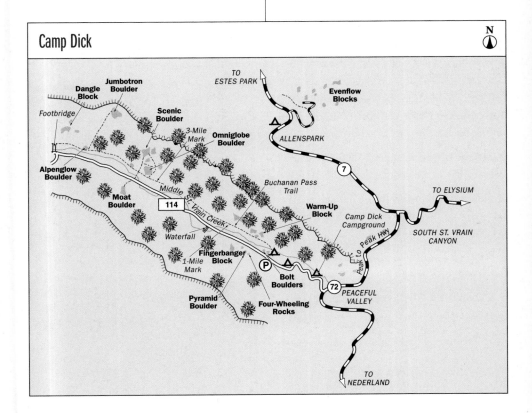

Camp Dick

N

TO ESTES PARK

Dangle Block
Jumbotron Boulder
Footbridge
Scenic Boulder
3-Mile Mark
Omniglobe Boulder
Evenflow Blocks
ALLENSPARK
Alpenglow Boulder
Middle
Moat Boulder
114
St. Vrain Creek
Buchanan Pass Trail
7
TO ELYSIUM
Waterfall
Warm-Up Block
Camp Dick Campground
SOUTH ST. VRAIN CANYON
Fingerbanger Block
1-Mile Mark
P
Bolt Boulders
72
PEACEFUL VALLEY
Pyramid Boulder
Four-Wheeling Rocks
Peak to Peak Hwy

TO NEDERLAND

Bolt Boulders

Follow the dirt road a short distance west from the parking area and you will see these boulders on the right side of the road in the brush. Good landings abound.

Thunder Bolt Boulder ▲

This is the best boulder of the three in this area. It is also the tallest and has a clean white granite surface on its north face.

1. UK Hockey Night V6 (hb) Climb the arête on the far-left side of the north face.

2. Legend of the Drunken Master V7 (hb) Climb right of a black streak up the corner.

3. Sidepull Sammy V3 (hb) Climb the north face right of *Legend of the Drunken Master* via layaways.

4. Shorty V2 Climb the far right side of the north face.

5. Slabs V0–V3 Climb the various slabs facing the road.

Traverse Boulder ▶

You can find this trailside rock after hiking along the Buchanan Pass Trail several hun-

dred yards. Cross the bridge over the creek, east of the Bolt Boulders area, north of the parking lot. Head west down the trail.

1. The Traverse V4 Traverse from left to right along the boulder's slopers on the southwest face.

2. Hour Glass V3 Climb up the middle of the southwest face into the groove up the top.

Fridge Block ◄

This block is up behind Traverse Boulder to the northwest.

1. Icebox V1 Climb up the middle of the southwest face.

Warm-Up Area

Hike farther west along the trail and you will run into these blocks. Many straight-up problems as well as traverses can be done on these trailside rocks.

Warm-Up Block ▼

1. East Slab V0 Climb up the left side of the east face.

Four-Wheeling Rocks

These rocks are along or just off the roadway as you head west from the parking lot and the Bolt Boulders area.

Pyramid Boulder

Continue up the road for 0.5 mile from the Bolt Boulders and park in a clearing (if you drove). Hike south about 120 feet along a deer trail and you will see this boulder.

1. Warmth V0 Climb up the far-left side to the top utilizing a crystal.

2. Treetop Flyer V5 (hb) Climb the right-leaning crack.

3. Mr. Clean V7 Climb up the blackened prow.

Fingerbanger Block ▼

Continue west up the road from the Pyramid Boulder parking for 0.2 mile to a campsite clearing. Hike due south a few feet to this nice-looking block.

1. Pete's Party Pudding V1 On the left side of the south face is a shorter crimpy leap problem.

2. Matt's Dirty Fingers V3 Climb the seam through the black streak in the center of the south face.

3. Slopus V0 Climb the arête on the right side of the south face.

4. Drop Kick Murphy V4 Climb the finger crack on the east face.

5. LeFingerbanger V7 Climb from the rail to the rounded arête then up and left.

6. Pattycake V6 Climb up the overhanging blackened scoop.

Omniglobe Area

This area is approximately 2.2 miles west of Fingerbanger Block, or 3 miles from the parking area. There is a parking spot at the 3-mile mark on the right side of the road. Moat Block is found just south of this parking area. Omniglobe Boulder, Fork Boulder, Scenic Boulder, and Huge Boulders (not described) are across the stream to the north, east, and west.

Moat Block

A couple of miles west of Fingerbanger Block, 3.1-miles from the parking lot, this block is characterized by a watery northwest side. It is a large block with quality problems.

1. Fortress V4 Climb up the middle of the east face, angling left up the edge system.

2. Wizards V6 Climb the northeast prow.

3. Warlocks V5 Climb the north face above the moat to the blackened scoop.

4. Witches V6 Climb above the right side of the moat to the slab, then up to the ramp on the right.

Omniglobe Boulder ▼

If you are approaching in a four-wheel-drive vehicle, park at the 3-mile marker, hike northwest, cross the streambed, and continue west until you intersect with the Buchanan Pass Trail. From the main trail follow a faint trail northeast to the boulder.

If you are approaching on foot along the Buchanan Pass Trail, look for the parking spot at the 3-mile marker down on the road and continue another 200 yards (five minutes), and then head right to the boulder.

Look for the cairns. Omniglobe is a massive boulder of clean white and gray granite in a forest setting. It has face, crack, and big roofs.

1. Dogfight V6 Climb out the north cave from the undercling on the left side.

2. Put Some Hair Around It V8 Climb out the north cave just right of *Dogfight,* utilizing slopers.

3. Schwagg V6 (hb) Climb out the north cave just right of *Put Some Hair Around It,* utilizing pinches.

4. Gonjar V3 (hb) Climb out right of the north cave past double tiers in the black streak.

5. VBGV V1 (hb) Climb from the V in the white face of the west face.

6. Tricky Stick V2 (hb) Climb the laybacks right of *VBGV.*

7. Theo's Problem V6 (hb) Climb small edges left of the tree on the west face.

Omniglobe Boulder
(southwest face)

8. Maxi-Pad V4 (hb) Climb from the rail on the southeast face, out the cave across the prow.

9. Cleaner's Call V7 (hb) Climb to the lip right of *Maxi-Pad*.

10. Sweet Emily V8 (hb) Climb out and up just right of *Cleaner's Call*.

11. Southeast Face V2 (hb) Climb out the rail directly below the right side of the upper roof.

12. Omni V4 (hb) Climb out the prow on the far-left side of the south face just right of the upper roof.

13. Ominous V5 (hb) Climb up the thin crack angling to the arête on the east face.

14. Raggedy Man V4 (hb) Climb from the ground rock, up the right angling ramp.

15. Raggedy Ann V0 Climb up the corner behind the tree on the east face.

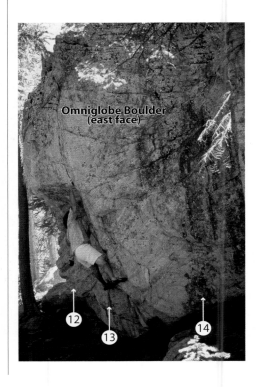

Omniglobe Boulder
(east face)

Fork Boulder

From Omniglobe Boulder, hike north through the forest and you will come across this overhanging block.

1. Ball That Jack V5 (hb) Climb up the scoop in the middle of the north-facing overhang.

Scenic Boulders

To find this cluster of boulders continue from Fork Boulder and Omniglobe Boulder upslope to the northwest. The rock ranges from granite to a gray, high-quality alpine-style conglomerate.

Parallellogram Boulder

This rectangular boulder forms the east wall of the corridor. It has some nice warm-up face routes on its west face.

The Uber-Pyramid

This large boulder forms the western portion of the corridor. It has some interesting highballs.

Scenic Boulder

This boulder hosts nice problems in an awesome setting. It has an extensive overhanging southeast-facing wall. It is at the western end of the area, up on a ledge system.

1. I Love Dick V7 (hb) Climb up the right side of the boulder's south face.

2. Swallow This V5 (hb) Climb the finger seam in the corner on the left side of the east face.

3. Easy Highball V2 (hb) Climb the face right of *Swallow This* on the right side of the east face.

4. We Gotta Save Them Critters V5 (hb) Climb the face on the far-right side of the east face.

Alpenglow Boulder ▼

Get back on the Buchanan Pass Trail and continue west for ten minutes. You will see this nice boulder on the right, next to the trail, sitting by itself in the clearing. Use this as a marker for where you want to head upslope to Jumbotron Boulder. The views are

inspiring, and there are fun problems around its faces.

1. Alpenprow V2 Climb the prow on the southwest edge of the boulder.

Jumbotron Boulder

From Alpenglow Boulder, hike up to the northeast on a faint trail. Jumbotron is a huge boulder in a nice setting.

1. Get to the Point V3 Climb the right-leaning roof to the arête on the west face, go right, around the corner from the hole.

2. Jumbo Arête V2 Climb the southwestern arête.

3. Mumbo Jumbo V4 Climb from deep in the cave on the southeastern notch up and left.

4. Jumbo Shrimp V0 Climb out the short roof on the southeast edge of the boulder.

5. Dead Teletubbies V5 Climb out the left side of the cave on the northeast face, utilizing slopers.

6. Uncle Mike's Late Show V4 Climb out the right side of the cave via small edges.

7. Casual Corner V2 Climb the corner on the left side of the cave on the northwest face.

8. Ken's Party Pudding V7 Climb from within the cave's left side.

9. The Orifice V2 Climb out positive holds from within the cave, just right of *Ken's Party Pudding*.

10. Dick's Party Pudding V4 Climb out the right side of the cave.

Dangle Block ▼

This block is approximately 200 yards up the Buchanan Pass Trail to the west of Alpenglow Boulder. From the trail you can see it on the slope to the north.

1. By the Balls V1 Climb up the ramp and face on the far-left side of the south face.

2. Wangle V5 Climb up the steep face to the shelf just right of the tree.

BOULDER AREA

Residents as well as visitors to the Boulder area are fortunate to have one of the world's greatest concentrations of boulders to climb on and explore. Variations in rock type, holds, steepness, and environment provide bouldering and training possibilities for climbers of all abilities.

Traditionally, areas such as Eldorado Canyon and Flagstaff Mountain have been the hot spots for the area's bouldering enthusiasts, and for good reason. However, there are many more areas throughout the Flatirons that offer premium bouldering. The excellent rock quality and beauty of these boulders and their surroundings offer experiences I hope you will enjoy and help preserve for many generations to come.

A few of the areas near Boulder have seasonal raptor closures. The closures at present are in effect from February 1 through July 31. These areas are the Third Flatiron, Sacred Cliffs, Skunk Canyon, Fern Canyon, and

Boulder Area Overview

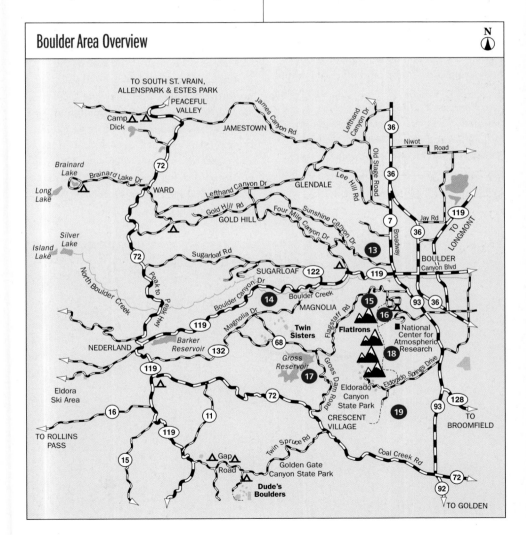

Shadow Canyon. Find alternate destinations during these times. Get updates from authorities (www.bouldercolorado.gov), because the closures are sometimes lifted early.

There are also Habitat Conservation Areas that are not off limits for access, but a permit is required. It is free of charge and can be printed at www.co.boulder.co.us/open space/. Detailed maps are also available that show boulders and areas requiring a permit.

If you are visiting Boulder and the weather turns bad (or even if it doesn't), consider visiting the Spot Bouldering Gym. This is Boulder's premier indoor bouldering gym and offers an excellent artificial bouldering experience. It is also home to many national bouldering competitions and other fun events. To find the Spot, get on Arapahoe Avenue and turn north on Thirtieth Street. Follow Thirtieth Street a few blocks to a right on Walnut Street. Follow Walnut to a left on Thirty-second Street, and follow it to a right on Prairie Street. Take Prairie up a block and you will see the gym on the right.

13 MOUNT SANITAS

This spiny ridge of west-facing outcrops is filled with moderate boulder problems that have good landings. A short hike uphill to the ridge takes you to a pine-scented sandstone bouldering area featuring enough rock to please all levels of ability.

Directions: To reach Mount Sanitas you must locate Colorado Highway 93 (Broadway) in Boulder. Take Broadway to Mapleton Street, just north of the Pearl Street Mall downtown. Take Mapleton west toward the mountains. The small city park with its pavilion and fire pit is located about half a block west of Memorial Hospital at the base of the foothills. Park near the shelter and walk north over a footbridge, following the trail around to the west (left) and uphill until you reach the main ridge. This north-stretching ridge is filled with cracks, faces, and arêtes and makes an enjoyable after-work place to go. Just look along the walls for the chalk marks to find the many well-tracked problems this fun place has to offer.

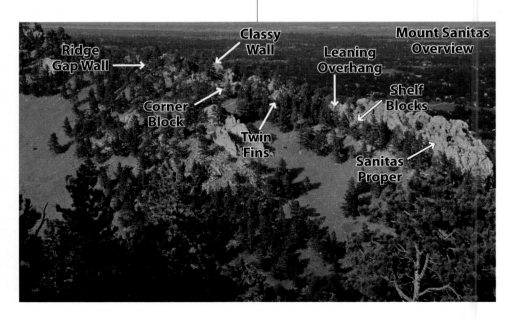

Shelf Blocks

These blocks are about a half mile from the trailhead. Walk onto the shelf.

North Shelf Block ▼

1. Shelving Traverse V2 Traverse the blocks from north to south.

2. The Layaway V1 Climb up the face on the far-left side via laybacks.

3. Bulging Crack V2 (hb) Climb up the crack and over the bulge.

4. Tree Left Face V1 Climb the face just left of the tree, right of *Bulging Crack*.

5. V0 Corner V0 Climb the face and corner right of the tree.

6. V0 Slot V0 Climb the slot right of the Corner.

7. Face the Right V0 This block is somewhat connected to North Shelf Block and located on the shelf to the south. Climb the face up the middle of the block to its highest point.

Leaning Overhang ▼

From the North Shelf Blocks, walk up and around to the north, to the east side of the Sanitas Proper. This excellent bouldering apparatus is hanging on an eastern shelf and has great landings.

1. The Leaning Overhang V5 (B1+) Climb out the overhang to the right, utilizing the best edges available. Other eliminates are also worthwhile.

Twin Fins

Continue upslope, a short way from the Sanitas Proper and its North and South Shelf Blocks, along the trail, and you can't miss these classic dakota fins. One sits to the right of the trail (the lower fin), and one sits above and behind the other. Both offer great fun.

East Fin ▼

This fin is located just behind and to the east of West Fin.

1. Traverser V1 Traverse the wall.

2. Flake V0 Climb up the layback system.

3. Face V0 Climb up the middle of the face.

4. Face Route V0 Climb up the far-right side of the fin.

West Fin ▼

This is the westernmost fin along the trail.

1. Traverse Fin V2 Traverse the lower portion of the fin.

2. Undercling Fin V0 Start off the undercling and climb up the left side of the face.

3. Crack in the Fin V0 Climb the crack on its west face.

4. Other One V1 Climb the face immediately right of *Crack in the Fin*.

5. Right One V0 Climb the face on the far-right side.

Corner Block ◀

Hike a short way up the trail from the Fins and you come to this blocky spire of dakota on the right side of the trail.

1. Overhanger V3 Climb the steep face on the far-left side of the block.

2. The Prow V2 Climb the prow of the block.

3. Bulgy V0 Climb the far-right bulge of the block.

Classy Wall ▼

Immediately up from and behind Corner Block, you see this sheer-edged wall.

1. Central Left V1 Climb up the left side of the wall.

2. Central Right V1 Climb up the right side of the wall.

14 BOULDER CANYON

Boulder Canyon is rich with fine granite and offers a large number of single- and multi-pitch routes. Boulder fields of this quality granite are limited, but in recent years there has been a lot of development and new discoveries. The well-known bouldering that exists in Boulder Canyon is located mostly at the bases of the larger formations, with some scattered in the trees along the creek or in secluded gullies.

The Wafer, located up across the road to the southwest from the Dome, is worthwhile, as are the Canyon Block Boulders. Cob Rock has a large talus field on its north-facing slopes and offers some good boulders and blocks (some that are yet to be sent). Farther up the canyon you will not want to miss Graham Boulder, hidden creekside a short way from the roadside. This nice, granite dud offers challenging problems for all ability levels. The Patio traverse is an excellent place to train in any weather and is at the base of Bell Buttress, a short way across the creek, sitting in seclusion on a scenic shelf.

Farther up the road are the Animal Boulders, just west of Animal World Rock. Many quality problems are found here. Next are the High Energy Blocks, also sitting in seclusion on the shelves up above High Energy Crag. Farther on is the Coney Island Area, located on both sides of the road. The Nip and Tuck crags are also hot spots for the advanced boulderer, with problems that have become quite classic, including *The Barrio Traverse,* an awesome roof traverse with unlimited variations.

These destinations are capped off by Castle Rock, which hosts several classic Gill problems such as *The Acrobat Overhang* and *The Gill Crack.* More recent attractions within this area are the creekside Castle Rock Cube and Hardboiled Block. Even farther up the canyon are the Forest Boulders, a great place to escape the summer heat or the lower areas.

Boulder Canyon offers an excellent bouldering experience with refreshing Boulder Creek close by and plenty of places to roam and explore.

Directions: To reach Boulder Canyon, locate Highway 93 (Broadway in Boulder) and take it to Canyon Boulevard. Go west on Canyon Boulevard (Highway 119) straight into Boulder Canyon. All mileages are given from the intersection of Broadway and Canyon Boulevard.

Boulder Canyon Mileages

Elephant Buttress	0.5 mile
Dome Boulder	1.6 miles
Tunnel	2.8 miles
Mental Rock	4.8 miles
Eagle Rock	6.2 miles
Cob Rock	6.6 miles
Graham Boulder	7.4 miles
Boulder Falls	7.6 miles
Mine Shaft Block	7.8 miles
Bell Buttress/The Patio	8.1 miles
Vampire/Animal World	8.6 miles
Easter Rock	9.0 miles
High Energy Crag	9.1 miles
Coney Island	9.2 miles
Nip and Tuck	10.5 miles
Castle Rock	11.8 miles
Surprising Crag	12.4 miles
Barker Reservoir	13.7 miles

Boulder Canyon

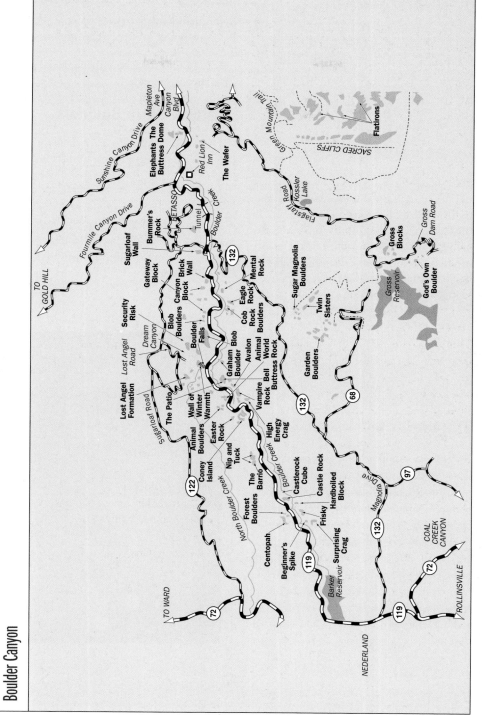

N

Elephant Buttress
Area/Lower Canyon

As you enter Boulder Canyon, there is a large four-point buttress on the right (north) side of the road called the Elephant Buttress. Northwest of this buttress is a prominent granite dome appropriately named the Dome. Just past these granite masses are two road cuts. Park at the road cut to access these areas.

Dome Boulder

This minicliff is south of the Dome's summit and offers moderate traverses and highballs. Drive 1.6 miles from the intersection of Broadway and Canyon Boulevard and park in the large parking area just past the road cut. Hike up the south side of the Dome for ten minutes, through a gap to the area.

Bridge Wall

This section of wall is on the left side of the large road cut. Park, head toward the creek, cross the bridge, and you will see a nice section that can be bouldered up and exited before going too high.

The Wafer ▶

This granite chunk can be seen upslope to the south, on the slope above and across the road from the Elephant Buttress and the Dome. It is on the east side of the first road cut and can be accessed by driving past the road cut and parking in the large parking area on the left (same as for the Dome). From the parking area, hike upslope on a faint trail that leads over the ridge to the southeast. The Wafer is located out to the south among the granite slabs and is readily distinguishable as you skirt around the slabs.

1. Espresso Wafer V2 Climb up the left-angling arête on the right side of the block.

2. Dolly Madison V1 Climb the face to the right traversing ledge system, then to the top.

3. Food Club V5 Climb the underside of the left arête to the top.

Canyon Block Boulders

These boulders are located just above the road and in the gully west of the Canyon Block formation. Good, isolated granite duds are found here. Drive up the canyon 5.6 miles and park on the right. Hike up as if going to Canyon Block but stay in the gully and follow it up the slope that leads behind to the west of the ridgeline that holds Canyon Block.

Cranial Boulder ▲

This nice boulder, split by a diagonal crack, is up the west gully from Canyon Block. Hike up the gully for ten minutes, or until you run into this boulder.

1. Angular Gyrus V3 Climb up the crack to the slopey shelf on the southwest side of the boulder.

2. Cerebral V2 Climb up the bulge and slab on the southeast side of the boulder.

Cob Rock Boulders/Middle Canyon

The blocks and boulders below Cob Rock offer a variety of classic problems, some of which have recently received a lot of attention due to the state-of-the-art standard of bouldering occurring at Mount Evans as well as at Rocky Mountain National Park's world-class areas such as Emerald Lake and Lake Hiyaha. Drive up the canyon 6.6 miles and park on the left (south) side of the road below the cliff. You can see Cob Rock and its fall line of boulders from the road.

Mast Block ▲

You can see this severely overhanging block at the lower end of the talus line. It has a point protruding from its north face.

1. Tied to the Mast V12? Climb the severely overhanging north side of the block.

Cob Block ▲

This block, with an overhanging northwest arête, is to the left and above Mast Block.

1. Corn on the Cob V4 (hb) Climb the leaning northwest arête.

Stacked Block ▲

This block is down at the base of the talus field, 100 feet east of Mast Block.

1. Pit Arête V2 Climb the arête from out of the pit on the east side of the rock.

Graham Boulder ▲

From the Cob Rock Boulders, drive a short way up the road toward Boulder Falls. At the Boulder Falls 1,000 feet sign, pull off on the opposite side of the road and park. At this point, you are approximately 7.4 miles up from Canyon Boulevard and Broadway. You can see the granite boulder within the trees on the south side, across Boulder Creek to the southeast from the pull off. Hike back east 200 feet and you will see the boulder.

1. Graham Arête V11 This is a short but difficult problem. Climbs up the north-facing arête, utilizing smears and crimps to gain the top.

2. West Face Left V1 Climb up the left side of the west face to good holds above.

3. Capps Face V6 Climb up thin holds in the center of the west face.

4. BH Arête V10 Climb up the prow-like arête on the right side of the west face.

Bell Buttress Area

The Patio ▼

This 50-foot traverse wall is below Bell Buttress, across from Practice Rock, 8.1 miles from Ninth Street. It is a nice refuge from the rain and offers a great pump relatively close to the road. Drive up the canyon 8.1 miles from Broadway and Canyon Boulevard and park on the right. Cross the creek to the south and head up to the shelf that has the caved traverse wall.

1. One Way Trip V4 Traverse from left to right across the 50-foot length of the wall.

2. Round About V6 Traverse back and forth across the 50-foot length.

Mine Shaft Block

Continue a short way up the road from Boulder Falls, 7.8 miles from Canyon Boulevard and Broadway, and park in a large lot on the right side of the road. An old mine shaft that has been sealed recently can be seen in the slope to the north. The block is located just down and left of the mine shaft–looking threshold.

1. Mine Shaft Arête V2 Climb up the right side of the block, utilizing the arête.

2. Mine Men V3 Climb up the face and crack left of *Mine Shaft Arête.*

Animal World Area

The Animal Boulders are just west of Animal World Rock, across the road from the Black Widow Slabs. Park as for Vampire Rock and Animal World, approximately 8.6 miles from Broadway and Canyon Boulevard. Cross the road and go approximately 25 yards west along the road. Head upslope into the trees and you will see this boulder pack sitting at the base of a broken cliff band.

Animal Block ◄

This prominent cubed block, the left of the three, is removed from the wall above.

1. Magnetism V2 Climb the left side of the south face.

2. Magnet V3 Climb the flake on the south face.

Animal Planet Block ▼

This block is just to the right of Animal Block and forms a cove with it.

1. Crocodile Hunter V2 Climb the middle of the south face.

Animal Spire ▲

This pinnacled boulder is within the trees to the right of Animal Block. It has a severe overhanging west side and a highball south and east side.

1. Magic Arête V6 (hb) Climb the overhang and arête on the southwest corner.

Easter Rock Block

This large block is in the trees to the west of the Easter Rock formation, approximately 9.0 miles up Boulder Canyon. Park as for Easter Rock and hike 200 feet up the steep slope to the west side of Easter Rock. The block is within the trees on the far southwest end of the Easter Rock formation.

High Energy Blocks

These blocks are on the shelf system to the right of the main High Energy Crag formation, across from Easter Rock at 9.1 miles up the canyon. Park as for Easter Rock at 9.0 miles, then hike up the right side of High Energy Crag to a point above the main cliff band and you will find these prominent blocks.

Energy Rock

This rock sits on the slabby shelf to the right of the prominent blocks.

1. To the Point V1 Climb up the middle of the east face.

Energy Block

This is the middle of the three blocks. A less-steep rock sits on its left, and Energy Rock is on its right.

1. Energy Arête V2 Climb up the northwest arête.

Coney Island Area

These boulders are below the main Coney Island Cliff, located approximately 9.2 miles up Boulder Canyon. The first boulder is creekside, while the others are below the first and second tiers of the shelved formation. Park at the small pullout on the south side of the road across from the cliff, or drive farther west to a larger pullout also on the south side of the road.

Fish Block

This block is creekside on the south side of the road below the formation, just above the creek.

1. Fisher V3 Climb up the middle of the south face.

Separator Block ▲

This block is below the first tier of the formation to the right (east) within the trees. Hike up the left side of the formation, cut to the east below the first set of sport climbs, and you will see this overhanging leaning block.

1. Up and Over V4 Climb out the overhangs of the block up and onto the slab.

Dragonfly Block ▲

This boulder is above the first tier of the Coney Island formation. Hike up the trail on the west side of the formation, past the first set of sport climbs on the lower tier. Continue to the upper headwall and head east to the ridge gap and shelf. The isolated boulder sits atop the ridge below the west side of the headwall.

1. Angry Dragon V7 From down low, climb up the dihedral roof system on the south side of the boulder.

2. Mod Arête V1 Climb up the arête and face on the left side of the east face.

3. Up and Away V1 Climb the crack and face on the north side.

Nip and Tuck/The Barrio

Approximately 10.5 miles up Boulder Canyon, on the right (north) side, you encounter Nip and Tuck. These two masses are separated by a gully that separates the western mass (Nip) from the eastern one (Tuck).

Nip

This is the western formation. It has an excellent face route on the left edge of the south face.

1. Gill's Bulges V5 Climb the sloping holds.

The Barrio ▲

At the far-left side of the Nip rock, behind the guardrail, look for a severely overhanging roof system with good-looking holds skirting diagonally to the upper right.

1. The Barrio Traverse V7 Start on the lower left end and traverse up to the right. Other variations exist.

Tuck ▶

This is the eastern formation, with a prominent overhanging, sheer wall with crack and arête.

1. Caddis V10 (hb) Climb the granite, right-leaning seam, left of the arête, through the bulge to the face above. Follow the bolts.

2. Touch Me I'm Sick V7 (hb) Climb the severely overhanging east wall, utilizing the arête and crack. This problem requires incredible state-of-the-art moves.

Castle Rock Area

You can see Castle Rock on the south side of the road at approximately 11.8 miles up Boulder Canyon. Turn south onto the access road that borders Castle Rock's west side and follow it south then around to the east, just past the main formation's south end. Cross the bridge and park.

Castle Rock

From the parking area, go around the west end of Castle Rock and locate the large south face. John Gill established many daring feats on this sheer granite bouldering wall.

1. The Acrobat Overhang V5 This is a problem of sheer finger strength. A doorjamb fingertip hang is practically necessary to pull this one off. Located on the far-left side of the south face.

2. The Gill Crack V5 (hb) Today most people toprope this and for a good reason. The crack is on the southwest face of Castle Rock, at the base of the wall, to the right of *The Acrobat Overhang*. Walk up a short slope from the dirt road and see this incredible crack.

To Castle Rock

Dirt Road

Boulder Creek

Castle Rock Cube ▲

From the parking area, look to the north across Boulder Creek and you will see this nice cube sitting along the creek's shore.

1. Standard Bulge V5 Climb up the roofed bulge on the north face of the boulder.

2. The Citadel V8 Climb up the prow from down low on the northwest corner of the cube.

3. Hit Hard Tactics V7 Climb the overhanging arête on the southwest corner of the cube.

Hardboiled Block ▶

This block is west of Castle Rock, below the Ice Falls Area. It offers a good lowball start onto a crimpy sheer face. Park at Castle Rock (11.8 miles) and hike up Highway 119 for 0.4 mile, then cross the creek to the south. (Parking is forbidden in front of the Ice Falls Area.) The block sits in a talus jumble and is the best and most obvious of the blocks.

1. Hardboiled V11 From a sit-down start, climb up the overhang to the sheer face on the west side of the block.

Forest Boulders

These boulders are on the north side of the road approximately 12.3 miles up from Broadway and Canyon Boulevard (west of Castle Rock and the Hardboiled Block). Park on the right side of Highway 119 at 12.3 miles and walk upslope into the fall line of boulders. You can find many good problems amid the forest.

Line Block ▼

This prominent block is 100 yards upslope to the northwest of the small boulders you encounter just off the road in the forest. It is characterized by a seam/layback crack that splits its south face. Other boulders in this vicinity are also worthwhile.

1. The Line V3 (hb) Climb the splitting line up the south face of the towering block.

Beginner's Spike

This rock is up the road from Castle Rock, on the east side of Surprising Crag, 12.4 miles from Broadway and Canyon Boulevard. Drive up the canyon 0.6 miles west of Castle Rock and park in the pullout on the south (left) side of the road, below Surprising Crag. Hike east a short way and cross the creek, aiming for the talus. The rock sits on the left, amid the talus.

1. The Beginner V0 Climb up the west side of the spike.

Garden Boulders

To find the Garden Boulders drive approximately 4.6 miles up Boulder Canyon from Broadway, then turn south on Magnolia Drive and drive to its crest. The road turns to dirt at this point, and soon you will see Twin Sisters, two prominent formations to the south. Continue west on the dirt road, then turn left (south) onto County Road 68. Drive approximately 2 miles, over the creek bed. The road eventually turns into a moderate four-wheel-drive road. Continue along the rough road to a national forest parking

area. Park and hike east, then down the road to a point where the road takes a sharp curve back to the south. At the start of the curve, head out into the brush due east for a short way, crossing a small creek bed to a gully that heads up to the north. Follow the gully to the first set of boulders.

Boss Man Boulder

You encounter this large boulder when you arrive at the boulderfield. Most problems are found on its south face.

1. Poussin V9 Climb the seam on the left side of the south face.

2. Premium V11 Start as for *Poussin* and climb up the leaning arête to the right.

3. The Boss Man V11 Climb from the pocket to a long move to the sloper on the right side of the south face.

4. Capone V5 Climb up the southeast face from the rounded flake.

5. Empty Plate V3 Climb up the middle of the northwest face.

Invisible Man Boulder

This boulder is to the southwest of Boss Man Boulder. Problems are found on its south face.

1. Unnamed Arête V3 Climb the arête on the left side of the south face.

2. The Invisible Man V4 Climb crystals and undercling in the middle of the south face.

3. Hedge Clippers V6 Climb the arête on the right side of the south face.

Ladies Block

This is the smaller block just northeast of Boss Man Boulder. It offers a clean arête on its southwest corner.

1. For the Ladies V2 Climb the arête on the southwest corner.

Arrowhead Boulder ◄

This boulder is found upslope to the north from Boss Man Boulder, Invisible Man Boulder, and Ladies Block. It is characterized by a steep, slightly overhanging south face.

1. Arrowhead Arête V9 Climb up the south face utilizing both arêtes.

2. White Tee Arête V2 From down low, climb up the prow and face on the left side of the east face.

Cracked Boulder ▼

This large boulder, up to the north from Arrowhead Boulder, is characterized by a wide crack that splits the boulder.

1. Magoo V5 Climb the arête on the right side of the wide crack on the southwest face.

2. Limb It V10 Climb from the flake up and right on the left side of the east face.

Cracked Boulder (east face)

Magnolia Boulder

This boulder is up to the north from Cracked Boulder. Squeeze under the cave slot on the west side of Cracked Boulder to reach it.

1. Magnolia Arête V6 Climb up the arête via side pulls on the southwest corner.

2. Fear Factor V3 Climb the edges on the right side of the north face, left of the dead tree stump.

Sugar Magnolia Boulders

These fine boulders are northeast of the northernmost Twin Sister formation. From the Garden Boulders area, you must hike north on National Forest land and locate the faint trail system that eventually skirts the east side of the Twin Sisters. The hike takes approximately forty-five minutes. You can see the boulders downslope to the northeast from the far north formation. The farthest east boulders of the lot

3. B Block Steeze V3 Climb the edge up the middle of the east face.

Private Road

To Magnolia Drive

Private Property

Private Property

Aboriginal Boulder

Sugar Magnolia Boulders

To Twin Sisters

National Forest

border private property, so you must remain discreet and respectful.

Aboriginal Boulder ▼

This perfect granite boulder is at the tail end of the boulder slope that sits within a forested meadow. Its sheer south and east faces offer problems rivaling that of the Millennium Block of Matthews/Winters Park. The west face offers excellent slab climbing.

1. Normal Slab V1 Climb up the middle of the west-facing slab.

2. Arête SlabV1 Climb up the right side of the west slab utilizing the arête.

3. Abnormal Arête V3 Climb up the left arête on the south face.

4. Aboriginal Traverse V9 Traverse the wall from left to right.

5. Aboriginal Face V7 Climb up the center of the north face.

6. Diggerdido V3 Climb up the shorter face to the right of *Aboriginal Face.*

7. Undermove V2 Climb up the right side of the north face.

8. Sugar Magnolia V2 Climb up a variety of variations on the east face.

Dream Canyon Boulders

These boulders are in and around Upper Dream Canyon off Sugarloaf Road and offer a change of pace from the wealth of sport climbing in the canyon. From Broadway and Canyon Boulevard, drive up Boulder Canyon Drive (Highway 119) 4.8 miles, take a right onto Sugarloaf Road, and head uphill 3 miles to a left on Lost Angel Road. Follow the dirt road up and around to a parking area that sits above the canyon walls. Park and hike down into Upper Dream Canyon for the Oceanic Bouldering Wall. Hike south from the parking area for the Midnight Bouldering Wall, along a trail system at the top of the formation,

following the trail around to the southeast to the Midnight Rock formation.

Oceanic Bouldering Wall ▼

This bouldering wall is across the creek to the west, directly across from the Oceanic Wall. Hike up the slope 75 feet into the trees and you will find this wall.

1. Earth Wall V1 Climb up the middle of the scooping wall with good edges.

2. Earth Crack V1 Climb up the corner to the right of *Earth Wall*.

3. Ocean Arête V2 Climb up the arête on the right side of the corner.

Dream Boulder

This boulder sits on the west bank of the creek, across from the right side of the Oceanic Wall.

1. Dream Arête V? Climb the overhang and arête on the northwest side of the boulder.

Universal Bouldering Wall

This wall is located along the trail that leads to Universal Crag, on the north side of the creek, across from the north end of the Lost Angel formation. It has a good traverse across its east face, as well as a few problems to its top.

1. Universal Traverse V3 Traverse the wall from right to left.

Midnight Bouldering Wall ▼

This clean granite section of Midnight Rock is below and to the right of the Grande Finale sport climb. Hike to Midnight Rock, skirt its base to the east over the ridge gap, and you will see the wall.

1. Midnight V4 Climb out the middle of the granite protrusion's south face.

15 FLAGSTAFF MOUNTAIN

When visiting or living in the picturesque city of Boulder, Colorado, one should not miss the historic boulders of Flagstaff Mountain. The easy access by car has made this natural playground an area favorite. Spread out magically amid the pine-scented, forested slopes is an awesome array of short, demanding problems for all levels of ability. The conglomerate sandstone boulders often resemble mini-Flatiron formations that are usually quite solid. Flakes, pockets, edges, pebbles, and crystals appear on the well-rounded rocks to create an unlimited variety of challenges. Many climbers have found this exciting area to be a little rough on the fingertips at first, but with a bit of conditioning, the fingers will begin to adapt by forming nice calluses. Flagstaff has been the early training ground for many of the area's top climbers.

Directions: To find this bouldering area, locate Baseline Road, which runs east-west through the city of Boulder. Go west on Baseline until you reach the foot of Flagstaff Mountain. From here, Baseline takes a sharp curve up and to the north and turns into Flagstaff Road. The mileage markings used in this book begin at a small bridge, located where the road curves to the north at the base of the mountain. A pleasant foot trail leads up the mountain and is located just past this bridge on the west side of the road. A daily parks pass is required for non-local visitors.

Cloud Shadow Area

Capstan Rock ▶

On the north side of the road, about 1.5 miles up Flagstaff Road, in the center of a

hairpin turn, there is this prominent spire with a pointy summit and an obvious curving crack on its south face. Numerous great problems of various length and difficulty make this rock one of the many sought-after boulders on the mountain. Descend on the north side, careful of the road.

1. Northwest Edges V2 This overhanging problem climbs off the edge of the road and up the northwest face via small edges. The rounded top requires a committing summit move.

2. West Face V1 (hb) This ascends the west face of Capstan with some interesting pockets and layaways.

3. South Crack V2 (hb) This ascends the obvious finger crack on the south face of the rock via pin scars from an early-'50s aid ascent.

4. South Overhang V2-V4 This climbs the bulge just to the right of *South Crack*. A few variations have been done on this bulge. One

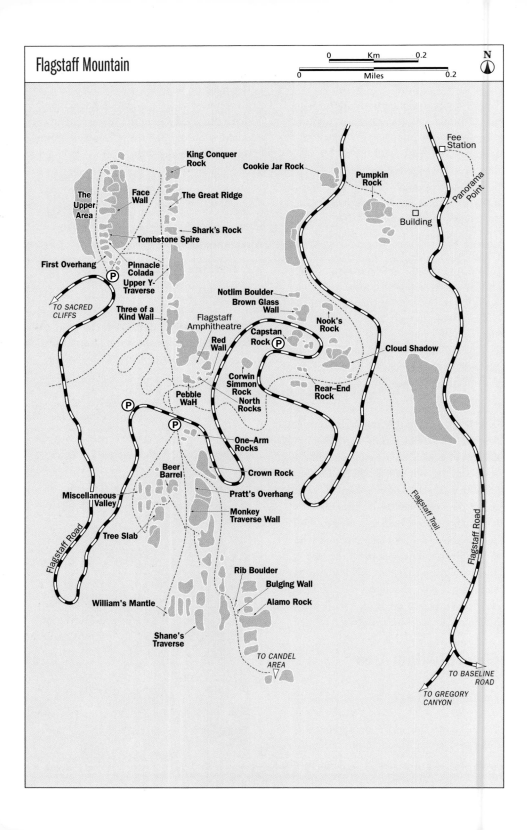

Flagstaff Mountain

0   Km   0.2

0   Miles   0.2

N

King Conquer Rock

Cookie Jar Rock

Pumpkin Rock

Fee Station

Panorama Point

The Upper Area

Face Wall

The Great Ridge

Building

Shark's Rock

Tombstone Spire

First Overhang

Pinnacle Colada

Upper Y-Traverse

TO SACRED CLIFFS

Three of a Kind Wall

Notlim Boulder

Brown Glass Wall

Nook's Rock

Flagstaff Amphitheatre

Red Wall

Capstan Rock

Cloud Shadow

Corwin Simmon Rock

Rear-End Rock

Pebble WaH

North Rocks

One-Arm Rocks

Beer Barrel

Miscellaneous Valley

Crown Rock

Pratt's Overhang

Monkey Traverse Wall

Flagstaff Road

Flagstaff Trail

Tree Slab

Flagstaff Road

Rib Boulder

Bulging Wall

Alamo Rock

William's Mantle

Shane's Traverse

TO CANDEL AREA

TO BASELINE ROAD

TO GREGORY CANYON

reaches left off a hole to a sloping edge, another reaches up statically to the right off a crystal and a hole, and another problem lunges off the holds up to the left or right.

5. Just Right V7 This climbs the severe overhang to the right of *South Overhang*. Pull onto the face with layaway moves, then reach with your right hand, avoiding the pocket to the small holds at top. The top moves offer some delicate thin-edged balance moves.

6. Diverse Traverse V2–V5 This fingery traverse moves along the bottom of the rock from an undercling at *Just Right* all the way past *South Crack* to *Northwest Edges,* then back, if your endurance allows. The small finger holes are reminiscent of climbing at Buoux in France.

Notlim Boulder ▼

Down the slope to the north of Road Sign Rock there is an interesting boulder with a very bizarre route up its northern face.

1. Hollow's Way V8 Fingertip your way up this desperate overhanging barn door layback.

Rear-End Rock

From Capstan Rock walk south, downhill, and a short way east along the main trail to find this split boulder.

1. Left Bulge V4 Climb the bulging face left of the crack via a tricky mantel.

2. Crack Crack V3 This jams the south crack of the formation.

Cloud Shadow (East End)

At the first hairpin curve, a few feet up the road from Capstan and below the road to the southeast, you see the incredible Cloud Shadow formation. A very unique traverse with solution pockets is located on the formation's south face, as well as several difficult, bulging face problems.

1. Bob's Pull V5 Halfway across *Cloud Shadow Traverse* look for a nice circular pocket that you can cram both hands into. From here, place your left foot up onto a polished downsloping ramp and crank in a dynamic motion up and slightly left for a large solution pocket.

2. Cloud Shadow Traverse V4 There are a few different ways to traverse this wall, one staying fairly high across the pockets, and one staying very low. From *Consideration,* traverse to the left until you cannot hold on any longer.

3. Lower Bulge Traverse V9 From *Contemplation* to *East Inside Corner,* this demanding traverse may be the hardest traverse Flagstaff has to offer.

Cloud Shadow
(east end)

4. Contemplation V2 (hb) Follow a seam curving to the left, then proceed with caution straight above.

5. Moderate Bulge V0 Right of *Lower Bulge Traverse* at the far-right, east end of the formation, grab a large hole, get this as an undercling, and make a long extended reach to the top.

6. Reverse Consideration V4 This is the same as *Consideration,* except that you switch hands in the hole and reach up with the other hand. A whole different balance point is created with this move.

7. Consideration V3 (B1) On the right side of the wall, left of the bulge routes, at another bulging section is the deep hole. From the hole, reach up to a good edge with your right hand, then up to a sharp smaller edge with your left, then reach to the top of the angling shelf.

8. Trice V10 Just right of *Consideration* is a sloping finger pocket approximately 8 feet up in an overhanging bulge.

9. Bob's Bulge V5 Right of *Consideration* and *Trice* is a prominent bulge above an undercling. Throw a heel over the bulge and proceed up the traversing shelf.

10. East Inside Corner V0 On the far-east side of the traversing wall there is a small corner.

Cloud Shadow (West End)

1. Launching Pad V4 On the very far-left side of the wall there is a difficult reach problem that launches off a small crystal up to a finger edge. Since the first ascent, the crystal has broken, creating a new challenge.

2. Dandy Line V5 This strenuous problem climbs the steep face right of *Launching Pad* and just left of *Hagan's Wall* via a small pebble.

3. Hagan's Wall V5 (B1+)

Right of *Dandy Line* there is another bulging wall with a small flake for one hand and a solution pocket that fits two fingers for the other. Crank off the small boulder to a sloping hold above and work this to the top.

4. Miar's Face V6

Ascend this strenuous, overhanging face just right of *Hagan's Wall*.

5. Hand Traverse V2

On the left side of *Cloud Shadow Traverse*, right of *Hagan's Wall*, there is a left-angling ramp leading upward. Hand traverse this to a difficult reach out left.

The Alcove

Slightly uphill behind the south face of Cloud Shadow there is an alcove with some very excellent problems.

1. Sailor's Delight V1 (hb)

This is located up above the alcove on a prominent bulging roof. See photo at right.

The Alcove

2. East Overhang V2 This is an obvious roof problem on the west side of the alcove.

3. Crack Allegro V1 Below *Sailor's Delight,* on a north-facing wall in the alcove, there is this right-leaning crack.

4. Allegro Bulge V2 Climb the bulge right of *Crack Allegro* to a mantel on the top.

Golf Club Boulder ▲

On the far-east end of Cloud Shadow there is a prominent blob that looks like a golf club when looking at it from the west.

1. The Angler V2 This is a strenuous hand-and-finger traverse from the east side of the blob to the far-south side.

2. The Roof V1 On the west side there is an overhang that is surmounted via a heel hook.

Pratt's Overhang Area

One-Arm Rocks

These two boulders sit together just off the road on the south side, after a sharp curve 1.6 miles up Flagstaff Road. Many variations ascend these fun boulders, which are mostly known for their steep one-arm problems.

4. Stone Ground V3 This climbs the face between *Pratt's Overhang* and *Smith's Overhang.*

5. Smith's Overhang V5 (B1-) To the right of *Pratt's Overhang* is a severely thin overhanging face with a prominent layback flake.

6. Gill Swing V4 This is a superdynamic move that goes off a small layback hold right of *Smith's Overhang* and shoots for the top.

7. Crystal Corner V2 Just right of *Smith's Overhang* is a small overhanging arête with a prominent crystal on it. Layback the corner to the crystal, then move up to the top via a high step.

8. Gully V0 To the right of *Crystal Corner* is a gully that can be mantled or face climbed.

1. One-Arm Overhang V3 On the east rocks, west-facing overhang there is a one-arm problem that climbs into the small dihedral above the overhang.

2. Right Hand Mantel V2 This one-arm problem climbs the north face of the west rock using a small crystal as a foothold while pressing into a one-arm mantel off a small edge.

Pratt's Overhang ▶

From the One-Arm Rocks, walk a few hundred feet along a path leading south from the parking area and you soon discover this west-facing, overhanging formation with several classic problems.

1. Pratt's Mantel V2 This is most directly done as a straightforward mantel, although many variations using small edges have also been accomplished.

2. Aerial Burial V3 From some small holds below the shelf on *Pratt's Mantel,* double lunge up for the shelf. Variations do exist.

3. Pratt's Overhang V2 To the right of the mantel shelf there is a right-slanting slot. Climb this via some awkward moves. Many variations exist.

Monkey Traverse Wall ▲

Farther down the trail, south of Pratt's Overhang, is a sunny west-facing, overhanging outcrop with a variety of traverses and roof problems. This is probably the most popular area of all the Flagstaff boulders. When first arriving at Flagstaff it is a good place to get the local beta, becoming familiar with the rock, and perhaps meet a climbing partner.

1. Monkey Traverse V4 This is the obvious chalked-up traverse that goes from right to left and back again. Your endurance will grow the more you apply yourself to this routine. Many other contrived variations on this traverse exist, some very hard.

2. West Overhang V1 (hb) Just slightly left of the *Monkey Traverse* midsection there is an obvious roof problem.

3. Million Dollar Spider V4 On the far-south end of the traverse there are a few overhanging problems. Grab for a pinch in the overhang and reach for the top.

Beer Barrel

From the parking area 1.6 miles up Flagstaff Road, where the trail that leads to Pratt's Overhang Area goes straight, drop down to the southwest until you see a picnic table. Just west of this table is the Beer Barrel rock. Many incredible problems and rock formations lie beyond.

1. West Traverse V3 On the west face of Beer Barrel there is a great overhanging flake system. Traverse this back and forth for a good pump.

2. Southwest Corner V0 This classic layback system is a very enjoyable problem.

3. South Face V0 Climb the good edges up the south face to an overhanging bulge crack. Several other variations on the south face of the rock are possible.

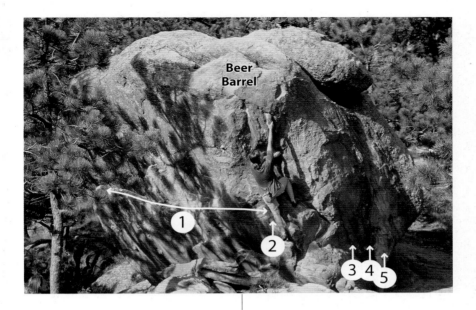

4. Pinch Pebble V5 Climb to the left of *Polling Pebble Route* using only two pebbles.

5. Polling Pebble Route V5 (B1/+) This climbs the bulge on the southeast corner of the formation via some very small holds where the famous pebble used to exist. This pebble was the largest on the face and withstood thirty years of pulling before it was pulled off.

Distant Dancer Pinnacle ▶

This is the pointy spire just southwest of Beer Barrel. Easy access to its summit is found on its north face.

1. West Overhang V1–V4 Many variations on the west side of the pinnacle are possible. Start as low as possible in the shelf.

2. Red Horn Overhang V1 On the southwest side of the spire is an overhanging corner. Layback this corner up to the summit.

3. Distant Dancer 5.12 V6 (xhb) This exciting problem ascends the south face of the spire via laybacks, underclings, and long reaches with a swing. Can be toproped.

Tree Slab ▲

Down the hill to the south of Distant Dancer Pinnacle is a smooth west-facing slab with many great problems up it.

1. Classic Line V0 Behind the tree is an obvious face. This was done one-handed in the '60s.

2. Layback Crack V0 Right of the tree is a fun layback crack with a small challenge.

3. Slab Traverse V0 Move across this traverse of the slab one-handed for an excellent challenge. It is hardest if the climber stays close to the ground.

Miscellaneous Valley

This group of formations is located below and to the north of Tree Slab. The west-facing rocks have many good problems.

Bulging Crack Wall

From Beer Barrel, hike around to the north to the trail below. This wall sits on the north edge of the outcrop along the lower trail.

1. Left Bulge V0 To the left of the crack there is this enjoyable bulge problem.

2. Leaning Jam V1 This is the crack out of the bulge on the left side of the wall.

The Alamo Rock Area

South of Crown Rock and southeast, above Monkey Traverse Wall there is a foot path leading to the south following the summit ridge way. After about 50 yards, the large Alamo Rock formation comes into view with its rounded summit and overhanging west side. The east face resembles a Flatiron-like slab, offering moderate access to its summit.

Rib Boulder ▲

Below and slightly northwest of Alamo Rock, there is a small cubical boulder with some fun routes on its sides.

1. The Crease V0 Climb the flaky crease on the west end of the boulder.

2. Arête It V1 Climb the arête on the southwest corner.

3. Face It V0 Climb the face to the right of the arête.

Bulging Wall ▼

Just east of the Rib Boulder is a bulging wall with a prominent finger crack. This sits below Alamo Rock and is connected to its lower northwest face.

1. Bulging Face V1 Left of the finger crack is a bulging face route.

2. Dalke Finger Crack V1 Climb the finger and hand crack in the wall.

3. Rib Right V0 Right of the finger crack is a nice face with good holds.

4. Arrows Traverse V4 Go back and forth along the lower portion of Bulging Wall.

5. Diamond Face V3 Below the overhanging crack on the west face of Alamo Rock, immediately to the northwest, there is a vertical south-facing wall with small edges.

The Candel Area

This is a ridge of broken boulders and slabs southeast of Alamo Rock. Hike up and behind Alamo Rock and head south along the summit ridge.

The Jug ▲

Follow a faint trail south along the ridge, south of Alamo Rock, to a dead tree—a formation with a finger crack on its west side is located to the right of this dead tree. From this crack hike south around the corner. The Jug is a west-facing wall with a gray ramp rock on its left.

1. The Ramp V1 Climb the southwest-facing, narrow gray slab.

2. Red Streak V1 On the northwest face there is a red-streaked wall. Climb this to the top.

Sunshine Slab

Just to the right and farther downhill is a large southwest-facing slabby wall.

1. Michael's Face V2 Directly behind the tree is a thin face with crystals.

Pebble Wall Area

Pebble Wall ▲

From the parking area around the curve from Crown Rock, 1.6 miles up Flagstaff Road, walk uphill to the north on the Flagstaff Trail for a few hundred feet. Look in the trees on the right to find this incredible well-rounded boulder. Many pebbles and crystals lace the walls.

1. North Face V0 This problem skirts left of *North Overhang,* avoiding its crux moves.

2. North Overhang V3 On the north side there is a prominent overhang with many pebbles.

3. West Overhang V3 On the northwest edge there is a climb up a prow.

4. Southwest Corner V0 This laybacks the rounded corner up from *Southwest Face.*

5. Over Yourself Traverse V10 Traverse the lower portion of the south and west face.

6. Southwest Face V3 Another delicate face with a little more exposure.

7. High Step V1 On the right side of *Direct South Face,* there is another pebbly face.

8. Direct South Face V3 (B1) Right of *High Step,* left of the mantel crystal, there is a steep pebbly face that starts off a root.

9. Crystal Mantel V2 There are several ways to mantle this obvious large crystal on the far-right side of the south face.

10. Original Route V0 On the southeast corner of the boulder there is a face ending with an undercling. Start near the small boulder.

North Rocks ▶

Just east of the Pebble Wall there are two boulders with an unlimited variety of good problems.

1. Left Rock V0 Climb up the middle of the west face of the northernmost rock.

2. Right Rock V1 Climb up the left side of the southernmost rock via slopey crystals.

Red Wall ▼

Just behind and to the east of the North Rocks there is an interesting, smooth, south–facing vertical wall with very small edges on it. Some of Flagstaff's hardest problems lie on this wall.

1. Left Side V1 Climb the far-left side via a small finger pocket.

2. Center Left V3 This tight move reaches up for an obvious hole with your right hand and then extends for a pinch crystal.

3. Standard Route V3 Instead of reaching the hole with your right hand, try it with your left.

4. Direct V5 Just right of *Standard Route* there is a difficult problem that starts with a small pebble for your left hand and a dish or cup hold for your right. Reach up to a good edge then a small finger niche.

5. Right Side V4 (B1) On the right side of the wall, near a tree, there is this classic hard problem that goes off a cup with your left hand to a long reach to a crystal niche with your right.

6. Far-Right Side V3 Just behind the tree there is a face problem that reaches over from the right to the holds atop *Right Side.*

The Flagstaff Amphitheatre

This enclosed outcropping can be found just to the north of Pebble Wall and is packed with many splendid problems.

Right Side Rock ▲

This is the rock found on the right (east) side of the two Amphitheatre rocks. All problems exit up and to the left.

1. The Overhanging Hand Traverse (hb) V1

Follow the large finger holds up and right.

2. Gill Direct V4 (hb)

(B1) From some small edges right of *The*

Overhanging Hand Traverse, ascend up and slightly right to some good holds at the lip.

3. South Bulge V1

On the right side of the wall there are edged shelves leading to the top.

4. South Corner V1

On the right side of the wall there is a short overhanging corner.

Left Side Rock ▼

This is the left-side (south) rock that forms the Amphitheatre.

1. High Overhang V0 (hb)

On the far-left side, up the slot, there is a scary reach problem off a high boulder, which finishes by mantling the airy lip.

2. South Face Left Side V3

An obvious corner/arête with some small edges.

3. Finger Trip V5

A difficult mantel problem right of *South Face Left Side.*

4. Briggs Route V3

Another thin pebbled face that starts up the leaning corner.

5. Direct South Face V3

From the slab under the base, climb the small pebbles.

6. Crystal Swing V2

A leap to a large pebble on the right side.

1. South Undercling V3 At the lower south end of this formation, immediately down to the left of Left Side Rock, there is a steep face with an undercling.

2. Big Overhang V2 (hb) The problem climbs the large overhanging block on the north end of the formation and is uphill, around to the north of the Amphitheatre.

The Great Ridge Area

This is a series of west-facing overhanging walls and spires uphill to the north of Pebble Wall. There are many classic problems here as well as some excellent traverses.

Three of a Kind Wall ▼

This is the first formation at the lower south end of the Great Ridge Area. You can play on three serious face problems and a low traverse here.

1. The Face V3 On the left side of the west face there is a soft, high-quality sandstone face. Be careful of the loose flakes.

Overhang Wall ▲

When leaving the Amphitheatre, head southwest and continue up the hill to the north to this wall of overhanging problems.

2. Kaptain Face V5 Right of *The Face* there is another thin face.

3. Round Pebble V4 (hb) Right of *Kaptain Face* there is another problem ascending a thin seam via laybacks on small edges to a good edge and pebble.

4. High Flake V4 (hb) On the right side, just to the left of a groove/trough, there is a prominent flake extending up and to the left. From the top of the flake reach up for a small crystal.

5. The Groove V0 An obvious groove with a fun challenge.

6. Bulging Slab V3 At the start of the Great Ridge Area, on the far-right side of Three of a Kind Wall, there is a sloping traverse that leads to a groove. This problem climbs up the sloping slab at the start of *The Traverse*.

7. The Traverse V5 Starting from the far-right side of the wall, traverse across to the flake.

Upper Y-Traverse ▼

Uphill from Three of a Kind Wall there is another large outcropping with an overhanging west wall and a well-chalked traverse skirting its base. A Y-shaped crack is visible in the gap.

1. Upper Y-Traverse V3 This great traverse is considered one of the best on Flagstaff.

2. Y Right Face V0 Climb the big-hold face right of the Y-slots.

3. Pinch Bulge V3 At the far-right end of the wall there is a good finger flake in the overhang. From this flake, reach up with your left hand to a pinch layback on the arête, then reach for the top.

4. Direct Mantel V4 Left of the pinch problem there is an obvious mantel shelf.

Shark's Rock ▲

Up from the Upper Y-Traverse, there is a spire with a vertical corner on its southwest face.

1. Direct West V4 Climb up the middle of the west face.

2. West Arête V3 Climb the southwest corner.

Little Flatiron

This describes the small spire just uphill to the north from Shark's Rock.

1. Leany Face V1 This ascends the left overhanging face.

2. Right Arête V3 This difficult problem takes the overhanging arête on the southwest corner.

King Conquer Rock ▲

This is the large blocky formation at the top of the Great Ridge Area and is loaded with many excellent problems, including a classic overhanging jam crack.

1. King Conquer Overhang V3 (hb) This is the overhanging crack that splits the block.

2. Face Out V5 (B1+) Right of the crack there is an overhanging face with very small, sharp edges.

3. Southwest Layback V1 On the far-right side there is an overhanging layback.

4. Conquer Traverse V6 (B2-) This is a low traverse along the King Conquer formation.

The Upper Area

This is the high point of the Flagstaff boulders, located up the road around a curve from the Pratt parking area.

First Overhang ▲

At the second hairpin, uphill past the Crown Rock parking area, look for a classic boulder sitting at the northeast edge of a parking area.

1. Masochism Tango V6 On the far-left side of the rock there is an overhanging arête.

2. Center Route V7 The center of the face between *First Overhang* and *Masochism Tango*.

3. First Overhang V5 (B1+) This is a problem on the right side of the southwest face.

Pinnacle Colada ▶

This is the first prominent rectangular pinnacle uphill and to the north of First Overhang.

1. Standard Route V0 (hb) On the left side of the west face there is a right-leaning corner.

2. Pebble Reach V3 (hb) There is a steep face on the right side with a pebble high up.

3. Southwest Corner V3 On the southwest corner of the formation there is a vertical arête.

4. South Face V0 On the south face there is a short face problem with a good flake up top.

5. Colada Traverse V4 Traverse across the overhang on the bottom of the pinnacle.

Tombstone Spire ▲

Just to the north of Pinnacle Colada is another, smaller rectangular pinnacle with good routes.

1. Triple Bulge V2 On the northwest corner of the pinnacle there is an obvious bulging arête.

2. West Side V0 On the west face of the pinnacle there is a good route with large holds.

3. Southwest Bulge V1 Climb the south-west corner of the spire.

Face Wall ▲

Just north of Tombstone Spire there is a bouldering wall with trees very close to its south face.

1. West Roof V1 On the west side there is an obvious overhang with little edges.

2. Left Side V3 (hb) On the left side of the south face there is a delicate face problem.

3. Center V3 (hb) On the south face of the wall there is a delicate face going up the middle.

4. Horan's Traverse V6 (B2-) Traverse across the lower wall from the far right to the left, finishing with *West Roof.*

16 SACRED CLIFFS (WEST RIDGE OF GREEN MOUNTAIN)

This extensive, spiny band of blocks, spires, and boulders is located on the west ridge of Green Mountain. It is to the southwest of Flagstaff Mountain and west of the Fourth and Fifth Flatirons, Skunk Canyon, and Dinosaur Mountain. Permits are required for Habitat Conservation areas. These are available at www.co.boulder.co.us/openspace/.

Directions: Moderate access to these cliffs is gained by driving up Flagstaff Road (Baseline Road turns into Flagstaff Road) approximately 2.5 miles from the base of the mountain where Baseline Road meets the Gregory Canyon turnoff. Drive past the Flagstaff summit up toward Gross Reservoir. At the crest of the road, just after the final hairpin turn, you encounter the trailhead known as Green Mountain West Ridge. This trail, approximately 1.0 mile long, will take you directly up to the Northern Spine of the Sacred

Sacred Cliffs

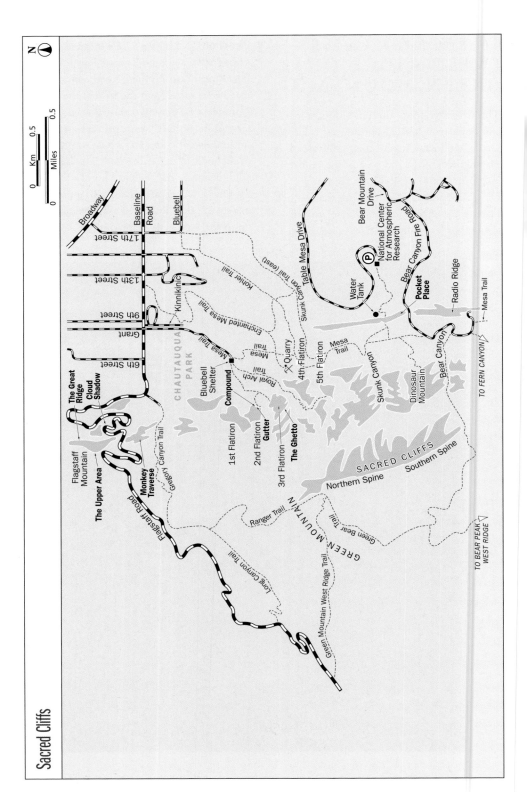

Cliffs. From a point just short of the summit, you can access the Trail Rocks, Balarney Stones, Land of Oz, Teton Area, Sunset Blocks, Ridgebreak Boulders, Southern Spine, Garden Wall Area, Eden Rocks, Stonehenge Area, and Hobbit Area.

Northern Spine

The Sacred Cliffs are broken up into two sections seperated by a rockless saddle. The Northern Spine consists of smaller summit blocks and spires compared to the larger Southern Spine formations. Below the summit rocks of the Northern Spine there is an awesome array of quality blocks and boulders. Each bouldering area follows prominent fall lines of rock that have broken away from the summit rocks and tumbled downslope in a somewhat regular fashion. The bouldering areas, north to south, are the Trail Rocks, Balarney Stones, Land of Oz, Sunset Blocks, and Ridgebreak Boulders. Each are accessed by hiking the western slopes, very close to the summit ridges.

The Trail Rocks

These are located north of the Balarney Stones, main fall line, along the trail leading up and close to the summit of Green Mountain's West Ridge.

East And West Blobs

These boulders are along the trail leading to the summit of Green Mountain's West Ridge. Steep problems exist on their north and west faces. The west sides are more slabby, while the north faces are slightly overhung.

East Blob

1. North Ace V4 (B1) Climb up the far-left side of the north face.

2. North Case V7 On the far-right side of the north face, start with an undercling and edge in the overhang and reach for the better edges.

West Blob

1. Crystal Left V3 Climb up the far-left side of the north face and mantel.

2. West Arête V2 Climb up the west face, utilizing the arête to the slab.

Sacred Cliffs Detail

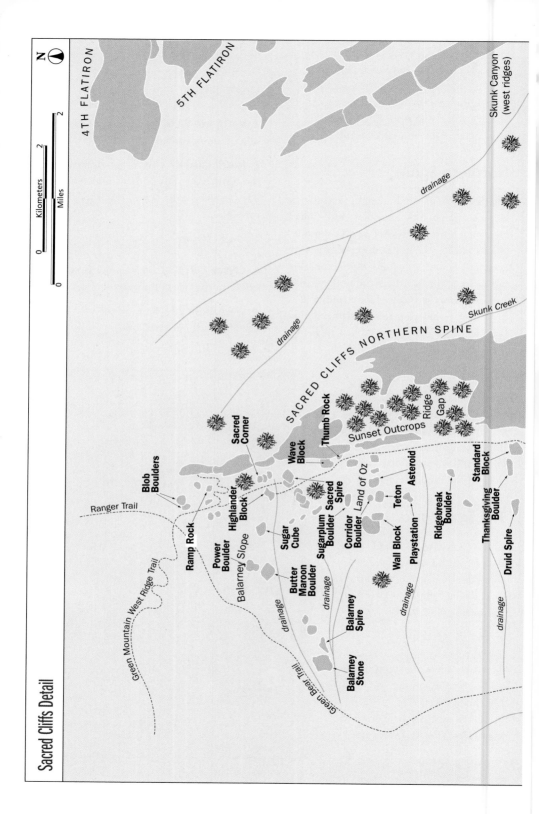

4TH FLATIRON

5TH FLATIRON

Skunk Canyon (west ridges)

drainage

drainage

Skunk Creek

SACRED CLIFFS NORTHERN SPINE

Sunset Outcrops Ridge Gap

Thumb Rock

Sacred Corner

Wave Block

Blob Boulders

Ranger Trail

Highlander Block

Land of Oz

Sacred Spire

Asteroid

Power Boulder

Ramp Rock

Sugar Cube

Sugarplum Boulder

Corridor Boulder

Teton

Standard Block

Balarney Slope

Butter Maroon Boulder

Wall Block

Playstation

Ridgebreak Boulder

Thanksgiving Boulder

Green Mountain West Ridge Trail

drainage

drainage

Balarney Spire

drainage

Druid Spire

Green Bear Trail

Balarney Stone

N

0   Kilometers   2

0   Miles   2

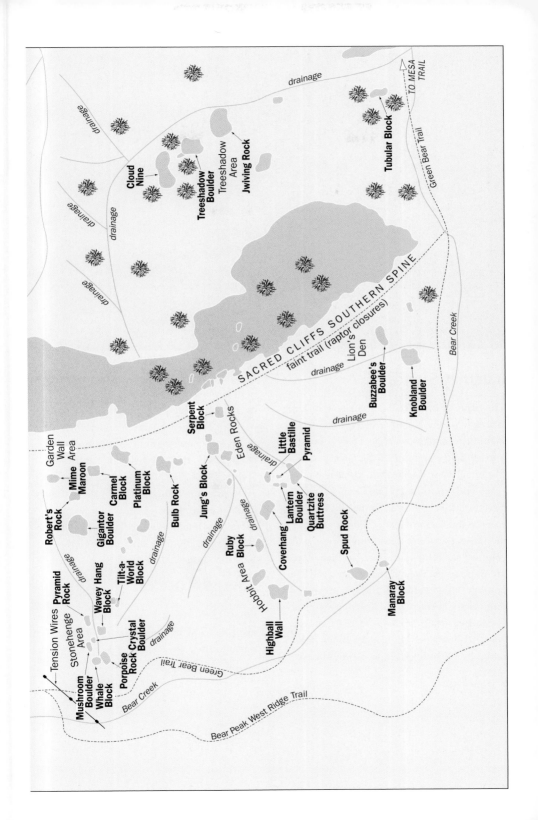

Balarney Stones

This array of boulders and blocks is amazing. You may hardly believe what you are seeing within this bouldered slope. From a point just below the summit of the Green Mountain West Ridge Trail, locate Ramp Rock and continue up off the main trail directly to the south for about 100 feet until you see the Sacred Corner. This is the first of the Balarney Stones. From this corner, you begin to see more and more boulders down the slope to the west through the trees. The boulder slope extends all the way to the bottom (west), eventually intersecting with the Green Bear Trail. After the Sacred Corner, you encounter the Highlander Block, followed by Cucumber Rock. Below this, you find the Sugar Cube, a nice cube-shaped boulder. From the Sugar Cube, keep descending the fall line until you see Butter Maroon Boulder (a large boulder with steep north, west, and south faces). Immediately below this is the crystal-lined, overhanging Walrus Block. Farther down the slope about 100 yards you will come across the Balarney Spire and the Balarney Stone. These two rocks are something to see and offer unique challenges with great landings, as all the Balarney Stones do.

Sacred Corner

From Ramp Rock, head due south off the main trail and, in approximately 100 feet, you run into these great bouldering walls.

North Wall

This makes up the northern side of the corner, forming a slot between the two walls.

1. Suspicion V2 Climb up the left side of the south face.

2. Riff-Raff V3 Climb the face right of *Suspicion*.

3. Love Triangles V0 Climb the pinchy groove up the middle of the face.

4. Sinister V2 Climb the right side of the south face, utilizing the arête.

South Wall

This rock makes up the south side of the corner.

1. Karen's Crack V0 Layback the crack in the corner of the slot.

2. Pathological Arête V0 Climb out of the slot, up and right to the arête.

3. Cola V0 Climb the left side of the west face via large crystals.

4. Peppy Slab V3 Climb up the center of the west face.

5. Addictive V3 Climb the right side of the west face via a scoop.

6. Princess of Darkness V3 Climb the south face just right of the arête.

7. Three Strikes V0 Climb up the center of the south face.

Highlander Block ▼

This cubical boulder is about 20 feet below Sacred Corner.

1. The Highlander V2 Follow the left-facing corners on the left side.

2. Highlander Arête V3 (hb) Climb the arête on the far-right side.

Cucumber Rock

Just below the Highlander Block there is a cluster of boulders. Cucumber Rock is a pickle-shaped spire to the left and is the northernmost of the lot.

1. Squash Wall V0 Climb up the middle of the west face.

Sugar Cube ▼

This awesome boulder is found down in the trees about 60 yards below Highlander Block. It offers great problems with good landings and is the first of the surprises that lie ahead. Descend its summit from the east.

1. Saintly One V5 (hb) Climb up the middle of the west face.

2. Middleman V4 (hb) Ascend the west face to the left of the crack.

3. The Flying Overhang V3 (B1) (hb) Follows the crack to the top.

4. Mat Mover V2 Climb the far-right side of the south face.

Butter Maroon Boulder ▼

To reach this boulder, hike downslope from the junction where the Green Mountain West Ridge Trail intersects the Ranger and Green Bear Trails. Head down the Green Bear Trail a short way to where it levels out in a nice forested section. The boulder sits just off to the left (south) side. Descend to the east.

1. Land O'Boulders V5 (hb) Climb the far-left side of the northwest face, starting off small edges in the overhang and eventually reaching larger holds at the top.

2. Peregrine V6–V7 (hb) Climb the overhanging face left of the arête joining the crack.

3. Sweet Arête V4 (hb) Climb the arête to the crack above.

4. Buffalo Gold V4 (B1) (hb) Climb the layaway crack to the holds above.

5. Parkay V5 (hb) Climb the steep south face to the right of the layaway crack.

6. Butter Rum V3 Climb the far-right side of south face.

Balarney Spire

This is a prominent, pointy-topped rock set kindly on soft ground. It is found downslope from Butter Maroon Boulder. Good problems exist across its north face. A few very enjoyable highballs exist on the left side. Exit to the south.

1. Clover V0 (hb) Climb the far-left side of the north face via the large pockets.

2. Spireman V3 (hb) Climb up the center of the north face to the very point at the top.

3. Four Leaf Clover V3 Climb the face via edges just right of *Spireman*. Exit right off shelf.

4. Irishman V4 Climb the thin north face just left of the tree.

5. Lucky V3 Climb the north face behind the tree via nice edges.

6. Shamrock V2 Climb the north face right of the tree line.

Balarney Stone

This is a favorite big block within the Flatiron Range, comparable with Square Rock on Dinosaur Mountain. It is located immediately right of the spire. Descend to the south.

1. End Game V4 (hb) Climb the arête on the far-left side of the east face, left of the dihedral.

Balarney Stone

2. Dihedral Man V3 (hb) Climb the dihedral on the left side of the east face.

3. The Leprechaun V? (hb) Climb the water-mark up the center of the east face.

4. Northern Lights V2 (hb) Climb the arête on the northeast corner.

5. North Face V4 Climb the north face via crystals just right of the arête.

6. Big Dipper V2 Climb the north face via pods and crystals.

7. Falling to Earth V2 Climb the north face just right of *Big Dipper.*

8. Balarney V3 Climb up the face on the right side via small edges.

9. No Balarney V0 Climb the far-right side of the north face.

Note: There is good traversing on this block, as well as many easier highball slab problems found on the west side.

Land of Oz

From very near the summit of the Green Mountain West Ridge Trail, locate Ramp Rock and head south, staying close to the top of the ridge; continue past the Sacred Corner, located at the top of the Balarney Stones. A faint trail makes its way across to this area, where you first encounter the Sacred Spire (not described). A wide variety of problems exist on the many rocks found within this secluded boulder pack.

NOTE: This area is off-limits during nesting season, which begins on February 1 and lasts through July 31. Find alternate destinations at this time.

The Asteroid Blocks

Just below the Teton Area, there are some boulders with excellent moderate to difficult problems around them. Escape off the summits to the east.

Middle Asteroid ▲

This is the middle block.

1. Comet Crack V3 (B1) Climb the crack on the left side of the west face.

2. Gnarly Tree V7 Ascend the face, right of center, via a crystal reach.

Note: Excellent slab problems from V0 to V3 are on the north face.

West Asteroid ▶

This block is located immediately west of Middle Asteroid.

1. West One V1 Climb up the middle of the west face.

The Teton

This prominent Teton-shaped rock rises out above the scattered boulders and offers a great landmark from which one can access other boulders. It is found immediately south of the Asteroids. The east side of the rock is the most practical way up, although problems have been seen on its south and west faces.

1. Mangy Moose V3 (hb) Climb the sheer face on the far-right side of the west face, exiting to the right short of the summit.

2. Grande V2 (hb) Climb up the center of the southeast face via crystals.

3. Tits Ville V0 (hb) Climb the crack line on the middle of the east face.

4. The Hostel V4 (hb) Climb the arête on the northeast corner.

Sunset Blocks

On the far-right (south) summit of the northern spine, the cliff thins out into short blocks and outcrops. These beautifully boulderable formations are well worth the visit and a great place to have a ridgetop picnic or sunset bouldering session. Some of the rock shapes are reminiscent of those on Flagstaff Mountain, although the rock is a bit smoother.

Sunset Cube

Before reaching the end of the Sacred Cliffs Northern Spine, you see this blackened cube. The north face has a hanging start onto its steep face.

1. Black Ice V6–V7 Pull onto the north face via small crimpy crystals.

2. Blackened Arête V4 Climb the leaning arête on the northwest edge.

Sunset Spike ▼

This pinnacle is located on the far-right summit ridge just before its tail end. Hike due south from Sunset Cube for about 50 yards.

1. Southside Jahosa V0 Climb the south face of the pinnacle.

1. **Arêtes Away V2** Climb the arête on the far-left side of the outcrop.

2. **Cracking Up V2** Climb the overhanging crack on the left side.

3. **Crystal Dyno V7–V8** Utilize the large crystal in the center of the face.

4. **Sunscreen V1** Climb up the right side of the outcrop, left of the block.

Sunset Dice Block

Sunset Dice is to your left when you face Sunset Outcrop.

1. **Nice and Easy V0** Climb up the south face.

Sunset Outcrop Block

This ridgetop outcrop makes up the very far-right, southern end of the Sacred Cliffs Northern Spine. Many good problems are found on its overhanging west face. Hike south along the ridge, past an outcrop with highball cracks.

Ridgebreak Boulders

These boulders are directly below and slightly right of the Sunset Blocks, where the summit ridge becomes a rockless saddle. Excellent bouldering is offered on boulders unique to this particular ridge zone. Head downslope to discover several good rocks.

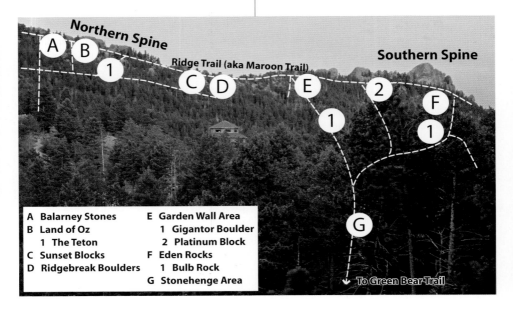

A **Balarney Stones**
B **Land of Oz**
  1 **The Teton**
C **Sunset Blocks**
D **Ridgebreak Boulders**
E **Garden Wall Area**
  1 **Gigantor Boulder**
  2 **Platinum Block**
F **Eden Rocks**
  1 **Bulb Rock**
G **Stonehenge Area**

Southern Spine

This portion of the Sacred Cliffs is characterized by well-endowed fall lines of boulders situated below the large spire-like formations. The descending boulders are scattered throughout the trees and are most easily reached by traversing from the Northern Spine Ridge Trail, following it to the south. You will first encounter, on the far-left north-ernmost portion of the Southern Spine, the Garden Wall Area blocks and boulders: Standard Block, Thanksgiving Boulder, Druid Spire, Mime Maroon, Carmel Block, Robert's Rock, Gigantor Boulder, and Platinum Block. Farther south along the summit you find, just below the ridgetop, Eden Rocks: Bulb Rock, Jung's Block and Boulder, Hobbit Block, Arrowhead Rock, the Coin, and Serpent Block.

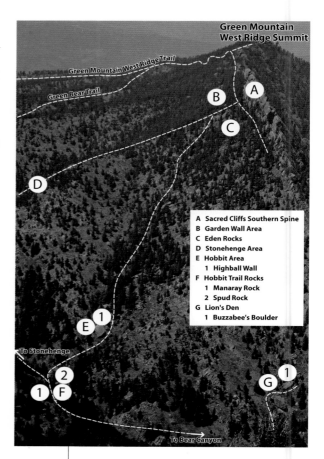

A Sacred Cliffs Southern Spine
B Garden Wall Area
C Eden Rocks
D Stonehenge Area
E Hobbit Area
  1 Highball Wall
F Hobbit Trail Rocks
  1 Manaray Rock
  2 Spud Rock
G Lion's Den
  1 Buzzabee's Boulder

Garden Wall Area

This array of boulders and blocks is located at the far-northern summit of the Sacred Cliffs Southern Spine. Hike to a point just below the first large formations of the spine. The first block you see is the Standard Block. This awesome block is hard to miss, for its cubical shape with good landings is one you might dream about. Just below, you cross Thanksgiving Boulder. Its steep south face is covered with crystals and edges. Farther below and to the north you find the Druid Spire (not described). Directly across to the southeast you reach the Mime Maroon (not described), consisting of

extremely thin and steep face routes up its west side. Just up and right is the Carmel Block (not described), with a fun, semi-highball center route up its west overhang. Below the Mime and slightly right you will eventually run into Robert's Rock (not described), with an overhanging west face and very challenging problems. Below this is Gigantor Boulder, which has awesome problems on its south side, as well as a classic trad overhang on its west face. Platinum Block is located across the slope to the south approximately 75 yards from the Carmel Block. Its west face is hidden within the trees and offers great overhanging problems.

Standard Block ▲

This block is visible from the summit ridge trail at the beginning of the Southern Spine's north end. The blocks don't get much better than this. Descend from the large crystalled east face.

1. Wavey V2 Climb the left side of south face.

2. The Groove V3 Climb the south face via pockets and an undercling right of *Wavey*.

3. Stylin' V3 Climb up the laybacks and edges just right of *The Groove*.

4. Standard Shield V2 (B1-) Climb the varnished shield via layaway pockets.

5. Crystalled Scoop V4 Climb the obvious crystal-lined scoop of the southeast corner.

6. Crystal Arête V0 Climb up crystals right of the *Crystalled Scoop*.

7. Short Crystal V0 Climb up crystals on the center of the east face.

Garden Wall Area
1 Standard Block
2 Thanksgiving Boulder
3 Druid Spire
4 Carmel Block
5 Mime Maroom
6 Robert's Rock
7 Gigantor Boulder
8 Platinum Boulder

Stonehenge Area
1 Whale Block
2 Porpoise Spire
3 Mushroom Boulder
4 Crystal Boulder
5 Wavey Hang Block
6 Pyramid Rock
7 Tilt-a-World

Thanksgiving Boulder ▲

This boulder is located immediately down-slope to the north from the Standard Block. Many challenging and somewhat thin problems utilizing crystals and small edges have been established.

1. Mashed Potatoes V5 Climb the south-west nose of the south face.

2. Turkey Bird V6 Climb the south face, right of *Mashed Potatoes,* utilizing underclings and crystals.

3. Gravy V4 Climb up the center of the south face via pockets and crystals.

4. Stuffing V1 Climb the right side of the south face via good holds.

Gigantor Boulder ▶

Down below Mime Maroon and Robert's Rock, you eventually run into a giant boulder with an extremely overhanging west face, somewhat more like a roof. The flake system out the west side of this roof goes at 5.12 and is then bouldered out. On the south side of this huge overhang, there is a problem that offers good holds up the steep bulging wall. Exit to the east. This is perhaps the largest boulder in the Maroon Garden.

Gigantor Roof 5.12

Note: From this boulder you can descend down toward the bottom of the gully, toward the Green Bear Trail, to reach the Stonehenge Area.

1. Tobar V7 (hb) Climb the steep, overhanging, bulging south wall of the boulder.

2. The Surf V7 Climb up the left side of the south face, out the bulges.

Platinum Block ▼

This awesome block has a severely overhanging west face hidden in the trees. It offers some of the best overhanging bouldering in the garden. It is located across the gully to the south from the heart of the Garden Wall Area, sitting downslope below the summit ridge. Exit its east side.

1. Plato's Arête V6 Climb up the arête on the far-left side.

2. Socrate's Overhang V5 (B1+) Climb up the wall right of *Plato's Arête,* starting down low.

3. Pop Overhangs V2 Several variations are possible out this midsection.

4. Main Hang V5 Climb out the overhang, right of *Pop Overhangs,* starting right and reaching out to the left. A difficult large crystal pinch is utilized at the lip.

5. Platinum Overhang V8 Climb the big overhang right of *Main Hang.*

6. Platinum Traverse V12? Traverse from the right to the left.

Eden Rocks

This spread of blocks and boulders is found at the high point on the south end of the Southern Spine just before it descends down into the far-west end of Bear Canyon. The

boulders and blocks here begin a southwestern fall line of rock that eventually works its way down, intersecting the Green Bear Trail below. Many rocks appear along this fall line, but the cream of the crop sits high up on the summit ridge. Its lower portion, close to the Green Bear Trail, is the Hobbit Area. From the high point of the Southern Spine, descend down to the northwest until you come across a nice meadow break with a cluster of good-quality boulders sitting just north of the ridge crest. The first boulder encountered on the east side of the cluster is the Sheer Maroon (not described) followed by Bulb Rock to the north and the Hobnail Boulder to the south.

Bulb Rock ▼

Immediately north of Sheer Maroon, and somewhat attached, you find this large,

problem-endowed, dome-shaped rock. Traversing is also an option. Exit to the east.

1. Lantern V6 Climb up the thin face on the far-left side of the west face.

2. Cervazi General V2 Climb layback seam to the right of *Lantern*.

3. Western Flake V2 (hb) Climb the flake route in the center of the face.

4. Western Electric V6–V7 Climb the sheer microslab, on the right side.

5. Slabs Away V3 Climb the thin slab to the left of the crack.

6. Southern Crack V1 Climb the crack line on the south face.

7. Slabbo V4 Climb the slab on the right side of the crack.

Jung's Block

From Bulb Rock, head due south for approximately 100 feet and you run into these fine rocks. From up top, once you reach the ridgecrest of the Sacred Cliffs Southern Spine, at a point where you can see down south into the far-west end of Bear Canyon, descend the meadowed slope to the southwest. Jung's Block and Boulder are sitting on the crest below. They are somewhat hard to see when approaching from the north. The bouldering is found in a southeast-facing cove formed by the two blocks. Jung's Block is the more southwestern of the two.

1. South Overhanger V6 (hb) On the south face of the block there is a steep, somewhat overhanging face with good holds.

2. Pocket Arête V3 Climb to the top via pockets on the southeast arête.

3. Crystal's Wall V0–V2 This is the first of a series of short, fun problems starting on the far-left (south) end of the block, moving then to the right (north) end of the block. Pick and choose a variation.

Jung's Boulder ▶

This is the perfectly steep and varied boulder on the north end of the alcove. A few very difficult problems are found on the south face.

1. Animus V5 Climb the west face of the block via small crystals and edges.

2. Analysand V6 Climb the southwest arête.

3. Anima V8 (B2) Climb the steep, south-facing corner, utilizing the thin seam.

Arrowhead Rock ▲

This interesting rock resembles a giant arrowhead and is located up against and below the tall overhanging summit block formation of the Southern Spine. From Jung's Block, head uphill and slightly south until up against the summit towers. The rock offers a few excellent face problems. A spotter and crash pad are very helpful.

1. Crazyhorse V5 (B1+) Climb up the middle of the south face.

The Coin ▲

This circular rock is located immediately south, across from Arrowhead Rock and connected to the main formation.

1. Coin Toss V1 (hb) Climb the north face of the rock, starting on its right side, and then up and left.

3. Northern Son V3 Climb up the middle of the north face via small edges.

The Stonehenge Area

From the junction where the Green Mountain West Ridge Trail meets the Green Bear Trail, hike down to the bottom of the Green Bear Trail, eventually heading due south. Just past the junction of the Bear Peak Trail and Green Bear Trail, the trail begins to rise a bit and then goes under the tension wires. Once at the top of the knoll, almost directly below the tension wires, head out to the east, skirting around to the southeast on the northern slope above the gully. Once around the short ridge break, look down into the gully to see the first Stonehenge rocks.

Whale Block

This is the first maroon block you see when descending into and hiking up the gully to the east. Its sheer west face has challenging, short-but-sweet problems. Whale Block is the northernmost block of the two, making up the northwest-facing alcove.

1. The Spout V2 On the far-left, northern end, climb to the top via a hole.

2. Save the Whale V2 Climb the good set of edges to the top.

3. Monowhale V6 From a strenuous mono pull, reach the top.

Serpent Block ▲

Just below the Coin to the northwest, down and somewhat hidden amid the brush, is this entrancing block, which offers daring problems up its south face. Its north face also offers steep face problems with a more reasonable landing. Exit to the east.

1. Apple's Way V4 (hb) Climb the short corner line on the left side of the south face.

2. Original Line V3 (hb) Climb the center of the south face via good edges. Starts from the right side.

4. Right On V1 Climb up the far-right end of the block.

Porpoise Spire

This rock is located immediately south of Whale Block and forms the southern end of the northwest-facing alcove. Good problems exist on its north face. Exit to the south.

1. Dolphin Free V4 (hb) From a strenuous undercling on the left end of the north face, extend up to good edges with the left hand and then work up the layback system.

2. The Porpoise V5 (hb) From the undercling on the right, reach across to the left, then up.

3. No Porpoise V0 This is a great bucket haul up and over the right side of the rock.

Mushroom Boulder ▼

This magnificent boulder is found immediately up from Whale Block and Porpoise Spire and forms the northern wall of this southwest-facing alcove. Difficult problems, including a classic traverse, are to be found.

1. Huecoed Shroom V1 Climb the left side of the west face via pockets.

2. Crystaled One V2 Climb the center of the west face, pulling on with a crystal and edge.

3. Shroom's Arête V3 Climb the arête on the southwest corner.

4. Magic Mushroom V4 Beginning on two crystals, reach up for the pocketed edge.

5. Hooka V6 Layback and extend to the top, reaching the shallow pocket.

6. The Mushroom V4 From the large undercling, reach up to the seam, then pocket.

7. Mushroom Traverse V4–V6 Start on the right or left and traverse back and forth. Finish with *Magic Mushroom* or *The Mushroom* for added difficulty.

Crystal Boulder ▼

This dome-shaped boulder is located immediately east, somewhat attached to Mushroom Boulder.

1. Crystal Crimper V7 Climb up the center of west face utilizing the small crystals.

Tilt-a-World Block ▼

From the Crystal Boulder, hike a short ways uphill to the south and you run right into this challenging block. On the way you will pass the Wavey Hang Block and Pyramid Rock (not described).

1. Superduper V6 Starting from the big layback edge, pull and reach up to the next ledge.

2. Grande Central V8 Climb up the center of east face using laybacks.

3. Superwoman V4 Climb up the right side of the east face.

Hobbit Area

This area is accessed in two ways. Hike up from the Bear Canyon Trail, past Bear Canyon to the west, past the Tree Shadow Area, until you reach the lower southern portion of the Sacred Cliffs Southern Spine, then continue up to the far west just before Stonehenge. The other way is from the Green Mountain West Ridge Trail. Take the Green Bear Trail downhill, past Stonehenge and around to the next ridge and fall line of rock. A block is visible on the east side of the trail just south of the gully line.

Hobbit Trail Rocks

These boulders are along the Bear Canyon Trail, approximately 100 yards west of the Sacred Cliffs Southern Spine, leading to the heart of the Hobbit Area.

Manaray Rock ▶

When approaching from Bear Canyon, continue hiking past the Sacred Cliffs Southern Spine, approximately 100 yards to the west, and you come across a meadowed area with an interesting little spire-like rock sitting on the west side of the trail. It has a sheer north face.

1. Manaray Face V5 Climb up the center of the sheer north face.

Spud Rock ▼

Across the trail to the east you can see this rock. It looks somewhat like a mini–tail end of a ridge.

1. The Spud V3 Climb up the left side of the south face.

Triangles Boulder ▲

To find this boulder continue upslope to the southeast of Highball Wall. Triangles Boulder is characterized by a left-leaning arête on its west face and a slab on the south.

1. Triangles Arête V3 Climb up the left-leaning arête on the southwest corner.

2. Love Triangles V5 Climb up the left side of the west face.

Lantern Boulder ▼

This oblong boulder is up to the northeast of Triangles Boulder, high above the Highball Wall.

1. Lantern V3 Climb up the left side of the west face.

2. Flashlight Crack V2 Climb up the right-angling crack on the west face.

3. Candle Light V4 Climb up the thin face to the right of the crack.

4. Matchlight V5 Climb up the face to the right of *Candle Light*.

Little Bastille ▲

This tower block is a short way upslope to the north of Lantern Boulder.

1. XM V5 (hb) Climb up the middle of the west face.

2. Bastille Arête V3 (hb) Climb up the right-hand arête on the west face.

Lion's Den

These boulders are found by hiking in from the east up the Bear Canyon Trail. Continue west on the Bear Canyon Trail, past the northern slopes of Bear Canyon's West Ridge, past the Sacred Cliffs Southern Spine, to the first gully coming off the slopes. A large, crystal-endowed boulder is visible north of the trail. Head up and behind this large boulder.

Buzzabee's Boulder ▼

This boulder is found up to the east behind the large boulder seen from the trail. Head upslope to the northeast. The south face of this boulder has awesome face routes.

1. Cigars V2 Climb the face on the far-left side of the boulder

2. Doobee V5 Climb up the center of the south face via small edges.

3. Microbrew V6 Climb up the steep, thin-edged face right of *Doobee*.

4. Rioriffic V4 Climb the steep wall on the far-right side of the boulder.

17 GROSS RESERVOIR

See map on page 111.

The bouldering found along Gross Dam Road on the east and south sides of the reservoir offers some of the Boulder area's most extreme granite problems. Four separate areas have been the main source of concentration: Hazard County, the Burn Area, Damnation Boulders, and the Freight Train. All are located off Gross Dam Road. Some of these areas are closed for revegetation due to fire. Please obey all posted signs and closure notices.

Directions: From the beginning of Flagstaff Road (where Baseline Road turns into Flagstaff Road), drive approximately 9.0 miles, past the summit of Flagstaff, past the Green Mountain West trailhead, and past the Walker Ranch trailhead. Continue west, winding down and around, then go left (south) on Gross Dam Road. Follow the dirt road south. The first area, Hazard County, is located down the road approximately 0.8 mile.

Hazard County

Hazard County is located 0.8 mile south of the intersection of Flagstaff Road and Gross Dam Road. Park at the pull off just before the left hairpin. Hike out to the southwest, toward the cliff top. You will find the boulders below.

Sound System ▲

From the parking area, hike out due west, then slightly right after 50 yards, and you will run into this fun area with a nice corner.

1. Sound System V0 Climb up the dihedral, then across to the left on the crack.

2. Boom Box V2 Climb the arête on the left.

150 yards from Sound System. Cross up and over the slab.

1. Falcon Crack V0 (hb) Climb the classic layback crack on the north side.

Faces Wall ▼

To find this wall with a great landing, continue down the road from the Hazard County parking area. Park in a spot near the next curve to the right. Look for a gated road leading off to the southwest. Hike 100 yards down the road, around to the southeast. The Faces Wall is hidden over the knoll to the south. Many variations exist on its south face. This is a great wintertime area.

Burn Area

To access this area, take Gross Dam Road south approximately 1 mile from Flagstaff Road. Drive past the left hairpin to a right curve and park on the left pull out. To reach the boulders, hike north and northeast.

Falcon Block ▲

To find this towering block with a layback crack on its left side, hike out to the south

Natural Apparatus Boulder ▼

You will find this fine boulder downhill through the trees to the northeast. Two pine trees frame the west face of the boulder.

1. Apparatus Arête V0 Climb the arête on the left side of the west face.

2. Hold On V2 Climb the face just right of *Apparatus Arête.*

3. Big Easy V0 Climb up the middle of the west face.

4. Natural One V3 From down low, climb up to the pocket, right of *Big Easy.*

5. Natural Arête V4 From down low, climb up the arête on the right side of the west face.

6. Flatiron Simulator V3 Climb the holds up the bolt ladder on the left side of the south face.

7. Party Tick V4 Climb the thin north face.

Sculptor's Block ▼

This block is 60 feet to the southeast of Natural Apparatus Boulder. It has a steep south face with challenging problems.

1. The Conundrum V9 (hb) Climb the seam on the north face.

2. West Wall V0 Climb a variety of easy up and downs.

3. Sands of Time V4 Climb up and over the roof on the southwest face.

4. Scooter V0 Climb the discontinuous seam on the right side of the southwest face.

5. Sculptor Crack V5 (hb) Climb the thin finger crack on the left side of the south face.

6. Tools V4 (hb) Climb the horizontal seams right of the center.

7. Hammer Down V7 (hb) Climb the thin face on the right side of the south face.

Freight Train Area ▲

This mini-cliff of blobbed granite is approximately 4 miles from Flagstaff Road on Gross Dam Road. Park on the left side of the road and hike south, parallel to the track. Skirt around the east side of the hillside for fifteen minutes, catching a faint cattle road. The road, or trail, will swing back around to the west. Follow this a few hundred feet, look out to the southeast, and you will see the mini-cliff.

1. Frog Lips V2 Climb the left-facing dihedral to the rails on the left side of the southwest face.

2. Pokemon V2 Climb up to the pocket on the left side of the face right of *Frog Lips*.

3. Prancing Cow V3 (hb) Climb up to the sloper right of *Pokemon*.

4. Chubby Bunny V7 (hb) From the shelf, climb up to the pinch and up in the middle of the face.

5. Chew, Chew V3 (hb) Climb the face to the right of the obvious crystal wash.

6. Tall Face (hb) Climb good holds with long reaches up the tallest portion of the face.

7. High Warm Up V1 (hb) Climb good holds to the airy topout to the right of *Tall Face*.

8. Buddha Belly V3 Climb the bulge to the right of *High Warm Up*.

18 THE FLATIRONS

Bluebell Area

This area consists of problems within the Second Flatiron and Third Flatiron, as well as the isolated boulders on the southern slopes of Bluebell Canyon. Within these famous and picturesque Flatirons, you find amazing rock slots such as the Compound, the Gutter, and the Ghetto, as well as the Satellite Boulders. At the mouth of Bluebell Canyon are the Tomato, the Egg, and the Potato. These boulders offer good, fun problems.

NOTE: The Third Flatiron is closed during raptor season and open from July 31 through February 1. Check with park regulations, for this could change over the years. Stiff fines are enforced. Find alternate destinations while the closures are in effect. Go to www.co.us/openspace/ for permits and information.

Directions: Locate Baseline Road in Boulder and drive due west to Grant Street, located just before the foot of the mountains. Turn left into Chautauqua Park. Parking is obvious. Hike up the paved road from the ranger cottage, located at the south end of the parking lot. This takes you up to the Bluebell Shelter. To reach the Satellite Boulders, the Gutter, and the Compound, take the Bluebell-Baird Trail up from the shelter to the north until you reach the Third Flatiron Climbing Access Trail. Take this trail up to the west. The trail winds up to the northeast side of the Third Flatiron. At that point you begin to see the Satellite Boulders scattered along the trail. To reach the Gutter and the Compound, continue to the north through the Satellite Boulders until you see the base of the Second Flatiron. The Gutter is visible down and right of the massive overhang protruding from the east slab. The Compound is slightly up and behind the Gutter.

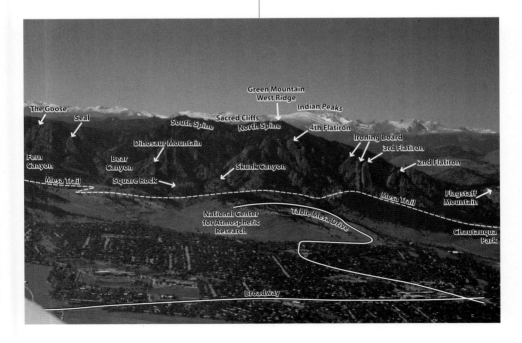

The Flatirons

0 — Km — 1
0 — Miles — 1

N

Flagstaff Road

Gregory Canyon Trail

TO BASELINE ROAD

CHAUTAUQUA PARK

Saddlerock Trail

1st Flatiron

2nd Flatiron

3rd Flatiron

4th Flatiron

5th Flatiron

Mesa Trail

Enchanted Mesa Trail

Kohler Trail

Long Canyon Trail

Ranger Trail

Green Mountain West Ridge Trail

Bro's Spire

Skunk Canyon Trail

Table Mesa Drive

Lehigh Street/Green Briar Boulevard

✗ Green Mountain

Yahman Boulder

Medicine Man Boulder

Green Bear Trail

faint trail (raptor closures)

SACRED CLIFFS

Skunk Canyon

Pocket Place

National Center for Atmospheric Research

Green Bear Trail

Square Rock

Bear Canyon

Bear Canyon Access Road

Radio Ridge

Bongo Boulder

Bear Peak West Ridge Trail

Megatron Boulder

The Goose

Fern Canyon Trail

Burgundy Boulder

North Shanahan Trail

The Slab

Mesa Meadows

Mesa Trail

South Shanahan Trail

Bear Peak ▲

Medal Maroon

South Boulder Peak ▲

Blue's Boulders

OPEN SPACE

PUBLIC LAND
PRIVATE LAND

Devil's Thumb

Shadow Canyon

Maiden

Big Bluestem Trail

BOULDER MOUNTAIN PARKS

Horan's Block

Aladin's Lamp

South Mesa Trail

Eldorado Trail

The Flatirons Detail

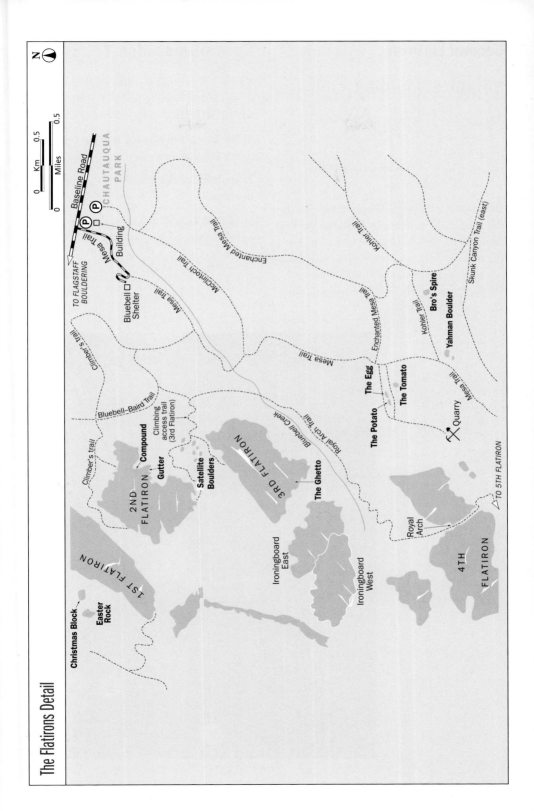

Second Flatiron

Satellite Boulders

This boulder pack has a number of good boulders and problems. This is a nice alternative to other areas such as Flagstaff and has a remote feel to it. The rock is somewhat coarse but manageable.

Directions: From Chautauqua Park, hike up the road to the south, up toward the Bluebell Shelter. Hike beyond the shelter and follow the trail to the Second and Third Flatirons. At the split continue on the Third Flatiron climbing access trail. The Satellites will begin to appear along the trail.

Sputnik Boulder ▼

You will first encounter this trailside boulder on the left side of the trail just north of the talus field. It has a steep slabby east face.

1. The Bleep Traverse V4 Traverse from right to left across the east face.

2. Sputnik One V1 Climb the face right of the crack.

3. Sputnik Two V0 Climb the slab to the right of *Sputnik One.*

Stardust Block ▲

This block is on the right side of the trail, up past Sputnik Boulder.

1. Aerogel V5 Traverse from far left to the right, then up to the top.

2. The Hard Traverse V5 Traverse farther right to the layback, then connect with the side block.

G-Friend Block

This lowball block is 30 feet up the trail from Stardust Block.

1. Girlfriend Traverse V4 Traverse from the off-width crack across the southwest face.

A-7 Boulder ▼

This boulder is on the left side of the trail and has an underbelly.

1. Face Full of Brian V8 From down low, climb up the slopey holds.

Best of Boulder County Boulder and Cap Stone

From A-7 Boulder, hike 75 feet upslope to the right and you will see this flat-top boulder with a larger block leaning up against its west side.

1. Ice Nine V8 Clims from down low, utilizing the arête on the east face.

2. Major Tom V3 Climb the face on the left end of the west face.

3. Balance in Nature V6 Climb from the dihedral across to the left.

4. Re-Entry V6 Climb the razor edge via underclings, right of *Balance in Nature.*

5. The Turning Point V9 This overhanging arête problem is found on the east face of Cap Stone, located next to and on top of the Best of Boulder County Boulder.

Upper Satellites

These isolated boulders are farther up the trail from the Lower Satellite Boulders. Continue up the trail 300 feet, then head toward the Second Flatiron. The boulders are on the south side of the Second Flatiron.

The Gutter ▲

This slot is located on the east side of the Second Flatiron below and slightly right (north) of the massive overhang protruding from its eastern slab. It offers an excellent overhanging roof problem that extends in an upper diagonaling manner in the slot.

1. Gutter Traverse V7 Traverse up the slot, starting down and right.

The Compound ▼

This somewhat bulging, double-bouldered slot of maroon is on the east side of the Second Flatiron above and right of the Gutter. It offers excellent traversing as well as overhanging problems out its bulging walls. Pick and choose a route.

1. Compound Traverse V6 Traverse the length of the two maroons.

Third Flatiron

The Ghetto

This awesome slot is on the western side of the Third Flatiron and is accessible via a west-side gully and short cliff leading to its secluded bench. Many excellent problems exiting its roofs exist, as well as the classic *Ghetto Traverse,* which skirts the big jugs hanging from the slot's lip.

Directions: From Chautauqua Park, head up the paved road to the Bluebell Shelter. Take the Royal Arch Trail, up through Bluebell Canyon, to a point past the west face of the Third Flatiron. At this point you must locate the gully leading up to the Third Flatiron's west face. Scan the west face for an elongated ledge system. A short face must be climbed to reach this shelf where the Ghetto is located.

Third Flatiron/Ghetto Area

N

West Bench

3RD FLATIRON

Winky Woo

East Ironing Board

The Ghetto Area

Queen Anne's Head

Access Face (VO)

Royal Arch Trail

TO CHAUTAUQUA PARK

Ghetto Traverse Rock ▲

This rock is the northernmost of the two rocks that make up the Ghetto.

1. Guanophobia V6 Climb the caved slot on the far-left side of the rock.

2. Inner Space V4 Climb the holds out the roof just right of *Guanophobia*.

3. Ghetto Traverse V3 (B1) Traverse up the lip, starting down low and right.

Dungeon Rock ▶

This rock is the southernmost rock of the Ghetto area.

1. Pebble Problem V3 Climb up the overhang, utilizing the pebbles on the far-right side.

2. Dr. Slut Pants V7 Climb the overhang right of *Pebble Problem*.

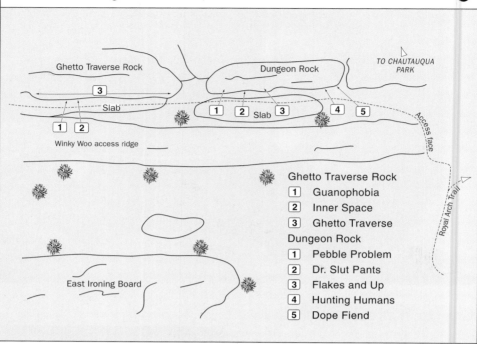

Ghetto Traverse Rock

Dungeon Rock

TO CHAUTAUQUA
PARK

3

Slab

1 2

Winky Woo access ridge

1 2 Slab 3

4 5

Access face

Royal Arch Trail

Ghetto Traverse Rock
1 Guanophobia
2 Inner Space
3 Ghetto Traverse

Dungeon Rock
1 Pebble Problem
2 Dr. Slut Pants
3 Flakes and Up
4 Hunting Humans
5 Dope Fiend

East Ironing Board

3. Flakes and Up V5 Climb the overhang right of *Dr. Slut Pants,* utilizing the flake system.

4. Hunting Humans V5 Starting down low, climb out the overhang located right of *Flakes and Up.*

5. Dope Fiend V5 Climb the overhang on the far-right side of the rock.

6. Anicostia Traverse V10 Traverse across Dungeon Rock.

Bluebell Canyon

The Tomato ◄

Take the Mesa Trail south (before the Bluebell Shelter), until you are just past the McClintoch Trail junction. Follow the thin trail heading up to the west and you soon run across this rock. Many fun, short problems surround this boulder.

V0   V0   V1

Fourth And Fifth Flatirons (Royal Meadows)

The boulders found amid these meadows are quite nice and offer a wide variety of classic challenges. All are located east of the Mesa Trail within the meadows of the Fourth and Fifth Flatirons and Skunk Canyon. Take the Mesa Trail from Chautauqua Park, past the Enchanted Mesa Trail junction, up toward the Skunk Canyon Trail.

Yahman Boulder

This boulder is found immediately to the south of the junction where the Kohler Trail meets the Mesa Trail.

1. Pink Floyds V4 Climb up the bulging south face of the boulder.

2. Yahman Traverse V5 Start either from the far-left or right and traverse back and forth along the crackline.

The Potato ▲

This small dome-shaped boulder is found immediately right (northwest) of the Tomato. Challenging problems are found on its north face. Exit to the south.

1. Left Spud V4 Climb up the left side of the bulge, utilizing a stem.

2. The Middle Spud V3 Reach up for the good holds right of *Left Spud*.

3. The Potato V6 Climb directly up the right side of the north face.

4. Right Spud V4 Climb up the far-right side of the north face.

Skunk Canyon

Skunk Canyon offers some very worthwhile boulders east and west of the main ridges of the inner canyon. Follow the creekbed from the east, up to and through the canyon, around to the north, and you come upon all of these boulders.

Directions: From the National Center for Atmospheric Research (NCAR) at the west end of Table Mesa Drive in Boulder, hike the NCAR Trail to the west, eventually intersecting the Mesa Trail. Head to the north, down past a gully, and then up to the heart of the canyon. Go to the east to access Bulge Boulder, Roof Rock (not described), and Medicine Man Boulder. Go to the west into the inner canyon and eventually through to the northwest for Rasta Boulder, Block Wall, and the Hueco Boulder.

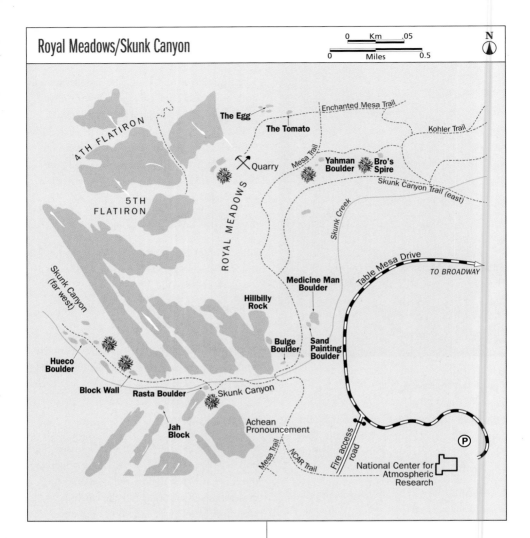

NOTE: All ridges behind Ridge One are closed for nesting from February 1 to July 31. Find alternate destinations during this time.

Bulge Boulder

From NCAR take the Mesa Trail north to the front of Skunk Canyon. This boulder is located on the northern slopes, east of the first ridges of Skunk Canyon.

1. Power Bulge V3 Climb up the middle of the southeast face.

Sand Painting Boulder

Continue east from the Roof Rock along the Mesa Trail until it turns to the north. After approximately 100 feet (hiking north), look down to the east to see the tops of these nice boulders. This boulder has challenging, steep face problems on its east face and is somewhat attached to Medicine Man Boulder.

1. Sands of Time V3 Climb up the middle of the east face.

Medicine Man Boulder ▼

This is one of the nicest boulders in the meadows east of Skunk Canyon. It is the large boulder down from and somewhat attached to the Sand Painting Boulder. Awesome overhanging problems with a very interesting little cave are found on its east side.

1. What's Up Doc V3 (hb) Climb up the left side of the boulder.

2. Love Solution V3 (hb) Climb up the center of the south face via the flake system.

3. Good Love V4 (hb) Start on the big bucket and climb out the top.

4. Panic Attack V3 Climb up the center of the east face.

5. Therapy Traverse V5 Start with the bucket and traverse to the right or start on the far right and traverse to the left, finishing with *Good Love.*

Rasta Boulder ▲

Head into the heart of Skunk Canyon, following the narrow trail along the side of the
creek, at times switching from one side to
the other. This prime boulder is found in the
trees, on the south side of the creek, below
the second ridge of Skunk Canyon.

1. Vibration Yeaho V6 (B2-) Climb up the
overhanging east face of the rock.

2. Dred Arête V4 Climb the northeast arête.

Jah Block ▲

This boulder is farther west on the slopes
above the creek.

1. Jah V4 Climb up the left side of the north
face.

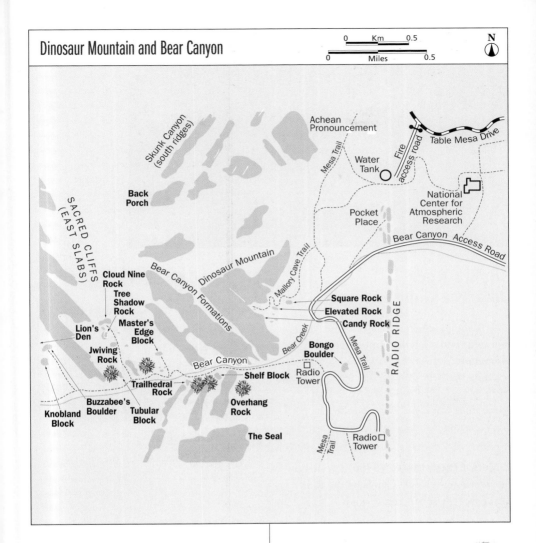

Dinosaur Mountain and Bear Canyon

0   Km   0.5

0   Miles   0.5

N

Map labels:
Skunk Canyon (south ridges)
Achean Pronouncement
Table Mesa Drive
Mesa Trail
Fire access road
Water Tank
National Center for Atmospheric Research
Back Porch
Pocket Place
SACRED CLIFFS (EAST SLABS)
Bear Canyon Access Road
Cloud Nine Rock
Tree Shadow Rock
Bear Canyon Formations
Dinosaur Mountain
Mallory Cave Trail
Square Rock
Elevated Rock
Candy Rock
RADIO RIDGE
Lion's Den
Master's Edge Block
Jwiving Rock
Bear Creek
Bongo Boulder
Mesa Trail
Trailhedral Rock
Bear Canyon
Shelf Block
Radio Tower
Buzzabee's Boulder
Tubular Block
Overhang Rock
Knobland Block
The Seal
Mesa Trail
Radio Tower

Dinosaur Mountain

Dinosaur Mountain consists of many rock formations making up the northern slopes of Bear Canyon. There is a good selection of boulders and blocks on its eastern slopes just up and west from the Mesa Trail.

Directions: From NCAR, hike due west, eventually catching the Mesa Trail to the south. At a point before Bear Canyon's access road, there is a trail heading up to the west (Mallory Cave Trail). Take this trail uphill and you find yourself staring at Square Rock. There are other boulders along the trail, past Square Rock.

Square Rock (aka The Cube) ▲

This beautiful block of maroon offers great toproping and a few highball problems. It is located just west of the Mesa Trail, before reaching the Bear Canyon dirt road. Take Mallory Cave Trail (from the Mesa Trail) uphill until you run straight into it. The descent route is found on the northwest corner via a tree climb.

1. Merest Excrescences V5 (hb) Located on the west side of block. Climb up the center of the face via small crimpy holds.

Elevated Rock ▼

Located uphill to the right (north) from Square Rock. It sits just left of the trail.

1. Edging Edgio V9 This starts in the overhang close to the ground on the far-left side of the rock, eventually reaching a very small crimper hold that must be utilized for a dyno to the top.

2. Slapshot V12 (B3) Climb the thin, overhanging, scoop-like face on the right side of the boulder.

Candy Block ▲

This nice block is up the trail to the south-west on the left side.

1. Candy Cane V6 Climb up just right of the center.

Holloway's Hangout

This boulder pack is located uphill from Square Rock and Elevated Rock. There are many good problems on isolated boulders, as well as ridge outcrops.

Bear Canyon

Bear Canyon offers some of the finest bouldering in the Flatiron Range, and lots of it. Boulders are found to the east and west of the inner canyon, as well as in the heart of it. In this book only the very best of the crop are described, starting with Bongo Boulder

to the east, excellent Shelf Block and Trailhedral Rock of the inner canyon, and Master's Edge Block, Tubular Block, Jwiving Rock, and Cloud Nine Rock to the west. You may also access the Sacred Cliffs Southern Spine from this trail, which leads up through the canyon and then out to the west, eventually intersecting the Sacred Cliffs' southern tail end.

Directions: From NCAR, hike up to the Mesa Trail and head south until you reach the Bear Canyon Access Road. Head to the east, down the road. Looking up and to the east, you see a hogback ridge extending from north to south. The road cuts through the point where Bear Creek has formed a canyon passage through the hogback. On the north side of the ridge, you find Pocket Place. A steep trail leads from the road up to its base. On the right side of the road you see Radio Ridge.

Radio Ridge ▲

This ridge offers an unlimited variety of boulder problems and traverses. It is seen extending to the south from the Bear Canyon Access Road.

1. Radio Waves Traverse V8–V9 Traverse the underside of the west face of Radio XI Rock, located approximately 50 yards downslope from the radio tower.

Bongo Boulder ▼

From the point where Bear Canyon Road (Mesa Trail) curves uphill to the south, continue up a short way until the road curves back around to the north. Look down to the north in the meadow to see this big boulder sitting within the hairpin. It offers one of the Boulder area's finest traverses.

1. Bongo Traverse V7 (B2) From good holds down right, traverse up and across the edges.

Shelf Block ▲

On the left (south) side of the trail, as you hike into the inner canyon, the boulders and blocks begin to appear frequently. This block has an obvious overhanging shelf system on its east side.

1. Tears Overhang V5 Climb up the center of the overhanging east face.

Trailhedral Rock ▲

At the far-west side of the boulders and blocks along the trail, there is an overhanging spire-like rock on the left (south) side of the trail. Difficult routes ascend its north face. Descend to the southwest along the ridge.

1. Hydrahedral V6 (hb) Climb the right-leaning dihedral on the north face (with arête) to the top.

2. Westside Arête V4 (hb) Climb the north-west arête and face of the rock.

Master's Edge Block ▲

Follow the Bear Canyon Trail to the west, past the canyon ridges. After passing the last ridge, follow the trail west for about 50 yards until you see a couple of small boulders sitting on the right (north) side. Look up and slightly right to see a prominent bouldering block up on the northern slopes. Scramble up to its base.

1. Jedi Knight V7 Climb the very thin face on the left side of the south-facing wall.

2. Master's Edge V3 Climb the arête on the far-right side of the block.

Jwiving Rock ▼

This beautiful rock is found upslope from Tubular Block (not described), around to the east in a shallow gully. After skirting the slope up and around to the northeast, follow the

western slope of the gully until you come to this, the best of the Flatiron maroons. Its south face offers amazing problems, including a traverse guaranteed to please. If you are in the area, also check out the nice traverses on Tree Shadow Rock and the crystals and pockets on Cloud Nine Rock.

1. Jwiving to Tears V1 Climb the short face on the far-left side.

2. Shadowed Paths V3 Climb up the center of the south face.

3. Twaversing V5 Begin on the right side of the rock and follow the crack line down and around to the left, connecting and finishing with *Shadowed Paths.*

Fern Canyon

Fern Canyon offers a wealth of bouldering up and through the narrows, as well as great meadow bouldering to the east.

Directions: Take Bear Canyon Road up past the Bear Canyon Trail cutoff and follow the Mesa Trail south until you reach the Fern Canyon Trail, which heads up to the west. To access Burgundy and Megatron Boulders, head up this trail to a point before the inner canyon and head off to the south for Burgundy and the north for Megatron.

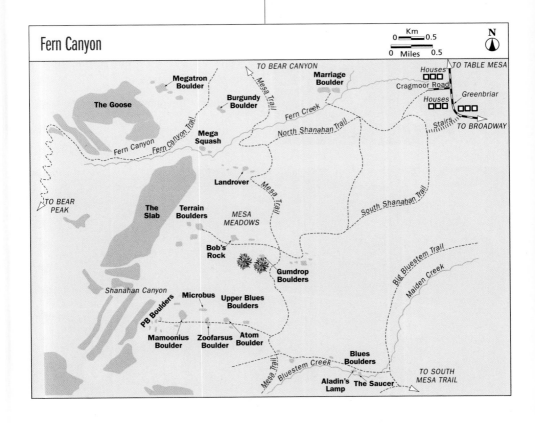

Megatron Boulder ▼

This boulder, sitting out below the south-eastern slopes of the Goose Flatiron, is located off to the north from the trail leading up to Fern Canyon's threshold. Several other interesting large rocks will be encountered before reaching this big boulder.

1. Kaptain's Route V3 Climb the steep, bulging face on the left side of the east face.

2. Holloway's Overhang V6 (hb) Climb out the large roof on the north side.

Burgundy Boulder ▼

This exceptionally nice boulder is located to the south of the Fern Canyon Trail out in the northeastern meadows of the Slab Flatiron. The demanding problems are found on its east face.

1. Burgundy Marooner V3 Climb the face and bulge on the far-left end.

2. Bottle of Red V4 (B1) Climb up over the bulge right of *Burgundy Marooner*.

3. Wine and Dine V4 Climb the thin overhang on the far-right end.

4. Burgundy Traverse V5 Start on the far-left end and traverse to the right, following a thin seam with small crimpy edges.

Fern Creek East

These boulders are located on the northern slopes just off Fern Creek, east of the Mesa Trail. Take North Shanahan Trail to a point just past the halfway junction and head off to the north on a faint road descending down to the north, eventually crossing the creek.

Shanahan Canyon/ Terrain Boulders

The Terrain Boulders offer a large concentration of boulders and blocks within a short distance of one another. The rock and problems are of the best quality with a variety of hold types. The forested surroundings offer a pleasant break from the sun during the warmer months. Many of the huge blocks are highball, but plenty of ground traverses exist as well.

Directions: To find the boulderfield, hike from the North Shanahan Trail Loop, which you can access from the east after parking at the dead end on Cragmoor Road. Hike west up the trail, eventually connecting to the North Shanahan Trail. Head west to the Mesa Trail and then go left (south) for approximately ten minutes to a point where it clears into a meadow on the right (west) side of the Mesa Trail. Hike up the north side of the meadow, following the ridgeline. You will encounter the small but challenging Peanut Boulder on the right. The Gumdrop is across the meadow just off the drainage to the southeast. Continue along this ridgeline for ten minutes to towering Bob's Rock, standing alone in an open field. The other boulders are up to the northwest from this point.

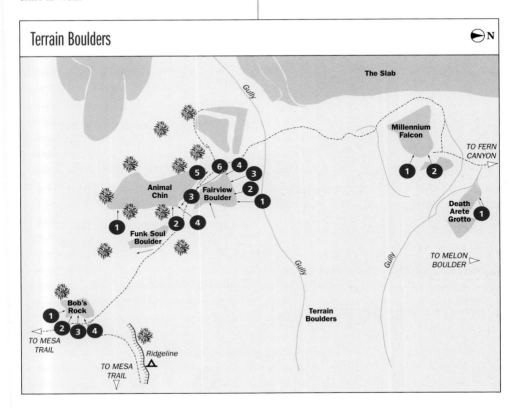

5. Trust Arête V5 (hb) Climb the arête on the southeast corner.

6. Bob's Wall V5 (hb) Climb up the left side of the east face.

Fairview Boulder

This massive block is upslope to the northwest of Bob's Rock. It gets its name from its prominent view, topping out the trees as seen from Fairview High School. Perhaps this was the developers' inspiration—they saw it from school and decided to check it out. Good problems abound on all sides.

1. Parasol V4 Climb up the left side of the northwest face via underclings to the bulge.

2. Ken Kenny's Whistle V5 Climb out the roof 10 feet right of *Parasol*.

3. Plush V5 Climb up to the pocket on the tall section of the northwest face.

4. Shag V2 Climb up the far-right side of the northwest face.

5. SFP V1 Climb up the southwest end of the block.

6. GFT V1 Traverse the face from left to right, right of the tree.

7. Kleine Schlampe V3 (hb) Climb from the horizontal around the corner left of the ponderosa.

8. Eara Fuchin Schmuckin V3 (hb) Climb the crack from down low, across to the left, then up top.

9. Shoots and Ladders V4 (hb) Climb out the crack to the right, over the bulge to the top.

Bob's Rock ▲

Uphill from Peanut Boulder, the forest thins out to an open fire-burned section of the slope. Bob's Rock is located within this tundra-like setting. It resembles a quality Flagstaff Mountain spire, like that of Capstan Rock. A great traverse skirts its south face. Exit to the north.

1.Golden Ticket V2 (B1-) Climb the steep face to the left of the crack.

2. Bob's Crack V0 This fun route climbs the crack on the south face.

3. Wanka Traverse V5 Traverse from left to right utilizing excellent pockets and edges.

4. Dude's Face V5 (hb) This highball south face offers good edges.

Fairview
Boulder

10. Snuff V1 Climb the northeastern arête behind the ponderosa.

Animal Chin Boulder ▶

This large pocketed boulder is a few feet southwest of Fairview Boulder. Highballs abound.

1. Ejector Seat V5 (hb) Climb the southeast corner behind the trees.

2. Solo Meister V4 (hb) Climb the extended wall left of the leaning prow, on the right side of the east face.

3. MBT V4 Traverse the north face from right to left.

4. Tower of Power V10 (hb) This leaning prow is an area classic and works its way up the various hold sequences on the prow.

5. It Satisfies V5 (hb) Climb from down low up the crack and overhang right of *Tower of Power.*

The Love Boat

This massive block is 200 yards upslope to the west of Fairview Boulder. Its east face has several classic highball problems.

1. Tall Boy V3 (hb) Climb the extended face right of the tree, in the middle of the east face.

2. Famous V4 (hb) Climb the smooth maroon wall right of *Tall Boy*.

3. Having a Moment V3 (hb) Climb up the quality scooped sequence and rock on the north face.

The Millennium Falcon ▼

This protruding rock of quality sandstone is 200 feet across the rock–packed forest and gully to the north of Fairview Boulder.

1. Hand Solo V3 (hb) Climb out the slot and overhang on the southeast face.

2. Spewbacca V4 (hb) Climb the severe overhang and prow of the northeast point.

3. Princess Layme V4 (hb) Climb the pocket and face right of *Spewbacca*.

Death Arête Grotto ▲

You will find this several minutes through the forest roughly to the north.

1. Alpine Pansy V5 (hb) Climb the obvious prow of the block.

Holly's Rock ▲

To find this rock, continue up into Shanahan Canyon, then head upslope and right to the ridgetop.

1. Holly's Face V5 Go up the middle of the east face.

Shanahan South

South Shanahan Trail: This trail takes you up to the Mesa Trail, just south of the Mesa Meadows. Just before reaching the Mesa Trail, at a point where the road takes a sharp curve heading upslope, you can see Medal Maroon off to the south in the trees.

Medal Maroon ▼

This beautiful piece of maroon is just east of the Mesa Trail off the South Shanahan upper trail. At a point where the South Shanahan Trail curves upslope, look to the south to see the back, north side of this gem.

1. South Face V5 Climb up the right side of the south face via small edges.

2. Corner Stone V2 Climb the southeast corner of the block.

3. Dice V3 Climb the east face just right of the southeast corner.

4. East Face V2 Climb up the center of the east face.

5. Swinger V0 On the far-right side of the east face, swing up to the top.

The Blues Boulders

This fall line of boulders offers secluded climbing sessions amid excellent boulders. Many isolated boulders appear along this Big Bluestem trailway with a refreshing small creek nearby. Each boulder offers an amazing amount of overhanging to vertical challenges.

Directions: The lower portion of this area is accessible via the South Mesa Trail, located before Eldorado Canyon off Highway 170. The upper boulders are accessible via the latter or Shanahan South Trail, west of the Mesa Trail. To reach the upper section from the South Mesa Trail, take Big Bluestem Trail up to Mesa Trail and then go right (north) for a short distance until you reach the next gully over. Take the gully up to the west until you run into the main boulders.

Aladin's Lamp

This boulder is the first challenging boulder of the far-east Blues Boulders. From the South Mesa Trail, head off to the north on the Big Bluestem Trail. Take this up a short way until you see a few boulders just down and off the trail to the left (south). Aladin's Lamp offers a fine array of problems in a beautifully scenic setting. In spring the flowing creek adds to the magnificence.

1. Genie V3 Start on the far-left side of the rock under the overhang and traverse across to the right, ending at a reach problem in the middle of the south face.

2. Magic Carpet V3 Climb up the big edges in the center of south face to a long reach for the top.

3. Climb Aladin V3 Climb up the right side of the south face via small edges.

Upper Blues Boulders

These awesome boulders are located west of the Mesa Trail from the Big Bluestem Trail junction. From the South Mesa Trail, take the Big Bluestem Trail up west to the Mesa Trail. Head right at the Mesa Trail junction (north) for a short distance to the next gully over. Follow this up west to the boulder pack.

Alternative Route: From the Terrain Boulders and Bob's Rock, you may hike to the south across the old trail, staying east of the steep slope until you reach the large Mamoonius Boulder. The trail is marked with cairns.

Atom Boulder ▼

From the Mesa Trail, head up to the west. After passing a spire-like rock up the gully, head west for a short distance until you come across this superfine chunk of maroon. Many great overhanging problems have been fashioned here.

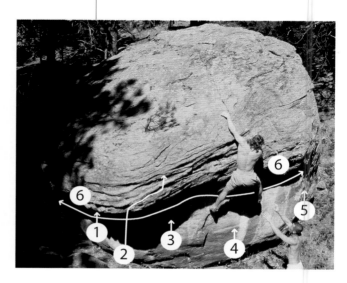

1. Doodlely Dud V5 (B1+) Starting on the far-left side with the crystals in the roof, climb to the top.

2. Curly Merl V4 Starting from the far left, traverse up and out right.

3. Mighty Dude V4 Climb the overhanging face right of *Curly Merl*.

4. Adam's Roof V2 Climb up the center of the overhanging east face via good holds.

5. Jumpin Gymnee V0 Climb up from the far-right side of east face.

6. Atom Traverse V7 Traverse the length of the boulder from right to left or left to right. Go back and forth for added difficulty.

Zoofarsus Boulder ▼

Continue up to the west for a short way until you run into this unique rock. Many problems and variations have been established.

1. Zooloo V4 Climb out the roof from the far-left side.

2. Zoofarsus Roof V4 (B1) Climb out the center of the boulder over the roof.

3. Zoofarsus Traverse V6 Traverse across left to right.

4. Zoo TV V8 Traverse from left to right finishing with *Zoofarsus Roof*.

5. Zooper Dooper V5 Traverse across from right to left and then out *Zooloo*.

Mamoonius Boulder ▲

1. Chaugle Pants V5 (hb) Climb up the left side of the south face to the dish above.

2. South Face Direct V3 (hb) Climb the flake to the slopey lip a few feet to the right of *Chaugle Pants*.

3. Crystal Reach V3 (hb) Climb the flake, then right to the large crystal.

4. Mamoonius Flake V3 (hb) Climb the crack on the sheer southwest face.

5. Easy Skeakin V0 (hb) Climb the jug haul right of *Mamoonius Flake*. This is also the down climb for the topout routes.

6. Crimp Wah V4 (hb) Climb the face just left of the southeast prow.

7. Southeast Arête V7 Climb the prow of the southeast corner.

8. Mamoon Traverse V6 (hb) Traverse in an upper diagonal direction from left to right.

9. Southeast Wall V5 (hb) Climb the smooth face from the block up to the seams.

10. East Arête V4 (hb) Climb up to pockets.

11. Mamoonia V3 Climb the left side of the east face over the bulge.

12 Moonbeam V6 Climb the leaning seam to the right of *Mamoonia*.

13. Squeezin' and Skeezin' V4 Climb the thin northeast face just right of the tree.

PB Boulders

This set of blocks is directly upgully to the west from the Upper Blues Boulders. They offer good problems on clean, hardened maroon sandstone. The first block is five minutes upgully from Mamoonius Boulder.

Pretty Boy Boulder

This is the first large boulder you encounter upgully.

1. Pretty Boy V7 Climb the sheer southwest arête of the block.

Big Orange Block

This large block is due west and is characterized by an orange-tinted north side.

1. Big Orange V1 (hb) Climb the lengthy wall on the left side of the north face.

2. Curious Orange V6 (hb) Climb from the block up the face.

3. Ornage Groove V0 Climb the groove on the right side of the north face.

Sag Wagon Block

This large block is just west of Big Orange Block. It is characterized by a blackened west face.

1. Sag and Bag V5 Climb up the south face just left of the tree.

2. Dueto's Pride (hb) Climb up the right side of the west face.

3. Black Wall V5 (hb) Climb up the middle of the west face.

4. Wagon Arête V8 Climb the overhanging corner on the north face.

The Pyramid

This triangular-shaped block is isolated just west of the previous blocks. Down climb the west groove.

1. Arête Master V1 Climb the prow on the west face.

2. Phillip's Slab V2 Climb the slab just left of the center.

3. Arête Meister V0 Climb the southwestern arête.

Mr. Gronky Block ▼

This cubed maroon gem is found up to the west 200 yards from the Mamoonius Boulder.

1. Funkarête V4 Climb the arête on the left side of the east face.

2. Slickhedral V5 Climb the flake and dihedral system on the east face.

3. One Trick Pony V5 Climb from the maroon flake, out left to the leaning arête.

4. The Full Gronky V7 Traverse from right to left and finish up the right-hand problem.

5. Mr. Gronky V5 Climb the sheer flake on the right side of the east face.

Mamooth Traverse Block

To find this large block, head due south from Mr. Gronky Block. Hike south, through the woods, over the hillside for five minutes until you see this chalk-laden block.

1. Mamooth Traverse V6 Traverse the east face from left to right.

Maiden Area

This section of the Flatirons is best accessed from the South Mesa Trail. Take the trail due west and follow the Mesa Trail markers. After several curves in the road, you run across a bulletin board sitting very close to an old wood ruin. The Maiden is visible off to the northwest from this point. Horan's Block is located just east of the Mesa Trail from this kiosk/wood-ruin point. Head due east into the trees. In approximately 100 feet, you encounter this block.

Horan's Block

This quality piece of maroon offers problems comparable to those of the Milton Boulder in Eldorado Canyon. From a point along the Mesa Trail, at a kiosk and wood ruin, head east from the main trail.

1. Horse with a Name V1 Undercling the flake on the far-left end.

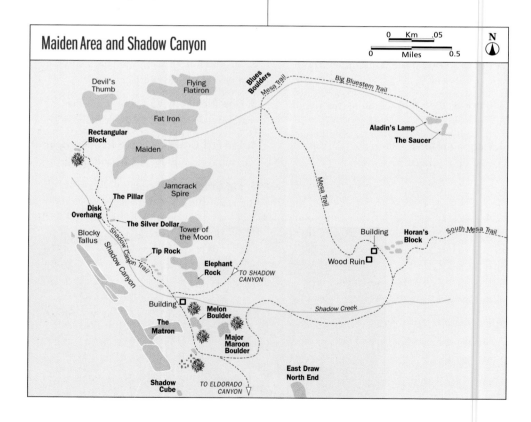

Maiden Area and Shadow Canyon

Horan's Block

2. Milestone V6 (B2-) Climb the thin-edged face right of the undercling flake.

3. At 40 V4 Climb up the thin-edged face on the right side via a high step.

4. Swing Out V1 From the far-right end of the block, step out and reach up for the top.

Shadow Canyon

Shadow Canyon offers an enormous variety of bouldering along its steep and winding trail. I have included only a few boulders, although there are many, many more that have been bouldered upon.

Directions: Hike in from the South Mesa Trail. Follow the Mesa Trail signs west until reaching the Shadow Canyon turnoff. This trail takes you around to the backside of the Flatirons, behind the Maiden and Devil's Thumb.

Elephant Rock

This small huecoed formation is found on the eastern slope of Shadow Canyon, just northeast of the intersection of South Mesa Trail and Shadow Canyon Trail. Hike as if going up Shadow Canyon and you will see this formation shaped like an elephant's head on the southwestern side of Bear Mountain (Bear Mountain makes up the eastern slope of Shadow Canyon).

The many huecos on the south face of Elephant Rock offer great bouldering traverses and vertical challenges.

Tip Rock

Found on the right side of the trail approximately fifteen minutes uptrail.

1. South Arête V1 Climb the south arête via a small pocket and layaways.

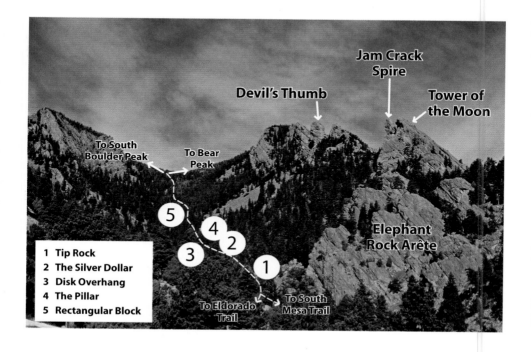

1 Tip Rock
2 The Silver Dollar
3 Disk Overhang
4 The Pillar
5 Rectangular Block

The Silver Dollar ▲

This oval-shaped slice of rock is found along the right side of the trail.

1. Silver Arête V4 (B1) Climb the southwest arête of the rock.

2. Coin Toss V2 Climb up the face just right of the arête and reach for the crack.

3. Tails It Is V1 Climb up the far-right side of the rock.

The Pillar

Found up along the trail, behind the Silver Dollar a short way.

1. Southwest Arête V1 Climb the arête.

2. South Slab V0 Climb the south face of the block.

Rectangular Block

Continue up the trail for several hundred feet from the Silver Dollar and you come across this classic block. This is located at the top portion of the Shadow Canyon Trail. The trail cuts right in front of its north face.

1. Rectangle V1 Climb the far-left side of the north face.

2. Going Rectangular V1 Climb up the center of the north face.

3. Right Rectangular V0 Climb the far-right side of the north face.

Matron East

These boulders are located just off the trail (dirt road) leading up to the Shadow Canyon Trail junction from the Eldorado or South Mesa Trail. The meadow setting that these boulders are found in is awesome—a great place to have a bouldering picnic.

Melon Boulder ◄

This boulder is located just off the main trail to the east, before a hut at the beginning of the Shadow Canyon Trail. Difficult face climbs abound.

1. The Edge V4 From the left side of the east face, climb to the top.

2. Underlying Dynamics V5 (B1+) From the undercling, reach up to small edges then up to the top.

3. Dicey Slab V4 Start right of the undercling and climb to the top.

4. Melon Arête V2 Coming in from the right, reach up to the top.

5. Blind Melon Corner V2 Climb the classic corner on the right side.

Major Maroon Boulder (West Face) ▼

This large boulder is located downhill, across the meadow, to the east of Melon Boulder.

The west face offers good, hard face problems with perfect landings. The south face offers some fun highball routes in the V0 range. The east face offers a few exciting problems on its northeast corner. Exit the west face.

1. Indirect West V3 Climb the far-left side of the featured west face.

2. Direct West V4 Climb up the middle of the featured west face.

3. Hangout V3 Climb up the right side of the west face.

4. Easy Edge V2 Climb up the far-right side via good edges.

5. Rollin V0 Climb to the right of *Easy Edge* via a high-step rollover.

Major Maroon Boulder (South Face) ▲

These are pocketed high problems on the south face.

1. Thumbs Up V1 (hb) Climb the pocketed face on the far-left side.

2. Angel's Thumb V1 (hb) Climb the left-angling crack system.

Major Maroon Boulder (Northeast Face)

There are a few problems climbing up from the face and arête of the boulder.

1. Sheer Twist V3 Start on left side of the arête and climb up to the right.

2. Twist to Shout V4 Climb straight up the arête, exiting on the right.
Note: A great traverse from northeast corner to west face exists.

Shadow Cube ▼

On the trail leading down to Eldorado Canyon from Shadow Canyon and the Mesa Trail, you come across a few gullies to the west. Shadow Cube lies in the trees of the first gully south of the Matron. A few small boulders are visible as you come down the gully. Shadow Cube is hidden in the trees and not visible from the main trail. You may also access this boulder by coming up from Eldorado Canyon via a trailway from out the northeast section of town.

1. Cubular V1 Climb the cube, utilizing the flake on the southeast corner.

2. Prime Face V6 Climb up the left side of the east face.

3. Three Leaves V4 (B1) Climb the face and arête on the right side.

4. Craig's Arête V1 Climb to top, utilizing the far-right arête and slab.

19 ELDORADO CANYON

Eldorado Canyon's high-quality, hardened sandstone has attracted climbers from all parts of the globe. Many rock routes with crux moves resembling boulder problems are found amid this vertical paradise. Classic routes such as *PsychoRoof, Genesis,* and *Rainbow Wall,* to name a few, reflect bouldering moves executed high above the ground. These physically as well as mentally challenging routes are considered by the serious climber as mere extensions of difficult moves developed and trained for on boulders close to the ground, many of which are located within the heart of Eldorado Canyon.

Eldorado's boulder problems are among the best found along the Front Range, with the rock type to match. Boulder problems have been fashioned at the bases of the prominent formations as well as the many isolated boulders and blocks spread along South Boulder Creek and up its slopes. Most of these are of a hardened maroon, quality sandstone. The bouldering is extremely enjoyable for all levels of ability at any time of the year.

Directions: Go south out of Boulder on Highway 93 (Broadway). In just a few miles, locate the stop light at the intersection of Highway 93 and Highway 170/Eldorado Springs Drive. The ELDORADO STATE PARK sign at the intersection directs you to the west. Head west on Eldorado Springs Drive for approximately 3.3 miles, through the town of Eldorado Springs, until you run straight into the state park. There is an entrance station with a park official willing to collect your entrance fee. For those enjoying the canyon on a regular basis, an annual pass to the Colorado State Parks system is recommended. Otherwise, daily passes are available.

Eldorado Canyon (East)

N

Shadow Cube

Talus

TO SHADOW CANYON

Old Mesa Trail

Sofa Patrol Wall
Highwire Wall
Center Ring Wall
Stratum Block
Lengthy Block
Low Traverse Rock

Ridge Slope Block

Houses

ELDORADO SPRINGS

Pool

Entrance Station

Houses

TO KID BOULDERS APPROX 2 MILES

TO GOLDEN NUGGET AREA APPROX 1.5 MILES

Shirt Tail Peak 7,243'

Rotwand Wall

Hawk Eagle Ridge

Wind Tower

Whale's Tail

Rincon Wall

Redgarden Wall

Cinch Block

West Ridge

Poly Block

Redgarden Boulders

River Block

Cap Block

Mental Maroon

Quartz Ridge

West World Boulders

Water Boulder

Kankakee

The Bastille

Cement Platform

Restroom

Patio

Peanuts Wall

Lion's Turf Boulders

Peanuts Boulder

Peanuts Block

Rolling Stone Boulder

Dog Town Boulder

Milton Boulder

Supremacy Slab

Gill Boulder

South Boulder Creek

South Boulder Creek

Rattlesnake Gulch Trail (Hotel Run Trail)

TO ELDORADO WEST BOULDERS

Eldorado Trail

Sun Valley Boulders

Visitor Center

TO HOTEL RUIN

P

Eldorado Springs Drive

Kid Boulders

Now that some of us older boulderers have young ones, I thought I'd add this favorite "little people's" bouldering area where for years I brought my toddlers to hike and climb (of course now they would rather go skateboarding). Here you can expose the young beginner to the techniques and safety of bouldering. You can teach them the bouldering experience: how to spot, how to use the natural face holds, how to layback, how a bouldering pad works, and so on. Check it out; it is truly a natural playground for the kids.

Most of the boulders have two or three moves to the top, while one is a perfect 7-footer with a challenging steep face. A larger prominent block sits in the meadow to the southwest of the miniboulders. A few good problems have been done on this block. They are perfect for the progression to larger boulders, should the youngsters choose to do so as they advance.

Directions: Follow the directions to Eldorado Canyon, turning west off Highway 93 onto Eldorado Springs Drive. Drive about a mile and park at the South Mesa trailhead, located down on the right. From the parking area, head north up Mesa Trail. (The trail at this point is actually an access road.) Hike north for about ten minutes, until you see the large block sitting in the trail loop. The miniboulders are found behind this block to the northeast.

Kids Boulder ▼

This short boulder is on the far-east end of the boulderfield. There are two or three moves to the top. Drop the pad below the south face and have fun.

1. The Layback V0 Climb up the little layback flake on the south face.

2. Pocket and Huecos V0 Climb up the left side of the south face.

Mini Maroon ▲

This 7-foot boulder is found to the west of the Kids Boulder and offers a more challenging south headwall.

1. The Shield V0 Climb up the center of the south face.

Eldorado Canyon East

East Draw

This hogback ridge rises out of the east end of the little town of Eldorado Springs, just east of the Eldorado Canyon State Park entrance. A good wintertime designation, it is full of traverses and overhanging problems, as well as a few isolated boulders on its western slopes. The Sofa Patrol Wall is perhaps the gem of the lot and offers good highball or toproping challenges up its west face.

To find the rocks from the main parking area at Eldorado Canyon, take Shadow Canyon Trail (Old Mesa Trail), on the northeast end of the housing units. Hike north to a point beyond the center of the hogback, then angle up and back to the southeast to the ridgetop. No public parking is allowed in Eldorado Springs. Be courteous of the townfolk.

Sofa Patrol Wall ▶

This colorful, sheer wall of perfect, almost quartzite-type rock is at the north end of the hogback. It is the best wall on the hogback and a good starting point for the problems that follow down along the ridge to the southeast. This is usually toproped but has recently had a few bouldered-out ascents. The landings are good, but many pads were stacked for the ascents. A toprope is seriously recommended.

1. Sofa Patrol V5 (xhb) Climb up the good edge on the left side of the west face.

2. Couch Potato V6 (xhb) Climb the thin face to the right of *Sofa Patrol*.

Highwire Wall

This highball wall is to the right of Sofa Patrol Wall and offers a lengthy 20-foot topout.

1. Pervertical Sanctuary V2 (hb) Climb the thin crack on the left side of the diamond-shaped wall.

2. D1 V4 (hb) Climb up the middle of the diamond face.

3. King of Swords V2 Climb good holds on the right side of the wall.

Center Ring Wall

This traverse wall offers an excellent pump across the 50-foot overhanging wall, as well as some challenging straight-up problems. Hike downslope to the southeast and until you see an old barbed wire fence at the right end of the wall.

1. Hooey's Back Porch V3 (hb) Climb up from the horizontal on the left side of the wall.

2. Pig-Dog V6 Climb the steep overhang a few feet to the right of *Hooey's Back Porch*.

3. Pig Nose V3 Climb the large holds up the right side of the lengthy overhang.

4. Barbed Wire Traverse V7 Traverse along the base of the wall from right to left.

Ridge Slope Block

This nice cube of sandstone is downslope approximately 200 feet from Center Ring Wall. It sits just off the hogback out to the west, slightly downslope.

1. Crimpster V5 Climb up the left side of the sheer southwest face, right of the prow.

2. Jama V3 Climb up the middle of the southwest face.

Stratum Block

This block is closer to the hogback than Ridge Slope Block. It is a solar collector.

1. Sun Tan V2 (hb) Climb up the left side of the south face, up the tan rock, right of the arête.

2. Black Dike V1 (hb) Climb the blackened section left of the center.

3. Scoopy Doo V3 Climb the scoop up the middle of the block.

4. Curving Arête V2 Climb the arête on the right side of the block.

5. Cracker Jack V1 Climb the crack system on the east side.

Lengthy Block

This highball block is within the hogback, down to the southeast of the previous blocks and just north of Low Traverse Rock.

1. The End V2 (hb) Climb diagonally across the west face to a scary topout.

Low Traverse Rock

This good rock is just south of Lengthy Block and offers nice holds for a good pump.

1. Le Crack V2 Climb the classic crack on the left side of the rock.

2. Le Face V4 Climb the steep face to the right of the crack.

3. Low Traverse V6 Traverse across the rock from right to left.

Eldorado Canyon—Inner Canyon

The Bastille ▼

Just up the road from the entrance parking area, on the south side of the road, is the towering Bastille. In prime season you will see groups of people standing along the side of the road watching and pointing up at the entertaining boulderers and climbers. The base of the Bastille has excellent bouldering and is best known for its long traverse that skirts the base.

1. The Shield V4 (hb) From the east end of the Bastille's south face, walk up the road approximately 25 feet to find a smooth vertical face with small layback edges on it. Crank your way up the 20-foot face.

2. Shield Traverse V3 At the base of the Shield there is a delicate traverse with a stretchy move. This is probably the single hardest part of *Lower Bastille Traverse*.

3. Micro Traverse V6 To the right of *Shield Traverse* there is a delicate little edge traverse problem that skirts the ground. Stay low below the obvious rampway.

4. March of Dimes Direct V2 Approximately 20 feet from *Micro Traverse* there is an obvious crack with a small undercling reach in it. Make the reach and proceed to the prominent left-angling finger crack (hb), or exit immediately to the right and down.

5. Zorro Crack V3 (hb) Just to the left of *March of Dimes Direct* is a very thin right-angling crack that intersects the upper finger crack from *March of Dimes Direct*.

6. Flake Left V2 To the right of *March of Dimes Direct,* after the traverse breaks up a bit, there is a short left-leaning flake with a thin crack paralleling it on its left. Avoid the

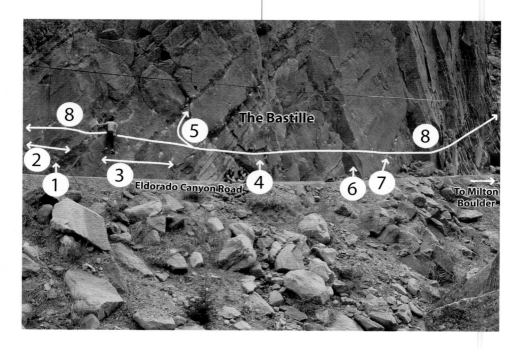

flake on the right and ascend this delicate crack.

7. Sloper Face V2 Just right of *Flake Left,* to the right of the flake, is a small right-angling ramp system with some bolt holes at its start. Without getting too off-balance or tangled up, try to mantel your way up and across this.

8. Lower Bastille Traverse V3 (B1) From the far-left side of the north-facing wall, traverse across the base to the scree field on the far-right side.

Wind Tower ▼

From the entrance parking area, walk west a short way, past the steel gate to the footbridge that leads you to the north side of the creek. The Wind Tower is visible to the northeast from the bridge. After crossing the bridge, take a right, down the trail to the

east, where you find some excellent problems at the base of this large tower of rock.

1. Wind Tower Lower Traverse V3 This mostly moderate traverse starts on the far-west side of the south face just below the *Crystal Lift* route and traverses the entire south face.

2. Crystal Lift V2 A polished arête with a small hollow flake at the start and a small crystal part way up. The balancey reach for the top is a real thrill.

3. South Wall V2 There are many variations on this steep wall just right of *Crystal Lift.* The easiest is found up a sort of groove on the left side; the middle face is classic; and the right side is a good challenge.

4. Gold Rush V4 Across the gap from *Crystal Lift* and *South Wall* is a golden-colored, smooth vertical wall with some small edges. Crank away and mantel the top.

Wind Tower Pillar ▲

You can find this pillared block leaning up against the west side of Wind Tower, just south of Salvation Roof.

1. Wind Arête V1 (hb) Climb the arête to the south slab on the right side of the north face.

2. Wind Overhang V? (hb) Climb the overhanging face and arête on the east underbelly of the pillar.

Hawk Eagle Block

This block is across the gully to the west from Cinch Block and sits up against the slab that leads down the east side of the Redgarden Wall.

1. Cinch V0 Climb from down right up and across to the left on the southwest face.

Whale's Tail ▲

From the north side of the footbridge, hang a left to arrive at the base of this large formation. Whale's Tail is most famous for its large cave at the base of its west end. Some of the best bouldering is found in and around this monumental cave. The rock here is very solid and has a slick nature due to years of polishing by the river. The polished stone makes for an interesting type of bouldering, one that takes strength combined with steadiness to be successful. Of special note is the fact that all of the routes along this south face have been bouldered out by a few daring local boulderers. Although ropes are most seriously recommended for a few of these dangerously high ball (xhb) boulder problems, they will be included for historical reasons.

Corners Area

This area encompasses the eastern portion of Whale's Tail from *Spoof* to *Mantel Man*.

1. Mantel Man V2–V3 As you walk west a few feet along the eastern base of Whale's Tail, you come across a polished sloping mantel shelf. You can climb this mantel in various ways. One way uses an undercling and a one-arm mantel, and the other uses a straight-on, two-handed push.

2. Slipper Face V2 Just to the left of *Mantel Man* there is a vertical face with an undercling start leading to a downsloping ledge system. Climb up and exit right.

3. Dihedral 1 V2 (hb) Just left of *Slipper Face* is a small corner with some barn door moves. You can go left or right to exit.

4. Slick Traverse V5 Just above the ground, starting at *Dihedral 1* traverse across to *Mantel Man*.

5. Throw Back V3 (hb) Left of *Dihedral 1* there is an overhanging face with an arête on the left wall. Climb this and exit right.

6. Scary Cling V3 (hb) Just left of *Throw Back* there is a vertical wall with an interesting move at the top.

7. Dihedral 2 V0 (hb) Just left of *Scary Cling* there is a classic dihedral with a block overhang. Climb up and over, then down climb.

8. Just Left V0 (hb) Just to the left of *Dihedral 2* there is an overhanging face with good holds. Exit *Dihedral 2*.

9. Pocket Bulge V1 (hb) Left of *Just Left* is a bulging wall with an obvious pocket about 10 feet up.

10. Amputee Love 5.12 V6 (xhb) Start to the left of pocket bulge, right of *Spoof* ramp, and climb the steep, overhanging face via slopey edges.

Creek Slab ▼

Across the trail from *Mantel Man* on Whale's Tail, there is a big boulder with a smooth northeast-facing slab. Many problems exist on this slab, as well as many little edges. Most problems are in the V0 to V1 range.

Creek Boulder

Just west of Creek Slab, there is a nice rounded boulder with a difficult east-facing bulge. In high-water season the start is submerged.

1. East Bulge V5 (B1+) From the sandy beach below the retaining wall you will notice an east-facing bulge with some delicate layback edges. Climb up and mantel.

The Cave Area

These boulder problems are found in and around the cave's threshold. Continue west along the base of Whale's Tail and you can't miss this cave.

1. Cave Traverse V7 From the back of the cave traverse out toward the opening via laybacks, underclings, knee locks, and iron cross moves.

2. Threshold Traverse V4 Traverse the outer threshold of the cave close to the ground.

3. The Monument 5.12 V5 (xhb) Undercling up and out, finishing at the top of *Horangutan*.

4. Horangutan 5.12 V5 (xhb) Begin at the mouth of the cave on the big holds and climb up and out diagonally left.

5. Around the World V3 (B1) On the east side of the cave, at its opening, there is a polished wall. This is the rightmost section of *Cave Traverse*. Traverse in a circular direction, utilizing the good but angling edge system.

6. Ironman V6 Left of *Around the World*, climb up small holds with an iron cross and reach out right of the bulge to the big jugs of *Around the World*.

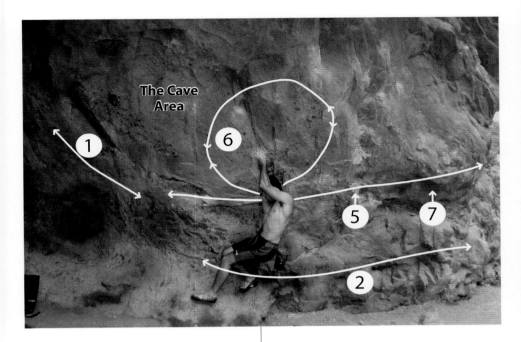
The Cave Area

7. **Vertical Polish V3** In the middle of *Around the World* there is a face with some small edges that can be ascended by utilizing a tricky mantel.

N.E.D. Wall

Outside the cave to the west is a beautiful wall with a wide variety of problems.

1. **N.E.D. 5.12 V5 (xhb)** Climb out the severe overhang via dynamic moves up and left of the cave's threshold.

2. **Off the Couch V1** Below and slightly left of the *N.E.D.* roof there is a slightly overhanging face with some nice little jugs on it. Exit right, or left to *Clementine.*

3. **Clementine V0 (hb)** Just left of *Off the Couch* is an obvious crack line that fades left onto some polished ledges.

4. **Lunge Break V2 (B1-)** Just left of *Clementine* directly across from the northeast corner of the cement platform, there is a

bulging, sloping ledge system. There are many different eliminates to gain the sloping ledges, including a double lunge.

5. **Double Lunge V6** From two good holds, left of the start of *Lunge Break,* soar up with two hands, latch onto the sloping edges, and finish *Lunge Break.*

6. **Smooth One V8** This problem climbs up from the left of *Double Lunge* utilizing very small edges in the bulge.

Platform Block

This block is immediately west of the far southwest corner of Whale's Tail, forming somewhat of a cave between the two.

1. **The Arête V2** Just left and slightly south, almost touching the *Lunge Break* problem, there is a short arête with a tricky heel hook move.

2. **Micro Pull V7** To the immediate left of *The Arête* there is a short bulging wall. Feel

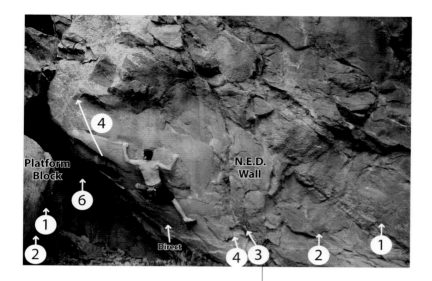

up for the micro edges if you can reach them and pull to the top.

3. The Layback V0 From a sitting position left of *Micro Pull* there is a short layback problem.

Close to the Edge Blocks ▼

Immediately up and left of N.E.D. Wall, above Platform Block, there are two elongated blocks. The lower block offers several difficult mantels as well as a traverse that is linked with the upper block. The upper block has an upward-diagonaling arête.

1. Mondoman Traverse V6 From the far-west edge of the lower rock, traverse across and then link upward with *Close to the Edge*.

2. Close to the Edge V4 (B1) This upper-diagonal, right-leaning arête's edge traverse makes its way up the upper block.

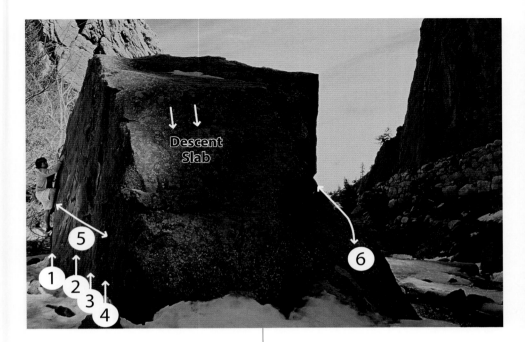

Water Boulder ▲

From the cement platform at the southwest corner of Whale's Tail, the trail continues west along the creek. After about 50 feet, near a small cement dam, you discover this nice block with a sheer northwest face. Many problems exist all around this, including an exciting traverse over the water.

1. East Arête V2 On the easternmost edge of the boulder there is a right-leaning face.

2. Center Route V3 This is a tricky layaway problem up the center.

3. West Side V2 Just right of *Center Route* there is another small-edged challenge.

4. Undercling Face V1 On the far-right side of the boulder there is a fun undercling route that consists of a high step and long reach.

5. Water Boulder Traverse V4 This is a traverse of the lower northwest face of the boulder. Little edges and footholds make this a great challenge. On the west side of the rock, there is a fun low-angle slab with some good friction. This is also the easiest descent from the top.

6. Over Water Traverse V1 On the south face of the boulder, over the water, there is a nice set of holds that can be traversed and ascended via a small layback system. Start west and head east and up.

Crank Rock ▲

This overhanging block is located upcreek from Water Boulder on the same (north) side. Follow the trail slightly uphill and then cut across a faint path leading down along the creek. This south-facing wall emerges from out of the creek bed. In spring and midsummer the base will most likely be underwater. Can be toproped.

1. Crankakee V3 (hb) On the south face of the rock, climb the overhanging face via sloping holds. Other variations exist.

River Block ▶

Getting back to the main trail, on the north side of the creek, follow it west past the lower south end of the Redgarden Wall for about 200 feet. From here drop down toward the creek to this massive block, which sits

along the creek bed. Look for challenging problems on its south and east faces. Can be toproped.

1. Gunk Roof V1 On the upper slope of the east side of the block, hidden in the bush somewhat, there is an incredible set of good holds leading out right to the dicey lip. The ground is close enough for comfort.

2. Kiss of Life V7 (hb) On the lower east side of the block is a large roof with a little jam in it. From here, you must reach up to the sloping ledge and mantel to a stance. The rest is airy but moderate.

3. Eastern Priest V4 (hb) On the south face of the boulder, just out of the creek, there is an overhanging face with some scary reaches.

4. Fall Line V0 Left of *Eastern Priest* there is a classic crack. Laybacking this line is a true delight.

Redgarden Boulders

These blocks are located along the trail that leads up the west side of Redgarden Wall.

They are of the best quality and offer steep to overhanging problems on their west faces. Other blocks are located to the west below and above Kloof Alcove.

O'Donnell's Block ▲

You will find this block on the right side of the trail after you've hiked about ten minutes upslope. It has a shelfy, slightly overhanging southwest face just above the trail.

1. O'Donnell's Route V2 (hb) Climb up to the large shelf, then up on the right side of the southwest face.

2. Trail Wall V2 (hb) Climb up the thin face on the left side of the southwest face.

Ledge Boulder

This boulder protrudes from the wall up on a shelf 10 feet above the trail. Hike several feet up the trail from O'Donnell's Block to a point where the trail splits off to the west for Kloof Alcove. Look up to the right to see this overhanging boulder sitting on the ledge system 10 feet above. The boulder sticks out from the lower part of the wall, yet it's connected to it. Scramble up to the ledge.

1. Eldo Wall V2 Climb the overhang on the right side of the boulder.

2. Maroon Plate V5 Climb up the left side of the boulder.

3. Shelf Traverse V5 Traverse the overhanging face from left to right.

Redgarden Block ▼

This high-quality, slightly overhanging block is a few feet up the trail on the right side. It has a colorful southwest face.

1. Redgarden Arête V6 Climb up the face and arête on the right side of the southwest face.

2. Redgarden Wall V7–8 Climb up the small crimps up the middle of the southwest face.

Kloof Block ▲

This nice block of Eldorado maroon is just above Kloof Alcove, west of the Redgarden Wall Trail. Hike due west from Redgarden Block, toward Kloof Alcove. The block sits above the alcove to the north.

1. Eldo Arête V1 (hb) Climb the face and arête on the right side of the south face.

Pure Maroon Block

This awesome edge-filled block is hidden in the trees, approximately 75 feet upslope to the north of Kloof Block. It has a steep and edgy east face on perfect rock.

1. Pure Face V0–V1 Climb a variety of edges up any part of the east face.

2. Pure Traverse V1 Traverse the east face from right to left, then up.

Fall Line Block

This block is downslope from the south entrance into Kloof Alcove.

1. Fall Line V2 Climb up the middle of the west face.

The Pancake ▼

This pillared, thin-sliced block is at the base of the southeast side of West Ridge, a few feet above the base trail that leads from east to west on the north side of South Boulder Creek.

1. Pancake Arête V1 Climb up the arête and face on the left side of the south face.

2. The Pancake V2 Climb up the middle of the south face.

Milton Area

Milton Boulder ▼

This is one of Eldorado's true prizes and is located about 200 yards up the road from the Bastille. The boulder sits along the north side of the road with a blank looking southwest face. Many incredible routes are all around this gem. Some of Eldorado's most difficult face problems have been fashioned here.

1. Ridge Face V0 On the far-left side of the west face there is a thin slab with some delicate moves.

2. Layaway V0 This is probably the easiest way to ascend the west face. Start out on a big step just off the ground and follow the laybacks up and right, around the overhang at the top.

3. Micro Slab V6 To the right of *Layaway* there is a thin slab with no footholds and very small edges. Climb up and exit right.

4. Standard V1 To the right of *Micro Slab* there is a thin face following a crack.

5. Undercling Route V3 To the right of *Standard* there is a conspicuous undercling that can be used to gain the upper slopes of the boulder.

6. Smeary Thing V7 Immediately right of *Undercling Route* there is a strenuous friction problem that ascends the scoop. Start by pinching the arête, throw a smeary stem out right, reach a small layaway just inches right of the undercling, and reach for the slopey shelf above a mantel.

7. Donna V4 This was named for the graffiti once below its face. To the right of *Smeary Thing* there is another thin finger problem that uses a two-finger, left-handed nitch. High step and reach for the top, then mantel.

8. Milton V4 (B1) This is the center problem on the southwest face and was named after the writing once on the southwest wall,

hence the boulder's name, as well. Pull on the face with a good layback and reach up for an obvious crystal and edge, then go for the top and mantel.

9. Milton Hop V3 This is a run-and-jump problem, up the *Milton* face that latches the mantel shelf.

10. Layreach V5 Immediately right of *Milton* there is a good right-hand layback hold. Smear up to this and crank to the top.

11. Never Say Never V10 (B2+) This is the blank-looking scooping face to the right of *Milton*.

12. Guerin Buttress V9 This thin problem laybacks the prow right of *Never Say Never*.

13. Micro Sheer V9 On the south face of the boulder there is an improbable-looking face that crimps small holds to the top.

14. Leaning Arête V0 On the south side of the boulder, just right of *Micro Sheer*, there is a left-leaning arête. Keep your body on the left side and traverse up to the top.

15. Milton Upper Traverse V3 On the top edge of the southwest face you can traverse back and forth until totally pumped.

East Slab

On the east side of Milton Boulder there is an excellent beginner's slab with many variations, including "no hands" for a good challenge.

Eye Drop Boulder ▲

This boulder is across the road to the south from Milton Boulder. It sits on top of a platform block.

1. Pete's Arête V6 Climb the dueling arêtes on the north prow of the boulder.

Overhang Block ▲

This large block with an overhanging north side is behind to the left (southeast) of Eye Drop Boulder.

1. Bob's Arête V2 (hb) Climb the arête and overhanging face on the left side of the north face.

Dimension Boulder ▲

This scenic boulder is up the talus to the southeast of Overhang Block. It has an overhanging southwest arête that rises out of a hole.

1. Dimension Arête V7 Climb the crimpy overhanging arête from down low, up and left, finishing on the northwest prow.

2. Dimension V3 Start at the far-left side of the west face and traverse to the right, then up the northwest prow.

Sharma's Roof Block

This slice of rock, leaning on top of a smaller block to form a severe overhanging roof, is found up the talus a short way to the south-west from Dimension Boulder.

1. Sharma's Roof V12 Climb out the roof on the northwest underside of the block.

The Patio ▶

This pyramid-shaped block is up the talus to the south of Sharma's Roof Block. Fowler Trail is just above its summit.

1. Patio Arête V1
Climb up the arête on the left side of the north face.

2. The Patio V1 Climb up the middle of the north face.

West World Boulders

Across from Milton Boulder to the north, upslope in the trees, is a cluster of boulders. During high water you must access this area by crossing the footbridge toward Whale's Tail, heading west down the main trail, and continuing past the West Ridge. In low-water season you can access the area by crossing the creek at Milton Boulder.

Lower West Ridge ▼

On the lower southern end of the West Ridge there is an awesome traverse skirting the base. Hike uphill on the main trail past the West Ridge. The traverse is found along the trail about 100 feet up from the creek.

1. West Ridge Traverse V6 Follow the crack line from right to left.

2. Terminator Version V7 Start on the crystalline wall right of the crack line adding several meters of hard crystal crimping in the bulging wall, finishing with *West Ridge Traverse*.

Tofu Block

You can see this rectangular-shaped block across the creek to the northeast from Milton Boulder.

1. Tofu Arête V0 Climb up the southwest arête of the block.

Cascade Boulder ▲

This boulder is accessible only during low-water season, usually beginning in early fall. It sits upstream and on the north side along the bank about 50 feet west of Milton Boulder.

1. Cascade Face V1 Climb the sheer–edged face of the south side, just off the creek.

Park Tech Boulder ▼

This short but sweet boulder is 150 feet upstream from Milton Boulder. It is nestled in the trees approximately 50 feet to the north of the creek.

1. Funky V4 Climb the arête and seam on the left side of the south face.

2. Tone's Warm-up V2 Climb the right-angling crack on the left.

3. Park Tech V5 Climb the small crimpy face with a toss for the top on the right side of the south face.

West World Boulder ▲

Hike west from Lower West Ridge, off the main trail toward the trees, to discover this obvious roof-like overhang with a good flake system leading out its lip.

1. Germ-Free Adolescence V5 (B1+) (hb) Climb the extreme south-facing roof with a tree close by. Yard on the flake system to the edges in the roof. The scary part is turning the lip.

2. Here Comes Sickness V8 (hb) This problem climbs the *Germ-Free Adolescence* overhang (from a sitting position) connecting to the top.

3. The Day the World Turned Day-Glo V5 Just to the left of *Germ-Free Adolescence* there is a bulging wall with a delicate move to gain the top.

4. Genetic Engineering V5 This is another bulge problem just to the left of the *Day Glo* bulge.

Roofus Block (West Face) ▼

This block is located just west of West World Boulder (the one with *Germ-Free Adolescence* on it) and offers an overhanging south face and a sheer west face.

1. Sheep Thrills V3 Climb up the left side of the west face.

2. When the Chips Are Down V9 (hb) Climb up the middle of the west face, right of *Sheep Thrills*.

3. Collin's Highball V3 (hb) Climb up the arête on the right side of the west face.

4. High Ho V0 (hb) Climb the arête, then onto the southwest slab.

The High Spire

This lengthy block is behind to the north of West World Boulder. It is attached to another block to the west, and there is a descent route between the two.

1. Squealer V4 Climb up the left side of the west face via good edges.

2. Feeler V5 Climb up the middle of the west face.

3. Three Beers V4 Climb up and left from the southwest prow.

4. Two Beers V3 Climb straight up from the southwest prow.

5. Stratosfear V2 (hb) This lengthy crack is climbed on the south face.

6. Klingon V0 (hb) Climb the good hold on the east face of the block.

Sail Boulder

This leaning boulder is up to the northwest from the previous blocks.

1. Sail Away V2 Climb up the west face.

Jammer Boulder

This boulder is to the northwest of Sail Boulder and sits behind a large fallen tree.

1. Wammer Jammer V5 Climb the arête and face of the southeast corner.

Spotless Boulder ▼

To find this boulder, hike north of the Roofus Block approximately 150 feet across the slope to the north. The boulder has a corner feature on its southwest face.

1. Venus and the Razor Blades V2 Climb the right side of the face within the gap.

2. Don't Touch I-man Locks V3 Climb up the middle of the face.

3. Punky Reggae Party V1 Climb up the left side of the face within the gap.

4. V-Locks V? Climb the corner flake on the left side of the west face.

West-End Block ▲

This nice block is several feet due west from Spotless Boulder and offers a sheer south face.

1. West End Tavern V2 Climb up the left side of the west face, right of the tree.

2. Sloppy Seconds V5 Climb up the middle of the south face.

3. Dilemma V3 Climb up the right side of the south face.

Tree Hug Block

This block is within the trees to the northeast of Spotless Boulder.

1. In Between V1 Climb the arête and face on the right side of the south face.

Meister Boulder

This large boulder is upslope about 150 feet northeast of Spotless Boulder and sits below a massive block that is up to the north.

1. Meister V7 (hb) Climb up the left side of the east face.

Massive Block ▼

This massive block is just upslope from Meister Boulder and has a blank overhanging south face.

1. Massive Traverse V4 Traverse the left rail of the left side of the south face.

Eldorado Flatiron ◄

Continue upslope to the north from Massive Block another 75 yards until you see this flatiron-shaped rock.

1. Eldo Flats V1 (hb) Climb up the middle of the south face; other variations on the right and left can also be done.

Lego Block

From Eldorado Flatiron, continue upslope to the southeast 50 yards and you will see this cubed block.

1. Legoland V2 Climb the left prow on the left side of the west face.

2. Legoland Traverse V3 Traverse the south and west face from left to right.

Ridge Top Block ▼

This awesome block is at the ridge cap that sits on the left side of the trail as it peaks.

1. Ridge Cap Arête V4 Climb the arching arête, starting down left and arching up right.

2. Ridge Wall V2 Climbs up the center of the east overhang.

South Boulder Creek Boulder ▲

This nice boulder is hidden in the trees. It is just offshore on the east side of the creek, at a point where the quartz ridge that is north-west of West World Boulder bottoms out.

1. Creek Arête V2 Climb the arête and face on the left side of the north face.

2. Creek Overhang V2 From down low, climb out the east overhang.

The Playground ▲

Up the road from Milton Boulder, to the point where the road levels off and turns to the north, a road cut is encountered. On the road cut's south side, a short way upslope to the west and facing southwest, there is a quartzite wall with good problems, including a 140-foot traverse.

1. Natural Pro Traverse V3 Starting at the lower right end of the formation, traverse low for 140 feet up the slope. For an extra pump, traverse back down the slope. Other more difficult eliminations exist.

Fowler Trail Boulders

From the small parking lot for the Playground, head up to the south and then east along the Fowler Trail, past the Rattlesnake Gulch junction for about 100 feet. These boulders are located up on the right and down to the left, somewhat close to the trail.

Rolling Stone Rock ▼

From Milton Boulder, head uproad to the west and catch the Fowler Trail heading back east past the Rattlesnake Trail junction for approximately 100 feet. This unique boulder is visible from the trail when looking up on the southern slope. The boulder's postion allows for difficult traversing up its leaning eastern arête.

1. High Traverse V6 Start on the far right and traverse the boulder, staying up and along the lip.

2. Sticky Fingers V7 Start as for *High Traverse* but drop down into the roof holds and then across low.

3. Rolling Roof V4 From a sitting position, climb up and out to the top, then across to the left for finish.

4. Stoned Roof V3 Climb the roof via large holds in the ceiling; finish by traversing left.

Peanuts Boulders

These boulders are located on the south slope of the canyon near Peanuts Wall.

Peanuts Block

This leaning block is out in the trees approximately 100 feet due west of Upper Peanuts Wall and Sunrider Arête.

1. Peanuts Arête V3 (hb) Climb up the northeast arête.

2. Peanuts Face V2 Climb up the middle of the east side.

Lion's Turf Boulders

These boulders and blocks are on the eastern slopes just off the east side of Upper Peanuts Wall. Many problems have been done.

Peanuts Boulder

From the east slab of Upper Peanuts Wall, hike about 100 yards east across the talus field. Peanuts Boulder is hidden in the trees and offers climbing on excellent welded tuff, a unique rock type for the area. Edges, crystals, and pockets can be found on its overhanging east face.

1. Peapod V3 Climb up the left side of the east face.

2. Pea Soup V5 Climb up just right of *Peapod*.

3. Nut Shell V6 Climb up the middle of the east face.

4. Peanuts V4 Climb up the right side of the east face.

Dog Town Boulder ▼

This classic block sits isolated amid the massive talus west of Peanuts Wall. Hike up Fowler Trail and hang a right on Hotel Ruin Trail. Hike up 100 feet to the west, until you are below the talus. Then head upslope to the south 10 yards, until you see the block.

1. Dog Arête V6 Climb the arête on the left side of the north face.

2. Dog Town V4 Climb up the middle of the north face.

3. Doggy Dog V3 Climb the right side of the north face.

Supremacy Slab ◄

From Milton Boulder continue up the road past the Playground and road cut, then down to the intersection at the bridge over Eldorado Creek. Supremacy Slab is along the side of the road, on the left, where the road takes a turn to the left before the bridge. A fun traverse along its base offers good warm-ups and eliminates.

Water Rock ▼

From the bridge near Supremacy Slab, look to the southwest to see this rock sitting on the east side of the creek with its oval-shaped west face.

1. West Scoop V0 (hb) This is the obvious west face with a crystal jug halfway up the face. Many other variations are possible.

Gill Boulder ▲

This challenging, very diverse boulder is hidden in the trees just northeast of the bridge. All sides of this classic blocky boulder have great problems with good landings. Descend on the west side via a tree step.

West Face Gill Boulder

1. Western Slab V0 On the southwest corner of the boulder there is a narrow slab leading to the top.

2. Ament's Wall V4 Right of the prominent descent tree is a vertical wall with a hard move off some small edges eventually reaching the top.

North Face Gill Boulder

3. Gill Face V4 (B1) Around to the left of *Ament's Wall* there is a smooth vertical wall immediately left of the northwest corner.

4. Baldwin Face V5 Left of *Gill Face* about 10 feet there is a thin-edged face. Move up and right.

5. Standard Route V3–V4 This is the obvious vertical face up the center of the sheer north face.

6. Horan Face V6 Just left of *Standard Route* there is a set of small edges. Climb up and slightly right, finishing at the top of *Standard Route*.

7. Northeast Reach V0 On the northeast corner of the boulder there is an exciting route that starts out with some great edges with a long reach to the top.

East Face Gill Boulder

1. East Dihedral V0 On the east side of the boulder there is an obvious dihedral leading up to the top.

2. Southeast Corner V0 This short but fun route climbs the southeast corner via some laybacks.

3. East Side Traverse V0 This is a good traverse that skirts the east face of the boulder, the most difficult section being at the north end.

South Face Gill Boulder

1. South Left V3 On the left side of the slab there's a thin face that is gained with a small toe pocket and high step.

2. South Center V4 This is a very difficult thin-edged face up the center of the slab.

3. South Right V3 On the far-right side of the thin slab there's a delicate face requiring a thumbs-down push and small step.

Eldorado West

These are the numerous boulders that line the slopes and valleys to the north and west of Rincon Wall. These include Sun Valley, Musical Boulders, Lower and Upper Physical Boulders, Metaphysical Boulders, and Sobo Boulders. Many world-class problems have been established in this vast bouldering para-dise. Bouldering is good all year round, with the best time being fall and winter.

All of these areas are accessible from the main Eldorado Trail, starting just above the visitor center located in the northwest end of the park. Don't miss West Egg and East Egg of the Musical Boulders, as well as Lightning Spire with the infamous *Midnight Freightening* problems. Other excellent options are Nightmare Block in the Physical Boulders and *Sky Eye Arête* in the Lower Sobo Boulders.

Rincon Boulders

You can see Rincon boulders downslope due west of Rincon Wall. You can also see them off Eldorado Road, several hundred yards upslope to the east across the road from Supremacy Slab. Hike west up Eldorado Trail. At the switchback just before the climbing access trail and the sign to Rincon Wall, head south across the talus into the trees. You encounter Point Block just south of the talus in the trees. To find Tree Disk, continue south through the trees.

Surf Traverse Wall ▲

To find this awesome section of maroon rock, head farther south to a point below the Rincon Wall. It is characterized by an upward-traversing north face along a horizontal crack system.

1.Surf Traverse V3 Traverse in an upward-angling direction across the crack on the north face.

Mental Maroon Block ▼

This prime block is 75 feet southeast of Surf Traverse Wall, in an opening below Rincon Wall's western slopes.

1. North Wall V3 Climb up the left side of the north face with a slopey topout.

2. Mental Arête V5 (hb) Climb up the overhanging prow on the northwest corner of the block.

3. Think V1 Climb up the middle of the west face on the block just right of the block.

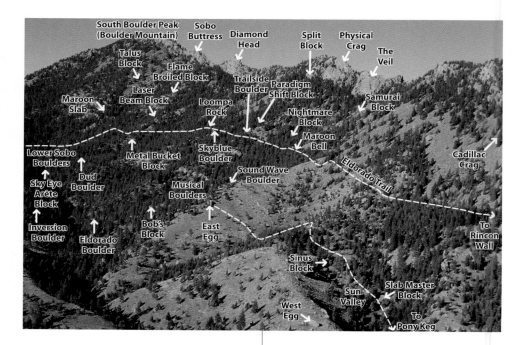

Sun Valley

Sun Valley is located down low and can be accessed at a point after you hike up the Eldorado Trail for about five minutes. A well-tracked trail splits off to the left of the main trail, just after a wood fence, and leads you to the heart of Sun Valley.

Ron's Keg ▼

This is another short-but-sweet boulder that sits in a friendly secluded meadow a short way up the trail.

1. Chip's Arête V2 Climb up the northwest arête.

Eldorado Canyon (West)

N

South Boulder Peak

Upper Sobo Boulders

Diamond Head

Diamond Head Area

The Veil

Physical Crag

Teepee Rock

Cadillac Crag

Rincon Wall

Shirt Tail Peak

The Potatoe Chip

West Ridge

West Ridge

Redgarden Wall

The Bastille

Sobo Buttress

Sky Area

Physical Boulders

Musical Boulders

West Egg

Trailside Boulders

Lower Physical Boulders

Metaphysicals

Sinus Block

Master

Slab Block

Tree Block

East Egg

Ron's Keg

Rincon Boulders

Flying Saucer

Cap Block

Mental Maroon

Marrow Traverse

Gill Boulder

Milton Boulder

Supremacy Slab

West World Boulders

The Playground

Eldorado Trail

Eldorado Trail

Sun Valley Trail

Visitor Center

2. Ron's Pony Keg Traverse V5 Traverse from right to left across the north and west side of the boulder.

3. Easy V0 Climb the crack on the northwest side.

4. Horn's Mudda V2 Climb the horn to a pinch, then up on the northwest prow.

5. Southwest Arête V2 Climb the southwest arête

6. Southside V3 Climb up the south face.

7. Direct South V5 Climb up from the hueco on the south face, then over the bulge.

8. Waterway V0 Climb the water slot on the south face.

Pony Keg ▼

This is the neighboring boulder east of Ron's Keg. Difficult problems abound.

1. Lefty V2 Climb across the rail on the north face, then up.

2. Center Route V4 Climb up the middle of the north face.

3. Fingertip Traverse V6 Climb across the seam on the northwest face.

4. High Traverse V5 Traverse the sloped rail of the north face.

5. Northwest Corner V5 Climb the crystal and seam of the northwest corner.

6. Woody's Pebble V6 Climb the thin bulge left of the southwest prow.

7. Rail Yard V2 Climb the crack out to the right.

8. Pony Keg Traverse V8 Traverse across the boulder.

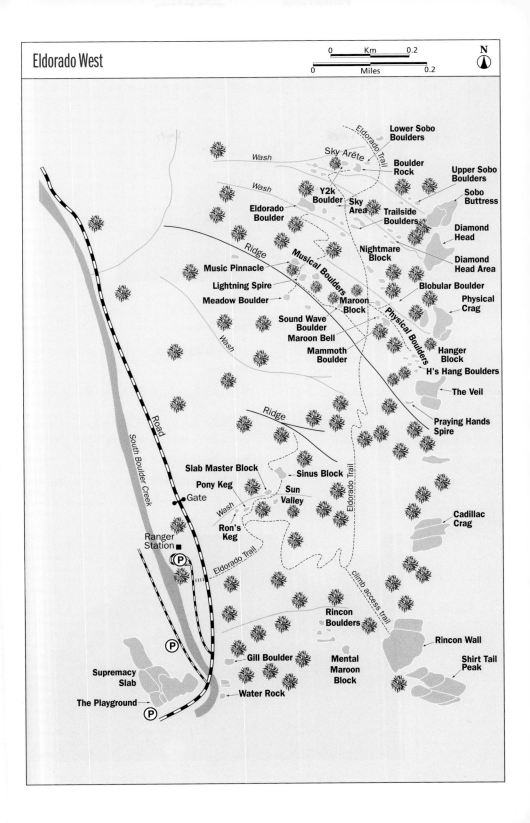

Eldorado West

0 Km 0.2

0 Miles 0.2

N

Lower Sobo Boulders

Sky Arête

Eldorado Trail

Wash

Boulder Rock

Upper Sobo Boulders

Sobo Buttress

Y2k Boulder

Sky Area

Trailside Boulders

Eldorado Boulder

Diamond Head

Wash

Ridge

Musical Boulders

Nightmare Block

Diamond Head Area

Music Pinnacle

Blobular Boulder

Lightning Spire

Maroon Block

Physical Crag

Meadow Boulder

Sound Wave Boulder

Physical Boulders

Maroon Bell

Hanger Block

Wash

Mammoth Boulder

H's Hang Boulders

The Veil

Ridge

Praying Hands Spire

Road

Slab Master Block

Sinus Block

South Boulder Creek

Pony Keg

Sun Valley

Eldorado Trail

Gate

Cadillac Crag

Ron's Keg

Wash

Ranger Station

P

Eldorado Trail

climb access trail

Rincon Boulders

P

Rincon Wall

Gill Boulder

Mental Maroon Block

Shirt Tail Peak

Supremacy Slab

The Playground

Water Rock

P

West Egg ▲

To find this nice boulder, hike up and over the slope to the north of Pony Keg. The boulder sits in the flat over the hillside. Be discreet as there is housing in the distance. This boulder is the farthest west of the Musical Boulders. A few short but good problems are also on the east face.

1. Egg Prow V3 Climb up the left prow of the west face.

2. Egg Beater V2 Climb up the middle of the west face.

3. Egg O V3 Climb up the right side of the west face.

Slab Master Block ▼

Continue east up the trail for 200 feet until you see this steep, thin slabby block on the right side of the trail.

1. Slab Master V6 Climb up the middle of the west-facing slab.

Sinus Block ◄

Continue up the trail another 100 yards to a point where the trail begins a steep incline to the north. The block is on the left.

1. Sinus Traverse V4 Traverse the horizontal crack from right to left.

2. Sinus Highball V5 (hb) Climb up the crack then onto the steep southwest prow and face.

Musical Boulders

You can see this classic line of premium fountain sandstone on the ridge out north from the first rise out of Sun Valley. Many world-class problems abound. The setting is meadowesque with good landings and views. Continue up the steep section of the Eldorado Trail from Sinus Block to the rise of the ridge. Follow the trail from the ridgetop, down north into the gully, then upslope to the boulders on the hillside above.

East Egg

This towering boulder dominates the skyline of the Musical Boulders. Problems—mostly of a highball nature—are on all sides. The west side offers more slabby challenges; the east is sheer and crimpy.

1. Descent Route V0 Easy way up or down the boulder. Climb the northwest slab.

2. West Face Left V1 (hb) Climb the hue-coed slab on the left side of the west face.

3. West Face Center V2 (hb) Climb the lengthier small-edged center of the west face.

4. Unknown V? Climb the blackened section, on the right side of the west face, left of *Southwest Prow.*

5. Southwest Prow V0 (hb) Climb the southwestern prow.

6. The Walrus V5 (hb) Climb the thin, less than vertical left side of the east face, right of the prow.

7. Eggman V3 (hb) Climb the sheer, green section up the middle of the east face.

8. Steak Knife V4 Climb the crimpy face on the right side of the east face, a few feet left of the northeast prow.

Lightning Spire ▲

This nice boulder is within the trees about 200 feet up to the northeast of East Egg. It has a thin overhanging east face with world-class boulder problems.

1. JB's Prow V6 Climb up the left side of the south face from a shallow pocket, up and out to the prow.

2. Midnight Frightening V9 (hb) Climb from the crack on the left side of the east face, then up the middle layback system.

3. Midnight Express V10 (hb) Climb up the middle of the east face, with a thin, crimpy start.

4. Adam's Prow V5 (hb) Climb the prow on the right side of the east face, finishing on the north slab.

Music Pinnacle ▲

This is another nice hardened-sandstone boulder with lengthy problems around its sides. It is downslope 20 feet northwest of Lightning Spire.

1. Original Line V0 (hb) Climb the face just left of the cracks on the east face.

2. The Cracks V2 (hb) Climb up the cracks on the left side of the east face.

3. Bob's Day Off V3 (hb) Climb the thin slab right of the cracks.

4. Far Side V2 (hb) Climb the rounded prow left of the tree, on the right side of the east face.

5. Huecos V0 (hb) Climb up huecoed northwest face.

6. West Crack V5 (hb) Climb the crack and groove on the west face.

Sound Wave Boulder ▲

This short-but-sweet boulder offers an excellent traverse across its east side. Easy ups are found on its south side. The boulder is uphill a short way from Lightning Spire.

1. Sound Wave Traverse V3 Traverse across the east face from left to right.

Eldorado Boulder

This is a massive boulder with great routes and problems around its sides. It is in the gully 200 feet northeast of Lightning Spire. Other boulder abound.

1. The Scooper V1 Climb up the scooped-out wall on the right side of the west face.

2. Eldorado Corner V5 (xhb) Climb up the steep and thin corner in the middle of the west face.

Physical Boulders

To find these boulders and blocks, continue along the West Eldorado Trail, located upslope from Musical Boulders. This is the trail that is used to access Rincon Wall. From the Rincon Wall turnoff, continue across to the north, reaching a point that looks down to Musical Boulders to the west. Continue down the trail from this high point, eventually heading into the trees. Once in the tree-dense section of the trail, head upslope to the east approximately 50 yards, until you run into the classic Nightmare Block. Other boulders are found up to the southeast and northeast of this landmark block.

Maroon Bell ▼

This sweet rock is located just above the trail on the right as you head through the forested area. It has a steep west face with a thin crack and flake system that splits it.

1. Maroon Bell V1 Climb up the center line in the middle of the west face.

9. Bob's Find V3 (hb)

Climb up the good holds in the middle of the west face.

10. My Liver Talks V6 (hb)

Climb the pseudoarête at a point where the rock changes from dark to light.

11. Optimator V3 (hb)

Climb from the center out right through side clings where rock change occurs, then up to jug.

12. You Can Do It V1 (hb) Climb from the pinnacle hold a few feet left of the farthermost right arêtes.

13. Ants V2 (hb) Climb up from the right arête to the slabby topout.

Nightmare Block ▲

This perfect block of maroon sandstone is above the trail and is characterized by an overhanging west face. The extremely featured west face allows for a problem every other foot up and across the face. Also known as Maroon Block.

1. Lip Service V5 Traverse the lip of from the north face around to and across the lip of the west face, mantel finish.

2. Eric's Deceit V4 Climb the whitened corner on the north side.

3. All Dogs Die V3 Climb the face just left of the arête on the north face.

4. Nightmare Traverse V10 Traverse across the west face from left to right.

5. Sentinel Rain V2 Climb the arête on the left side of the west face.

6. Gumby Hell V2 Climb from the arête out to the side cling right.

7. One Cig Make It Murder V5

Climb the maroon face 6 feet right of *Gumby Hell*.

8. Standard Nightmare V5 (hb)

Climb the face just left of the center.

Hanger Block ▼

This cubed boulder is upslope to the southeast from Nightmare Block. Hike approximately 200 feet up to this block. It has a nice southeastern arête, with a blank overhanging wall to the left.

1. Hanger Arête V2 Climb the southeastern arête.

Carpedium Block ◄

This one of many blocks is found down the draw, on its north side, facing south. Trees surround most of the boulders.

1. Carpedium V4 Climb the southwest prow, with a semidynamic finish.

Trailside Boulders

The Trailside Boulders start along the Eldorado Trail and continue upslope toward the Diamond Head formation. From the Nightmare Block turnoff, hike the main Eldorado Trail 200 feet north until you see the first massive, rounded, and elongated Trailside Boulder.

Trailside Boulder ▼

This large, rounded, and elongated boulder is just off the trail to the right (east). Its west end brushes the trailside.

1. The Dish V6 Climb the dished-out slab on the right side of the north face.

2. Super Hero V7 Climb up the bulging face, with horizontal breaks on the left side of the north face.

Lower Physical Boulders

These boulders and blocks are downslope to the northeast of the Upper Physical Boulders. Continue down the draw to the west and keep your eyes open for the boulders, which are spread about.

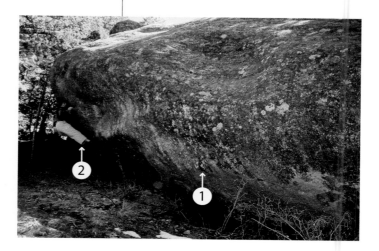

Trailside Alcove Block

This block also sits along the trail on the right (east) side, just north of Trailside Boulder. It leans up against another block to its southeast.

1. Alcove Arête V4 Climb up the leaning arête on the southeast edge of the block.

2. Middle Alcove V7 Climb up the overhanging middle of the southeast wall.

Paradigm Shift Block ▼

This is another quality maroon block, which is indigenous to Eldorado West. Hike upslope 150 feet from the trail beyond a few large boulders until you run into this steep block.

1. Paradigm Shift V6 Climb up the steep center of the west face.

Skyblue Boulder ▲

This lone boulder towers downslope to the left of the main trail about 50 feet and is obscured from the east by trees that surround its east side. From Trailside Boulder, hike 50 yards up the Eldorado Trail to the north. Hike downslope to the left just after a scenic rocky point. Descend the east tree.

1. North One V4 Climb up the thin north face.

2. Katydid Arête V3 (hb) Climb the left arête of the west face.

3. Skyblue V2 (hb) Climb up the center of the west face.

4. Skyblue Arête V4 (hb) Climb up the right arête of the west face.

5. Katididn't V3 Climb up the slabby, yet steep south face.

6. East One V4 Climb up the east shield, between the trees.

Sky Area

This area is 75 feet up the Eldorado Trail from Skyblue Boulder. You can see a smooth shielded boulder, Loompa Rock, above the trail on the right. Other boulders are located upslope, beyond Lumpa Rock to the east.

Loompa Rock

Loompa Rock is a nice shielded rock above the trail to the east. It has a red tint to it.

1. Loompa Reach V3 Climb up the center of the shielded north side to the prow.

Oompa Block

This fine block of quality maroon is 100 feet upslope to the east from Loompa Rock.

1. Oompa Traverse V5 Start on the lower left end of the west face and climb up the arête, then traverse the lip to the right and mantel finish on the far-right side.

2. Oompa Loompa V7 Climb from the horizontal edge up to the top on the right side of the west face.

Teepee Rock ▲

To reach this teepee-shaped rock from Oompa Block, continue upslope to the east around a few small boulders.

1. Teepee V2 Climb the face and right arête on the north face.

Metaphysical Boulders

This large line of boulders and blocks is located another five to ten minutes north from the Sky Area on the main trail. Look for a block on the right with a slab capped with an overhanging headwall. Follow the draw upslope for a few minutes, until you run into a cluster of good boulders and blocks. Other blocks are located downslope to the left of the trail. Check www.co.boulder.us/openspace/ for permit information.

Laser Beam Block

Hike up the draw for several minutes until you run into this block that has a perfect finger crack that splits its west face.

1. Laser Beam Crack V4 Climb from down low up the crack that splits the west face.

Flame Broiled Block ▲

This blackened-by-nature block is upslope toward the Veil. It sits in the thick forest at a point where the cliffs begin to terrace out in a steep format, eventually heightening to the sheer formation. These formations are unusual in the area and are a sight to see. This boulder has a west face that is as good as it gets and a traverse that alone is worth the venture. The routes are like those on the Maroon Block but twice as overhanging. Pick and chose your line.

The Flame ▶

This blocked section of the line of rocks that surround this area has a distinct lichen flame. The north face is a gem.

1. The Flame V3 Climb up the lichen flame of the north face.

Lower Sobo Boulders

This awesome area is located up and down the main Eldorado Trail north of Metal Bucket Block. Hike farther north/northeast for five to ten minutes. At a point where the trail peaks and then turns east, hike downslope 75 yards, following the left hillside. Mushroom Boulder is just east of an old flattened cow fence. Dud Boulder is another 75 feet downslope to the southwest. The prize Sky Eye Arête Block is in the gully due north of the Dud Boulder. Permit required.

Mushroom Boulder

This large boulder is downslope near the old cow fence. It has good problems on its south and north faces.

1. Mushroom Bulge V7 Climb up the overhanging Flagstaff-like bulge on the southwest corner.

Dud Boulder ▼

This perfect boulder is 75 feet downslope to the southwest from Mushroom Boulder. It has welded-tuff crystals on its north and west faces. Descend the tree on the southeast side.

1. Watermarks V5 Climb the thin groove on the left side of the north face.

2. Shield V5–V6 Climb up the crimpy center of the north face.

3. Major Dude V5 Climb the crystal and edge on the right side of the north face.

4. Crystalline V1 (hb) Climb the crystal-lined northwest end of the boulder.

5. Beginner's Flake V0 Climb up the flake to the slab on the right side of the west face.

Pond Boulder

This pleasant surprise is located in a hidden alcove of boulders, down in the gully due north of Dud Boulder. Hike down and around the west end into the alcove.

1. Pond Traverse V4 Traverse the west side of the boulder from left to right.

2. Ponder V4 Climb out the roof to the slab in the middle of the west face.

3. Babbling Pond V2 Climb up the right side of the west face.

Skyeye Arête Block

This towering pillar of clean maroon offers what is perhaps the best bouldering arête in the Flatirons and Eldorado Range—if not the state.

1. Skyeye Arête V4 (hb) Climb the beautiful arête of the west face. Starts out thin and balanced, then jugs out at the top.

Spearhead Block

This is the pointy rock just left of Sky Eye Arête Block.

1. Spearhead V7–V8 Climb up the sheer northwest face of the block.

Inversion Boulder ▼

This rounded boulder is down the gully wash to the west of Sky Eye Arête Block. Hike 150 yards, until you run into the boulder sitting on the south side of the wash.

1. Inversion V12 Climb the round corner and arête on the northeast edge of the boulder.

Upper Sobo Boulders

This area is located on the east side of the
Eldorado Trail and follows a line of boulders
that stretches into the talus that comes off
the southwestern slope of South Boulder
(Sobo) Buttress. From the point where you
descend to the Dud Boulder and Sky Eye
Arête Block, continue northeast down the
main trail to a point where it bottoms out,
then head out west. At the switchback, head
east on a faint trail, staying on the left side of
the draw. You will encounter many boulders
along this huge stretch. Permit required.

Maroon Slab ▼

This perfect slab is 200 yards up the wash,
within a cluster of other good boulders.

1. Maroon V0 Climb up the right side of the
west slab.

Talus Zone Block ▲

Continue upslope from Maroon Slab and
into the talus field. At a point where the
slope levels out, but not yet at the top, you
will see a huge towering block. Hike around
its south end and up behind it. The block's
east and north sides have good problems.

1. Zone Crack V3 From down low, climb up
the thin crack on the right side of the overhanging east face.

Talus Block ▲

This block sits on the talus's north side and offers an awesome south overhang with a perfect landing. The views are some of Eldorado West's best.

1. Talus Overhang V6 Climb up the right side of the south face to a slopey lip, then slab topout.

Mickey Mouse Meadows (East)

This meadow offers isolated boulders with good landings. The best time of year to boulder on these rocks is late fall and throughout the winter months. Other times of year, the grass is too high and there are too many mosquitos.

Directions: Just before entering the town of Eldorado Springs on Eldorado Springs Drive (see directions to Eldorado Canyon), there is

a road leading off to the south (left) from the main road. It is marked with a small sign that reads YOGA at its beginning. Turn up this road and take it to the end. There is a small parking area at the trailhead for this now-official open space area. The boulders ahead lie on the left side of the dirt-road trail. The first boulder, Honey Maroon Boulder, is about 200 yards ahead on the east side of the small creek. Moby Dick Rock is best accessed by hiking farther up the road around several curves until it heads back to the south.

Honey Maroon Boulder ▼

This is the first of the worthwhile boulders up the road on the left (east) side of the creek. Many good problems are found, including a classic overhanging crack on its northwest corner.

1. The Scoop V4 Climb the scooping north face of the boulder to crystals above.

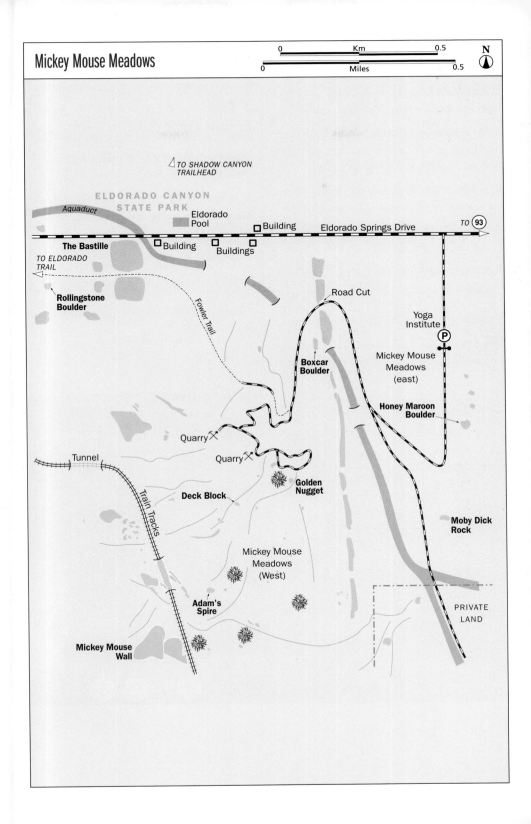

Mickey Mouse Meadows

0   Km   0.5
0   Miles   0.5

N

TO SHADOW CANYON
TRAILHEAD

ELDORADO CANYON
STATE PARK

Aquaduct

Eldorado
Pool

Building

Eldorado Springs Drive   TO 93

The Bastille

Building

Buildings

TO ELDORADO
TRAIL

Rollingstone
Boulder

Road Cut

Fowler Trail

Yoga
Institute

P

Boxcar
Boulder

Mickey Mouse
Meadows
(east)

Honey Maroon
Boulder

Quarry

Quarry

Tunnel

Golden
Nugget

Deck Block

Train Tracks

Moby Dick
Rock

Mickey Mouse
Meadows
(West)

Adam's
Spire

PRIVATE
LAND

Mickey Mouse
Wall

2. Pebbled Shield V4 Start in the crack and reach out left to crystals.

3. Earth Crack V2 (B1-) Climb the classic crack on the northwest corner.

4. Honey Maroon Overhang V8 Climb the overhanging west face via a crimpy pull start, then to a small layback and then jug.

5. Honey Route V3 Climb the crystally face on the southwest corner of the boulder.

6. Moon V2 Climb the left side of the south face using the ground flake for a foot hold.

7. Honeymoon V1 Climb the right side of the south face via good holds.

Moby Dick Rock

Continue up the road around the curves eventually heading back to the south. Head south to a point where the road begins to level out. The rock is located off the road to the east, approximately 100 yards across the meadow.

Moby Dick South Face

1. Moby Dude V1 Climb up the left side of the overhanging shield.

2. Air Jordan V3 Plant feet and hands firmly below the shield and double-dyno.

3. Ahab V2 Climb up the right side of the shield via small holds.

Moby Dick North Face

Several classic V0 slab lines can be done on this north side.

Mickey Mouse Meadows (West)

The boulders found in these meadows are quite amazing, offering incredible face climbing on vertical to slightly overhanging walls.

Directions: You can access these boulders by continuing up the road from Honey Maroon Boulder. However, instead of heading back to the south from the curves, you continue to the north up and through the road cut toward the old quarries (see map). The other way, which is usually my choice, is to park at the Fowler trailhead in the back of Eldorado Canyon and take the trail up to the east, past the Bastille, through the ridge that cuts around to the south. You must then take a right heading up the dirt road toward the old quarries, up to the Mickey Mouse Wall trailhead. The first boulder, the Golden Nugget, is located a few feet up the Mickey Mouse Trail just as you leave the dirt road and come onto the thin pathway. Adam's Spire is found a ways up the Mickey Mouse Wall Trail, across the meadow where the trail levels out just before it turns steeply uphill heading to the wall.

Golden Nugget ▼

This excellent gem of a boulder is located just beside the beginning of the Mickey Mouse Wall Trail, shortly after leaving the dirt road. Look to the right (southeast) side of the boulder, which sits very close to the trail, for many V0 slabs. The west and north sides offer the steep problems.

1. Ripples V3 Start on the far-left side of the north face and traverse to the right, finishing up the bulge.

2. Nipples V2 Climb out the center of the bulging north face wall.

3. The Bump V3 Climb the right side of the north face via crystal pinching.

4. The Nugget V4 (B1) Climb up the northwest corner, utilizing small edges.

5. Golden One V3 Climb the first line of small crystals right of *The Nugget*.

6. Pebble Hop V1 Climb up the center of the west face via big pebbles.

7. Gold Digger V4 A thin single crystal is utilized to gain the top.

8. Golden Girl V2 From the good pocket reach up to the edges and pebbles.

9. Fools Gold V1 Climb the crystals and edges on the right side of the west face.

10. She Like Gold V1 Climb the far-right side of the west face.

11. Necklace V1 Climb the vertical slab on the far-right side of the west face.

12. Golden Nugget Traverse V12 From the far-right side of the west face, traverse to the left, finishing on the north face.

Adam's Spire ▼

This spire-shaped rock is found by heading up to the Mickey Mouse Wall Trail from the Golden Nugget until the trail levels out in a nice meadow with small boulders. The spire is just before the trees, up to the west across the meadow.

1. Adam's Face V0 Climb up the south face, left of the crack.

2. Eastern Project V0 Climb up the middle of the east face.

GOLDEN AREA

The town of Golden is tucked up against the foothills west of Denver. Clear Creek flows down from the Continental Divide and is located at the northwest end of town. On the northeast side is North Table Mountain, with 75-foot volcanic outcrops. On the southwest side are the hardened maroon sandstone boulders and blocks of Matthews-Winters Park. A short distance farther to the south is the awesome bouldering of Morrison Wall.

While in the area, consider visiting the boulders on North Table Mountain.

This area is on the northeastern end of Golden. A band of solid volcanic rock characterizes this tabletop butte. You can find many good single-pitch climbs here. Most of the bouldering occurs at the base of the many routes, although a few additional bouldering areas are spread out on the slopes.

The Stacks are fun pinnacles to boulder.

To find them, hike to the far-north end of the main band of cliffs. At the point where the main cliff peters out, hike down to the small band of rocks that includes these stacked rocks. The Pillar is on the left side of the shortened band of rocks. Try *The Pill* (V0) on the west face. The Smoke Stack is a more broken rock stack on the far-right side of the band. Smokey (V0) goes up the west face.

Directions: To reach Golden from Denver, take Interstate 70 due west toward the mountains. I-70 catches the south end of Golden. Take the Golden/Morrison exit, which comes just before the foothills. Exit and head north for Table Mountain, Lower Clear Creek Canyon, or Golden Gate Canyon State Park. Head south for Matthews-Winters Park or the Morrison Wall bouldering areas.

If approaching from Boulder, head south on Highway 93 approximately 12 miles to the north end of Golden.

20 GOLDEN GATE CANYON STATE PARK

This area is characterized by large clean-white granite domes that stretch from north to south behind the foothills of the Front Range. One can only imagine the boulders and blocks that must be hidden within the dense forests that lie below the main formations. So far, very little has been discovered and/or bouldered upon, save for Dude's Boulders and the Golden Gate Road Blocks.

Directions: To find Golden Gate Canyon State Park, take Highway 46 (Golden Gate Canyon Road) west from Highway 93, at the north end of Golden and north of Clear Creek Canyon. Drive west on Highway 46 approximately 12 miles. The road winds up

Golden Area Overview

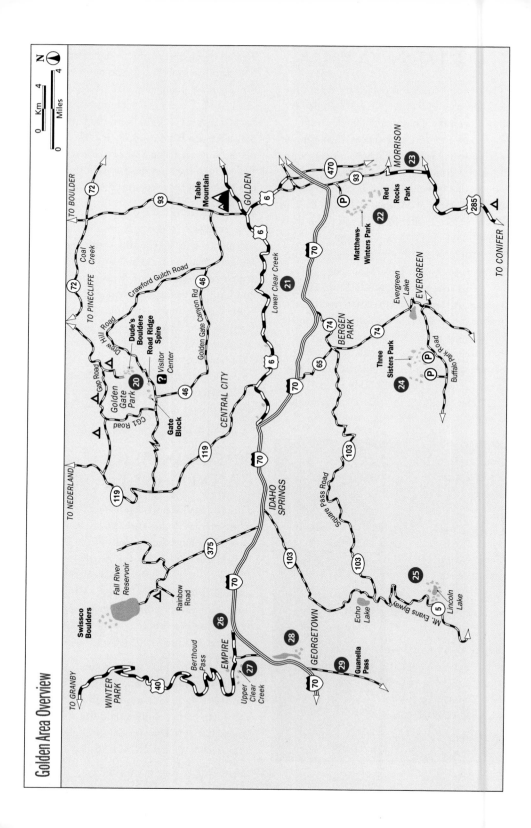

Golden Gate Canyon State Park

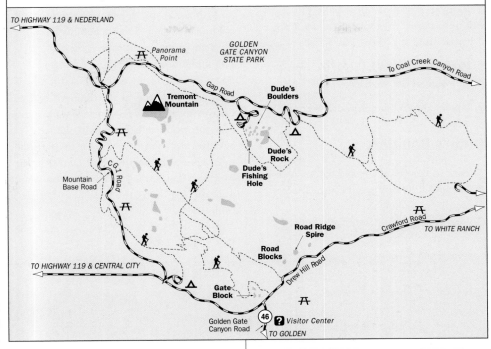

TO HIGHWAY 119 & NEDERLAND

Panorama Point

GOLDEN GATE CANYON STATE PARK

Gap Road

To Coal Creek Canyon Road

Tremont Mountain

Dude's Boulders

Dude's Rock

Dude's Fishing Hole

C.G.1 Road

Mountain Base Road

Crawford Road

TO WHITE RANCH

Road Ridge Spire

Road Blocks

TO HIGHWAY 119 & CENTRAL CITY

Drew Hill Road

Gate Block

Golden Gate Canyon Road

46

Visitor Center

TO GOLDEN

and around to the west and runs right into Golden Gate State Park. A day-use fee is required. There is great camping throughout the park.

Golden Gate Road Blocks

These blocks are on the slopes on the north side of Drew Hill Road, to the east and north of the south end visitor center.

Road Ridge Spire ▶

This nice piece of granite is on the northern slopes above Drew Hill Road, approximately 1 mile east of the intersection with Golden Gate Canyon Road and just east of the south entrance kiosk and visitor center.

1. The Peak V0 Climb up the middle of the east face.

Gate Block

You can see this block upslope to the northeast from the intersection of Golden Gate Canyon Road and Drew Hill Road.

1. Move Out Arête V1 Climb the arête on the left side of the west face.

2. Movin' On V0 Climb up the west face.

Dude's Boulders

These excellent boulders and blocks are on the slopes to the north and east of Dude's Fishing Hole. Follow the directions to Golden Gate Canyon State Park, locate CG1 Road, and follow it north to the intersection of CG1 Road and Gap Road. Go right (east) on Gap Road and follow it to a right (south) at Dude's Fishing Hole turnoff. Drive past the campgrounds and park at the Dude's Fishing Hole trailhead. Hike a short way down the trail to the dirt road and follow it southwest 200 yards to the fishing hole. Look upslope to the east and you will see the large rock formation called Dude's Rock. The boulders are a short way upslope within the trees seen to the northwest of Dude's Rock west face. You can see an obvious boulder pack sticking out of the trees; head for this landmark.

Rugby Boulder ◄

This boulder is on the right (south) end of the boulder pack.

1. Holdless Arête V8 Climb up the smooth prow on the left side of the north face.

Dude's Boulder ▼

This boulder is just left of Rugby Boulder and offers a nice traverse and bulging problems on its west face. Around to the north is a short classic crack.

1. Dude's Traverse V5 Traverse from good holds on the left across to the right, finishing up the bulge.

2. Dude's Overhang V4 Climb the bulging overhang to sloper top.

3. The Dude Project V? Climb the leaning crack on left side of the west face.

4. Dude's Line V1 Climb the thin crack on the north face.

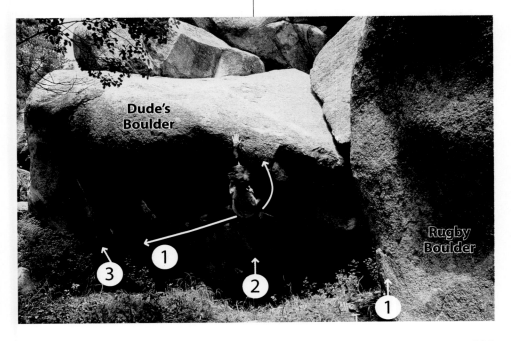

Obtuse Block ◄

To find this clean granite block scramble up
the boulder pack, up and behind Dude's
Boulder, near the top. This block and Hey
Dude Block form a short corridor.

1. Obtuse V4 Start in the pit on the southeast side of the block and climb the open
book.

Hey Dude Block ▼

This block is just above Obtuse Block. It has
an overhanging west face.

1. Hey Dude V2 Climb good holds on the
left side of the west face.

2. Big Dude V5 Climb up the thin crimps
right of *Hey Dude*.

Leaning Block

This nice granite wall is upslope and left of the top of Dude's Boulders. Scramble 100 feet upslope to more block forms. You can play on and around other miniwalls around this block.

1. Leaning Meaning V4 Climb up the left-leaning west face to the top.

Gap Boulders

These boulders are approximately 100 yards due north of the top of Dude's Boulders. Many problems on a wide variety of boulders have been done.

Gap Rock

This rock is at the lower north end of the boulders here. A leaning ramp corner characterizes its north face; the steep west side has face routes.

1. Gap Exit V4 Climb a short way up the ramp on the north side, exit up and right out the bulge.

2. Noprow V2 Climb up the northwest prow and face.

21 CLEAR CREEK CANYON

This 18-mile stretch of canyon has an unlimited source of bouldering rock. The unique granite with a swirled white, black, and gray tone is often quite solid. You can find boulders along the road and creekbed, as well as up on the slopes. They are often hidden from sight. Some of the best areas are far off the road, hidden in side canyons. Take caution if you cross the creek during high-country run-off season. The canyon is best in late fall and early winter, when the creek can be easily crossed at most points.

Lower Clear Creek is located on Highway 6 as you head west through the foothills in northwestern Golden. Mileage is given from the intersection of Highway 93 and Highway 6. Upper Clear Creek, along Interstate 70, will be described later. If you continue west on Highway 6 through Clear Creek Canyon, you will eventually merge with I-70. Check the sign at the beginning of the canyon for current rules and regulations.

Clear Creek Canyon

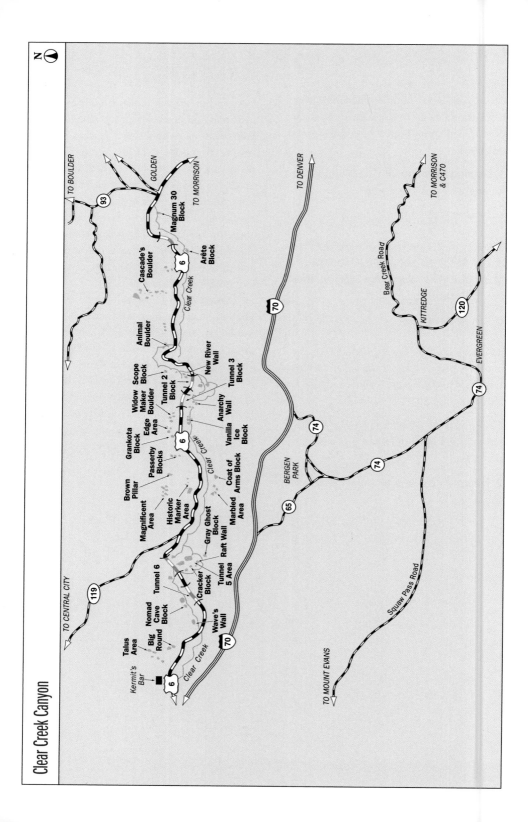

Magnum 30 Block ▲

This is the first worthy block you will encounter. From Highway 93, it is 0.6 mile west on Highway 6. This rock is a good example of the kind of rock that exists throughout the canyon.

At 0.6 mile, park on the left side of the road at the CLEAR CREEK CANYON NEXT 10 MILES sign. Head across the creek to the prominent block, which is somewhat hidden in the trees and upstream to the right.

1. East Face V0 Climb the variety of slab variations on the easy side of block.

2. Magnum 30 V5 Climb the northeast corner utilizing small edges and the crack.

3. Magnum Shield V5 Climb prominent shield of the far-left side of the north face.

4. Concave V3 Climb up the middle of concaved wall on the north face.

5. Magnum Traverse V6 Traverse from the right side of the north face to the east-side slab.

Arête Block

This block is located approximately 1.9 miles up the canyon. Pull off on the left shoulder just before the road becomes paved. Cross the river to the block.

1. The Arête V4 Climb the northeast arête.

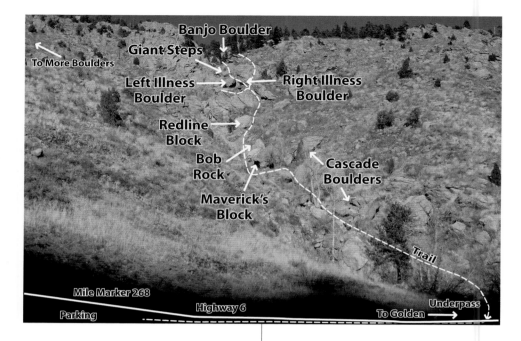

The Cascade Boulders and Lower Canyon Areas

The Cascade Boulders are located about another mile up Highway 6 from the Arête Block (a total of 3.7 miles west of the intersection of Highway 93 and Highway 6). Park on the left side of the road. Look for mile marker 268.

Look up to the north and you will see this large fall line of rock cascading down the slope from high above. Hike up the gully, starting at its base; follow it up the wash to the boulders. The Cascade Boulders are perhaps Clear Creek's most traveled and developed bouldering area. A wide range of problems abound. Expect lots of highballs or landings that are sloper washouts. The fall line faces south, which makes it very warm in the summer and perfect during the cold winter months.

Maverick's Block

After passing a few boulders on your right at the very low end of the gully, continue up a short way and you will see this solid block up and to the right. Many nice lines have been established on this highball block.

1. 41st Street V7 Climb the pyramid-shaped south face of the block.

2. Mavericks V5 (hb) Climb out the middle of the overhanging southwest face, above the small block attached to its base.

Maverick's Block

3. North Shore V9 Climb out from the far-left side of the southwest face, up and right, finishing with *Mavericks*.

Bob Rock ▼

Located up the wash another 40 feet from Maverick's Block.

1. Bob's the Man V4 Climb from a platform, up and out the middle of the northwest face.

2. Thin Red Line V5 Climb up the small edges on the southeast face to the finger crack.

3. Redline V3 (hb) Climb the corner system, then traverse across the crack.

Illness Area

Continue about 300 feet up the gully, past a few boulders, until you cross this cluster of boulders and blocks spread about the gully's slope, below a large rock formation. You can see smiley-face graffiti on the wall. Many problems are located within this cluster of rock. The Right and Left Illness Boulders sit side by side in the gully. They are located up and to the right of a big tree in the middle of the gully. Right Illness Boulder is on the east side and has a roof. Left Illness Boulder has a prominent slab on the west side that rises to a point. Good landings and sunshine make this a nice destination.

Redline Block ▲

Continue straight upslope from Bob Rock and you will run into this block.

1. Red V2 Climb from the platform rock up the crack on the east face.

Right Illness Boulder ▼

1. Ebola V7 Traverse the lip of the overhang from right to left.

2. Viral V3 Climb from low down on the right side of the overhang, up and right.

3. Bacterial V5 Climb out left from *Viral*.

Left Illness Boulder ▼

The left (west) slab has an overhang on its east side.

1. Dead Lizard V1 (hb) Climb the southwest face.

2. Battling Seizure Robots V5 Climb up the golden prow.

3. Squid V8 Climb from the south face up left of the prow to the seam above.

Giant Steps

To find this cluster of highball boulders, continue upslope toward the big formation north of Left Illness Boulder.

Giant Steps Left

This brown-toned, massive block is on the left. It has highball faces with smooth landings.

1. The Moose V4 (hb) Climb the plates a few feet right of the northwest prow.

2. Speed Zoo V4 (hb) Climb the west face undercling route just right of the prow.

3. Master of Irony V3 Climb the prow of the northwest face.

4. Slaves of Truth V1 Climb the pocketed north face left of *Masters of Irony*.

Giant Steps Right

This highball boulder is on the right. It is characterized by a prominent arête left of a gnarly dead tree and a rounded crowned top.

1. Up with People V4 (hb) Climb the arête on the far-right side.

2. Il Precario V6 Climb the steep face right of the crack system.

3. La Fissura V1 (hb) Climb the dihedral in the middle of the wall.

4. Rolly Polly V5 Climb the steep face left of *La Fissura* right of the other corner.

5. Star Dive V0 Climb left of the most blackened corner to bolt up top.

6. Headbanger V6 Climb up the bulge left of *Star Dive*.

Banjo Boulder

To find this boulder, continue up the gully several hundred yards. As the gully ends, head up and around the bush onto the right side, then drop back down into the upper gully. You will find this boulder sitting in a meadowesque setting.

1. Sympathy V3 Climb the angling finger crack on the right a few feet left of the bush.

2. Courtesy V2 (hb) Climb up the center of the face to horizontal.

3. Rufus's Wonder Move V4 (hb) Climb from the horn over the roof to the scoop.

4. Banjos V6 Climb left out of the cave to the finger crack.

5. Sandcastle V8 Climb from within the cave up and left to the corner system, slapping for rounded holds, eventually gaining the horizontals.

6. Banjo Traverse V7 Traverse the entire cave.

7. The Dihedral V0 Climb the crack/corner system on the left side.

8. Eric's Highball V3 (hb) Climb the crack system then out left and up.

Animal Boulder ▲

Drive west another 0.8 mile on Highway 6 from the Cascade Boulders. Just after crossing the bridge, park in the pullout on the right side of the road. You can see the top portion of this block next to the road on the right. Scramble down toward the water chute to the overhang above the creek.

1. Animal V11 Climb out the severe overhang on the underbelly of the block.

Scope Block ▲

This perfectly shaped block has a steep east face. It is located 5.2 miles west on Highway 6 from Highway 93. Park at the large pulloff on the left side of the road, just before the curve in the passing lane. Look upslope to the west across the road and creek and you will see this prominent block of clean white granite.

1. Scope Left V1 Climb up the far-left side of the east face.

2. Telescope V10
Climb up the right side of the east face, utilizing the laybacks and microcrimps to the top.

This bouldering outcrop and cave is located just down and left of the well known *Sonic Youth* (5.13) corner system. Parking is found 6.1 miles west on Highway 6 from Highway 93. Look across the stream and locate the overhanging corner of *Sonic Youth*. Look down to the left and you will see a cave slot with a beautiful river-polished bulging head wall. Either cross at the Tyrolean, sometimes set up during run-off months, or hike up, cross the bridge, and hike back to the wall via a faint trail that descends down along cliff bands. The bouldering here is not topped out but rather utilizes only the lower portion of the cave and above.

1. Chilly V4 Climb out the right side of the cave, up left and down to exit.

2. Infinity V2 Climb out the right side of the overhanging corner.

3. Wet Carrot V3 Climb out the middle of the cave via a corner through the roof.

4. Than's Problemo V8 Climb out from the lip angling right to the cracks above.

5. Spinage V6 Climb out the angling roof system to the right end of the cave.

Tunnel 2 Block

Drive and park as for the New River Wall. Just before Tunnel 2, you can see the block from the road. Hike up and across the bridge and head back toward *Sonic Youth*. You can see the block on the north side, several hundred feet down the creek.

1. High Waters V6 Climb out the overhanging arête on the left side.

2. Aqua Huck V5 Climb the overhanging wall right of the arête.

3. Flash Flood V7 Climb the overhanging arête on the right side.

Tunnel 3 Blocks

You can see these blocks below Anarchy Wall, just south of Tunnel 3's west side. Drive approximately 6.7 miles west on Highway 6 from Highway 93, go through Tunnel 3, and park on the left, behind the guardrail. Look south and you will see the blocks on the flat. These are great beginner blocks, with low-angle slabs.

Anarchy Block

This is the small block just left of the two main slabby blocks.

1. Anarchor V1 Climb up the southwest face and prow of the block.

Block Slab North

This is the northernmost block with a low-angle west-facing slab. The west slabs are all V0.

1. South Wall V0 Climb up the sheer south wall of the block.

Block Slab South ▲

This is the southernmost block.

1. Low Angler V0 Climb up the middle of the west slab.

Grankota Block ▼

This nice piece of granite, reminiscent of a block of Dakota sandstone, is up the wash on the right (north) side of the road, approximately 7.8 miles up the canyon.

1. Grankota Traverse V4 Traverse the west face of the block.

2. Grankota Arête V2 Climb up the arête on the right side of the west face.

Passerby Blocks

Located 8 miles up the canyon from Highway 93. Park at the small pullout on the north side of the road, just before the guardrail. Hike back east and head up a notch in the gully. A smooth and blackened shielded piece of granite sits just right of the notch close to the road.

Awestruck Block ▼

Continue north through the notch and up the gully until you see this block upslope on the left.

1. Awestruck V4 Climb the face to the horizontal crack to the sloper slab on the left side of the west face.

2. Awed V7 Climb up the middle of the west face.

3. Awed Arête V5 Climb the overhanging arête on the right side of the west face.

Gray Block ▼

Continue up to the right around some trees to this beautiful block. Its east face has great vertical face problems.

1. Touch of Gray V2 Climb up the middle of the east face.

Knoll Area

This area is located on the north side of Highway 6 about 8.3 miles from Highway 93. You can see a prominent brown pillar upslope on the ridgeline. Park behind the guardrail on the south side of the road. Hike west about 100 yards and cross the road to a notch in the ridge. Head up the notch and wash to the boulders.

Brown Pillar

This pillar, located up on the ridgeline, is visible from the road. Look up to the northeast at the notch.

1. Brown Sugar V0 Climb up the south face of the pillar.

Coat of Arms Block ▼

This block is another 0.5 mile up the canyon (8.6 miles from Highway 93). Park on the south side of the road, a few hundred yards past the block. You will see the block across the river to the south. Hike back east and cross the creek to the south. The east side of the block has a sharp overhang with an awesome traverse across its lip.

1. Coat of Arms V4 Traverse across the overhang and lip from down right, to up and left across the lip.

Marbled Area

This area consists of quality white granite shelved with small boulders and blocks. Located on the left (south) side of the creek, it has a clean white-granite look unlike any area in the canyon. It is located 8.7 miles west on Highway 6 from Highway 93. Park on the south side of the road and cross over to the cliff bands.

The Marble ▲

You can see this fun block in the rock gathering on the right side of the cliff.

1. Marbles V1 Climb the crack and arête on the west face.

Power Tower ▶

This tower block, up on a nice ledge above the Marble, offers a leaning crack with a bulgy summit.

1. Tower Crack V3 (hb) Climb the left-angling crack on the northwest face. Exit right or left or up through the horizontals.

Historic Marker Area

This area is 9 miles up the canyon from Highway 93 on the north side of the road. Park in the area near the historic marker sign. Look upslope to the northeast, then hike upslope to the boulders sitting amid the cliffed ledge system.

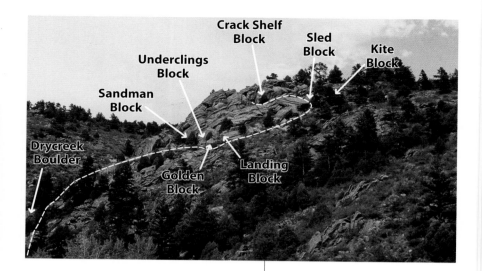

Magnificent Area

This area, located 9.4 miles from Highway 93, is the most promising of the new areas in Clear Creek Canyon. Park at Mayhem Creek in the large pullout area on the right (north) side of the road. Hike north up the narrow canyon toward the ridgeline of rock that stands in the distance to the northeast. A huge variety of boulders, blocks, and out-crops are found in this great ridgeline.

Drycreek Boulder ▼

This boulder is on the left side of the wash, across from the base of the ridgeline that leads up to the rest of the bouldering.

1. Drycreek Traverse V4 Traverse left from the far-right side of the boulder's east side, finishing on the far-left side of the south face.

2. Right of Way V1 Climb up the right side of the south face.

3. Flank V2 Climb up the middle of the east face.

Sandman Block ▲

This is the first prominent block you encounter as you hike upslope from the base of the fall line. It has excellent overhanging problems.

1. Sandman V6 Climb the angling edge system in the middle of the west face.

Underclings Block ▲

This blocked wall is just to the right of Sandman Block.

1. Undercling Man V4 Climb up the underclings on the left side of the west face.

Landing Block ▲

This block is just beyond Golden Block.

1. Landrover V2 Climb up the middle of the west face.

Sled Block

This block, located upslope beyond Landing Block, offers nice steep slab climbing.

1. Skiech V3 Climb up the middle of the west face.

Kite Block

This kite-shaped block is located upslope at the top of the fall line just beyond Sled Block.

1. Tree Top Flyer V1 Climb up the right side of the west face.

Crack Shelf Block ▶

To find this block, scramble a ledge system across to the northwest from Kite Block. You will find an awesome crack with a perfect ledged landing.

1. Alpha King Crack V3 (hb) Climb up the classic left-angling crack.

Nomad Cave Block ▼

This block is located 12.9 miles up the canyon from Highway 93, 1.3 miles from the intersection of Highway 6 and Highway 119. Continue west on Highway 6, through Tunnel 6, and park on the right side of the road. Look across the creek to the north and you will see Nomad Cave hidden behind the trees. The block is located just to the left (west) of the cave. A nice, clean, white pyramid-shaped rock sits down along the creek and has a good V0 south face that is worthwhile.

1. Southwest Overhang V8 Climb up the southwest edge of the block.

2. The Nomad V10 Climb the center of the south face.

Waves Wall

This wall is 13.1 miles from Highway 93, 1.5 miles from the intersection of Highway 6 and Highway 119. Continue driving west on Highway 6, through Tunnels 5 and 6 and 0.2 mile past Nomad Cave. Park on the right-shoulder pull off. Look down creekside to the north and you will see this solid river-polished overhanging scoop. During spring and summer run-off, the creek is too high to cross and the wall is submerged. During fall and winter, this has a nice sandy landing and can be accessed by hiking across the bridge ahead and heading back along the northern hillside to the wall.

1. The Surf V1 From down low, climb up the far-left side of the south face.

2. Hang Ten V2 Climb good holds to the horizontal with dyno finish just right of *The Surf.*

3. Body Surf V1 From the center prow, climb from the right, then cross the prow and up.

4. Balance V1 Finishes *Body Surf* up the prow.

5. Big Waves V2 Climb the pocket on the right side of the south face.

6. Captain Insano V7 Climb the thin right side of the scoop with a long dyno finish.

Big Round Boulders

These large boulders are on the right (north) side of the road approximately 0.2 mile from Waves Wall, just above the pull off. You can do good problems all over these.

Big Round

This is the large elongated boulder that dominates the cluster.

1. Biggy V2 (hb) Climb up the center of the roadside face.

Talus Talus Area

This large scattered fall line of boulders is located on the right (eastern) slopes of the canyon approximately 1.8 miles down the canyon from the intersection of Highway 6 and Highway 119, or 0.3 mile up the road from Waves Wall. There are lots of rocks and problems here.

22 MATTHEWS-WINTERS PARK

This unique area is loaded with solid, hardened sandstone blocks and boulders and is home to one of the Front Range's gems: the Millennium Block. The area also has a ridge cap and fall line of boulders as good as any great fall line along the Front Range.

To get to the area, take the Morrison exit just south of the Interstate 70 and Highway 6 intersection. Drive south about 100 yards and then turn west into the Matthews-Winters Park Open Space parking

area. Hike south down the well-groomed trail (Red Rocks Trail) along the Front Range for about twenty minutes. You will come to a split in the trail. For the Ridge Top Boulders, such as the Broadway Boulder, head up the Morrison Slide Trail; for the Lower Trail Boulders, such as the Millennium Block, go straight (east), following the Red Rocks Trail southeast around to the front (east) side of the ridge.

You may also drive farther south and head west on the far-north access road into Red Rocks Park. Drive west about 0.7 mile into Red Rocks and park at the Red Rocks

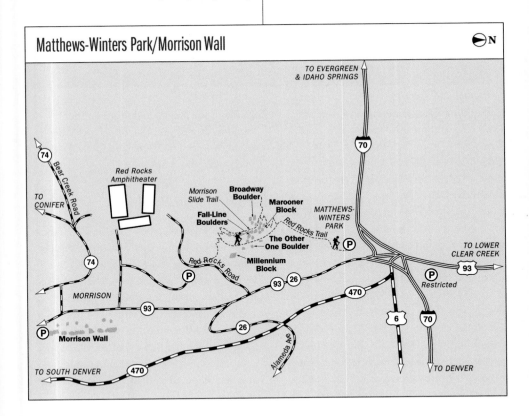

Ridge Gap · Plato Boulder · Morrison Slide Trail · To Broadway Boulder · Holdout Boulder · The Porch · Cave Boulder · Refracted Boulder · To Red Rocks Park · Red Rocks Trail · Clinton's Slab Boulder · To Matthews-Winters Parking Area · To The Other One Boulder 250 yards · To Millennium Block

trailhead parking area located on the left (east) side of the road. The trail is located across the road to the west of the parking lot. Take the Red Rocks Trail north up switchbacks to behind the first ridge. At the intersection with the Morrison Slide Trail, head to the left (west) on the Morrison Slide Trail for the Ridge Top Boulders. Follow the trail up to the top and across to the north. You will encounter Broadway Boulder at the north end of the plateau, just before it goes downslope. For the Millennium Block, head to the right (east) on the Red Rocks Trail and then climb up to a gap in the ridge and around to the north on the east side until you see the fall line of maroon rock. This is a twenty- to thirty-minute hike. The first significant block you'll see along the trail is the

Millennium Block, downslope in the meadow to the east. The other rocks are more or less to the west, upslope from the main trail.

Lower Trail Boulders

To reach these boulders take the Red Rocks Trail, whether from the Matthews-Winters Park trailhead parking area or the Red Rocks trailhead parking area. The trail leads around east to the front side of the first ridge. The boulders are either below, as in the case of the Millennium Block, the Other One Boulder, and Shoebox Block, or above the trail, as in the case of Clinton's Slab Boulder, the Refracted Boulder, or the Cave Boulder.

Millennium Block ▼

This special erratic of quality, hardened maroon sandstone is located east of the main trail, a lone block sitting in the meadow below. Upon further observation you will see that this is the lowest block of a large number of rocks within the fall line that comes from the ridge cap above. You can find vertical to slightly overhanging face problems on the north and east faces; the south and west faces are more moderate. Many of the problems, especially on the left side of the north face, are marginal highballs (hb) with flat landings.

1. Revelation V1 Climb out the far-right side of the hueco on the north face up to the arête.

2. Revolution V2 Climb straight up from the middle hueco on the right side of the north face.

3. Lono V3 Climb up from the left side of the hueco on the north face.

4. Second Coming V4 Climb the pockets left of the hueco to the top.

5. Old Bones V6 Climb from the horizontal bucket, up and right to the pocket, then good edges and a pinch.

6. Moon Child V10 Climb straight up from the horizontal bucket on the right side of the north face.

7. Ghost Dance V6 (hb) A classic line up the left side of the north face via crimpers and pockets with a daring topout.

8. Terminate with Extreme Prejudice V8 Climb the right side of the northeast face from the prominent hueco up through the black streak.

9. Black Heart V9 Lunge up to big shelf, then climb up.

10. Pocket Problem V9 Climb the pockets up the northeast face.

11. Cannibal Dance V7 Climb the right-angling line to the sloper pocket on the right side of the east face.

12. Desert V2 Climb the white-streaked wall.

13. Epiphany V5 Climb the southeastern arête.

14. B.C. V2 Climb the steep portion of the southeast face.

15. Starter Face V0 Climb the south face via slabs.

The Other One Boulder ▼

From the Millennium Boulder, hike approximately 250 yards north and you will see this round boulder with its pocketed south face.

1. Voodoo Child V5 (hb) Climb up from a horn on the far-right side of the south face to a nice pocket, then over the bulges to the top.

2. Little Wing V3 (hb) Climb up the bulges from the pockets in the middle of the south face.

3. Angel V3 Climb from the pebble in the pocket up to the horizontal break left of *Little Wing.*

4. Other Dyno V2 Dyno off the horizontal on the left side of the south face.

5. Vee-Wonderful V1 Climb up from the hole on far-left side of the south face.

6. Other One's Traverse V0 Traverse from far left out to the right.

Shoebox Block

Continue northwest from the Other One Boulder until you come across this rectangular block. It has great warm-up face climbs on its east face.

More Problems on East Face

Clinton's Slab Boulder

Hike upslope west of the trail to this slabby boulder that has many casual slab problems all over its south side.

Refracted Boulder ▲

This boulder is just upslope to the west of Clinton's Slab Boulder. It has a bright reddish maroon appearance with solid rock and good landings.

1. Refracted V4 Climb the finger crack on right side of the south face.

2. Monomaniac V5 Climb the reddened face left of the finger crack.

3. Proud Prow V2 Climb the seam up the prow.

4. Pain V6 Climb the gnarly crack up the east prow.

5. Thin Face V5 Climb up the thin white scoop of the south face.

6. Suburban Skyline V1 Climb the ramp system on the left side of the south face.

Ridgetop Boulders East

You can reach these rocks by taking the high trails from either direction and accessing the ridge cap of maroon from above by descending through a ridge gap, down and around to the north side of the east-facing ridge line. Broadway Boulder is located on the north end of the plateau off the trail, on top, within the trees.

Holdout Boulder

From the descent through the ridge gap, this is the first protruding boulder you will encounter on the left. It has a bulging red-dened north face.

1. The Holdout V8 (hb) Climb up the black streak on the north face via a small finger pocket.

2. Holdout Traverse V5 Traverse the west side of the boulder to the left across the horizontal break.

3. Holdy Moldy V2 Climb up the south face.

Plato Boulder

This boulder is located just north of Holdout Boulder. It has a clean northeastern arête.

1. F Plato V4 (hb) Climb up the northeast arête utilizing pebbles and crimps.

The Porch

The Porch is located a few rocks to the north of Plato Boulder and is characterized by an extensive black-and-white streaked wall that has a little cave making up its base.

1. Donkey Traverse V6 Traverse from the far right to the left, around to the south face, finishing in the big hole.

The Ticket

Continue north about 300 feet to an obvious prow.

1. The Ticket V6 Climb out of the cave to the lip via underclings and a seam.

Broadway Boulder ▲

From the very north end of the trail on top of the plateau, head south from the trail through the trees approximately 50 feet. This is a high rounded boulder that has a courser texture than the lower rocks.

1. Travercity V4 Traverse from the right (north) face to the west face pockets.

2. Mean Green V0 (hb) Climb the green slab on the north face.

3. Marcelo's Madness V7 Traverse from the right to the left on the south face, beginning at the northeast edge.

4. Horizontal Boop V3 (hb) Climb up the right side of the south face.

5. Pocket Pool V3 Climb the steep south face just right of the tree.

To Red Rocks Park

Morrison Slide Trail

Marooner Block

Broadway Boulder

The Shoe Block

The Block

1

To Matthews-Winters Parking Area →

Ridgetop Boulders Northeast

To reach these blocks and boulders, descend through the boulder pack from the far-northeast end of the ridgetop. You will find many boulders as you hike a short 50 feet downslope, eventually swinging around to the east side, eventually meeting up with the Ridge Top East Boulders. From the top of the trail on the northeast end of the plateau, descend down and around to these boulders.

The Block ▶

This block is just below the trail top to the east.

1. Blocker V1 Climb the north face.

Marooner Block ◀

You can find this nice piece of maroon at the far-north end of the ridgeline. It form a wall with other blocks.

1. The Maroon Face V6 Climb up the right side of the east face.

2. Mariner V1 Climb the left arête and face of the east face.

3. Tranquil Traverse V3 Traverse from left to right across the east face.

The Shoe Block ▼

This block is a short way downslope and northeast of Marooner Block. It has a white streak in the middle of its southeast face.

1. Shoe String V7 (hb) Climb up the middle of the southeast face to the horizontal break, then up to the top.

2. Shoe Horn V4 Climb the arête on the far-right side of the southeast face.

23 MORRISON WALL

For quality winter bouldering along the Front Range, the incredible overhanging outcrop of Morrison Wall is hard to beat. The smooth south-facing sandstone walls are a favorite for many boulderers. The severely overhanging walls are packed with good problems that involve traverses, overhangs, arêtes, and sheer-face routes, as well as several excellent topropes. Some of the toprope climbs overhang 40 feet. The area has long been a training ground for local rock jocks and has become the breeding ground for the young boulderer. Visit the Black Hole to test your abilities; these are some of the hardest anywhere. In recent years the south side has also become an alternative to the overworked north side and is surely worth a visit or two.

Directions: Take I-70 to the Morrison/Red Rocks exit. Head south past Red Rocks Park on Highway 26, which turns into Highway 93 and goes into the town of

Morrison, where it ends at a stoplight in the middle of town. From this light head left (east), drive a couple blocks, and park on the right side of the road. Look east and you will see the massive hogback. Hike up diagonally from the lower south end to the north along the base of the wall.

Another way to reach the area from I-70 is to exit onto Highway 470. Take Highway 470 south and exit at Morrison Road (Highway 8). Drive west about 0.3 mile, through the notch of the hogback, until you see the parking on the left.

The Black Hole

This is a cave/hole blackened by years of campfires, although it has been a long time since anyone has had a fire here. It is located a few hundred feet upslope from the southernmost end of the hogback. Many strenuous problems and variations have been set here.

1. Flake's Overhang V3 Climb from the far-right side deep in the cave and climb out spaced holds.

2. Cytogrinder V8 Traverse from low jugs up and out the roof utilizing slopers and crimps.

3. Helicopter V5 Climbs the roof utilizing the prow to the right of the crack.

4. Bearshears Crack V1 Climb the leaning crack line out the roof.

5. McTwist V3 Climb from the crack utilizing small holds.

6. Tendonitis Traverse V5 Traverse small crimps into the *Bearshears Crack*.

Many other variations and extended traverses have been done within the Black Hole and its surroundings. They range from V7 to V11.

Wisdom Cave

This cave is located above the Black Hole to the left, on the other side of a boulder that separates the two.

1. Wisdom Simulator V7 Climb from the right side of the cave and traverse across to the left, all the way to the upper area.

Main Hangs

You will encounter this along the trail. Descend down, then up to the left from the Black Hole. It offers straight-up problems and long traverses as well as many variations.

1. Psycho Simulator V3 Traverse the entire distance of the Main Hangs.

2. Holloway's Way V7 Climb the severe overhang to the right of the prominent Twist and Shout right-angling roof crack.

3. Willow's Wart V5 Climb from the lower right, across to the left, utilizing a variety of hold sequences.

4. Biceps Are Bigger V6 Another unique variation on the same wall.

Many other variations that range from V5 to V9 have been done along this overhanging section of the wall. In addition, a handful of V4-V5 toprope problems have been done out the overhangs above.

Hairy Scary Wall

This is the next overhanging section of the wall upslope to the left of the Main Hangs area.

1. Hairy Scary Traverse V2 Traverse the lip of the entire area from right to left.

2. The Stretcher V5 (hb) Stretch up and out from the left side of the traverse wall.

3. Hairball V1 Climb out dihedral on far-right side of the traverse, then out left to sloper pinches.

4. Dihedral V0 Climb up and out the dihedral on the far-right side.

Other variations exist, as well as some good toprope problems out the overhangs above, which range from V4 to V6.

Sailor's Delight Block ▲

This is a prominent blocked pinnacle that has an overhang on its west face. Hike up the trail about 30 feet and you will see this trailside.

1. Sailor's Delight V2 (hb) Climb up and out the flake, then to jugs over the roof on the west side.

The Cockpit

This cave is located up behind Sailor's Delight Block to the northeast.

1. Pit Overhang V0 From a sit, climb out the middle of the overhang.

The Slice Block

This block is down below Sailor's Delight Block. It is characterized by a south-facing slab that sits between the arêtes.

1. The Slice V0 Climb up the middle of the south face.

2. West Slice V1 Climb up west face.

Tree Slab ▼

This short slab sits next to the trees 30 feet north of the Cockpit.

1. Tree Slab Traverse V3 Traverse across the slab, avoiding its top.

2. Corner O V0 Climb the face right of the left-side arête.

3. Holds Traverse V0 Traverse the left-diagonaling break from the right.

Magnum Wall

This undercut, thin slabby chunk is around the corner to the north another 30 feet from Tree Slab.

1. Magnum Force V5 Climb from the uncut overhang, reach up the middle of the slab on micro-edges, then pull onto the slab.

2. Magnum PI V4 From down low, climb up and out the crack and arête.

Spike Rock

This spiked block, directly below Magnum Wall, is characterized by a leaning arête on its west face and an overhang on its north face.

1. Cocaine Corner V1 Climb the left-leaning arête on the west face.

2. Spike Overhang V2 Climb out the overhang on the north face.

Best Area

This is located up a short gully that leads to a secluded shelf left of Magnum Wall. The overhangs here are exposed and highball.

Bowling Ball Wall

This pocket-featured wall is left of a gully that is up and north from Magnum Wall. You will find lots of face variations here.

1. Bowling Ball Center V? (hb) Climb up the middle of the west face.

Nautilus Workout Area

This area is up from Magnum Wall and Bowling Ball Wall, at the farthest north end of the bouldering section. It features a large cave that offers toprope and highball routes that come out in all directions. An arête with large holds is located on its left side.

1. The Corner V0 (hb) Climb the huge horizontals and pocket up the left side of the cave. Best to climb up several feet and then down climb.

2. Nautilus Traverse V3 Traverse from the cave on the right to the south face's far-left side.

3. Fun Face V0 Climb up face just left of *The Corner*.

4. League V0 Climb up the center of the south face left of *Fun Face*.

5. Nemo V0 Climb up the far-left side of the south face.

Sharp's Arête Area

Farther down to the north, you will see this area, which has a prominent high arête. Several toprope problems have been done on and around this area.

Outback Arête

This is another toprope arête, even farther north than Sharp's Arête Area. It juts out of the hogback.

Morrison Southside

From Morrison Wall look south and you will see this broken boulderfield flowing off the hogback. To get there from the main parking area at Morrison Wall, hike or drive 0.1 mile east and take a right (south) on Soda Lakes Road. Park at the trailhead on the right and hike upslope to the west. Follow the thin trail around to the northwest to a notch that leads to its west side.

Slab Block

This is a prominent, north-facing slabby block just upslope to the southwest.

1. Arête Right V2 (hb) Climb the slab and arête on the right side of the north face.

2. Center Game V4 (hb) Climb up the middle of the north face.

3. Left Way V4 (hb) Climb the left side of the north face.

Tunnel Block

From Slab Block, head upslope until you see the rock that has right-angling cracks. This

rock sits atop Tunnel Block, making Tunnel Block the lower of the two and the support base.

1. Left Tunnel V2 Climb up roof on the south face.

2. Right Hang V1 Climb up the northeast side to the horizontal break over the roof.

Double Arête Block

Located above Tunnel Block to the south, this block is characterized by a double arête on its east face.

1. Double Arête V6 Climb the double arêtes on the east face from down low.

Square Block ▼

This perfect block is located upslope to the south from Double Arête Block. Its shape and quality are hard to beat. This block is as good as a block can get, with a splitter finger crack up the middle of its north face.

1. Western World V1 Climb the pockets up the white-rock section of the west face.

2. H-Arête V3 (hb) Climb the northwestern arête of the block.

3. Bearshear's Crack V3 (hb) Climb the finger crack up the center of the north face.

4. Bob's Arête V2 (hb) Climb the face and arête on the left side of the north face.

5. Done Deal Dyno V3 Dyno up from the bottom of the crack to the top on the southeast side.

6. Little Ones V0 Climb the crack on the southeast face.

Many other boulders, blocks, and problems exist around these choice rocks.

24 ALDERFER/THREE SISTERS PARK

This open space park just northwest of the Evergreen town center is a great escape from the more crowded Front Range areas. Amid the granite domes and pine forests you will find a large array of boulders scattered throughout the hillsides. Most of them are easily accessed along the wandering trail system.

Directions: From Golden, take I-70 west into the hills. Continue past Genesee Park to the El Rancho exit (Highway 74). Take Highway 74 southwest through Bergen Park, past Squaw Pass Road. (Squaw Pass Road will take you west to the Mount Evans Echo Lake area.) Continue south on Highway 74, past Evergreen Lake, to a stoplight in the center of Evergreen. Take a right at the light and continue south on Highway 73 until you reach the next stoplight at Buffalo Park Road. Turn right and travel about 1.5 miles, past the high school, to the parking lot. Look for the ALDERFER/THREE SISTERS park sign. From this parking lot, you can access the trail system that leads to all the areas. You can usually find a trail map at the trailhead. For the Homestead Trail/Elephant Park area, continue another 0.5 mile past this parking lot and turn right into the parking lot for that area.

The Eggs

This line of boulders and blocks is one of the more popular destinations, with solid friendly rock textures and a variety of good problems.

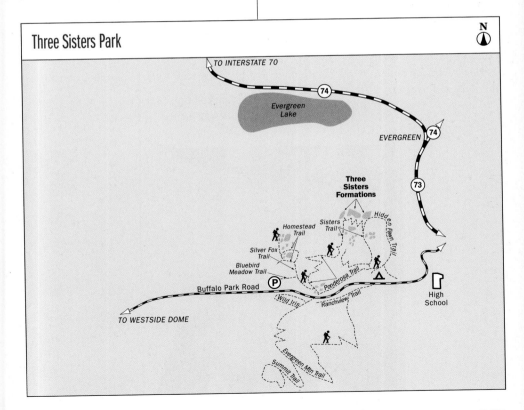

Three Sisters Park

N

TO INTERSTATE 70

74

Evergreen Lake

EVERGREEN · 74

73

Three Sisters Formations

Homestead Trail

Sisters Trail

Hidden Fawn Trail

Silver Fox Trail

Bluebird Meadow Trail

Buffalo Park Road · P

Ponderosa Trail

Wild Iris

Ranchview Trail

High School

TO WESTSIDE DOME

Evergreen Mtn Trail

Summit Trail

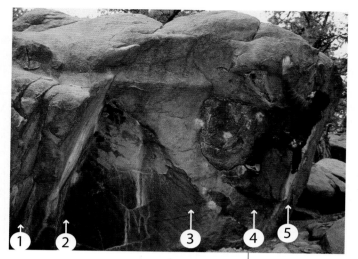

Trailside Egg ◀

This obvious south-facing, overhanging concave block sits just right of the trail.

1. Eggman V0 Climb the far-left side of the south face.

2. Egg Beater V1 Stem up the dihedral.

3. Golden Egg V4 Climb from the undercling out the roof in the gold rock.

Hike from the parking lot, starting on the Sisters/Hidden Fawn Trail for a few minutes, then hang a right on the Hidden Fawn Trail. Follow the trail around for about ten minutes, until you run into the Trailside Egg block, which sits just off the trail a few yards on the right side. There will be chalk marks on its south face. You can find the other boulders scattered about the hillside up to the right and beyond.

4. Black Breaker V3 Climb out the overhang in the blackened rock.

5. Egg White V0 Climb out the right side of the south face, up the white streak.

Cracked Egg ▼

Hike upslope another 90 feet, until you see this block with a crack splitting its west face.

1. Cracked Egg Crack V2 Climb the prominent crack on the west face.

Scrambled Egg ▲

Continue southeast for a short distance and you will see this blob.

1. Upper D V3 Climb across the right-angling crack system from the right to the left and up.

2. Roundabout V1 Climb up from the right side of the south face.

White Egg ▶

This block is located due south from Scrambled Egg and is characterized by a sheer scooping north face.

1. Scooped Wall V1 (hb) Climb from the left side of the north face via good holds and undercling.

2. White Night V2 (hb) Climb up the center of the north face, then slightly left and up.

Egg and I Boulder ▲

This is an extremely appealing boulder, located up and beyond White Egg block. It is characterized by a scooped-out obtuse corner on its south face.

1. Slabin on the Face V0 Climb the southwest slab left of the tree.

2. Eggs Benny V6 Climb up the scooped dihedral on the south face.

3. Egg Bernardo V4 Climb the prow on the far-right side of the south face.

4. Eggs Florentine V0 Climb up the low-angle east face.

East Sister Boulders

These boulders are located along and about the base of the easternmost Sisters formation.

From the parking area, take the Sisters Trail up to the base.

Beak Boulder

This overhanging boulder has a great traverse across its lips, as well as good roof and mantle problems.

1. Beak Traverse V2 Traverse across the lip from right to left.

2. Beak Roof V3 From down low, climb up and out the roof.

Middle Sisters Boulders

This large gathering of boulders and blocks is located downslope, just off the top of the middle Sisters formation. From the east parking area, take the Sisters Trail up to the Sisters formations.

Round Up Block ◄

This spired block is in the trees below the middle formation, just off the trail.

1. Round Up V3 Climb up the southeast prow.

The Elephant Area

Located down a smooth fall line below the Brother's Lookout formation (across to the south of the Sisters), these blackened soft sandstone boulders are a pleasant surprise.

Elephant Boulder ▼

This boulder is located out in the meadow at the lower end of the wash from the Brother's Lookout, just north of the middle section of the Ponderosa Trail.

1. Elephant V4 Climb the southeast prow via sloper holds and dishes.

2. Le Elephant V6 Climb up the southwest face.

Ponderosa Boulders

From the parking lot, hike west along the south leg of the Ponderosa Trail for approximately fifteen to twenty minutes, until you see this stretch of boulders and blocks. Some are trailside, while others are closer to the roadway.

The Spire ◄

This spire is on the left (south) side of the Ponderosa Trail, just before it intersects with the Silver Fox Trail. Spot it out in the trees.

1. Spire West V4 Climb up right of the center of the west face.

2. Spire Arête V5 (hb) Climb up the southwest arête.

Silver Fox Boulders

From the parking lot, hike west along the south leg of the Ponderosa Trail for fifteen minutes. Then take the Silver Fox Trail, staying to the northwest. You can see the boulder just off the trail on the right, and you will see more while heading upslope toward the outcrop.

Main Boulder ▼

This boulder is just off the trail to the right as you are heading slightly upslope on the Silver Fox Trail. It offers a great traverse on its north side.

1. Main Traverse V3 Traverse from the west side, across the lip and face, to the far-left side of the north face.

2. Upsidaisy V1 Climb up the far-left side of the north face.

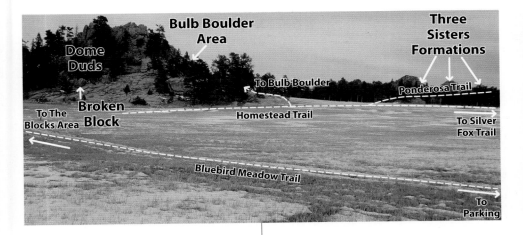

Bulb Boulder
Area

Three
Sisters
Formations

Dome
Duds

To Bulb Boulder

Ponderosa Trail

Broken
Block

To The
Blocks Area

Homestead Trail

To Silver
Fox Trail

Bluebird Meadow Trail

To
Parking

Three Sisters Westside Dome

To reach these boulders it is best to drive farther west on Buffalo Park Road. Drive about
1.4 miles from the main Three Sisters parking lot and hang a right on Le Masters
Road. Drive a short way and turn right into
the parking lot. Look north and you will see
some domes out across the field. The boulders and blocks are spread out and around
these dome formations.

Dome Duds

These boulders and blocks are found around
the dome formations' base and slabs.
Boulders are found around its circumference.

Broken Block

This block is on the southwest section of the
dome, up on its slabs.

1. Broken Arête V1 Climb up the southwest
arête of the block.

Bulb Boulder ▶

This boulder is on the north side of the
dome, amid many great minicliffs that offer
excellent bouldering.

1. Bulb Bulge V5 Climb up the left-side
bulge on the west face.

The Blocks Area

To find these blocks, which are on flat
ground, hike due north from the northwest
side of the dome formation. Hike past a
few outcroppings and you will run into the
blocked cove.

Anteater Block

This block is the westernmost of the two main blocks and is characterized by an over-hanging northwest arête.

1. Anteater V10 Climb up the northwest arête.

Cross Block

This block, which has a crack system that forms a cross on its west face, is just east of Anteater Block.

1. Crossfire V6 Climb up the northeast arête.

2. Cross Country V5 Climb up the northwest prow.

3. Cross Walk V3 Climb up the crack in the middle of the west face.

4. Crossword V1 Climb up the right side of the west face.

25 MOUNT EVANS

This alpine bouldering area consists of a number of independent areas within the Mount Evans Wilderness. The granite is of the best quality, with a number of test pieces throughout. Cracks, arêtes, and steep to overhanging faces abound. Much of the bouldering is located just off the creeks and lakes of the wilderness area, making for a truly pristine setting.

There are a few worthwhile isolated boulders just off Highway 103 on the way to Echo Lake. The most infamous area, the Chicago Basin, with four distinct areas, is located just south of the Idaho Springs Reservoir, along the Chicago Lakes Trail. This is a world-class area. Don't miss the Bierstadt Block, the Magnificent Block, and the Dali Block of Area A. The Lincoln Lake area is also of special interest and has a wealth of clean, white granite boulders with good landings.

Directions: From I-70, take the Idaho Springs/Mt. Evans exit and head south up Highway 103 to Echo Lake. From Echo Lake, follow the trail southwest around the lake and catch the Chicago Lakes Trail at the southwest end of the lake. Hike down the trail for fifteen to twenty minutes, until you come to a dirt road that leads northeast-southwest. Go left and hike approximately 1 mile up the road, past the reservoir, to where the road ends. The Chicago Lakes Trail resumes at this point. Hike southwest up the trail for fifteen minutes, passing a nice boulder on the right. At a point where you see the large rock formations on the left, veer onto a faint trail that leads into the scrub brush. Cross the creek and continue southwest on the faint trail, until you run into the first set of boulders and blocks. This is Area A. Area B is farther up the valley on the left. Area C is up the valley on the right side, and Area D is farther up the valley above tree line.

To reach the Lincoln Lake boulders (Lincoln Park), drive past Echo Lake toward the Mount Evans Byway entrance station. Just before the entrance on the left, you will see a campground. Park outside the campground and hike through it to the south until you catch the wilderness trail on its south end. Hike up and then down this trail for two hours until you reach the Lincoln Lake turn, which is marked with a sign. Go right (west) approximately 1 mile. This will take you to the east shores of Lincoln Lake. Hike around the southwest shore of the lake to the west shore. To the west, you will see the massive boulder and talus field that begins at the west shore and rises upslope to the west. This is a much more involved hike than for the Chicago Basin boulders. An earlier start is recommended, as well as proper gear for alpine conditions.

Mt. Evans Area

N

TO GEORGETOWN

70

70
TO DENVER

IDAHO SPRINGS

103

188
Logical Block

South Chicago Creek Boulder

West Chicago Creek

247

103

Lake Edith

West Chicago Creek

South Chicago Creek

Squaw Pass

103
TO EVERGREEN

Echo Lake

Switchback Block

Trail 46

Roadside Block

Idaho Springs Reservoir

Cracked Block

Trail 57

5

Trailside Block

Area A

480 Rd.

Area C

Chicago Lakes Trail

Area B

Trail 45

195

Chicago Lakes

Mt. Evans Byway

Lincoln Lake

Trail 44

Area D

Lincoln Park Boulders

Summit Lake

Mount Evans Wildlife Area

Mt. Evans 14,264'

Trail 82

Mt. Bierstadt 14,060'

Chicago Creek Boulders

Logical Block ▼

This nice block is located off Highway 103 just past the West Chicago Creek Campground/Lake Edith turnoff. From Idaho Springs, drive southwest on Highway 103 approximately 6 miles and park at the hairpin turn just past the West Chicago Creek campground turnoff. Hike south up the dirt road about 200 yards, until you see the granite outcropping on the right. The block sits below the formation on its southeast end.

1. Logical Arête V7 Climb up the leaning, southwestern arête.

2. Illogical Face V2 Climb up the left side of the west side.

South Chicago Creek Boulder

This boulder is just below the right side of the road, up from *Logical Block*. Drive another 3 miles up the road from the hairpin turn to a small pull off on the right, just before the South Chicago Creek picnic area and trailhead. Hike 50 feet downslope.

1. Chicago V0 Climb up the middle of the north face.

2. Chicago Traverse V4 Traverse the boulder from the left side of the north face, across to the far-right side of the southwest face.

Chicago Basin Areas

This world-class area is full of solid granite boulders and blocks. Hike the Chicago Lakes Trail from Echo Lake, past the Idaho Springs Reservoir, to the first areas (see directions above). This is an approximately one-hour trek. The first four boulders described are located along the way to Chicago Basin.

Switchback Block

This block is located out in the talus field at a point where the Chicago Lakes Trail (when going down the first and lengthy switchback from Echo Lake) switches back downslope. Hike out into the talus a short way and you will see this block within the talus.

1. September Overhang V1 Climb up the good edges in bulge on the left side of the east face.

2. September Face V2 Climb up the middle of the south face.

Cracked Block ▲

This perfect block is within the forest, south-east from the point on the Chicago Lakes Trail where the trail from Echo Lake bottoms out

and intersects with the road/trail that leads up to Idaho Springs Reservoir and Chicago Basin. Just before you cross the footbridge over Chicago Creek, head southeast about 100 yards into the woods, until you see this block, which is split by a finger crack.

1. Cracked Block Crack V2 Climb up the crack that splits the north face.

2. Cracked Up Traverse V5 From down low, climb out from the cave, out to the right, finishing up the crack.

Roadside Block ▼

This block is on the left side of the road as you head up to Idaho Springs Reservoir and Chicago Basin.

1. Road Shield V? Climb the thin left side of the road face.

2. Road Haul V0 Climb up good holds on the right side of the road face.

Trailside Block ◄

This prominent boulder is on the right side of the trail as you head up the Chicago Lakes Trail from the end-of-the-road part of the trail. This block is a good indication that the other boulders and its side trail are getting close.

1. Trail Mix V4 Climb up the middle of the southwest face.

2. Trail Prow V1 Climb up the southwest prow.

3. Trail Worthy V5 Climb up the right side of the east face.

4. The Shell V4 Climb up the shield on the right side of the east face.

Area A

This is the first of the four developed areas. It has many good problems on awesome granite.

Bierstadt Block ▲

This is the first major block you will encounter. Its east side, along the trail, forms a tunnel that leads to other boulders beyond.

1. Bierstadt V10 This is the east-facing blackened overhang with counter pull, lay-away within the tunnel.

2. Beeriest Arête V2 Climb the southeast arête of the block.

3. Painter's Face V2 (hb) Climb up the south-facing slab.

Landing Block

This is the shorter block just south of Bierstadt Block.

1. Random Progression V7 Climb up the leaning arête on the right side of the east face.

2. Timeline V2 (hb) Climb up the left side of the west-facing slab.

3. Last of the Ohitians V3 (hb) Climb up the left side of the slab.

Ladder Block ▲

This block is located just south of Landing Block and has a great classic problem up the middle of the east face.

1. Indian Ladder V2 Climb the middle of the east face on good holds.

Wedge Block

This is a good piece of rock that lies just south of Ladder Block.

1. Mental Pollution V11 Climb the severely overhanging south side, utilizing the side pulls.

Think Pink Block

This is an elongated block with quality rock on its north face. It is characterized by a pastel-looking sheer face. Hike up through the scrub brush trail to the block located up and east of Ladder Block.

1. Think Pink V6 Climb up the left side of the north face.

2. Pinky Fest V? Climb the thin set of crimps on the far-left side of the north face.

Magnificent Block ▲

To find this gem of a block, hike southeast 200 feet up and through the scrub brush. It is characterized by a thin, squiggly tips crack on the right side of its east face.

1. Pat's Arête V7 Climb the leaning arête on the north side from down low, turning onto the slab above.

2. Seraut Crack V8 Climb up the crimpy crack on the right side of the east face.

3. Jiggles V7 Climb the left side of the east face. Start left and move right and up.

B's Block

This square block with a good landing is located upslope to the south from Magnificent Block.

1. Black Wash V3 Climb up the black streak in the middle of the south face.

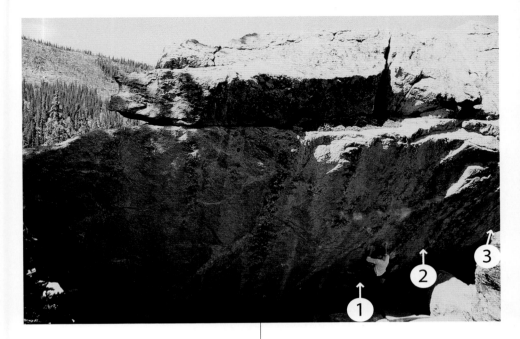

Dali Boulder

Continue upslope about 200 feet on the faint trail and you will come across this awesome block. It is characterized by an elongated, perfectly overhanging east wall. World-class problems abound.

1. Dali V5 Climb the thin overhanging to a rail break in the center of the east face.

2. The Lama V1 Climb the crack right of *Dali*.

3. Lime Face V13 Climb the small crimps out the overhang 10 feet right of the crack.

4. Lime Wall V12 Climb up the thin overhanging face to the slab above on the far-right side of the east face.

Area B

This is the next spread of boulders up from Area A. Good rock and problems abound.

Arête Block

1. City Walls of Dying Dreams V10 Climb the 25-foot-long perfect arête on the right side of the face.

2. All Dogs Go to Evans V9 Climb up and out the left-leaning arête.

Area C

Le Block

1. Gray Arête V5 Climb the arête on the block.

2. Goodman's Arête V6

3. Deception V9

Area D

This area is located at the high point of this escarpment at 12,000 feet. The area has a fragile ecosystem, so please minimize your impact.

The Big Four

1. Slander V11
2. Salad Toss V11
3. The Nothing V8
4. Dihedral Project V?
5. Hotep V6

Area D Block

1. Area D Arête V11 Climb the left-leaning gray green lichen arête.

Lincoln Park

This area is located at the northeast end of Lincoln Lake and extends to its western shores and up the talus slope. Many boulders and blocks abound. From the Echo Lake parking area, hike south toward the campground. Go past the campground and con-tinue along Trail 57. Then go right (west) on Trail 45, heading up to Lincoln Lake. The boulders are spread about the lake and upslope to the west and southwest. This has been broken into three areas.

Greener Grass Area

This area is up and over the first rise from the northeastern shores of Lincoln Lake.

Tier Boulder

From the southeast shore of Lincoln Lake, hike south over the hill and then southwest down through the junipers. You will find this nice boulder sitting among other smaller boulders.

1. Tier Left V2 Climb up the left side of the west overhang.

2. Tier Right V1 Climb up the right side of the west face.

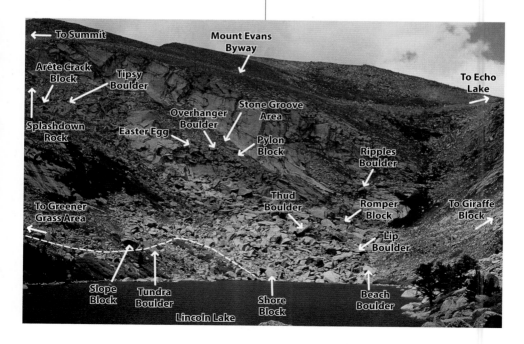

Pointer Rock ◄

This fun rock is located slightly upslope, 20 feet northwest of Tier Boulder.

1. The Pointer V3 Climb up the south face.

Rise Block ▼

This classic block is up and left a few feet from Pointer Rock.

1. The Rise V3 Climb up the right side of the east face.

2. Rise Above V4 Climb the arête on the left side of the east face.

Beach Boulders

These are the boulders located around the lakeside, and there are plenty of them.

Slope Block ▼

This large block is located upslope on the south side of the lake's west end. It is the obvious block that sits a good 75 feet above the lake's southwestern slopes, removed to the southeast from the main shoreline rocks.

1. Lakeside V4 Climb the left side of the north face.

2. Taluside V4 Climb up the left side of the west face.

Tundra Boulder

This boulder is 20 feet west of Slope Block.

1. Rolling Tundra V1 Climb up the middle of the northeast face.

2. Grassy Traverse V4 Traverse the northeast face from right to left.

Shore Block

This pointy block is located along the shoreline, just northwest of Tundra Boulder, and is the first shoreline block you encounter from the east.

1. Boa Shores V1 Climb up the southeastern arête.

Beach Boulder ▼

This overhanging boulder is on the northwest side of the lake, just above the shoreline.

1. Beach Party V3 Climb the middle of the east face.

2. Beach Blanket V2 Traverse across the east lip from right to left.

Land of Plenty Boulders

These boulders and blocks are above Beach Boulder, within the talus pack. This description is vague, so keep your eyes open for the rocks and use pictures for comparison.

Ripples Boulder ▲

This boulder is located upslope in the talus. It sits in a smooth section separated from the talus pack.

1. Ripples V5 Climb up just to the right of the middle of the east face.

2. Ripples Traverse V1 Traverse the lip from right to left.

Romper Block ▼

This crack-split block is above the Ripples Boulders at a point where a slight meadow forms.

1. Romper Room V0 Climb the left side of the east face.

2. Romper Crack V0 Climb up the crack corner on the east face.

3. Zoom V1 Climb the right side of the east face.

Strike Zone Boulders

These boulders and blocks are found in the upper end of the talus field to the right and left, below the crag.

Stone Groove Area

These boulders are on the far-right side of the upper talus slope, above the main pack and below the right (north) end of the crag.

Groove Block

This block is in the center of the Stone Groove Area and offers good face problems.

1. Stone Groove V4 Climb the middle of the northeast face.

Overhanger Boulder ▼

This nice boulder is located farther to the left of the Stone Groove Area and is characterized by an overhanging south face.

1. Slab Ho V2 (hb) Climb up the middle of the east slab.

2. Overhanger V4 Climb up the overhanging right side of the south face.

UPPER CLEAR CREEK / BERTHOUD PASS AREA

The Upper Clear Creek areas are located on Interstate 70 west of Evergreen, Highway 6, (Lower Clear Creek), and Idaho Springs. Continue past Idaho Springs for the areas including Dumont, Empire, Berthoud Falls, Jones Pass, Berthoud Pass, Georgetown, and Silver Plume.

Directions: Drive west on I-70 toward Idaho Springs or, if coming out of Lower Clear Creek, continue west on Highway 6 until it merges onto I-70, just past Kermit's roadside tavern. For the first area, Dumont, continue past Idaho Springs to the next major exit (a weigh station) for Dumont. There are a Starbucks, a Conoco, a Burger King, and the state weigh station on the right. Exit and head west on the frontage road. To find the other areas, continue west on I-70 and then follow Highway 40 north toward Berthoud Pass and Winter Park. To find Georgetown continue on I-70 a few miles past Highway 40.

26 DUMONT

You can see these blocks upslope on the right (north) as you travel west on the frontage road from the Burger King in Dumont. The Weigh Station Rocks are a few hundred yards to the west. Slim's Slope is approximately 1 mile west, just before the underpass. Park on the right side of the road. Look up to the northwest and you will see this fall line of quality granite blocks high up on the slopes.

The Pancake ▼

This steep chunk of clean, white granite sits just up off the frontage road on the north side of I-70, east of Dumont.

1. Syrup Crack V1 Climb the left-angling crack on the southwest face.

2. Jemima V5 Climb the face just right of the crack.

3. Log Cabin V1 Climb the steep southeastern arête.

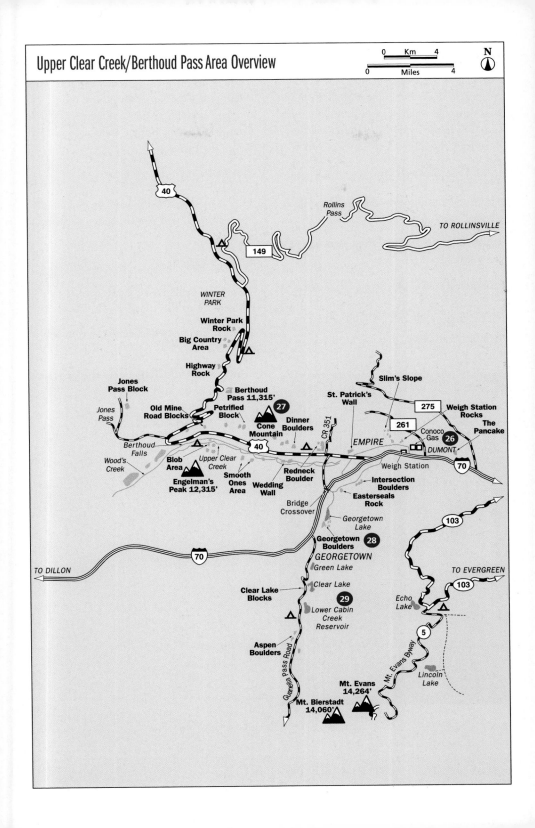

Upper Clear Creek/Berthoud Pass Area Overview

Weigh Station Rocks

These rocks are located a short way from the weigh station on the frontage road. Continue west from the weigh station about 200 yards and look to the right (north). You will see these rocks just above the frontage road.

Overload Spire

This is the tall spire you can see above the frontage road.

1. Overload V1 (hb) Climb the left side of the south face.

Scale Block ▼

This block is located behind the spire.

1. Scale Arête V3 Climb the southeast arête.

Slim's Slope

This fall line of rocks is located up and above the slopes to the northwest, above the frontage road. Drive for approximately 1 mile from the Dumont Burger King and park just before the underpass.

Approach Rocks

As you head upslope toward the Sheer and Proper Block, you will see these warm up rocks.

The Sheer

This south-facing vertical slab has a great problem on its sheer face.

1. Sheer Elegance V1 Climb the thin slab of the south face.

2. Side Show V0 Climb either the right or left edges of the rock.

27 EMPIRE/CONE MOUNTAIN

See map on page 341.

The Empire areas are located on the slopes near the town of Empire. To reach Empire, take I-70 west and exit onto Highway 40.

To find the Cone Mountain areas, follow Highway 40 toward Empire. Cone Mountain is north of Empire and begins at a point where the road starts a steep incline. There are bouldering areas all along this stretch, all the way to Berthoud Pass and beyond.

Empire Areas

These areas are located near the town of Empire.

St. Patrick's Wall

St. Patrick's Wall is located upslope to the north just before you merge off the I-70 exit ramp onto Highway 40 toward Empire. Stop at the sign, cross Highway 40 to the west, and park in the pull off. Look upslope due northeast from here and you will see this clean-cut wall. Hike upslope from the far left and then back to the wall. This is the largest clean section of rock. A few topropes are found on the high end of the west face.

1. St. Patty's Traverse V4 Traverse from the shorter end of the wall, on the far-left side, and move across to the right end of the higher section of the wall. Eliminate the top shelf on the shorter end for added difficulty.

Redneck Boulder ▲

To reach this rock, drive through Empire (beware of speed traps) to the far-north end and park on the shoulder just past a stoplight and the post office on the right. Look upslope to the right and you will spot this round dud.

1. Redneck Hero V3 Climb up the left side of the south face.

2. The Hick V4 Climb up the middle of the south face.

3. Alabama Getaway V3 Climb up the right side of the south face.

Cone Mountain Area

From the post office and stoplight on the far west end of Empire, drive west on Highway 40. Park at a large pull off on the left side of the road,. The boulders, blocks, and outcrops described here are on both sides of Highway 40; some are downslope toward Upper Clear Creek, while others are upslope toward the main formations.

Wedding Wall

This south-facing wall is located just below the south side of Highway 40. From the first parking pull off, where there are tension wires, hike down under the wires to the south until you come across this somewhat highball bouldering wall. Many problems across the wall have been done, including a lengthy traverse across the entire west face.

1. Wedding Wall Traverse V5 Traverse the wall from left to right.

2. Wedding Overhang V2 (hb) Climb over the bulged roof to top.

Dinner Boulders

These boulders and blocks are located up on an isolated shelf just above Highway 40 to the north. Drive to the pull off on the left (south) side of the road, park, and then hike north across the road. Hike up to a gap through a gully that has cairns. Head up north and then back south up to the shelf.

Tock Block

This block is among the trees to the north-west of Road Prow.

1. Tick V2 Climb the middle of the south face.

2. Tock V2 Climb the arête on the left side of the south face.

One-Night Stand Boulder ▲

From the stoplight at the far west end of Empire, continue west approximately 2 miles and you will see a national forest sign. Park on the right-hand shoulder at the sign and head upslope to the northwest for about ten minutes, until you run across this nice black-and-white-striped granite block.

1. One-Night Stand V3 Climb up the left side of the southeast face.

2. Piano Man V4 Climbs up the middle of the south face.

3. Vocalized Seduction V3 Climb up the right side of the south face.

4. Broken Rubber V3 Traverse across the north face from left to right.

5. Soho V4 Climb up the left side of the north face, angling toward its center and up.

Road Prow ▲

This overhanging block is on the shelf just above Highway 40. From Tock Block, hike toward the road slope to find this quality block.

1. Prowess V6 Climb up the overhanging face and arête on the left side of the west face.

Cone Boulders

This is a large fall line of rock located below the formation. Many excellent problems have been done here.

Cone Rock

This pointy-top rock is about 200 feet to the left of the Dinner Boulders. It sits in the trees on the southwest end of the large talus field.

1. Cone Arête V1 Climb up the leaning arête on the south face.

Lantern Block

This large block, upslope through the trees, is characterized by an overhanging north side and a steep west face.

1. The Lantern Arête V11 Climb up the arching arête on the north face.

2. Candylight V3 Climb up the left side of the west face.

Creekside Boulders

From the pull off for the Dinner Boulders, hike down and across the creek and head to its west side. Hike up or down creek for the boulders.

Arête Block

From the parking pull off, follow the trail down to the southeast, cross the creek, and then head to the left until you see this nice arête just offshore.

1. Arg Arête V3 Climb the arête just offshore.

Bart's Overhang

This overhanging block sits along the creek, west from Arête Block. It offers good overhanging problems just offshore.

1. Bart's Overhang V4 (hb) Climb up the middle of the north face.

Woods Boulders

These boulders and blocks are in the woods across the creek to the northwest of the previously described creekside rocks. Hike north through the woods and you will find these boulders.

Perfect Block ▼

This is a small, perfect, block-shaped block with an appealing arête on its northwest corner.

1. Daylight Arête V4 Climb the northwestern arête.

2. Daynight V0 Climb the right side of the west face.

Wheel Rock ▼

This rock is located just down to the northwest from Perfect Block. It has a quartz blackened south face.

1. Quartz V1 Climb up the middle of the south face.

Petrified Blocks

These small outcrops of unique super-quality granite are located upslope and north of Highway 40. From the stoplight and post office in Empire, drive west on Highway 40. Drive just past the Cone Mountain massif and park on the left side of the road, across from a guardrail. Cross the road toward the guardrail and hike up and behind it to the north through the woods for about five to ten minutes. You will run into this unique area.

Mini Wall

This is the first minicliff on the left side of the area. It offers excellent face problems.

1. Days End V2 Climb up the left side of the wall.

2. Removed V4 Climb up just right of *Days End*.

Petrified Block ▼

This is possibly the most incredible small rock I have seen in Colorado. It is characterized by a south-facing 15-foot wall with a splitter crack running through its midsection. A white, diagonal quartz streak angles through the crack making an X. The quartz streak looks like a petrified log.

1. Petrified Crack V3 (hb) Climb the finger crack to the top.

Smooth Ones Area

Drive west on Highway 40 several miles from Empire and park at a clearing and bend in the creek on the left side of the road. Cross the creek and you will see these smooth granite mounds.

Concave Boulder

This boulder is just across the creek at ground level. It has a crack that goes through its north face.

1. The Crack V1 Climb the crack on the north face.

The Granite Dune

Continue upslope behind Concave Boulder about 100 feet, until you see this blank-looking granite chunk.

1. Dune Left V0 Climb the angling edge system from the left side to the right and up.

2. Dune Central V7 Climb small micro-edges up the middle of the north face.

3. Done Dune V? Climb the right side of the north face.

Blob Area

From the Smooth Ones Area, drive another 0.5 mile up the road, pull off to the left, drive down a short road to a primitive group campsite, and park. Hike due west across the creek and head upslope into the forest. After about 100 feet, you will run into the first of these boulders.

The Blob

This is the first boulder upslope from the creek. It has a blobby rounded look to it.

1. The Blob V2 Climb up the middle of the north face.

2. Blob West Traverse V5 Traverse the north face from left to right.

Wave Block ▼

This gray block with an overhanging west face is directly behind the Blob to the southwest.

1. The Wave Traverse V3 Traverse the west face from right to left.

2. The Wave V4 From down low, climb up the middle of the west face.

28 GEORGETOWN BOULDERS

See map on page 341.

Yes, there is bouldering on the slopes of Georgetown. Much of it is located southwest of Georgetown Lake, while there are other boulders up Guanella Pass Road. Exit I-70 at Georgetown. Drive south on the road that leads to the foot of the mountain. Take a left and follow the road east to a parking spot above and beyond the house on the left side of the trailhead. The trail starts east of the house and heads off to the east. It is an old mining and logging road that goes on for miles. Hike up the trail for about fifteen minutes. Keep an eye downslope and you will see these blocks to the left.

Pocket Block ▼

This is the tall block with a pocketed north face.

1. Strange Condition V2 Climb the left side of the north face

2. Valentine's Day Massacre V4 Climb up the middle via pockets.

3. Cellular Savage V3 Climb the right side of the face, left of the right-leaning corner.

Graystone Block ▼

This block is west of Pocket Block and has a rectangular shape.

1. Verbal Retaliation V2 Climb the far-left side of the north face.

2. Barney Fife V3 Climb the face to the right of *Verbal Retaliation*.

3. Entrapment V3 Climb up the middle of the north face.

4. Envelopment V1 Climb the slab to the right of *Entrapment*.

5. The Dungeon V2 Climb the arête on the far-right (west) end of the block.

29 GUANELLA PASS

This alpine bouldering area has a lot to offer. It is a great adventure away from the towns below. From I-70 take the Georgetown exit and head into Georgetown. Turn right at the gas station and head west to the town center. You can access Guanella Pass via a winding uphill road (Guanella Pass Road) that begins at the far-west end of Georgetown.

Lower Areas

Curve Block ▼

Drive 2.7 miles south on Guanella Pass Road. Park on the left side of the road within the curve. Look down to the immediate south and you will see this massive block.

1. Georgetown Arête V3 Climb the right-leaning arête on the left side of the east face.

Power Boulders

Drive another 0.8 mile, or 3.5 miles from the beginning of Guanella Pass Road, to where the road levels out at a small lake that has a house on its east end. Drive past the lake and park on the right. Look north and you will see a talus area that has some nice-looking blocks.

Striped Block ▼

This nice block has two arching, horizontal white pegmatite stripes on its south face.

1. Candy Stripe V0 Climb the left side of the south face.

2. Stripes V1 Climb up the middle of the south face.

Guanella Pass

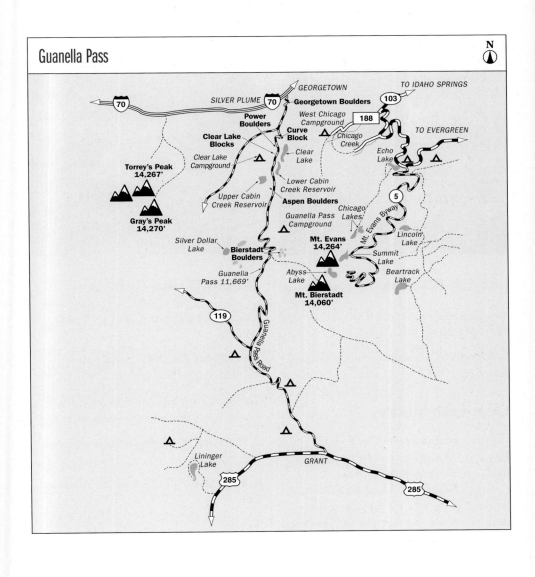

N

TO IDAHO SPRINGS

GEORGETOWN

SILVER PLUME

70 · **70**

Georgetown Boulders

103

TO EVERGREEN

Power Boulders

West Chicago Campground

188

Clear Lake Blocks

Curve Block

Chicago Creek

Clear Lake Campground

Clear Lake

Echo Lake

Torrey's Peak 14,267'

Lower Cabin Creek Reservoir

5

Upper Cabin Creek Reservoir

Aspen Boulders

Chicago Lakes

Gray's Peak 14,270'

Guanella Pass Campground

Lincoln Lake

Silver Dollar Lake

Bierstadt Boulders

Mt. Evans 14,264'

Mt. Evans Byway

Summit Lake

Guanelia Pass 11,669'

Abyss Lake

Beartrack Lake

Mt. Bierstadt 14,060'

119

Guanella Pass Road

Lininger Lake

GRANT

285

285

Launch Block ▲

This gray blackened block is located just east of Striped Block.

1. Rocket V1 Climb up the middle of the west face.

Clear Lake Blocks

Continue west another 0.6 mile on Guanella Pass Road (4.4 miles from the base of the road) and turn into the Clear Lake Campground and Day Use Area. Park at the west end of the lake and hike along the shoreline toward the dam. You will see these nice blocks on the northeast side of the lake. Depending on the time of year, the rocks may be inaccessible due to high water. This is a fee area.

Precipitation Cube ▲

This is a cube-shaped block with a steep south face.

1. Blackened Face V3 Climb the steep middle of the south face.

2. Alright Prow V2 Climb the prow and face on the far-right side of the south face.

3. The Bump V0 Climb the slab of the east side.

4. Black Shield V0 Climb up the northeast face.

Shore Block ▲

This dark gray block is the easternmost rock of the group. It sits nicely on the sand-pebbled beach. It has an overhang on its west face and a slabby southwest face.

1. Beach Roof V1 Climb up and over the roof on the left side of the west face.

2. Shoreline V1 Traverse around the entire block.

Aspen Boulders

From Clear Lake, head another 0.4 mile farther west on Guanella Pass Road (6.8 miles from the beginning of the road) and park on the left side of the road or at the pull off just ahead. You can see these boulders on the right side, just off the dirt road and within the aspen trees. They are of a clean, white quality.

Rodeo Boulder ▲

This roadside boulder is pretty short.

1. Rodeo V1 Climb the crack on the right side of the west face.

Aspen Boulder ▼

This boulder is located just north of Rodeo Boulder and is surrounded by a few aspen trees.

1. Aspen Arête V5 Climb the arête and face on the left end of the west face.

2. Right Away V? Climb the face on the right side of the boulder.

3. Ramp V0 Climb up the northwest slab.

Up the Creek Boulder ◄

Continue west about 0.2 mile on Guanella Pass Road (7 miles from the start) and you will see a large block on the left side of the road. The creek runs around its southeastern side.

1. Kindred Spirit V7 (hb) Climb the steep left side of the face.

2. The Ghost V? (hb) Climb the right side of the face.

Bierstadt Boulders

Continue another 5 miles west on Guanella Pass Road and you will see the trailhead parking area for Mount Bierstadt. Hike as if you're going to hike up Bierstadt and look out to the southeast. You will see the boulders out amid the meadows and slopes.

Castle Rock Area Overview

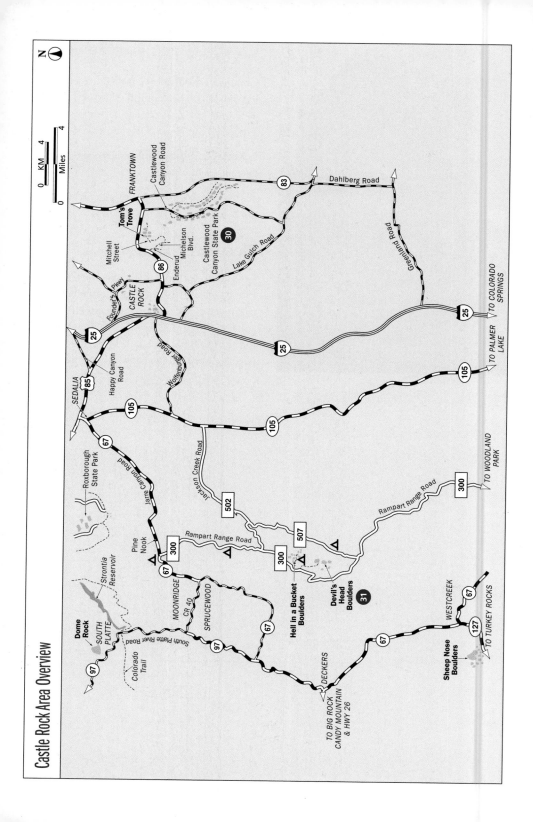

CASTLE ROCK AREA

30 CASTLEWOOD CANYON

This short cliffed canyon with Cherry Creek running through it has a wealth of bouldering. It is secluded within the rolling hills southeast of the town of Castle Rock. The canyon hosts numerous boulders, blocks, spires, and caves. The rock ranges from a unique Castlewood conglomerate with crystalline walls to smooth hardened sandstone, some creek polished. Many of the gems are hidden within the scrub oak.

Directions: Castlewood Canyon has two entrances—one on the east side, considered the main entry, and one on the west side. To reach either entrance, take Interstate 25 south from Denver and exit at Castle Rock, exit 182. You can see the Castle Rock formation on the left (east) side of the highway. Drive east over the interstate and take a right onto Wilcox Street, then a left on Fifth Street (Highway 86).

For access to the west entrance and the Five and Dime Area, Fontainebleau Area, and Central City, drive approximately 6.5 miles on Highway 86 and turn right onto Castlewood Canyon Road. Drive south about 2.3 miles and you will see the self-serve entry station on the right.

To access the Creekside Blocks, Trailside Boulders, Buddha Cave, and Berthoud Cave, continue down Highway 86, past Castlewood Canyon Road, to Franktown. Turn right (south) onto Highway 83 and drive about 4.7 miles and then turn right into the east entrance station. After paying the fee collected at this entrance, continue ahead and park. The parking lots are large and restrooms and picnic tables are available.

Five and Dime Area

This boulder slope is located on the west side of Castlewood Canyon Road, about 0.1 mile from the west entrance station. Park in the Homestead Trail parking lot on the left side of the road. From the lot, hike southwest and then head upslope to the right (west). Aim for a large pyramid-shaped rock at the top of the slope, just below the cliffs. You will see a prominent gray slab directly below.

The Slab

From the parking lot look slightly upslope to the southwest and you will see this large gray block, which has a north-facing slab.

1. Dihedarête V3 Climb the left side of the north face utilizing the arête.

2. Lichen Dark V2 Climb to the right of *Dihedarête*.

Castlewood Canyon State Park

N

TO CASTLE ROCK & AND INTERSTATE 25

86

86

TO FRANKTOWN

83

Ridge Line

Castlewood Canyon Road

Cherry Creek

West Entry

Ridgeline

Five And Dime Area

Fontainebleau Area

Nine Lives Area

Dungeon Area

Mini Cliff Area

Buoux Block

Sentry Blocks

Falls Wall

St. Patrick's Day Area

P

Leprachaun Corridor

Waterfall

The Drain

Berthoud Cave

The Corridor

White Boulder

Titanic Block

Turd Ball Tiers

The Cave Caves (Eastern World)

Phallic Spire

Ridgeline

Castlewood Canyon Road

Creekside Blocks/ Trailside Boulders

Lake Gulch Rim Trail

Cherry Creek

Picnic Area

P

83

East Entrance

7-11 Boulders

Hike upslope to the southwest from the lot across the road, and then go behind the Slab, winding around the scrub oak. This pair of boulders—Big Gulp to the west and Coffin Lid Block to the east—lean against one another to form a tunnel. Good overhangs and traverses characterize this shaded area.

Big Gulp

This is the western of the two boulders.

1. Big Gulp V3 Climb out the roof from down low on the west face.

2. Slurpee V2 Climb out the roof from down low, left of *Big Gulp*.

Coffin Lid Block

This is the eastern block of the two boulders.

1. Crystal Overhang V5 Climb out the crystals in the overhanging northeast corner.

2. Diehedral V0 Climb up the dihedral on the northwest face.

3. Southeast Face V0 Climb up the southeast face.

4. Pocket Block Traverse V8 Climb the pocket on the southwest face from down low, left, up, and across to the right.

Traverse Cave Rock

Continue upslope toward the pyramid-shaped rock and around to the left at the base of the cliff band and you will see this overhanging roofed rock.

1. Ted's Hole V6 Climb out the huge roof from the crack down low, up and out to the east side.

Puzzle Block

This fun block is 30 feet down and to the right of Traverse Cave Rock.

1. Ledge Reach V0 Climb up the pockets on the left side of the east face.

2. Corner Pockets V2 Climb the pockets right of *Ledge Reach.*

3. The Face V1 Climb the face right of *Corner Pockets.*

4. Behind Tree V0 Climb up the face behind the tree.

Square Away Block

This block is a few feet north of Puzzle Block.

1. The Point V0 Climb the pockets on the east arête.

2. Undercling Reach V2 Climb up the right of *The Point,* from the undercling and arête.

Fontainebleau Area

This area is named for the texture of the stone found here, which resembles the soft sandstone of France's premier bouldering area, Fontainebleau. To find this unique rock for Castlewood Canyon, drive about 0.7 mile from the west entrance station and park at the Climber's Trail parking lot. Hike west up the trail, to the split just below the cliff band. Take a right and, at the base of the Grocery Store Wall, walk north about 300 feet, until you pass a gap formed by a boulder close to the cliff. The boulders are scattered down to the north-northeast from this point.

Stage Boulder ▼

You will see this boulder out to the north once you pass the gap. It is characterized by a bulging east face that has a horizontal crack running across its upper section.

1. Exit Stage Left V2 Climb from down low over the bulge on the far-left side of the east face.

2. Exit Stage Right V3 Same as *Exit Stage Left* start, but exit up and right.

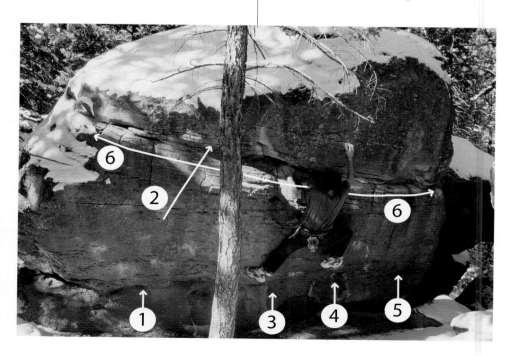

3. Up Staged V2 Climb up the middle of the east face.

4. Center Stage V2 Climb up just right of the middle of the east face.

5. Back Stage V0 Climb up the far-right side of the east face.

6. Hold Up Traverse V4 Traverse the easy face in any direction.

Fountain Lip Blocks ▼

These blocks are 30 feet downslope to the northeast of Stage Boulder. Two blocks, one leaning up against the other, characterize this group of blocks.

1. Fountain Lip Traverse V3 Climb the right-leaning arête of the west side of the north block.

2. Cave Route Direct V6 Climb out the overhang within the cave on the north block.

3. Toy Slab V0 Climb up the north-facing slab of the south block.

4. Toy Arête V1 Climb up the northwest arête of the south block.

Pac Man Rock

This rock is behind Fountain Lip Blocks, up to the southeast.

1. Rattled V3 From down low on the southwest side, climb the bulge to the top.

To Dungeon Area

Rim Rock Trail

Falls Wall

Buoux Block

North Sentry Block

Hank's Block

To St. Patrick's Area

Plate Rock

Orange Boulder

South Sentry Block

To Nine Lives Area

To Falls

Central City

This area encompasses several independent areas on the massive boulder-and-block slope on the east side of the canyon. The areas described are found to the north and south of the central Big Blocks Area. Drive approximately 1 mile from the east entrance station and park at the Falls trailhead on the left. Hike east down the trail and then south along the creekside trail, just past the wooden fence. Look for the waterfall above the creek and cross over its top to the other side.

Scramble down a short slope then up a gully to a faint north-south trail. Go straight up the slope to reach the Big Blocks Area. There are three prominent blocks. Two of them are next to each other (North Sentry Block and South Sentry Block), with the biggest of the three located up and behind these blocks. Buoux Block is named for its pocketed overhanging west face, which has good topropes on its sides. You will find anchors on top.

For the Saint Patrick's Day Area, you may continue south for several hundred yards past the Falls Wall along the base of the east rim, or you may continue on the Falls Trail along the creek up to the dam and then upslope to the northeast on a trail that leads to the east rim. The area is then just left of where the trail heads to the top of the rim.

For the Nine Lives Area, head north from the lower Big Blocks Area for approximately ten minutes. Just above the muddy creek bank, you will see a large block sitting just upslope. For Mini-Cliff, Scary Monster, Roof Pebble, or Dungeon, hike upslope from Buoux Block to the base of the wall and follow the base north for five to ten minutes, past the large overhangs that jut out of the cliff, to a lengthy wall with a perfect landing below. Scary Monsters is below the wall, down through the scrub oak. For the Dungeon Area, hike to the top of the cliff from Mini-Cliff, walk the rim to the north, and then head out west off the trail to a crevasse in the cliff band.

Big Blocks Area

After crossing the creek, head upslope toward the big block that has a prominent crack splitting its west face. The boulders and blocks are in close proximity to this landmark block.

North Sentry Block ▲

This is the northernmost block. A finger crack splits its west face.

1. Fingers V3 (hb) Climb the finger/hand crack on the west face.

2. Sentry Traverse V8 Traverse from the crack around the whole block ending at the crack.

South Sentry Block

This block is located due south of North Sentry Block.

1. South Sentry V? Climb up the right side of the west face.

Buoux Block

This massive block is located upslope to the east, down below the Falls Wall cliff band. It is characterized by a severely overhanging pocketed west face. Several toprope problems have been done on this face. Other slab problems can be done around its lower angled sides. Anchors on top.

1. Block Traverse V8 Traverse from the south side of the block around to the left, across the west face to the leaning crack system, which fades at the northwest corner.

2. Crack Traverse V3 Traverse the crack on the west face from right to left.

Central City South

These boulder and blocks are located to the right (south) of the Big Blocks Area of Central City.

Hank's Block ◄

This leaning block is located in the scrub oak near the upper cliff band, about 100 feet up-slope to the southeast of Buoux Block.

1. Hankenstein V5 Climb the west face up and right.

Hanky Panky Boulder ▼

This boulder is located downslope from Hank's Block.

1. Hanky Panky V2 Climb the north face of the boulder.

Orange Boulder ▲

This boulder is downslope to the southwest of Buoux Block. Descend about 150 feet to the large boulder.

1. Orangina V1 (hb) Climb up the center of the south face.

2. Orangeman Right V2 Climb up and right from *Orangina*.

Plate Rock ▶

This rock is across and to the south of Orange Boulder.

1. Highyeyah V2 (hb) Climb up the west side through a dished hold face.

2. The Tep V1 (hb) Climb the face right of the slot to the top.

3. Mumble V4 (hb) Climb the south face right of the arête on big pebbles.

4. Flakes V2 Climb up the flakes face on the south face.

5. North Roof V4 Climb over the roof on the north face.

Despicable Boulder ▲

This leaning block with a tree in front of it is downslope about 100 feet from Plate Rock.

1. Despicable Man V4 (hb) Climb the left side of the southwest face, past the horizontal break.

2. Dynasty V2 Dyno up from the whitened flake on the right side of the southwest face.

Falls Wall Far-Right Area

These fun problems are 200 yards to the right of Falls Wall and offer great pebble climbing at its base.

Blackened Bulge ▶

This pebbled bulge is on the right side of the wall, right of a cave slot, and climbs the wide black streak.

1. Wide Black Streak V1 Climb up the pebbles to the break.

Tandem Wall

This wall is just around the corner from Blackened Bulge.

1. Thin Black Streak V2 Climb from down low up the thin black streak, utilizing the pebble to the break.

St. Patrick's Day Area

To locate this fine area, hike several hundred yards southeast from the Big Blocks Area, past the far-right end of Falls Wall, continuing south. The boulders and blocks are at the base of the east rim and begin at a point where the rim breaks and curves around east and then continues south. The stretch of rock continues south and then hooks east, to the far-west end of the inner canyon. You will find a trail that leads up from the dam at the far-south end of the area. Good problems abound.

The Tear Drops

These are the first prominent blocks you will encounter in the St. Patrick's Day Area and are characterized by steep south and east faces with slabby tops.

Solar Diamond Block

This rock has a diamond-shaped top. It offers steep face problems on its south and east sides, behind the trees.

1. The Solar Collector V3 Climb up the south face.

2. Solar Power V4 Climb up the east face.

Tear Drop Block

This slabby top block is found just above Solar Diamond Block, up toward the ridgetop.

1. Tear Drop Face V3 Climb up the right side of the east face, up the clean, sheer section.

Dihedraled Wall ▲

Hike 75 feet south of Tear Drop Block, until you see this cornered section of wall.

1. The Face V2 Climb up the middle of the west face, left of the dihedral.

2. The Corner V1 Climb up the prominent dihedral.

3. The Pillar V4 Climb up the face and arête right of *The Corner.*

4. The Overhang V5 Climb up and out the overhang, out the block just left of *The Pillar.*

Smooth Bulged Boulder ▲

This boulder is to the right of Dihedraled Wall.

1. Smooth Bulge V3 Climb out the bulges on the north side.

2. The Prow V1 Climb up the northwest prow of the boulder.

St. Pat's Boulder ▲

This boulder is 50 feet south of Smooth Bulged Boulder, at the base of the cliff.

1. Shamrocker V4 Climb up the middle of the south face.

St. Pat's Corridor

This corridor of rock is 50 feet south of St. Pat's Boulder. It is characterized by a highball block on the east, an overhanging boulder on the north, a low-angled slab on the west, and a block on the south.

East Boulder

This boulder is on the east end of the corridor.

1. Under Tuck V3 Climb from down low, out the overhang on the south side of the boulder.

Sunny Block ▲

This large block makes up the east wall of the corridor. Many vertical challenges abound across its west face.

1. Sunshine V2 (hb) Climb the edges and crystals up the left side of the west face.

2. Sun Tan V2 (hb) Climb up the middle of the west face.

3. Sunnyside V2 Climb up the right side of the west face.

Proud Block ▲

This block is located at the south end of the corridor.

1. Proud Face V2 Climb up the middle of the east face.

2. Proud Prow V2 Climb up the prow on the northwest corner.

Central City North

These boulders and blocks are located north of the Big Blocks Area of Central City.

Mini-Cliff Area

From Buoux Block, head north at the base of the cliff band for about ten minutes; you will pass several gaps that lead up to the rim. Continue north along the cliff base, until you reach Mini-Cliff, which is characterized by an extensive west-facing vertical wall that has cracks and face routes.

Mini-Cliff ▲

1. Mini-Me V3 Climb up the far-right side of the wall, utilizing pebbles and finger holes.

2. Mini-You V1 Climb the crack on the right side of the wall.

3. Mini-Might V4 (hb) Climb the face with good pockets to slopers right of the tree.

4. Huge V4 (hb) Climb the face just left of the tree.

5. Donkey D V6 Climb up to the right of the black streak utilizing small pockets.

6. Little D V3 (hb) Climb up the black streak utilizing the small pebbles.

7. Big V0 Climb the left side of black streak utilizing huecos.

8. Biggy V0 Climb up the far-left side of the west face through big pockets right of the wide crack.

Dungeon Area

From Mini-Cliff, head up to the ridge gap, go to the rim, and head north for a few minutes down the Rim Rock Trail. At the point where the trail bends slightly east, hike west toward the slabs until you see a crevassed area. This is a small, secluded canyon that has blocks forming its side walls. The corridors within lead deep into caves. As you climb the problems, you can stem to the side walls to escape, if desired.

Dungeon Block ▲

This large block, sitting in the hole of the corridor, has a nice south wall with good problems.

1. The Dungeon V2 (hb) Climb the right side of the south face of the block.

2. Chains V3 (hb) Climb up the middle of the south face.

3. Bound V4 (hb) Climb the arête on the right side of the south face.

Nine Lives Area

This area is about five minutes north of the falls, below the Big Blocks Area of Central City. Hike north just above the mud-cliff banks of Cherry Creek until you see the first boulder upslope to the east.

The World's Sloppiest Boulder

This boulder is located just upslope to the east from the mud cliffs. It has a wavy, river-polished west face with sloper holds.

1. Wavy T V4 Traverse the west face from left to right.

2. Slopey Way V3 Climb the slopey west face just right of the crack.

Nine Lives Boulder

To find this boulder, hike 125 feet north of the World's Sloppiest Boulder. Nine Lives Boulder is 50 feet above the mud-cliffed creek on the east side. Hike about ten minutes from the falls, look upslope, and you will then see this large boulder, which has a nice west face.

1. Double Dick Dyno V6 (hb) Climb from the hueco to the corner in the center of the west face.

2. Tiny Tees V5 Climb the southwestern prow.

3. Southern Slim V1 (hb) Climb up the south face.

Pylon Block

This pillar of rock is 100 feet southeast of Nine Lives Boulder.

1. The Pillar V5 (hb) Climb the leaning north face, utilizing the pebbles.

White Boulder

To find this boulder, hike south along the creekside trail for ten minutes, passing the waterfall. You will see the boulder before the dam.

1. Bottom Up V2 Climb up the middle of the west face.

Note: The trail that heads northeast from the dam will take you to St. Pat's Corridor, the far-right (south) end of the St. Patrick's Day Area. Just before reaching the rim, cut out to the left (north) and wander around some interesting blocks of the corridor.

Inner Canyon Area

This extensive band of caves, boulders, and blocks is accessed from the east entrance via Highway 83 south of Franktown. Drive through the entrance station and park at the far-west end of the lot at the Canyon Point parking.

Hike down the Inner Canyon Trail, located to the northeast of the parking lot. Take this downslope into the canyon for a few minutes and cross the bridge.

The bouldering is located trailside as well as upslope to the north. For most of the bouldering, follow the trail west after the bridge.

Eastern World

These areas are located by heading east, west, or upslope to the north from the Inner Canyon Trail, north of the parking lot. The Cobble in a Blender is located at the top of the descent trail and is found by heading to the west along the shadowed south rim. The Cave Caves is located by crossing the bridge and heading upslope to the north and following the mini-cliff and blocked ridge base to the east around and above the big cave. Continue west down the trail and you will soon encounter the Phallic Spire, the Cigar, the Turd Ball Tiers and others described as follows.

Cobble in a Blender

To reach this rock from the parking area, cut off to the west at the point where you begin to descend into the canyon. Locate the base of the south rim and head west approximately 100 feet, to a notch that will allow you access down and west to a pile of trees and boulders.

1. Cobble in a Blender V? Traverse the crystalline wall from left to right, finishing up close to the tree.

The Cave Caves

This shelf of blocks is located across the canyon, just below the north rim and northwest of the bridge crossing. From the bridge, scramble upslope toward the north rim for the big cave. Hike west across the base of the cave and then head up to the shelf with the blocks above.

1. Jonah and the Whale V5 Traverse the southwest portion of the chambers behind the blocks. This route follows a horizontal-ledge system up and around to its top.

Western World

These are the caves, boulders, and blocks that are west and northwest of the bridge crossing. This area, loaded with problems, is pleasant any time of year.

Phallic Spire

This prominent, somewhat highball spire full of crystals and pockets sits trailside, just west of the bridge crossing.

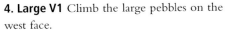

4. Large V1 Climb the large pebbles on the west face.

5. Circumcrack V1 Climb the crack on the left side of the south face.

6. Pebble Pussy V2 Climb the face just right of *Circumcrack,* utilizing the pebbles.

7. Pocket Rocket V1 Climb the pockets on the right side of the south face.

The Cigar

This cigar-shaped rock, approximately 200 yards west of the bridge past Phallic Spire, is located upslope through the brush to the northeast. It leans up against the north rim.

Traverse Wall

This west-facing wall is located just east of the Cigar.

1. Boner V2 (hb) Climb the southeastern prow of the spire.

2. Hard Up V1 (hb) Climb the pebbles and pockets up the center of the east side.

3. The Vein V0 (hb) Climb the north-facing crack.

Turd Ball Tiers

This tiered outcrop is just above an array of large boulders. To find it, hike about five minutes farther west down the Inner Canyon Trail, past two sets of wood stairs west of Phallic Spire. At the second set of wooden stairs, look upslope to the north and you will see these large boulders just below the cliff band. Hike upslope through the scrub and then beyond to the tiers.

Pocket Rocket Boulder ▲

This boulder, located within the boulderfield below the tiers to the southwest, has a steep north face.

1. Pocket Pussy V5 Climb the pocketed north face.

Turd Ball Une

This is a black–faced wall with large pebbles on its west face.

1. Turd Ball Une V2 (hb) Climb from large pebbles up the blackened west face.

Turd Ball Deux

This wall is located just above and to the left of Turd Ball Une. It has a gap on its west face.

1. Une V3 Climb the black streak in the center of the west face.

2. Deux V2 Climb the face to the right of the prow up to the large pocket.

Turd Ball Trois

This wall is located just east of Turd Ball Deux and has two prominent cracks on its elongated west face. There is a left, middle,

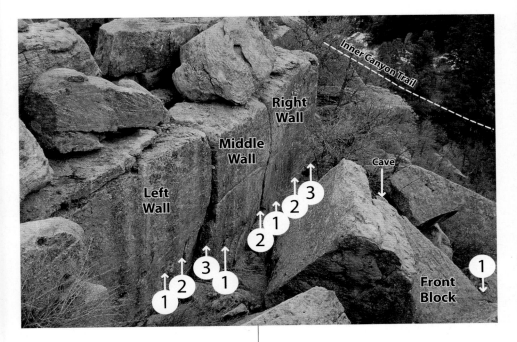

and right wall, as well as a separate block that sits in front.

Front Block

This block, located in front of Turd Ball Trois, has a nice leaning arête on its west side.

1. Merde Arête V4 Climb up the west-facing leaning arête.

Left Wall

1. Sloppea V2 Climb up the center of the face left of the crack.

2. Perpock V3 Climb the face left of the crack.

3. Give Me a Break V2 Climb the face to the right of the crack up to the break.

Middle Wall

This is the centerpiece of Turd Ball Trois, with many large crystals on the left side of its west face.

1. Midearth V3 Climb the face right of the southern crack to the big pebbles.

2. Poser V2 Climb the right side of the west face left of the prow.

Right Wall

This section is on the far right of Turd Ball Trois wall. It has lots of small pockets and pebbles lining its west face.

1. Small Wall Tim V3 Climb up the left side of this section.

2. Trickster's Wall V2 Climb up the middle of the west face, utilizing small features.

3. Snob Face V1 Climb the right side of the west face.

Tim's Boulder

Located directly below the power lines atop the north rim, this boulder has a white over-hanging southwest face with great problems.

From the Turd Ball Tiers outcrop, continue west along the Inner Canyon Trail until you see the tension wires overhead. Scramble upslope toward the north rim and locate the overhang below the ridgeline.

1. Tiger Woods V7 Climb out the left side of the overhanging southwest cave.

2. Pain V5 Climb out the center of the cave to a horizontal break.

3. Flakes of Wrath V3 Climb out the right side of the cave to a flake system.

Prow Boulder ▼

From Tim's Boulder continue a short way west along the Inner Canyon Trail. When you come to a set of wooden stairs, hike upslope from the upper set of stairs. You will come first to a long wall, appropriately named the Long Wall. Hike up and around to the right, heading for the north rim (the Corridor is just up and left behind the Long Wall), past a corner to this white-prowed boulder.

1. Proud Pile V2 Climb the crack on the right side of the southwest face.

2. Pile Proud V4 (hb) Climb the face right of the corner.

3. Kind Hole V1 (hb) Climb the crystals out over the bulge on the far-right side of the southwest face.

The Corridor

From the wooden stairs along the Inner Canyon Trail, hike up to the Long Wall. Head around and up to the right and follow the wall around to the left, behind and into a corridor. This area highlights the turning point, where the north rim takes a concave bend somewhat eastward (and is full of cave slots such as the Berthoud Cave) before connecting back to the north. The areas offer excellent vertical face problems on tanned green rock walls. Problems surrounding the Corridor's parameter are also good endeavors.

Titanic Block

This huge, prominent block dominates the area with a blackened west overhang. Many quality problems are found around this block's parameters.

1. Cave Blender V6 (hb) Climb within the cave eventually ascending the white face.

2. Kk Kay V5 Climb the scoop on the south face.

3. Emperor V6 (hb) Climb up the west face, utilizing the crack to the hole.

4. Monkey Pit V6 (hb) Climb out the pit to the arête, out right to pockets.

5. Monkey Slick V9 Climb out from the eastern cave.

6. Monkey Funky V3 Climb to the arête on the left, then out.

The Boxcar (East Face)

Titanic Block

Inner Canyon Trail

1

2

South Entrance

The Corridor

The Boxcar of Castlewood

This prominent block outlines the west side of the Corridor.

1. Scott's Wall V3 (hb) Climb the lightened black streak on the left side of the west face.

2. Scott's Folly V1 Climb up just left of the middle of the east face in the wide blackened drop.

Creekside Blocks

From the Corridor approach on the Inner Canyon Trail, head southwest across the creek to a nice set of white creek–polished blocks sitting in the meadow.

Meadow Boulder

This isolated boulder is south of the block pile in the meadow.

1. Meadow Arête V2 Climb the southwestern arête.

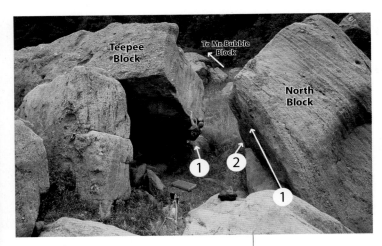

Teepee Block

This is the southern boulder of two blocks that lean up against each other. It has an overhanging west face that forms a tunnel apex.

1. TP V4 Climb up the leaning crack to the corner on the north face.

North Block

This is the block west of Teepee Block.

1. Flake It V1 Climb the large flake on the left side of the east face.

2. Corn V1 Climb up to the corner on the east face.

Mr. Bubble Block ▼

This is an interesting pebble-filled overhanging block that sits within the forest, southeast of Meadow Boulder. It has an east overhang with bowling-ball-size pebbles welded tuff.

1. The Shot Put V3 Climb up to the top from the large pebbles.

2. Bowling Ball Traverse V3 Traverse from left to right.

Trailside Boulders

These creek-washed rocks are located on the slope right of the trail. From the Corridor approach, continue west on the Inner Canyon Trail.

Trail Cube

This block is located upslope to the right, before the wooden stairs on the Inner Canyon Trail. It is characterized by a right-leaning crack on its west face.

1. Cubian V3 Climb the far-left side of the west face,

2. Trail It V1 Climb up the center of the west face left of the crack.

3. Cubian V2 Climb the face just right of the leaning crack.

Trailer Block ▼

This long-faced boulder sits on the right side of the trail as you continue west on the Inner Canyon Trail. You can see it past the wooden stairs, across and on the slope from the red footbridge.

1. Smooth V2 Climb the left side of the south face using the pie plates.

2. Middlemania V4 Climb up the middle of the south face.

Buddha and Berthoud Caves Area

This is an excellent south-facing cave area full of overhanging walls and roofs. It is hidden behind the trees and scrub, making it an excellent secluded workout area. Many of the problems here can be strenuous and crimpy at times. From the Inner Canyon Trail, approximately 350 feet beyond Trailer Block and past the meadow, ascend the slope. Passing a slab on the north, aim for a large dead tree up on the cliff above. The caves are below this dead tree to the left. Just before reaching the caves, you will come across a

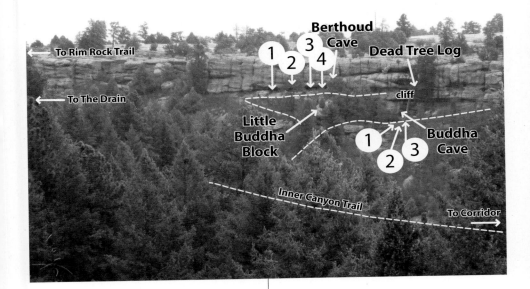

large block with an intriguing overhanging south face.

Little Buddha Block ▶

This large cube is just southwest of Buddha Cave. It is characterized by a classic problem up the center of its south face.

1. Solid Ways V2 Climb the middle of the west face.

2. Deuto's Face V? Climb the west face just left of the southwest corner.

3. Monkey Shots V7 Climb the southwestern arête.

4. Crystal Method V9 (hb) Climb up the center of the south face.

5. JT's Arête (hb) Climb the southeast arête of the block.

6. Deuto's Traverse V5 Traverse from the far-right side of the south face, across to the left, and around to the northwest corner.

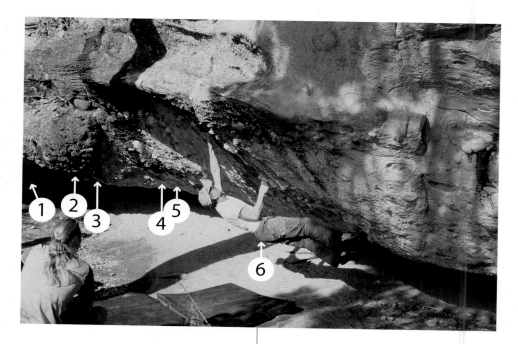

Buddha Cave ▲

This huge, roofed cave offers many difficult problems out its belly. It is located up to the northeast of Little Buddha Block. This is the easternmost slot of the caves, with more moderate overhangs compared to Berthoud Cave to the west.

1. The Buddha V4 Climb from the oval hueco and prow out to the corner on the far-left side of the cave.

2. Ned's Corner V5 Climb the overhang a few feet right of the latter to pebbles and corner.

3. Rounded Prow V2 Climb sloper prow from the pocket to the pebbles.

4. Sometimes Wet V2 Climb the black streak right of the drain.

5. Phil's Folly V5 Climb from the right side of the black streak to the pebble.

6. Butt Crystal V3 Climb from the horizontal pocket to a horn and pebble.

7. Swirly Face V3 Climb from the pillar to good holes.

Berthoud Cave ▲

This cave slot is up and around to the west of Buddha Cave. It has a good concentration of extreme problems ranging from V4 to V9.

1. After Berthoud V6 Climb from the large hueco on the left side of the cave out to the pod, then out left to the large pebble at the lip.

2. Giving Berthoud V8 Climb from deep in the cave out from the large hueco to the pod and then the crystal horizontal.

3. Berthoud Canal V5 Climb out the scooped section on the right side of the cave to the pockets and lip.

4. Berthoud Hips V7 Climb the overhanging buttress, right of the black crack, from the pod to crystals.

The Drain

This slot is characterized by overhanging, pebbled, and jugged features with a large visor that keeps the place dry even in the worst weather. The problems range from moderate to difficult. Hike farther west on the Inner Canyon Trail and before the bridge over the creek, head upslope to the north, aiming for the massive roof on the rim. The slot is located beneath the roof.

1. You Pay, Hot Tea V4 Climb from choppy landing out to the lip.

2. The Drain V2 Climb the good holds out the cave at a point where the ground below is flat.

3. The Full Drain V7 Traverse the entire slot utilizing pebbles, pockets, jugs, and huecos from right to left.

31 DEVIL'S HEAD BOULDERS

See map on page 356.

The Devil's Head Boulders are located along Rampart Range Road, a lengthy dirt road that runs north-south along the Rampart Mountain Range. Many boulders are scattered about. Several of the boulders are hidden in the forested sides of the road—some very close by, others involve a hike.

Directions: From Denver, head south on I-25 and exit at Happy Canyon Road (exit 187). Follow Happy Canyon Road west toward Highway 85. Then head west on Highway 85, toward the town of Sedalia, approximately 5.5 miles. In Sedalia, locate Jarre Canyon Road (Highway 67) and follow it southwest toward Pine Nook.

Approximately 1.5 miles past the Pine Nook junction, locate Rampart Range Road (Forest Road 300) and head left (south) off Highway 67. Rampart Range Road will lead you south, eventually to Woodland Park, which is west of Colorado Springs. The Devil's Head Boulders are located just east off the road, before the entrance to Devil's Head Campground; the rocks extend downslope to the southeast from there. Locate the road that leads to the campground and park on the left side of the road before the campground entrance.

Devil Duds

This first set of boulders is located about 100 feet east from the parking pull off. The boulder is mostly smooth with tiny edges, which makes for good sequences.

Devil's Dud Boulder ▼

Hike out to the clump of obvious boulder in the distance and you will see this round boulder that has a bulging east face.

1. Devil's in Dust V4 Climb up the left side of the southern prow.

2. Devil's Food V3 Climb the left side of the east face.

3. Devious V6 Climb up the middle of the east face.

4. Dirt Devil V5 Climb up right of center.

Dot Boulder ▼

This boulder is immediately south of Devil's Dud Boulder.

1. One Dot V3 Climb up the center of the north face.

2. Two Dot V3 Climb up the left side of the west face.

Divot Boulder

To find this boulder, hike northeast from Dot Boulder.

1. Divot V2 Climb up to the left of the slash.

2. The Slash V0 Climb up to the slash on the right side.

Gray Dome Boulder

This boulder is located across the road and parking to the west.

1. Shiny Slab V0–V3 Climb up the east-facing slab.

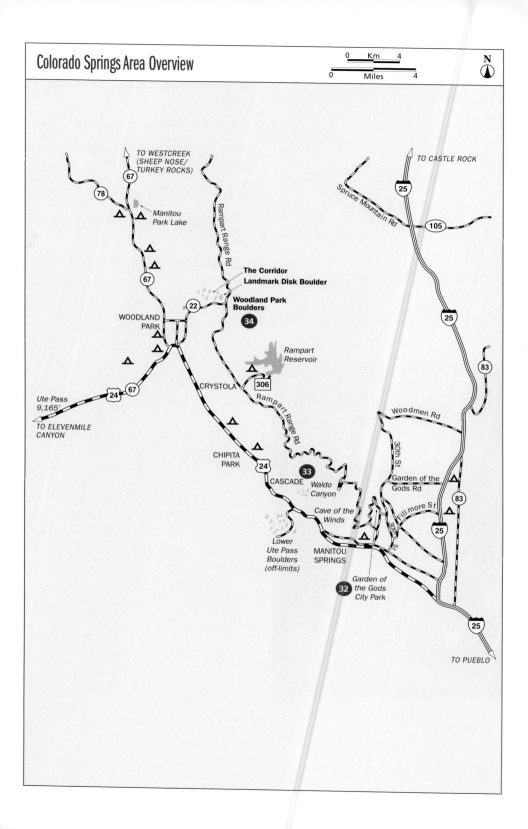

Colorado Springs Area Overview

0   Km   4

0   Miles   4

N

TO WESTCREEK
(SHEEP NOSE/
TURKEY ROCKS)

67

78

*Manitou
Park Lake*

Rampart Range Rd

67

22

The Corridor
Landmark Disk Boulder

Woodland Park
Boulders

34

WOODLAND
PARK

*Rampart
Reservoir*

CRYSTOLA

306

Rampart Range Rd

*Ute Pass
9,165*

24 67

TO ELEVENMILE
CANYON

CHIPITA
PARK

24

CASCADE

33

*Waldo
Canyon*

*Cave of the
Winds*

*Lower
Ute Pass
Boulders
(off-limits)*

MANITOU
SPRINGS

32

*Garden of
the Gods
City Park*

TO CASTLE ROCK

25

Spruce Mountain Rd

105

25

83

Woodmen Rd

30th St

Garden of the
Gods Rd

83

Fillmore St

30th St

25

25

TO PUEBLO

COLORADO SPRINGS AREA
32 GARDEN OF THE GODS

This soft sandstone area is easy to get to from northwestern Colorado Springs. The solid lower walls of the North and South Gateway Rocks offer some great traversing. The Cathedral Rock Area's east-side boulderfield, the Snake Pit, and the Gravity Slope offer good Dakota sandstone and problems with good landings. There are nice surroundings, with spires and towers throughout the city park. A majestic view of Pike's Peak to the southwest tops it off.

Directions: From Interstate 25 take the Garden of the Gods Road (exit 146) west. Follow this to a left onto 30th Street, which will take you to the entrance of the park.

North Gateway Rock

Within the park, two red sandstone formations dominate the skyline: North Gateway Rock to the north and South Gateway Rock to the south. The bouldering for North Gateway Rock is located on the west side. The rock is characterized by a pocket/holed west face just off the ground. Park at a large lot to the northeast and walk south around to the west side.

The Intermediate Area

This area is located on the right side of the west-facing wall. It offers frictiony pocket climbing above a sand landing.

1. Intermediate Traverse V1 Traverse the wall from the far right to the left.

The Blowouts

This is the pocketed/bucket wall on the left side, separated by a caved section. Chalk marks the traverse walls. One traverse goes to the left of the cave; the other goes to the right. Many endless variations from V0 to V11 are found here.

1. The Blowout V4 Traverse out the cave to the right on good pockets.

2. Blown Away V10 Traverse out left from the cave, tiling the smallest of pockets and holds.

South Gateway Rock

This is the other prominent red sandstone formation. You can find and access a hidden gap on its northeast side. Park in the lot across from North Gateway Rock and hike southeast down a cement trail between the two rocks. Hike approximately 175 feet south toward South Gateway Rock, through the bush to the gap. You can traverse the nice east-facing wall.

Garden of the Gods

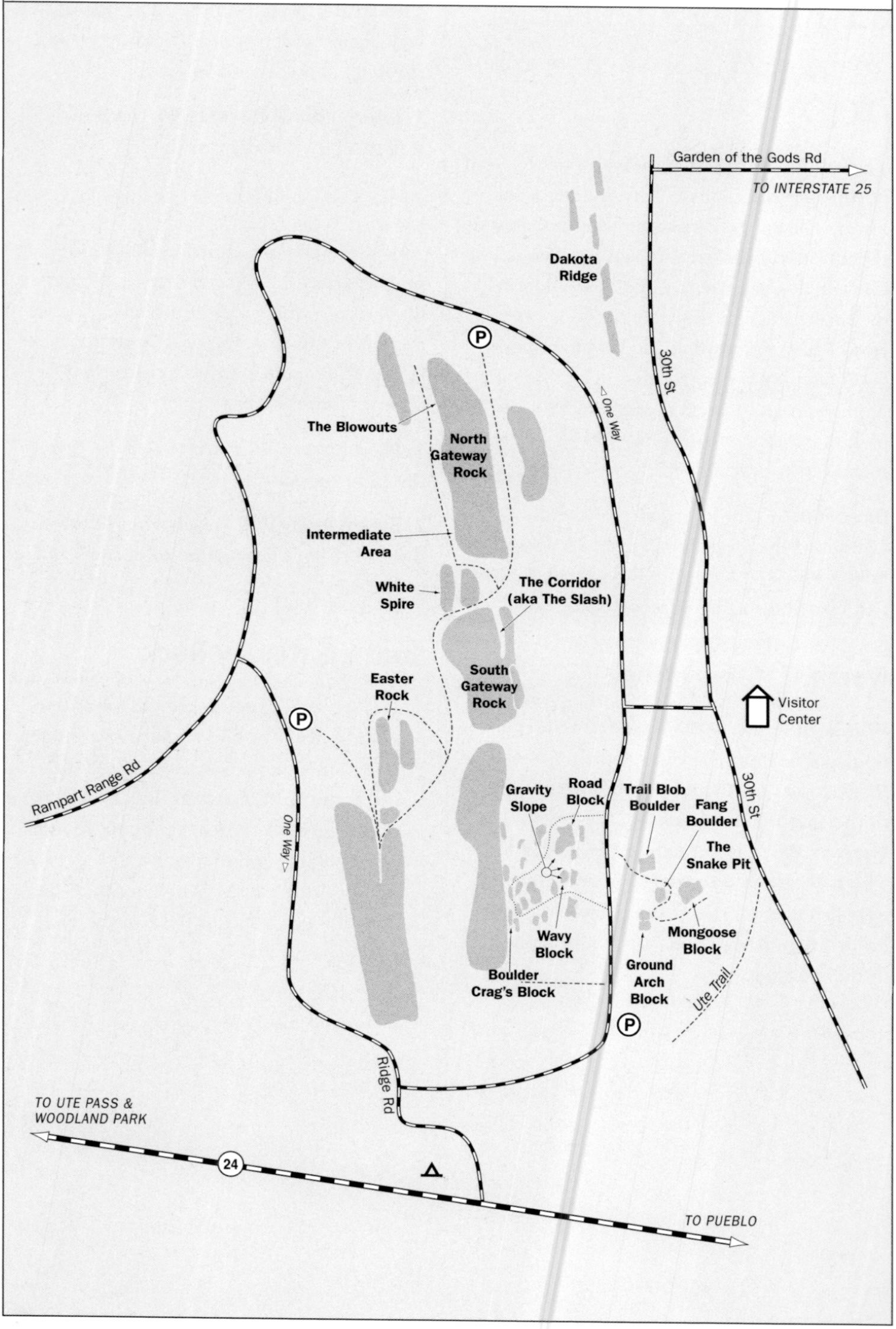

N

Garden of the Gods Rd

TO INTERSTATE 25

Dakota Ridge

30th St

One Way

P

The Blowouts

North Gateway Rock

Intermediate Area

White Spire

The Corridor (aka The Slash)

Easter Rock

South Gateway Rock

P

Rampart Range Rd

One Way

Visitor Center

30th St

Gravity Slope

Road Block

Trail Blob Boulder

Fang Boulder

The Snake Pit

Wavy Block

Ground Arch Block

Mongoose Block

Boulder Crag's Block

Ute Trail

P

Ridge Rd

TO UTE PASS & WOODLAND PARK

24

TO PUEBLO

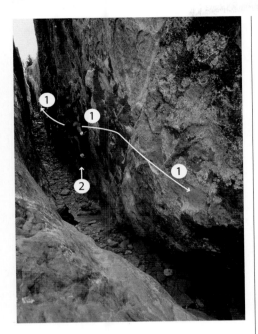

The Corridor ▲

1. The Corridor V4 Traverse across the entirety of the east wall of the gap.

2. The Alley V3 Climb up the middle of the east face of the corridor. Climb up to a safe height, then down. Other problems within the V0–V6 range can also be found here.

Cathedral Rock Area (aka Kindergarten Rock or Gray Rock)

This whitish gray formation with a pointy summit is located southeast of South Gateway Rock. On its eastern slopes you will find the Gravity Slope boulders and the Snake Pit. To find the area's parking lot, drive around the one-way loop and continue south from the main parking lot. Follow the road to the intersection at Ridge Road and head left, back up north, and park at the large parking area on the right. Hike north for

about five to ten minutes, until you see the line of boulders and blocks that come off the eastern slopes of the rock formation. The Gravity Slope boulders are on the left side of the road; the Snake Pit is on the right.

The Snake Pit

Locate the fall line of rock off Kindergarten Rock's eastern slope and follow it down to the right (east) side of the road. Here you will find the Snake Pit, the area's main draw. It has an awesome set of Dakota sandstone blocks with good landings and is just up and west of the Ute Trail, which travels north-south from the east side of the road.

Mongoose Block

This is the largest of the Snake Pit blocks and is the farthest east from the road, just west of the infamous Ute Trail. There are many sit-down starts, which add difficulty to these problems.

1. Northwest Sit V3 Climb from down low up the northwest face's left side.

2. The Corners V0 Climb the corners of the northwest corner.

3. Southwest Face V1 Climb the far-left side of the southwest face.

4. SW Right V2 Climb the left side of the southwest face, right of *Southwest Face*.

5. SW Center V2 Climb up the center of the southwest face.

6. SW Right V0 Climb the right side of the southwest face.

7. Nose Lunge V4 Dynamic move from off the southwest arête to top.

8. South Nose V2 Climb up the southwest arête.

9. SE Face V0 Climb up the overhanging southeast face.

10. SE Traverse V3 Traverse the southeast face.

Ground Arch Block

This block is located west of the Mongoose Block, just southwest of the Fang Boulder. A crack splits it. Many sit-down starts make this block difficult.

1. East Wall V0 Climb the east face.

2. The Crack V0 Climb the crack on the east face.

3. Flake Up V0 Climb the flake system on the west face.

4. Around the Block V3 Traverse around the entire block.

Fang Boulder

This boulder is just west of Mongoose Block.

1. Arêter V2 Climb up the southeastern arête.

2. East Wall V3 Climb up the center of the east face.

3. Arêteer V1 Climb the northeastern arête.

Trail Blob Boulder

This rather large boulder is northwest of Mongoose Block. It is disguised by thick brush. A traverse of its south and east faces is the draw.

1. Flato V1 Climb the left side of the southeast face.

2. Blob Traverse V? Traverse from the far-left side of the south face, across and around to the far-right side of the south face.

3. Ute Trail Traverse V6 Traverse from the right side of the east face to the left.

4. Sloper Dyno V5 Dyno off the slopers up to the top of the east face.

Gravity Slope

This fall line of rock is on the left (west) side of the road. The rocks extend from the base of the east-facing wall downslope to the road.

Wavy Block

This block is upslope to the west of the road, past a platform rock and into a slot. It has a wavy-looking east face.

1. Wavy Wall V0 Climb up the steep east face.

Boulder Crag's Block

This block is upslope to the west, just below Cathedral Rock's east face. It is left of the cone-shaped rock that has a nice east slab.

1. Crag's Traverse V3 Traverse the wall from left to right.

2. Crag's Face V0 Climb up the south face of the block.

3. Foolish Crag V0 Climb the right side of the east face.

Road Block

This nice block is due north of Gravity Slope's lower blocks. From Wavy Block, hike several yards north and you will see this block just above the road's western slope.

1. Road Rage V1 Climb the right side of the north face.

2. Serpent V1 Climb up the left side of the north face.

3. Road Runner V0 Climb the right side of the east face.

33 UTE PASS

See map on page 386.

This is an extensive area with a huge amount of varied granite boulders and blocks. The numerous areas are found along Highway 24 as it makes its way up Ute Pass. Some areas, such as the lower original Ute Pass Boulders (covered in the old Chockstone book *Colorado Front Range Bouldering: Southern Areas*), have been off-limits for some time now. But the boulder-filled slopes across the road, on the slopes of Waldo Canyon, are worthwhile. Continue up the pass and you will find many other areas that have been developed more recently. The rock offers an endless variety of solid crystalline faces, cracks, arêtes, corners, and overhangs, with a rock texture and type similar to the Buttermilks of California. You will find several campgrounds as you head up the pass. Most of the areas are located on the left (south) side of the highway, with only a few on the right (north) side.

Directions: From I-25 in Colorado Springs take exit 141 onto Highway 24. Head west on Highway 24 toward Manitou Springs. Go a few miles past Manitou Springs, until you reach the Waldo Canyon trailhead. Park on the right side of the highway. The old area (closed) is located southwest across the busy highway. The Waldo Canyon area is located upslope to the north.

Waldo Canyon

Head northeast on the trail from the Waldo Canyon parking lot, following it up and around to the north. The boulders are up on the ridgeline to the northwest, at a point on the trail where they are clearly seen. Hike up to the large colorful duds of crystalline granite. Major Dud is one of the best.

34 WOODLAND PARK

This enjoyable, yet sharp-edged area offers a good number of boulders and blocks that line the slopes of Rampart Range Road just northeast of the town of Woodland Park.

Directions: From Colorado Springs, take Highway 24 west to Woodland Park. Get off on Baldwin Street and go north. The road turns into County Road 22 and then Rampart Range Road. Drive up the road approximately 3.5 miles, until you see Landmark Disk Boulder up on the left. Park below the boulder and hike west, past the boulder about 250 feet, to the pillar-shaped blocks of the Corridor. You can also get to this area by heading south on Rampart Range Road from the Devil's Head Boulders.

Landmark Disk Boulder

You can see this boulder from the parking area upslope to the west. It is characterized by a disk-shaped slice of rock that angles atop a lower bump and a boulder.

1. The Diskette V0 Climb up the right-leaning edge of the disk's north side.

2. Support Slab V0 Climb up the middle of the support boulders west side.

The Corridor

Hike southwest up the trail about 250 feet to this pillared monument. Walk through the small canyon, which has Corridor Block on the right-hand side and Gargoyle Rock and Triathlon Block on its left-hand side.

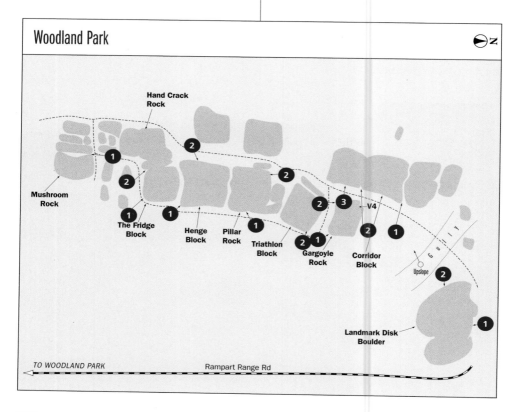

Woodland Park

Hand Crack Rock

Mushroom Rock

The Fridge Block

Henge Block

Pillar Rock

Triathlon Block

Gargoyle Rock

Corridor Block

Upslope

Landmark Disk Boulder

TO WOODLAND PARK

Rampart Range Rd

Corridor Block

This is the first block on the right side of the trail. It is characterized by two splitter cracks on the southeast side, creating three independent pillar-like sections.

1. The Pill V0 Climb the far-right finger crack.

2. The Thrill V1 Climb the far-left finger/hand crack.

3. The Mill V0 (hb) Climb the flake system just left of *The Thrill*.

Gargoyle Rock

Two rocks are located across from Corridor Block. Gargoyle Rock is the one on the left (north) side.

1. Yellow Wall V4 Climb the southeast arête.

2. Soleus Arête V4 Climb the northwest arête.

Triathlon Block

This block is to the right (south) of Gargoyle Rock.

1. Black Dihedral V? Climb the dark dihedral utilizing the arête.

2. Triathlete Arête V6 Climb the northeast arête.

3. Lay Up V2 Climb the layback crack on the southeast corner, where the two rocks meet.

Pillar Rock

This rock is somewhat connected to Triathlon Block by some small boulders.

1. Sit Crack V2 Climb from down low up the angling crack on the east face.

2. North Face Right V3 Climb the thin face on the right side of the north face.

Henge Block

This block is separated from Pillar Rock by only a small gap on the north side.

1. Katie's Face V5 Climb the far-right side of the south face, utilizing the arête.

2. The Henge V2 (hb) Climb up the west face.

The Fridge Block

This large block is just south of Henge Block and is separated into three sections by climbable cracks on its south face.

1. Katie's Arête V5 (hb) Highball up the southeast arête.

2. Cracker V0 Climb the far-left hand crack on the south face.

Mushroom Rock

This rock, south of the Fridge Block, has a nice roof on its north side.

1. Crackaroof V2 Climb the crack through the roof on the north face.

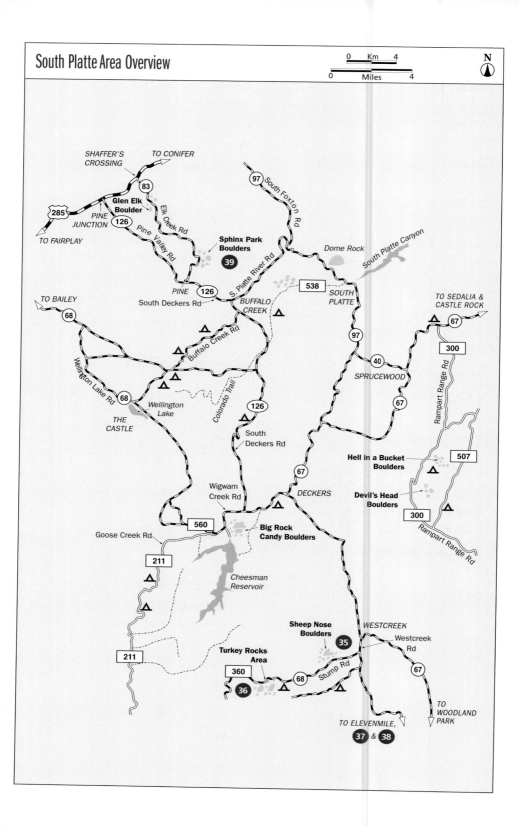

South Platte Area Overview

SOUTH PLATTE AREA

The South Platte offers a serene, somewhat secluded experience that is hard to beat. It is a complex area with granite boulders just about everywhere. The granite texture varies from bullet proof, to river polished, to crystalline, to blank or crumbly. The areas described here have an array of blocks and boulders that are usually spread about their larger formations. Areas such as Sheep Nose, Turkey Rock and Tail, Sphinx Park, Cynical Pinnacle, and Big Rock Candy Mountain are all worth visiting. All are accessed by traveling northwest of Woodland Park, up Highway 67 toward Westcreek, Dekkers, and beyond.

35 SHEEP NOSE BOULDERS

These boulders and blocks are on the southern slopes below the larger Sheep Nose formation. Granite ranging from 10 to 15 feet high is located about the forested slopes;

larger toprope blocks are closer to the main formation's base. You can access this complex of boulders via a nice trail system that heads up to the base of Sheep Nose. A wide variety of challenges await you, with crystal face cracks, corners, and arêtes. The infamous B1 Block (aka Air Jordan Block) is the area's gem, and many of the larger blocks have become reasonable highballs with stacks of pads for landing zones. Views of Pikes Peak also make this area breathtaking.

Directions: From Woodland Park and Highway 24, locate Highway 67 and head up to the right (north). Continue north on Highway 67 toward Westcreek. Once in Westcreek, drive to the stop sign and turn left (south) on Westcreek Road. Go 0.6 mile on Westcreek Road to a right on Stump Road (County Road 68). Follow CR 68 for 1.8 miles and park at a pull off on the right. Hike north up the broken road, past a fence to the trail, which is usually marked with a cairn. Hike up the trail for 10 minutes or so until you see the first boulders.

Sheep Nose East ▲

Slopes End Boulder

This is the first boulder you come across. It is characterized by its round shape and a crystal-lined water groove.

1. Scooper V0 Climb the groove on the southeast face.

Border Boulder ▲

This large boulder is located up the trail to the northwest of Sheep Nose East.

1. Border Face V4 (hb) Climb up the middle of the southwest face.

2. Border Prow V5 (hb) Climb up the prow on the right side of the southwest face.

Sheep Dud ▲

This nice boulder is located farther up the trail to the northwest of Border Boulder. You will find a layback flake on its west side.

1. The Flake Reach V2 Climb up the layback flake system on its west side.

Egg Drop Boulder ▼

This boulder is 20 feet upslope to the north of Sheep Dud.

1. Breaking Bulge V6 Climb up the left bulge of the south face.

Blank Block ▲

This sheer block is farther west from Sheep Dud.

1. Blank Arête V1 Climb up the west arête of the south face.

Slopes Beginning Boulder ▼

This boulder is just west of Blank Boulder. It marks the beginning of the old-area rocks. It has a horizontal crack on its cap.

1. Horizontal Central V3 Climb up the middle of the east face to the horizontal break.

Crystal's Boulder

This boulder is 100 feet upslope from Slopes Beginning Boulder. It. has a splitter crack on its north face.

1. Layback V4 Climb up the layaway on the right side of the east face.

2. Hand Crack V2 Climb the hand crack of the north face.

3. Higher V4 (hb) Climb up to the right of the flake system.

4. The Flake V3 (hb) Climb up the flake system on the left side of the boulder.

The Thumb

This boulder is upslope and 75 feet northwest of Slopes Beginning Boulder.

1. The Thumb V1 Climb up the southwest face.

Crack Boulder ▼

Hike 50 feet up the trail from the Thumb, until you see this rounded boulder with two splitter cracks on its south face.

1. Firecracker V4 Climb the crack on the left from down low.

2. Crank Crack V2 Climb up the crack to the right.

Moder Block ▼

Continue south approximately 50 feet from Crack Boulder, until you see this stumpy block.

1. Pyramid Flake V0 Climb up the flake on the west side.

2. Low Crack V1 Climb up the crack on the north face.

3. Undercling Traverse V1 Climb from the left side of the undercling, out right, then up.

Thinlay Boulder

This boulder is 30 feet south of Moder Block. A curving crack characterizes its southwest side.

1. Curving Crack V0 Climb the crack that curves from the south around to the west face.

2. Tree Pebbles V2 Climb to the left of the tree up the pebbly face.

The Fire Pit Area

This conglomeration of boulders and blocks is located west of the previously described boulders, below the talus pack. Hike west about 200 feet, until you see a boulder with a fire pit in close proximity.

Fire Pit Boulder

This boulder sits in close proximity to the fire pit.

1. Fire or Retire V4 Climb the overhanging, crimpy face on the right side of the south face, right of the fire pit.

2. Fire Pit Left V? Climb out the left side of the south face, utilizing a prow pinch.

Aside Block

This block is just west of Fire Pit Boulder. It has a crystal-filled east face.

1. Beer Jugs V0 Climb the jugs on the northeast face.

2. Crystal Seam V4 Climb up the southeast face, utilizing the crystals.

Slopey Top Block

This block is 30 feet northeast of Fire Pit Boulder. Its southwest side has a great mantle shelf.

1. Edge Pull V4 Climb up the arête on the southwest corner with a strenuous mantle up top.

Air Jordan Block (aka B1 Block) ▼

This block is a tall, perfect chuck of quality granite. It is a classic, and many boulderers seek it out. *Air Jordan* is a test piece for its grade, with a highball topout above a good landing. Hike about 100 feet slightly upslope to the northwest of Fire Pit Boulder, to the western edge of the talus. Down climb *Airbear*. A couple of other highball variations have been done on the right side of the southwest face. Bring a pad or use the bolt anchor on top.

1. Pebbled Arête V3 (hb) Climb the southwest arête, utilizing pebbles up top.

2. Air Jordan V5 (hb) Climb up the center of the west face to the undercling, then up to the top.

3. Air Left V4 (hb) Climb up the left side of the west face, left of Air Jordan's arête.

4. Wafer V3 (hb) Climb the northwest face up and left.

5. Airball Arête V3 (hb) Climb the arête on the northwest corner.

6. Airhall V2 Climb the north face just left of the northwest arête.

7. Airbear V0 Climb up the left side of the north face.

Sea of Hole ▼

This prominent block has a beautiful south-facing highball slab on its south face. You can find toprope anchors up top. Hike up to the northeast from Air Jordan Block.

1. Sea of Hole V2 (hb) Climb up the middle of the south slab.

2. Holey Moley V1 (hb) Climb the right side of the south face.

To Too Two

Stem Gem Rock ▲

This clean pyramid-shaped rock is upslope, beyond Sea of Hole and the talus cluster. Hike upslope to the northeast, behind Sea of Hole. Many large toprope blocks are located within the talus, just below the main Sheep Nose formation. Several of them are equipped with toprope anchors, home to many bouldering competitions.

1. Stem Gem V3 Climb up the middle of the south face.

36 TURKEY ROCKS AREA

The Turkey Rocks include Turkey Rock, Turkey Tail, and Turkey Perch. This is known as one of Colorado's premiere crack-climbing areas, but it also has some nice bouldering, most of which is still untapped. There is a nice spread of boulders in and around the area. The main areas are located on the north and south side of Turkey Rock, the north side of Turkey Tail, and the south side of Turkey Perch.

Directions: Follow the directions for the Sheep Nose Boulders. From there, continue southwest on Stump Road (CR 68) to a right turn onto Forest Road 360. Look for the sign for the Big Turkey and Turkey Rock Campgrounds. Drive toward the campground on FR 360 and park at the trailhead parking area on the south side of the campground (on the north side of the Turkey Tail and Turkey Rock formations). The hike to the base takes approximately fifteen minutes.

To locate the Turkey Rock Boulders, hike south from the trailhead. The Thanksgiving Boulders are located after hiking approximately 100 yards; they are to the right (west) within the burned forest. The boulders and blocks extend for 200 yards to the west, below the north face of Turkey Rock. This is perhaps the area's best cluster of boulders, with problems ranging from 10 to 15 feet with great landings. To reach the boulders and blocks on the south face, continue up the trail to the saddle between Turkey Rock and Turkey Perch and head to the southwest. The boulders are scattered below the south face of Turkey Rock.

To find the Turkey Tail Boulders, hike up the trail for 50 feet and you will see the boulders out to the left (east), extending all the way to the base of the north face of the Turkey Tail.

To find the Turkey Perch Boulders, hike south on the trail to the notch between Turkey Perch and Turkey Rock and head left (east) until you are below the south face of Turkey Perch. The boulders can be seen immediately to the southeast from Turkey Perch's south face.

37 ELEVENMILE CANYON

The granite boulders and blocks of the Elevenmile Canyon will satisfy any boulderer for days, weeks—even years. The countless boulders along the dammed South Platte River and mostly up on its northwestern slopes offer an unlimited source of problems, many of which are still to be sent. The River Blocks, Spy vs. Spy Area, and Spillway Boulders are a good start, but many more exist. Camping is plentiful, and you will find several user groups about. Many larger formations exist throughout the canyon. The river is treacherous during runoff months, and crossing can be limited. Late summer into fall is usually the best time of year for accessibility. Bring a kayak and fishing equipment. Mountain biking is fun as well.

Directions: From Woodland Park, drive west on Highway 24 to the small town of Lake George. From Lake George, locate the small sign pointing to Elevenmile Canyon (a small independently owned convenience store is on the southwest corner). Turn left (south) just before the convenience store and follow the road (Forest Road 96) around east then west to the canyon's entrance station. A day fee or camping fee will be assessed. From the entrance station, head west to the plentiful areas. The Canyon is 11 miles long, with some very interesting tunnels.

Elevenmile Canyon/Elevenmile Canyon Reservoir Areas

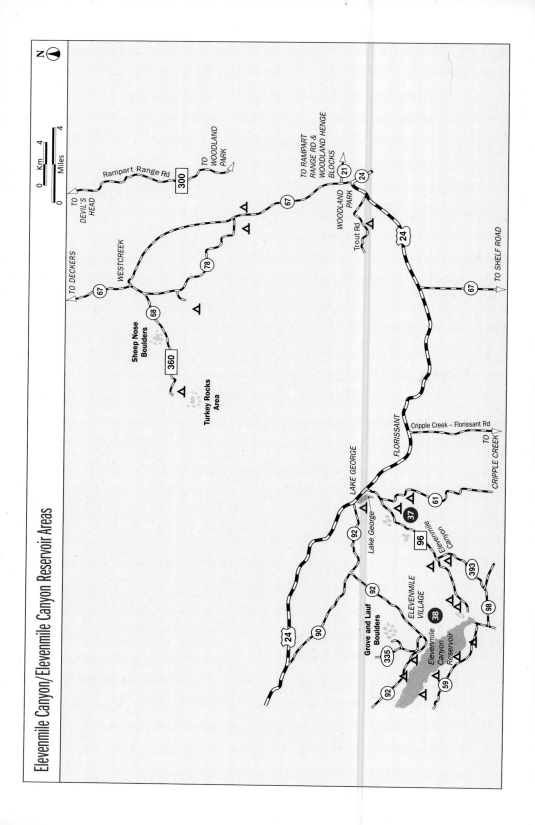

Spray Boulders

These boulders are found along the river approximately 2.4 miles from the entrance station. You can see the huge blocks under the overhangs, to the northwest, with a few to the east along the river.

Spray Boulder

This large boulder is below the overhanging bolted wall. It has an overhanging northwest face.

1. High and Mighty V6 Climb up the left side, utilizing the pie plates of the overhanging northwest face.

2. V Slot V8 Climb from the slot across to the right of the roof on the northwest face.

Satellite Boulder

This boulder is just downstream to the right of Spray Boulder.

1. Sit It Out V0 Climb from down low on the left side of the north face.

2. Arêtelite V1 Climb the northwest arête of the boulder.

Next River Boulder

This boulder is about 75 feet downstream to the right, close to the riverbank.

1. Riverway V3 Climbs up the overhanging east face.

Shore Blocks ▼

These boulders are in a meadowesque setting across the river to the northwest, approximately 4.3 miles from the entrance station. They offer good problems on nice granite.

Shore Block

This isolated roof block can be seen in the meadow across the river.

1. West Wall V0 Climb the good holds up the left side of the west face.

2. Zigzag Face V1 Climb up the cracks on the right side of the west face.

3. Block Roof V4 Climb out the roof on the south side of the block.

4. Arangerette V2 Climb the arête on the northwest corner.

5. Sizette V1 Climb to pockets via layaways up the southwest prow.

Shore Cube ◄

This cube is just east of the latter.

1. Boa Shores V4 Climb up the middle of the south face.

The River Blocks

These choice blocks are across the river to the northwest, approximately 7.5 miles from the entrance station. They have some of the most classic problems in the canyon, as well as great landings. They sit down below the road, just off the banks of the river. Bring a raft or wade across to them.

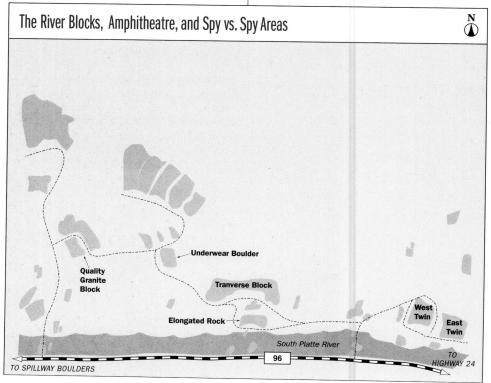

The River Blocks, Amphitheatre, and Spy vs. Spy Areas

N

Underwear Boulder

Quality
Granite
Block

Tranverse Block

Elongated Rock

West
Twin

East
Twin

South Platte River

96

TO
HIGHWAY 24

TO SPILLWAY BOULDERS

West Twin

This is the western block of the two. It has a large pine tree on its south side. Exit the top from the west side.

1. El Murray Right V5 Climb the layback line on the west face.

2. Thang V6 Climb up the left side of the west face.

3. Pinchy Corner V3 Climb up the prow on the northwest corner of the block.

4. Northern Exposure V2 Climb up the leaning dihedral on the right side of the north face.

5. Slot Arête V3 (hb) Climb up the prow on the north face within the slot.

East Twin

This is the eastern and choice block of the two. Its overhanging south face is just above the riverbank and inaccessible at times.

1. Triangle Face V2 (hb) Climb from a good hold on the left side of the south face and move to the slab and corner above.

2. West Corner V3 (hb) Climb the corner on the right side of the west face.

3. Bob's Wall V5 (hb) Climb up the leaning seam on the left side of the east face, utilizing thin crimps.

4. Pine Tree Left V1 (hb) Climb up the steep wall just left of the pine tree.

5. Pine Tree Right V4 (hb) Climb up the prow to the right of a pine tree.

6. Horan's Horizon V5 (hb) Climb thin edges up the far-left side of the north face, finishing to the right.

The Amphitheatre

This area is located 0.1 mile upstream to the west of the River Blocks. It has a secluded minicliff tucked upslope from the smaller blocks near the riverbank. Hike west approximately 500 feet from the River Blocks and locate a shortened block with an arch on its south face along the riverside. The minicliff is up behind this block.

Elongated Block

This shortened, elongated block is along the banks of the river.

1. The Arch V2 Climb from the undercling on the right side of the south face to the top.

Brian's Traverse Block ▼

This minicliff is upslope behind Elongated Block to the northwest.

East Twin

1. Black Corner V2 (hb) Climb up the blackened scoop.

2. Brian's High Traverse Crack V2 (hb)
Climb out the horizontal crack from left up and right.

Spy vs. Spy Area

This cluster of granite duds is found up behind the *Spy vs. Spy* route to the northeast. Continue west approximately 500 feet from the Amphitheatre until you see the first granite boulder upslope, and then head upslope to this quality granite dud. You can see *Spy vs. Spy* to the southwest at this point.

Underwear Boulder ▼

This clean, white granite boulder is the perfect height, with a vertical, somewhat-slabby north face.

1. Dog's Eye V3 Climb the far-right side of the north face, utilizing the laybacks.

2. Bear on the Slope V3 Climb the thin slab to the left of *Dog's Eye*.

3. Underwear Direct V3 Climb up the center of the face from the undercling.

4. Milligan's Way V3 Climb up the far-left side, utilizing the arête.

Quality Granite Block ◄

This block is located through a gap, approximately 50 feet west of Underwear Boulder.

1. Eastern Line V3 Climb up the far-right side of the block's east side, using some of the arête.

2. Due East V2 (hb) Climb up the edges in the center of the east face.

3. East Left V3 Climb up the left side of the east face right of the arête.

4. SE Prow V3 Climb the southeast arête.

Spillway Boulders

These boulders are at the far-west end of the canyon, approximately 8.5 miles from the entrance station. The boulders are scattered about the campground. If you can get a campsite, this is a great camp with the boulders in close proximity.

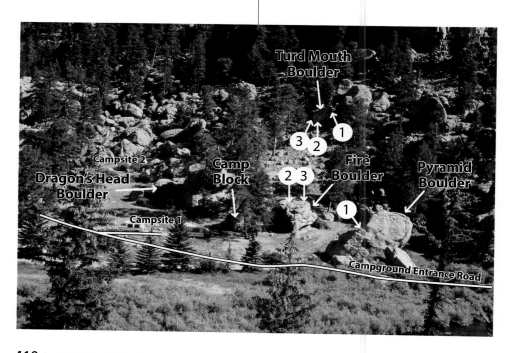

Pyramid Boulder ▲

This massive boulder is just west of campsite 1. It has a large, slabby west face with three prominent left-angling cracks.

1. Attention Campers V2 Climb from down low on the south face, up the crack, and onto the slab.

2. Triplet V1 (hb) Climb up the cracks on the northwest face.

Fire Boulder ▼

This is a nice-looking boulder that has been charred by the fire pit below its east face. It is east of campsite 1. You will find problems on its east side.

1. Fire Roof V2 Climb out the roof on the east face.

2. Firepit V4 (hb) Climb the crack system through the blackened east wall.

3. Firehose V1 Climb up the left side of the east face.

Camp Block

This block is located within campsite 1. Have a picnic on the table next to the problems.

1. Excuse Me V1 Climb out the bulging west face.

2. Pop Tent V0 Climb the prow on the right side of the east face.

3. Seam Sealer V2 Climb up the seam on the east face.

4. Smores V0 (hb) Climb up to the crack on the far-right side of the south face.

5. Campfire V2 (hb) Climb the thin line in the center of the south face.

6. Firewood V1 Climb the thin line on the left side of the south face, left of *Campfire*.

Dragon's Head Boulder

This is another massive boulder, located to the right of campsite 2. It is also another good place to have a picnic, as the table is close to the problems.

1. Dragon's Lair V3 Where the north slab comes down over an overhang, climb the overhang to the slab above.

2. Dragonfly V5 Climb the thin line right of *Dragon's Lair* up and left across the slab.

Boundaries Boulder

Within campsite 2 there are two boulders. The larger boulder is crumbly, and the smaller has few moderates.

1. East Throw V1 Climb up the east prow with a throw for the top.

2. Camphedral V0 Climb the moderate corner on the north side of the boulder.

Turd Mouth Boulder

This large boulder with a steep south face is located upslope to the northeast, about 50 feet from Dragon's Head Boulder.

1. Constipation V3 Climb up and out the left side of the bulging east face.

2. Indian Toilet Paper V? (hb) Climb the right-diagonaling crack system on the left side of the south face.

3. Turd Mouth Trois V? Climb up the far-left side of the south face, utilizing the face and crack.

38 ELEVENMILE CANYON RESERVOIR

See map on page 404.

Not to be confused with Elevenmile Canyon, this area is located farther west from the Lake George turnoff for Elevenmile Canyon. Although a fisherman's capital, this extensive area hosts nice bouldering on the north side of the reservoir amid the aspen forests. Much potential lies throughout this scenic wooded area that offers views of the majestic Colorado high country to the west.

Directions: Continue west on Highway 24, west of Lake George, approximately 0.7 mile past the turnoff for Elevenmile Canyon. Turn left onto County Road 92 and head toward Eleven Mile/Spring Mountain State Park. CR 92 continues almost 10 miles, to the ranger station entrance. Continue past the station's left side until you reach County Road 335. Continue about 1 mile on CR 335 and take a right onto a dirt road. Follow this road 0.8 mile, over a stony point and along a fence line. The Grove Boulders sit roadside and can be seen as you head west. For the Lauf Boulders, continue west another 1.4 miles and you will see them roadside just before the subdivision.

The Grove Boulders

Nestled a safe distance from the crowds, these boulders are within the aspen forest just off the side of the road.

Fence Boulder

As its name implies, this boulder is near the fence line. Down climb the south side.

1. Fence Me In V0 Climb the corner system on the west face.

2. Oh Fence V0 Climb the right side of the north-facing slab.

3. The Gate V2 Climb the seam in the center of the east face.

4. Post V1 Climb the far-left line on the east face.

5. Trespass V0 Climb the right side of the south face.

Grove Block

This crystalline block is 50 feet west of Fence Boulder.

1. Ouch V2 Climb the right side of the east face via a dyno.

2. Grover V4 Climb up the middle of the east face.

3. Map of England V3 Climb up the left side of the east face.

4. Straight Lace V1 Climb up the right side of the south face.

The Perfect Slab

From Grove Block continue west another 50 feet to this perfect slab boulder.

1. Perfect Slab V3 Climb up the center of the west face.

2. Bombs Away V3 Climb up the left side of the west face, right of the prow.

3. Slab Arête V1 Climb the arête, left of *Bombs Away.*

Lauf Boulders

These boulders are in the meadow north of the fence line, just before the subdivision. A scenic area with potential for more problems exists below the cliff band.

Another Roadside Boulder

This scenic boulder is 150 feet north of the road. It has a luring west face. Descend to the southwest.

1. White Caps Right V2 Climb the corner on the northeast face.

2. White Caps V5 Climb the classic arête of the northeast face.

3. Aspen Left V1 Climb the face left of the aspen tree on the east side.

4. Downclimb V0 Climb the arête on the southwest corner.

5. Classy Flake V2 Climb the classic flake system on the right side of the west face.

Last Lauf Spire

This triangular block rests upslope approximately 200 feet from Another Roadside Boulder.

1. Pyramid V2 Climb up slightly left of the center of the west face.

Lauf Block

This large block within the aspen grove is located 150 feet east of Another Roadside Boulder.

1. Higheast V0 (hb) Climb up the edgy east face.

2. Lauf's Prow V2 (hb) Climb the prow on the southeast corner.

3. Lauf Laugh V4 (hb) Climb up the left side of the south face.

4. Big Lauf V0 (hb) Climb the good holds up the west face.

Little Lauf Boulder

This boulder is attached to the west side of Lauf Block. It has an overhanging, bulging face.

1. Ich bin Hine V0 Climb the corner on the right side of boulder.

2. Ich bin Einfach Gut V5 Climb from down low, left of the bulge, up to the prow.

39 SPHINX PARK BOULDERS

See map on page 394.

The boulders here (mostly below the Sphinx Crack Rock formation) are plentiful and have been adeptly named Arêteland. This area may take the trophy for most cube-shaped rocks in any one area. The landmark Sphinx Rock formation has a world-class splitter crack that extends high up its northwest face. This was perhaps the country's first 5.13 crack line.

Directions: You can reach this area from both the north and the south. From the north, or the Denver/Boulder area, locate Highway 285 and travel west through the town of Conifer. Go left (southeast) at Pine Junction onto County Road 126 (Pine Valley Road). Follow CR 126 south 6.5 miles to the town of Pine. From Pine, turn left onto County Road 83. Drive 0.4 mile to a parking area on the left side of the road. You can access the Sphinx Rock formation and the blocks below by crossing the road to the east and scrambling up. The hike is about five minutes.

If you are coming from the south, or Woodland Park, continue northwest on Highway 67 to Dekkers. Then connect with CR 126 to the northwest, toward Pine.

Cynical Pinnacle Boulders

This fall line of rock has a wealth of bouldering and is located up the valley to the southeast of Sphinx Park.

Glen Elk Boulder ▶

This nice granite block sits in a meadow beside Elk Creek, on the south end of the small town of Glen Elk, just before the famous Bucksnort Inn.

Directions: From Highway 285, head southeast on CR 83 (Elk Creek Road) at Shaffers Crossing. Continue southeast through Glen Elk and just past the end of town, and then park at a small pull off. The block sits on the right side of the road, beside Elk Creek.

1. Buck's Seams V1 Climb the lines on the right side of the south face.

2. Buckaroo V0 Climb the far-left line of the south face.

3. Snort Flake V3 Climb the left-leaning flake on the far-right side of the west face.

4. The Cheater V4 Climb up the center of the west face, utilizing a cheat stone.

5. The Elk V6 From down low on the west face, climb up right of the corner.

6. Broken Elk V3 Climb up the dihedral on the west face.

7. Elk's Arête V1 Climb up the southwest arête.

CANON CITY/SHELF ROAD AREA

40 CANON CITY

These areas are just north of Canon City on the way to the Shelf Road climbing area. The first area is the Dakota Dam, located approximately 9 miles north of Highway 50, on the way north to Shelf Road. The others areas are below the cliffs and creek beds of Shelf Road.

Dakota Dam Boulders

Also known as the Dam Ruin Boulders, this nice array of blocks is located on the left and right sides of the road on the way to the Shelf Road climbing crags. From Highway 50, head north on Field Avenue (which eventually turns into Shelf Road) approximately 9 miles. Just after a curve in the road, you will see a stonewall ruin on the left side of the road. Park and hike upslope to the Dakota sandstone blocks behind the ruin. You will find a great traverse wall above, as well as many isolated boulders with good problems.

Traverse Block ▼

This massive block is the first block you will encounter behind the wall ruin. It has a great traverse on its south side.

1. Grand Traverse V5 Traverse from left to right across the south face. Many other harder eliminates can also be done.

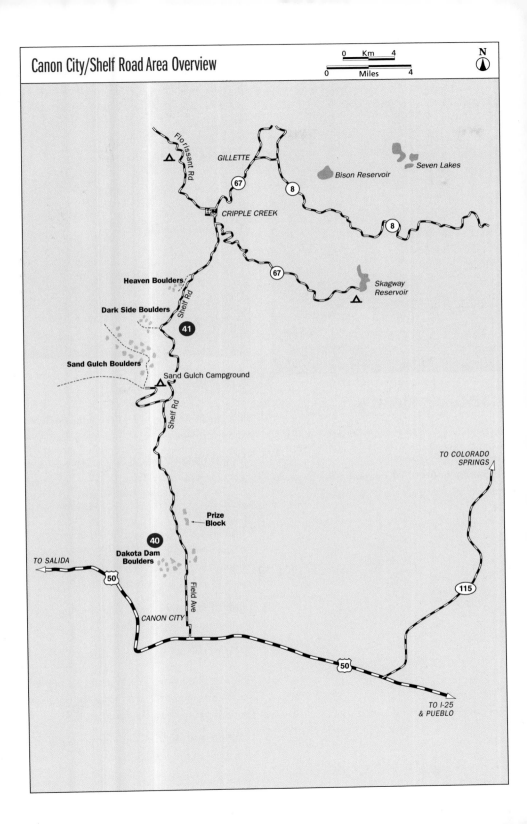

Canon City/Shelf Road Area Overview

N

0 Km 4
0 Miles 4

Florissant Rd

GILLETTE

Seven Lakes

Bison Reservoir

67

8

CRIPPLE CREEK

8

67

Heaven Boulders

Skagway Reservoir

Shelf Rd

Dark Side Boulders

41

Sand Gulch Boulders

Sand Gulch Campground

Shelf Rd

TO COLORADO SPRINGS

Prize Block

40

Dakota Dam Boulders

Field Ave

TO SALIDA

50

115

CANON CITY

50

TO I-25 & PUEBLO

Sandman Block ▲

This clean piece of Dakota is 10 feet west of Traverse Block.

1. Sandman Arête V3 Climb up the prow on the east face.

Support Block ▲

This block is connected to the left side of Sandman Block.

1. Right Wing V0 Climb up the arête on the right side of the east face.

Aerial Block

This highball wall is north of the Traverse, Sandman, and Support Blocks. A toprope is recommended. Other short but fun blocks are west and slightly upslope from Aerial Block.

1. Aerial Antics V3 Climb the steep line up the middle of the south face.

Slope Block

This roadside block is upslope on the opposite (right) side of the road from the parking for the Dakota Dam Boulders.

1. Swinger Arête V5 Climb up the northwest arête of the leaning block.

Prize Block ▲

Continue up the road a short distance and park in the pullout arch on the left side of the road. Look across to the east, slightly up-slope, and you will see this classic block of Dakota.

1. Prize Left V3 Climb up the left side of the west face.

2. Prize Central V2 Climb up the crack in the middle of the west face.

3. The Prize V2 Climb up the arête and face on the right side of the west face.

The Finger

To find this overhanging block, walk north approximately 100 yards along the ridgeline. The block is on top of the east-facing slope, just below the ridgeline.

1. The Finger V2 Start down low and climb up the face and arête. This utilizes both sides.

41 SHELF ROAD BOULDERS

See map on page 417.

At the end of the day at one of Colorado's premier sport-climbing areas, climbers always find themselves sitting about camp pondering what to do next. Well there is plenty of bouldering to seek out along the dry creek beds and slopes of the cliffs above. Like the steep cliffs above, the boulders are solid limestone with many edges and pockets. The creek bed boulders are at times polished and slick, while the slope boulders tend to be more frictiony and shaded.

Directions: Thus far there have been three distinct areas developed along Shelf Road. The first area includes the Sand Gulch Boulders, which are located down the trail from the campground. Drive approximately 12.7 miles on Field Avenue from Highway 50 to this campground. The Dark Side Boulders are located up the road another 1.8 miles from the campground. Park on the left side of the road and trend down to the creek bed. The third area, the Heaven Boulders, is north another 1.8 miles from the Dark Side Boulders. Parking is on the left, about 0.3 mile past the boulders.

Sand Gulch Boulders

These boulders are scattered about the creek bed and offer short problems that utilize edges, pockets, and cracks. They are found outside the Sand Gulch campground by hiking downslope on the climbers' trail into the creek bed. Follow the creek bed to the right. You will see the first boulders at the trail junction for the Contest Wall; they extend up the canyon from there.

Contest Block ▲

This block is across from the Contest Wall trailhead.

1. Shorty V2 Climb from down low up the southwest face of the block.

2. Contestant V1 Traverse the block from right to left.

Lengthy Block ▶

To find this block, hike farther north up the wash 20 feet from Contest Block, then head upslope a short way to the block.

1. Pocket Rocket V2 (hb) Climb up the right side of the west face to a large pocket above.

Black and Tan Block ▲

This block is farther up the wash from Lengthy Block, about 30 feet on the left. It has a steep east face that has a tan left side and a black right side.

1. Streak V4 Climb up the left side of the east face.

Porous Boulder

This black boulder is up the wash another 50 feet from Black and Tan Block.

1. Tree Squeeze V0 Climb up the middle of the north face.

Ball Boulder ▶

This black boulder is farther up the wash another 50 feet from Porous Boulder.

1. By The V1 Climb up the middle of the east face.

Wash Block ▲

This cubed block is 50 feet up the wash from Ball Boulder.

1. Laundry V0 Climb up the middle of the north face.

Sand Piper Boulder ▶

This boulder is located at a point where the boulders and blocks peter out. Hike up the wash another 100 feet from Wash Block and you will see this boulder.

1. Sandpiper V2 Climb the arête to the top.

Dark Side Boulders

The next area up the road to the north is a gathering of boulders down in the creek bed below the Dark Side cliff band. The boulders are taller than the Sand Gulch Boulders and offer some polished rocks within the creek bed.

Dark Star Boulder

This creekbed block is located about 75 feet up from the parking pull off. It is the block on the left and is taller than the one next to it.

1. The Ankler V1 Climb up the left side of the face.

2. Dark Star V2 (hb) Climb up just left of the center on the face.

Orchestra Block

This block is just right of Dark Star Boulder.

1. Orchestration V3 Climb up the pockets on the face.

2. Travesty V2 Traverse from left to the right across the face.

Short and Thin Block

This block is located west up the creek bed approximately 100 feet from Dark Star Boulder. It has a somewhat grassy top.

1. Dire Straights V0 Climb the face of the block.

2. Straights Traverse V5 Traverse the face from right to left.

White Slab Block

This prominent whitened slab that has a block to its left is approximately 100 feet farther west from Short and Thin Block.

1. Block Tock V1 Climb up the east face.

Tier Boulder

To find this boulder, walk up the creek another 100 feet west from White Slab Block. You will see it across the creek bed to the west. It is the farthest left of three.

1. Tears V2 Climb from down low up the arête.

2. Tires V0 Climb the face right of the arête.

3. Backside Pockets V1 Climb the pocket problem on the face.

Right On Block

This is the farthest right of three blocks. It has good arêtes and face problems.

1. Right On Arête V? Climb the arête.

Heaven Boulders

These boulders are located farther north up the road from the Dark Side Boulders at the end of the Shelf Road cliff band. You can see the boulders flowing off the slopes below the cliffs. They offer lots of good pocket bouldering.

East Block

This overhanging, white-striped block is the one furthest east from the parking area.

1. East's West V3 Climb up the right side of the west face.

2. West's East V0 Climb up the left side of the west face.

Middle East Block

Located southwest of East Block, this pocketed block has an overhanging east face and a steep north face.

1. Middle North V1 Climb up the center of the north face.

2. Pockets East V3 Climb from down low up and out the east overhang.

Black Boulder

Continue west 100 feet from Middle East Block, aiming for the road that leads to a black-faced boulder that has a large pine tree on its north side. The top is covered with undergrowth.

1. Dark V1 Climb up the right side of the west face.

2. Midnight V2 Climb up the left side of the west face.

3. Moonlight V6 Climb up the center of the north face, up the white streak via pockets.

4. Dark Side of the Moon V4 Climb up the left side of the north face via pockets.

5. The Abyss V0 Climb up the east face slab.

Black and White Block

Continue west another 150 feet from Black Boulder until you come to this elongated block that has black-and-white stripes on its northwest face.

1. Rock Scar V0 Climb up the northwest face to the right of the rock scar.

2. Rock Star V3 Climb up the white streaks on left side of the northwest face.

Pueblo Area

The Dakota sandstone rock layers that appear in irregular intervals along the Colorado Front Range are revealed in large quantities in the country that surrounds the city of Pueblo. Many small canyons, stand-alone boulders, and blocks of all shapes and sizes can be found here. They are full of face problems, pocket pulls, arêtes, dihedrals, corners, cracks, and traverses. Unfortunately, much of the bouldering potential is on private land, and the problems that have been done are either marginally accessible or altogether off-limits. However, because the quality of the boulders is so excellent, they are being noted in this guide with the hope that one day access will improve.

SKI COUNTRY BOULDERS

42 STEAMBOAT SPRINGS AREA

The Steamboat Springs area, like many Colorado ski towns, has bouldering scattered throughout its surrounding foothills and passes. This area usually has a late melt off, but by midsummer the hills are dry and the hot springs still wait. Fall, during aspen season, is the best time to visit for the bouldering. A few bouldering areas are readily available only minutes from Steamboat's town center. Some of it is found along the bases of climbing crags (Fish Creek Falls and Butcher Knife), while others are more peaceful and remote (east and west of Rabbit Ears Pass).

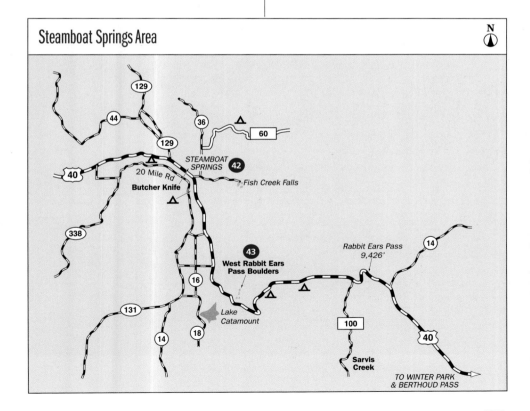

Steamboat Springs Area

N

129

44

36

60

129

STEAMBOAT
SPRINGS 42

40

20 Mile Rd

Butcher Knife

Fish Creek Falls

338

Rabbit Ears Pass
9,426'

14

43

**West Rabbit Ears
Pass Boulders**

16

100

131

Lake
Catamount

14   18

40

**Sarvis
Creek**

TO WINTER PARK
& BERTHOUD PASS

The author bouldering on the Waterside Block, Wolcott Boulders.

Directions: To reach Steamboat Springs from Denver, take Interstate 70 west, exit north on Highway 9 at Dillon, and take it to Highway 40, which goes northwest to Steamboat Springs. Another option from Denver is to take Highway 40 north across Berthoud Pass and through Winter Park to Steamboat Springs.

To reach Steamboat Springs from Grand Junction, take I-70 east, exit north on Highway 131, and then take Highway 40 north to Steamboat Springs.

Butcher Knife

This cliffy bouldering area close to town has traverse and steep face problems at the base. From Steamboat Springs, take Seventh Street to a right on Missouri, which will take you straight to the area. You will find a pull off where the road splits to the left. Hike over the bridge to the highball granite walls. This is a local toproping wall that has tempting highball potential. Stack the pads!

1. Butcher Traverse V? Climb the long traverse across the right side of the minicliff.

Fish Creek Falls

To find this scenic bouldering area, take Lincoln Avenue to a right on Third Street. Take another right on Fish Creek Falls Road and follow it approximately 3 miles to a pull off on the left. Hike the paved way parallel to the road and veer north on a stone trail for a couple hundred yards, until you see cliff band with blocks below. Fish Creek Falls is in the distance.

43 RABBIT EARS PASS

See map on page 425.

East Rabbit Ears Pass

This bouldering is located up close to the summit of Rabbit Ears Pass, southeast of Steamboat Springs. Follow Highway 40 toward Rabbit Ears Pass Summit.

Sarvis Creek

This is a forested bouldering area at 9,500 feet. Granite blocks are scattered within the forest and are full of a variety of challenges. From Steamboat Springs, drive up toward Rabbit Ears Pass and take a right (south) onto Forest Road 100 (Buffalo Park), about 0.4 mile before the summit. Continue south approximately 10 miles to a pull off on the left side of the dirt road. Follow the trail across the road into the forest and you will run across the boulders. The first blocks offer good problems, and more follow if you continue up the trail through a meadow and beyond.

Forest Blocks

These are the first blocks you come to within the forest. Many good problems abound.

Meadow Blocks

To find these blocks, continue up the trail from the Forest Blocks, past the meadow.

West Rabbit Ears Pass

This is a more remote, scenic, and peaceful destination. The boulderfield is just off a cliff band 200 feet downslope to the west from the top of the Rabbit Ears Pass Summit pull off. From the Steamboat Springs town center, take Highway 40 up to Rabbit Ears Pass Summit (9,426 feet). Park on the pass between mile markers 144 and 145 and hike downslope to the west for about 5 minutes. Go past the cliff band and look for the boulderfield.

Southwest Rabbit Ears Pass

The boulderfield here is somewhat untouched, but it is surely ready to be bouldered upon. From the walls closest to Highway 40, on the southwest side of the pass, hike downslope to the boulderfield.

Flat Top Block

This main attraction is located downslope south of Highway 40. It has a wide, flat top and a small roofed section.

1. Trashy V0 Climb up the far-left side of the south face.

2. Munjal Traverse V4 Climb from down low on the south face, across to the left, to the top.

3. Weather Report V5 Climb up the far-left side of the east face.

4. Show Me V5 Climb out the small roof on the northeast side, out from the left.

Six Shooter Boulder

This boulder is located downslope to the south from Flat Top Block. It is surrounded by many other boulders.

SUMMIT COUNTY

Summit County is famous for its many great ski resorts. Naturally, during winter months the nearby bouldering areas are immersed in snow. But in summer and fall they offer great bouldering in a beautiful setting. The mountainous environment offers a great escape from the hustle and bustle of the ever-sprawling Front Range. Most of the bouldering areas are west of the Eisenhower Tunnel and are accessed off Interstate 70.

44 FRISCO AREA

This area hosts two very unique and quality chunks of granite that have striped, solid, and smooth-edged stone. One of the main attractions, *Via the Hot One* (V9) on the Frisco Chunk, has some of the best rock and is worth visiting despite its location close to the interstate. Other bouldering areas are located south and west and offer minicliff-style bouldering.

Directions: To find the Frisco Boulders exit I-70 at Frisco (exit 201), following the exit up to the traffic circle, around to the right, and onto the frontage road. Follow the frontage road west and park at the Peaks Trail parking lot.

Frisco Boulders

Frisco Block

Located east of the Peaks Trail parking lot, this granite block has a black-and-white-striped overhanging south face. From the parking lot, walk east about 150 yards and look up on the left (north) side of the entrance ramp to see this block.

Summit County Area Overview

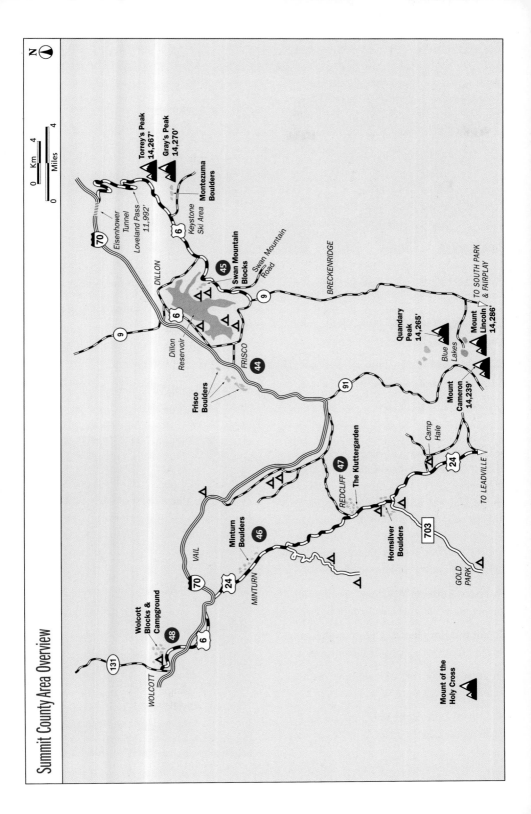

1. Far Left V2 Climb up the left side of the south face.

2. Middle Streaks V4 Climb up the middle of the south face.

3. Right Streaks V5 Climb up the right side of the south face.

Frisco Chunk ▶

This beautiful, overhanging chunk of quality gold and black striped stone is located up on a shelf, imbedded in the hillside just above the north side of I-70. Quality problems abound. To reach it, hike west from the parking lot toward the bottom of the exit ramp. At the last light post, look up to the right (north) and you will see this awesome chunk of rock. Scramble upslope to the shelf.

1. Frisco Buttress V7 Climb up the south-facing arête, utilizing small edges and slopers.

2. Via the Hot One V9 Climb up the scoop on the south face, right of the buttress.

3. Crystal Dike Left V1 Climb up the left side of the dike, right of *Via the Hot One*.

4. Crystal Dike Right V0 Climb the face right of the dike.

5. Ramp It V0 Climb up the ramp.

6. Streaker V1 (hb) Climb up the face right of the ramp.

7. Diesel Scoop V1 (hb) Climb up the scooped face left of the slab.

8. Higher Scoop V2 Climb up the scoop above *Diesel Scoop*.

45 SWAN MOUNTAIN BLOCKS

See map on page 429.

This is another area that has a lot of mini-cliff bouldering and a few blocks sitting aside the cliff band. The problems along the cliff band are mostly moderate but airy. The blocks are worthwhile.

Directions: From Frisco, drive east on Highway 6 toward the Keystone Ski Area. Turn right (southwest) onto Swan Mountain Road and drive approximately 2 miles to a right into the Swan Mountain Recreation Area. Park and then hike north about 500 feet up the dirt road on the right to a trail that heads northwest to the ridgeline. From the ridgeline hike downslope to the blocks.

The Pillar

This pillar is at the north end of the minicliffs.

1. Nice Jugs V0 (hb) Climb up the large holds on the west face of the pillar.

2. Pillar T V3 Traverse the pillar from the west face to the east face.

3. Pilate V1 (hb) Climb up the southeast arête.

The Slab Wall

This slabby wall is just above the blocks. It is a minicliff with many nice problems.

1. Slab Traverse V1 Traverse the slab from right to left.

2. Slab Crack V0 (hb) Climb the tall crack just right of the tree on the left side of the wall.

Swan Block

This block is located downslope from a prominent slab wall. Hike down a short way from an exit trail to the block.

Two Trees Block

This block is farther downslope from Swan Block. It has two trees in front of its face.

46 MINTURN BOULDERS

See map on page 429.

Although these boulders have a soft texture, they have recently been climbed enough to create some very solid, excellent problems. This area is a worthwhile experience in a pleasant setting with fun bouldering.

Directions: From Vail, go west on I-70 to exit 171. Go 0.3 mile south on Highway 24, toward Minturn, to the first left, which goes across the Eagle River. Follow the dirt road around to the south and drive approximately 1 mile to the far-south end of the boulder-field on the left. Park and walk back north. Some of the boulders are in the trees to the east; others are in the meadow.

The Gray Cube ▲

This cube-shaped gray block sits in the southern meadow. It has a few fun problems up its south face.

1. Cube's Arête V0 Climb the southeast arête.

2. Cube's Center V0 Climb up the center of the south face.

3. Cube's Slab V0 Climb up the far-left side of the south face.

Meadow Boulder ▼

This nice golden boulder sits in the meadow just off the road. It has a steep, leaning south face with good problems.

1. Golden Arête V1 Climb the right-leaning southwest arête.

2. Golden Age V0 Climb up the center of the south face up and over the cap.

47 REDCLIFF

See map on page 429.

This incredible boulderfield surrounded by pine and aspen trees is nestled just off the main road along an old side track. The boulders sit within a scattered iron yard that is more historic than unpleasant. The bouldering during fall, when the aspens are turning, is magnificent. Due to its high altitude, the area is usually snowed in after October.

Directions: From I-70 west of Vail, take Highway 24 (exit 171) south, past the Minturn Boulders, and continue up the pass toward the old mining town of Redcliff. Cross the bridge to the south and park at the far-south end of Redcliff in a convenient and large parking area. (Park away from the bus stop or you may be towed.) From the parking area, cross the road to the east. Follow the old side road that leads up and left into the heart of the Kluttergarden.

The Kluttergarden

This bouldering destination is located along the old road. Hike east from the main road for about five minutes, until you see the first set of boulders sitting roadside. You will also see many old machines within this area, hence the name Kluttergarden. These boulders have loads of fun problems on good stone.

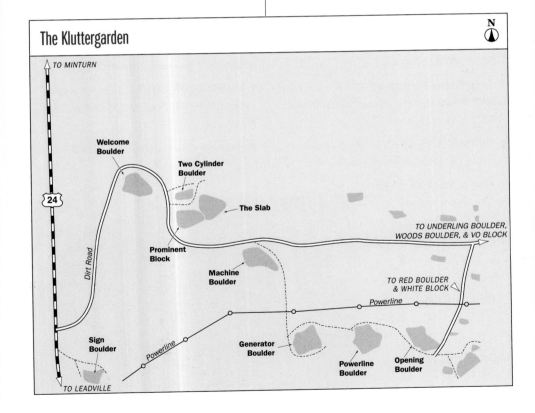

The Kluttergarden

N

TO MINTURN

24

Dirt Road

Welcome Boulder

Two Cylinder Boulder

The Slab

TO UNDERLING BOULDER, WOODS BOULDER, & VO BLOCK

Prominent Block

Machine Boulder

TO RED BOULDER & WHITE BLOCK

Powerline

Sign Boulder

Powerline

Generator Boulder

Powerline Boulder

Opening Boulder

TO LEADVILLE

Sign Boulder ▲

This lone boulder is located upslope, across the road from the parking area to the southeast. Its west face is steep with good, worthwhile problems.

1. Everywhere's a Sign V6 Climb up the left side of the south face, utilizing the southeast arête.

2. No Passing V5 Climb up the black stripes, utilizing the prow on the south face.

3. Men at Work V3 Climb up the southeast face.

4. Speed Limit V1 (hb) Climb up the ramp on the right side of the south face.

5. Mule Crossing V2 Climb the steep left side of the west face.

6. Deer Crossing V2 Climb up the west face just right of *Mule Crossing*.

Welcome Boulder ▼

This is the first boulder you reach after a five-minute hike up the old road. It is located on the right side of the road and is characterized by a southeast corner.

1. Howdy Overhang V5 Climb the overhanging west face from an undercling to a horizontal.

2. Hello V6 Climb the southeast, overhanging corner. Stem away.

3. Goodbye V6 From down low, climb up the rounded face right of the corner.

Two Cylinder Boulder

Just east across the track from Welcome Boulder is a set of three boulders. This is the smaller, left of the three. Problems start down low.

1. Choke V2 Climb up the left side of the north face.

2. Clutch V1 Climb up the left side of the south face.

3. Throttle V1 Climb from down low just left of *Clutch*.

4. Carburetor V1 Climb up the arête on the southeast side.

The Slab

This slabby boulder is north of Two Cylinder Boulder. The smooth, highball south slab has fun problems.

1. Blunt Arête V0 (hb) Climb the arête of the southwest corner.

2. Sun Slab V0 (hb) Climb up the south-facing slab, just left of center.

Prominent Block

This is the largest of the three blocks and is connected to the Slab.

1. The Face V2 Climb up the left side of the west face.

2. The Stare V3 Climb up the center of the west face.

3. Prominent Traverse V5 Climb from the scoop on the right side of the west face, across the slopers, to the far-left side.

4. Prominent Arête V1 From down low, climb up the southeast arête.

5. Prominent Crack V0 Climb up the crack on the east face.

Machine Boulder

This overhanging boulder is in isolation just up the road to the east from Two Cylinder Boulder, the Slab, and Prominent Block. Hike the road 100 feet and you will see it on the right side of the road.

1. The Machine V8 From down low, climb up the center of the overhanging north face, exiting left.

2. Fire Power V6 Climb up the center of the north face to the slab above.

3. Welcome to the Machine V6 Climb up right of the center to the center topout.

4. The Piston V4 Climb up the far-right side of the overhanging north face.

5. Cruise Control V0 Climb up the good holds on the right side of the west face.

6. The Brake V1 Climb up the left side of the south face.

Generator Boulder ▲

This large boulder is approximately 100 feet southeast of Machine Boulder. Walk toward and under the power lines to the overhanging southwest face of the rock.

1. Immortality V7 (hb) This highball climbs up from the far-left side of the southwest face to the corner topout.

2. Sticky Fingers V5 Climb up the center of the southwest face.

3. Anaphylactic V6 (hb) From the slot down low, move up and left of the latter.

4. Mortal Fingers V6 Climb from the center of the northwest face up to the pocketed slab.

5. Lip Hump V3 Climb up from the far-left side of the roof over the lip.

6. Tragedy Resides in You V6 (hb) Climb up from the right side of the roof to the right-facing dihedral.

Powerline Boulder

This nice boulder is located approximately 100 feet east of Generator Boulder.

1. Powerdyno V3 Dyno up the center of the north face left of a large hold.

2. Powerline Traverse V4 Traverse from the far-left side of the north face across to the west face seam.

3. Power Outage V1 Climb up the far-right slab of the west face, left of the crack.

4. Powercrack V0 Climb up the crack on the right side of the west face.

Opening Boulder ▼

Continue hiking 250 feet east along the power line above to a clearing in the trees.

1. Slabben V0 Climb up the slab on the northwest side.

2. Slopen V1 Climb up the right side of the northwest face.

3. Sliden V1 Climb up the right side of the southwest face.

4. Slappen V0 Climb up the center of the east face.

Woods Boulder ▲

Continue northeast beyond Opening Boulder, across a trail that leads into the forest, and you will run into this fine boulder.

1. The Axe V1 Climb up from down low on the far-left side of the northwest face.

2. The Wedge V0 Climb up the center of the scoop on the northwest face.

3. The Log V2 Climb up the face just right of the scoop.

4. Firewood V5 Traverse from right to left across the southwest face.

Underlying Boulder ▼

This boulder is located west of Woods Boulder and has many thin, delicate face problems, some in the V9–V10 range.

1. Underlying Traverse V9 Traverse from right to left across the north overhang.

2. Under Roof V5 Climb from down low out the north overhang.

V0 Block

From Underlying Boulder head back to the road that is located directly west. Hike 350 feet up the road, crossing under the power lines. Just before the downslope, hike northeast 50 feet and you will see this block.

1. The Arête V3 Climb up the arête on the south side of the block.

2. The Slabs V0 Climb up the slabs on the face.

Red Boulder ▼

This classic boulder is located upslope 100 feet east of V0 Block, within the trees.

1. Red Alert V0 (hb) Climb up the center of the west face.

2. Red Rain V3 (hb) Climb up the southwest arête.

3. Redman V1 (hb) Climb up the right side of the south side.

White Block ▼

This large block, located to the right (west) of Red Boulder, is characterized by a bulging roof on its west face.

1. Whitey V0 Climb up the left side of the north face.

2. Tighty V0 (hb) Climb up the dihedral on the north face.

3. White Knight V1 Climb over the left side of the bulge on the west face.

4. White Light V3 Climb out the right side of the bulge on the west face.

Hornsilver Boulders

The first of these boulders are located on the right side of the road, south of the Redcliff area, at the Hornsilver Day Use Area. The best boulders and blocks are located west across the stream at the base of the talus slope. Depending on the time of year and the amount of precipitation, this area is some-times submerged and swamped out, making it difficult to cross over to the western talus blocks. The campground has good boulder-ing (northeast across the road or south below Hornsilver Cliff). When not wet, this is a good area with an awesome array of boulder-ing. Views of Hornsilver Mountain at 11,570 feet can be seen to the east.

Directions: From Vail, go west on I-70 to exit 171 (Highway 24) and take Highway 24 south to Redcliff. Approximately 0.5 mile past the south end of Redcliff, pull off on the right side of the road at the day use area. The campground is another 0.5 mile south. The first boulder is located in a meadow beside the road. Others are across the stream to the west. The campground boulders are located to the northeast.

Hornsilver Block ▲

This landmark block has a few short prob-lems on its south face.

1. Middle V0 Climb the middle of the south face.

48 WOLCOTT BLOCKS

See map on page 429.

These gems are perhaps the most convenient blocks of Dakota sandstone in Colorado. They offer all the luxuries of camping close by, with a river down below and quality boulder problems with good landings. This is often a boulderer's rest area when traveling west from the Front Range or from the western slope to the east.

Directions: When driving east or west on I-70, exit at Wolcott (exit 157) and go to the second stop sign. Turn left onto Highway 6 and continue west 1.5 miles to the campground entrance. Park in the large lot outside the camp. The blocks are located north out in the meadow.

Picnic Block

To find this steep and short boulder, hike west from the parking lot, toward the boat launch and a picnic table on the far-west side of the campground.

1. Pignic V0 Climb up the center of the south face.

Fire Pit Block

Just east of Picnic Block is a block with a fire pit over its face.

1. Fire Pit V0 Climb up above the fire pit.

Big Block ▶

This three-body-lengths block is the prize contender of Wolcott, with many great problems up its sides. It is seen southeast of Fire Pit Block. Although these are highball ventures, you can resort to the bolts on top for a rope.

1. Blockyway V2 (hb) Climb up the northwest arête.

2. Crack of Desire V0 Climb up the crack on the west face.

3. Bob's Bulge V? Climb up the bulge right of the crack.

4. Casual V0 Climb up the right side of the south face.

5. In the Groove V0 (hb) Climb up the crack on the left side of the east face.

6. The Seam V1 (hb) Climb up the seam on the left side of the east face.

7. Black Streak V1 (hb) Climb up the crack within the black streak.

8. White Streaker V2 Climb up the thin seam on the right side of the east face.

9. Gluts Mega Maximus V7 (hb) Climb up the corner on the far-left side of the north face.

10. Maximus V8 (hb) Climb up the center of the north face.

11. Cirque Du Traverse V5 Traverse around the entirety of the block.

Waterside Block ▶

This beautiful golden-toned block sits east of Big Block. It is a few feet shorter, but it is another contender for quality at Wolcott, with awesome problems up its sides. Depending on the amount of precipitation, its north face may be submerged. Down climb the southwest corner.

1. Touch of Gray V0 Climb up the center of the west face.

2. Down and Off V0 Climb up the right side of the west face.

3. Golden Years V5 (hb) Climb up the golden left side of the south face.

4. In the Sun V2 (hb) Climb up the right side of the south face, utilizing the dihedral.

5. Bombay V1 (hb) Climb up the left side of the east face.

6. Underminer V1 (hb) Climb up the middle of the east face from the undercling.

Campsite Block

This split block that forms two blocks is found within campsite 1, the easternmost site.

1. Attention Campers V0 Climb up the crack and arête on the north block's west face.

2. Camp On V2 On the south block, from down low, climb up the northwest arête.

CARBONDALE/ NEW CASTLE AREA

The Carbondale area has a variety of bouldering that surrounds its neighboring towns of Redstone to the south and Basalt to the southeast. Redstone offers nice sandstone conglomerate blocks, some with solid crystalline-laced walls along a refreshing river. The Basalt area offers smooth sandstone boulders and granite boulders in a beautiful setting near a creek and lake. Camping is close by, which offers an alternative to driving farther south into the busy town of Aspen.

49 REDSTONE

These red sandstone crystalline blocks are located just north of Redstone's town center. They are divided into two distinct areas, parted only by the bending of the refreshing Crystal River. Some of the blocks are found along the river, while others are set amid the shady aspen forests. Boulderers will encounter a variety of steep faces with a multitude of hold types, as well as crystal crimping and workout traverses.

Directions: From Interstate 70 take the Glenwood Springs/Aspen exit and head south onto Highway 82. Follow Highway 82 to the Carbondale exit, then go south on

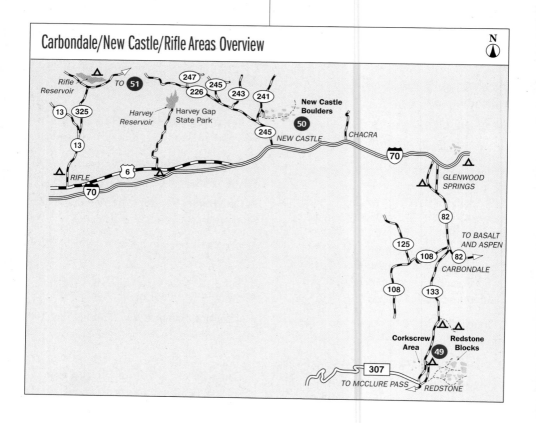

Carbondale/New Castle/Rifle Areas Overview

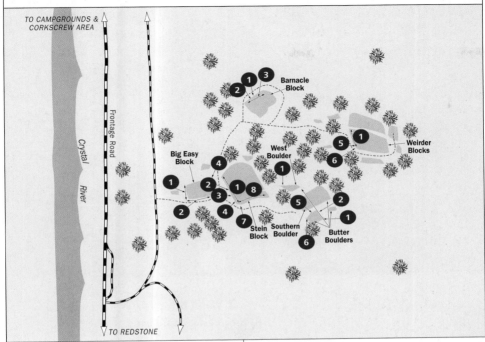

Highway 133 to the north end of Redstone. Before the town center, you will see a few distinct campgrounds on the left side of the road, one with full hookups and showers.

For the Corkscrew Area, park in the pull off just south of the north entrance into Redstone. The boulders are located on the west bank of the river.

For the Redstone Blocks, take a left onto the frontage road at the north end of Redstone and drive approximately 1 mile and park in the parking area just before the Redstone town sign. Locate the dirt road and hike on it 150 feet, to a left onto the single track. Follow the trail, eventually hiking along the fence line. Continue down the trail, past the end of the fence another 200 feet. Look for the faint climbers' trail that heads off to the right (east) into the thicket of trees. You will soon see the boulders within the aspen trees.

Corkscrew Area

This is the northernmost area, and the boulders and blocks are located along the banks of the Crystal River.

Corkscrew Block

How many bottles of wine have people drunk while gazing at the Crystal River from this block? This awesome block sits riverside and is endowed with many problem types.

1. Corkscrew Left V5 Climb up the pod to the slopers above on the left side of the east face.

2. Corkscrew V6 Climb up the center of the overhanging east face.

3. Main Squeeze V6 From down low, climb up the overhanging northeast arête.

4. Magazine Traverse V8 Traverse from *Main Squeeze* across left to *Corkscrew Left*.

5. Guns and Roses V6 Traverse down low across the northwest face.

6. Northwest Slab V2 (hb) Climb up the center of the northwest slab.

7. Worm Drive V4 (hb) Climb up the far-right side of the northwest face.

8. South Slab V3 (hb) Climb up the highball center of the south-facing slab.

The Pyramid

This is another riverside boulder just north of Corkscrew Block. Depending on the time of year and the amount of precipitation, this boulder may be submerged. Nonetheless, it has great challenges on crystalline faces.

1. Pyramid V6 Dyno up the southeast face.

2. Pyramid Traverse V7 Traverse from right to left across the boulder.

Immersion Block

The name says it all: This boulder may be immersed in water, or if you fall off the riverside face, you will be. This block is across the river to the southeast of Corkscrew Block.

1. Immersion Traverse V2 Traverse the block's top from left across to the right on the riverside. It's a splash.

2. Total Immersion V2 Climb up the clean northwest arête.

Splash Boulder ▲

This boulder is across the river and northeast of Corkscrew Block. Its west side is submerged.

1. Solid Ground V0 Climb the right side of the east face.

Redstone Blocks

These boulders and blocks are located in a pristine setting among the aspen trees, just north of Redstone's town center. Huge to medium boulders are full of excellent problems.

Big Easy Block

This is the first block you will see as you hike up the boulderer's trail through the aspens. It is located at a clearing, where you can see other rocks to the east. Traverses abound on this block.

1. The Front V6 Traverse the west face from left to right.

2. Big Easy V1 Traverse across the south face from left to right, ending on the far-right side of the east face.

3. Lowrider V10 Traverse as an eliminate, utilizing only the pebbles down low. Traverse the same distance as *Big Easy*.

4. Pocket Prob V2 Climb up the pockets and pebbles on the far-right side of the east face.

5. Biggy Arête V6 From down low, climb up the northeast arête.

Stein Block ▼

You can see this massive block across the clearing to the east of Big Easy Block. It sits among the aspen trees. A multitude of traverses and steep face problems exist on its west and south sides. Many variation exists across the south face, and contrived eliminates abound.

1. Slopenstein V6 Traverse across slopers from the far-left side of the west face to a large hold.

2. Gertrudestein V9 Climb up the west face just right of the aspen tree.

3. Arêtestein V7 Climb up the face to the left of the off-width.

4. Frankenstein V8 Climb up the dihedral, just right of the off-width.

5. Grisseltwist V10 Climb the dihedral, utilizing counter pulls.

6. Pinchenstein V4 From down low, climb up the face to the right of the dihedral, utilizing underclings and slopers.

7. Melonstein V6 Climb up the southwest prow.

8. Linkenstein V5 Traverse from the southwest prow across the south face to the right on large horizontals.

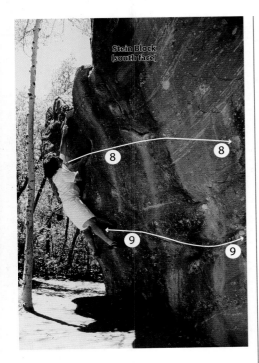

Stein Block
(south face)

9. Lowenstein V10 Traverse across the south face, utilizing the low holds.

10. Simplestein V0 Climb the best hold across the south face.

Barnacle Block

This large cube is approximately 100 feet upslope to the northeast of Stein Block. It has a crystalline northwest face and sits within the aspen forest.

1. Octopus V4 (hb) Climb up the center of the northwest face to large pebbles.

2. Pebble Affair V7 Climb up the northwest face to the right of *Octopus*.

3. Barnacle Traverse V7 Traverse the northwest face from far right across left to the northeastern arête.

Weirder Block ▼

This large block is upslope to the east of Barnacle Block and upslope to the northeast of Stein Block. It is obscured by aspen trees, so be patient in your search for it. Hike east approximately 100 feet through the trees on a boulderer's trail between Barnacle Block and Stein Block, until you see this large block.

1. High Traverse V2 Traverse across the west face from left to right.

2. Low Traverse V8 Traverse the sloper down low across the west face.

3. Weirdo V5 Climb up the left side of the west face.

4. Weird Al V7 Climb up the face just left of the crack.

5. Geek Crack V10 Climb the crack on the west face.

6. Geekatron V6 Climb up the face to the right of the crack.

Butter Boulders

This group of smaller boulders is located southwest of Weirder Block, southeast of

Barnacle Block, and east of Stein Block. Hike 50 feet downslope to the west of Weirder Block and then head due south about 100 feet through the trees, until you see these boulders.

West Boulder

This is the boulder that sits to the southwest as you approach from the north.

1. East Butter Overhang V6 Climb out the north face of the westernmost boulder.

Southern Boulder ◄ ▲

This is the southernmost boulder of the three. The majority of the problems are on its north face.

1. Left Arête V6 Climb up the southeastern arête of the east face.

2. Middle Arête V2 Climb up the left-angling arête on the northeast corner.

3. The Prow V7 Climb up the prow on the northeast corner.

4. The Scoop V2 Climb up the scoop on the left side of the north face.

5. Pocket Route V1 Climb up the pockets in the center of the north face.

6. Right Arête V1 Climb up the northwest arête.

50 NEW CASTLE (SANDS OF TIME BOULDERS)

See map on page 442.

This solid sandstone boulderfield is located amid the sage-filled meadows and juniper-filled landscape northwest of the small town of New Castle, west of Glenwood Springs. At a relatively low elevation, the conditions here are moderate year round and offer a great alternative to the areas east and south. The sandstone offers great problems that will intrigue even the most arrogant boulderer.

Directions: From Glenwood Springs, head west on I-70 approximately 11.5 miles to the New Castle exit (exit 105). Head west through the center of town and go right (north) onto County Road 245. Drive northwest on CR 245 out of town and go right (north) onto East Elk Creek Road (County Road 241). Take CR 241 north for about 0.3 mile and park at the pullout on the right. Backtrack by hiking up the road to a side road that switchbacks and follows a waterline to the upslope. Look for a pole rising from the first boulder on the slope.

51 RIFLE MOUNTAIN PARK

See map on page 442.

The limestone walls of Rifle Mountain offer good traverse training at their bases. Isolated boulders are a rarity within the canyon, so you may want to venture eastward to New Castle, where there are solid sandstone boulders. When staying at Rifle, though, bouldering offers an alternative to the multitude of sport routes that line the canyon walls.

Directions: From I-70 exit at New Castle (exit 105) and follow the road west through town, to a right on CR 245. Follow CR 245 northwest for approximately 12.3 miles, eventually turning into County Road 226, just before the right turn onto County Road 325. Head right (northeast) and follow CR 325 into Rifle Mountain Park.

You also may continue down I-70 from New Castle and take the Rifle exit. Follow Highway 13 north through the town of Rifle to a right onto CR 325. Follow CR 325 past the Rifle Gap Reservoir, staying right, and into Rifle Mountain Park.

The Wasteland

This section of limestone has a steep base below its bulging and overhanging upper section. The landings are flat and the traversing is a great pump. Drive 0.4 mile from the entrance kiosk and park on the left side of the road. Hike across the road to the limestone base.

1. Wasted Traverse V5 Traverse the limestone base of the wall from left to right.

Lower Tier

This overhanging section of limestone is located 0.1 mile from the Wasteland. Park in the pullout, walk up the trail to the base, then go right to the overhangs.

1. Tears Traverse V? Traverse the base from the third bolted route across to the left, ending in the center of the wall at the gray protrusion.

2. Teary Traverse V6 Traverse across the base from the far-left bolt line to the right, finishing at the holdless section.

Bauhaus Wall

This quality limestone cave is on the far-left side of the cliff and offers a multitude of variations from within it. Drive north another 0.3 mile from Lower Tier (0.4 from the Wasteland) and park on the right. Look for the bridge that crosses the creek, hike across, and head to the right and then take a left. Follow the trail 100 feet, until you see the climbers' trail that leads to the base of the wall. Hike to the base and follow it to the far-left end. You will see the small cave with chalk.

1. Bauhaus Overhang V5 Climb out the cave.

2. Bausit V8 Traverse across to the right from the far left bolt line on the cliff.

Anti-Phil Wall

Continue from the Bauhaus Wall another 0.3 mile north down the road to a picnic area pull off on the left. Hike across the creek via a log crossing and head right on the climbers' trail that leads to the base of the cliff. Follow the cliff band to the right to the table in the meadow. The traverse starts in the middle of the wall to the right of the picnic table. Other vertical boulder problems, topped out at 10 feet to a shelf break, are found farther to the right within the forest, before the dirt pile.

1. Anti-Phil Traverse V5 Traverse the base from its center, across to the left, to a ramp.

2. Lantz Problemo V? Climb up the middle of the 10-foot face.

BASALT AREA
52 BASALT BOULDERS

The boulders east of Basalt offer a reclusive bouldering experience that is a good escape from the hustle and bustle of Highway 82 and the Aspen area. They also offer alternative camping not too far from the Redstone area. The boulders are located along Frying Pan Road as you drive east toward Chapman Lake.

Directions: From Carbondale, take Highway 82 east to the town of Basalt. Look for the BASALT/RUEDI RESERVOIR sign on the right side of the road. Exit onto Midland Avenue and take it to Frying Pan Road (Forest Road 105). Head east on Frying Pan Road toward Ruedi Reservoir. The Rudy Boulders are located roadside on the way to the reservoir.

The Meredith Blocks appear near Meredith, just east of the reservoir.

Rudy Boulders

These boulders are located along Frying Pan Road a few miles east of Basalt, before the Reudi Reservoir. They sit roadside, almost opposite of each other. There is a large sandstone block on the left and an overhanging boulder on the right, near the creek.

Rudy Boulder

This is the leaning, overhanging sandstone boulder on the right side of the road, just off the creek.

1. Rudy's Overhang V4 From down low, climb up the right side of the northwest face, utilizing the arête.

Basal/Aspen Area Overview

Rude Block ▲

This tall sandstone block is on the left side of the road, just opposite of Rudy Boulder. You can see other blocks on the slopes above and along the north side of the road.

1. Rude Arête V2 Climb the left arête of the south face.

2. Rude Fisher V3 Climb up the middle of the south face.

3. Rude On V1 Climb up the right side of the north face.

53 CHAPMAN LAKE

There are plenty of boulders scattered about the forests and shores of Chapman Lake. Others are up toward Hagerman Pass. There are many problem types here, and the boulders have a fresh, low-traffic feel to them.

Directions: From Basalt, take Frying Pan Road (Forest Road 105) east, another 6 or so miles past Meredith, and take a right toward Chapman Lake and Campground. Park at the group-site gate and walk east on a dirt road that leads to the Chapman boulders. After hiking a short way, the first boulder, Numero Uno Boulder, will be on the right. Continue along the dirt road toward the campground and you will come across other boulders (including the Unknown Boulders).

Continue down the road, past the lake, until you see a sign on the right for campsite 22. Hike a short way up the trail to campsite 22 and you will begin to see boulders spread about. To find other boulders, take the right-hand trail just past the parking area upslope to the southeast approximately 500 feet. On the slope you will see the Canine Blocks, two blocks separated by a chimney.

Campsite 22 Boulders

These are around and about campsite 22.

Lone Boulder ▲

This isolated boulder is located across the trail and upslope to the west of the camp. It has a blackened south side.

1. Lone V0 Climb up the left side of the east face.

2. Own V3 Climb up the middle of the east face.

3. Money V0 Climb up the right side of the east face.

Hillside Boulders

These boulders are located upslope and are scattered about the hillside to the west of the Campsite 22 Boulders. Many fresh problems await.

Hillrod Boulder ▼

To find this boulder, hike west 200 feet up the trail from campsite 22 and then descend the hillside to the boulder. You also will encounter many other boulders.

1. Hillrod V1 Climb up the right prow of the west face.

2. Sloperod V4 Climb up the steep slab on the left side of the west face.

Group Site Boulders

To find these boulders. continue past the trail that leads to the Campsite 22 Boulders, hike up the dirt road to the east, cross into the group campsites, and continue farther east up the road until you see the boulders.

Hagerman Pass Boulders

These boulders are scattered throughout the west side of Hagerman Pass. Many problems await discovery.

Directions: Drive up Frying Pan Road (FR 105), past Chapman Lake, to a prominent hairpin turn. Continue driving northwest. Just past the Forest Road 505 turnoff, you will begin to see the boulders on the left side of the road.

Sunshine Boulder

This polished granite boulder sits up valley with a panoramic serene setting. It is located on the left side of the road within the brush, just past FR 505 as you travel up FR 105.

1. Sunny V5 From down low, climb up the far-left side of the west face.

2. Morning Star V6 Climb up to the corner on left side of the west face.

3. Sunshine V8 Climb up the right-leaning line in the center of the west face.

4. Glare V6 Climb the prow on the right side of the west face.

5. Blinded V2 Climb up the south face.

6. Alpenglow V4 Climb up the southeast face.

7. White Light Traverse V7? Traverse the west face from right to left.

ASPEN AREA

The famous celebrity hangout and tourist town of Aspen offers many things to do, both in town and in the nearby mountains. Aspen also has a local outdoor bouldering park located at the far-west end of the mall, near the Ute Mountaineer gear shop. Great problems exist on this artificial work of art. But if you're looking for a true bouldering experience, you must venture out of town to Independence Pass, which is packed with bouldering areas.

54 INDEPENDENCE PASS WEST

This side of the pass (west of the summit and southeast of Aspen) is a welcome escape from the busy town below. The alpine environment offers boulders, blocks, and minicliffs all along the winding and at times very narrow Highway 82. Access to most areas is a hop, skip, and a jump away, making this a perfect beat-the-heat summer area. The high elevation of 9,000 to 12,000 feet keeps the boulders crisp and frictiony. In winter the road is closed, although the lower-lying areas are accessible most times of the year. The road does not open again until late spring, sometimes early summer. Camping is available all along the way, with majestic views of the divide at the upper ends of the pass.

Directions: From Interstate 70, exit at Glenwood Springs and loop around south on Highway 82 toward Aspen. Drive southeast, past Carbondale and Basalt, into the heart of Aspen. Continue on Highway 82 (Original Street), past the intersection of Cooper Avenue and head southeast out of town. Mileages for bouldering are given from the intersection of Highway 82 and Original Street.

Check out the outdoor bouldering park in Aspen if you have time.

Independence Pass

0 Km 4
0 Miles 4

ASPEN

TO HIGHWAY 24

Mt. Massive 14,421'

Mt. Elbert 14,433'

Monitor Rock

La Plata Peak 14,336'

Lake

Twin Lakes

Perry Peaks Campground

Karma Cliff Boulders

Brie's Block
Katie's Block

Lackawanna Gulch

Independence Pass Summit 12,095'

Mountain Boy Boulders

James Brown Boulder

Bart Boulder

Bullfrog Boulders

Storm Boulder

Grotto's Wall Boulders

Sunset Boulder

The Boulder

Beetle Juice

Camp 5 Boulders

Hernando's Hideaway

Whirlpool Boulders

The Cube

Lincoln Creek Area

Ice Cube

World of Hurt

Weller Campground

Weller Slab

Jaws Boulders

Patrol Boulder

Roaring Fork River

Difficult Boulders

Difficult Campground

Castle Peak 14,245'

N

Patrol Boulder

This is located on the left side of the road, 2.8 miles from the intersection of Highway 82 and Original Street, just before mile marker 44.

1. Patrol Traverse V1 Traverse around the boulder.

Difficult Boulders

These boulders are located 3.6 miles from Highway 82 and Original Street. Turn right into the Difficult Campground and park at the day-use area. Hike southwest ten minutes, staying to the right at the trail junction. The boulders are along the trail on the right and left.

Difficult Right

This is the boulder on the right side of the trail.

1. The Traverse V1 Traverse the lip from right to left.

Difficult Left

This boulder is on the left side of the trail.

1. Trail Traverse V2 From down low traverse out the cove, then go up and left.

Jaws Boulders

To reach the Jaws Boulders from Highway 82 and Original Street, drive 7.7 miles up the pass and park at the parking area in a sharp curve. The boulders are located a short way downslope to the east just off the river.

Jaws Rock ▲

Park on the right side of the highway in the parking area. Hike downslope to the east and you will see this tall block close to the Roaring Fork River. You may want a toprope.

1. Killer Arête V3 (hb) Climb up the roof and arête on the east face.

2. Big Bite V1 (hb) Climb up the left side of the north face, left of the crack system.

3. Surfer V2 (hb) Climb up the crack on the north face.

Piranha Block

This block is located a few feet north of Jaws Rock.

1. Nibble V2 From down low, climb up the left side of the east face.

2. Chow Down V4 Climb up the center of the east face.

3. Piranha V5 From down low, climb up the arête on the right side of the east face.

Hernando's Hideaway

To find this area, continue up the pass from the Jaws Boulders parking area. Go 0.3 mile past the Weller Campground and park on the right side of the road. Hike 300 feet up the road and ascend a clean granite slab into the aspen forest. Continue through the groove to the northeast, hike the base of the black cliff band, and then go another 300 feet up above the cliff to the north. The problems are on the black cliff up to the right. Look for the chalk and the limitless variations in the over-hanging section of the cliff. These problems stay dry when it's raining.

1. Fernando's V0 Traverse down low from left to right.

2. Circle Game V6 Circle the wall from low to high across the face.

3. Hernando's Traverse V6 Climb the high route from right to left.

4. The Crescent V4 Climb up the left side of the face to the crescent.

5. Zernando's V2 Climb up the far-right side face.

Whirlpool Boulders

This area is another 0.9 mile up the pass from Jaws Rock (or 8.6 miles from Aspen), on the left side of the road. Park on the right, cross over the road to the trail that leads to Whirlpool Rock, and head left into the talus 100 feet to the area.

1. Whirlpool Arête V7 Climb the chalked-up overhanging arête above flat ground.

2. Vertical Challenges V1 Climb up the steep face right of *Whirlpool Arête*.

Grotto Wall Boulders

These are located 9.2 miles from Aspen. Park on the left after going around a hairpin turn. From the parking area you can see Lower Grotto Wall, with the clean white dihedral systems, upslope. Look west and you will see the talus field full of blocks and boulders. A few have excellent problems and reasonable landings.

Parking Lot Block

This block is in the parking area just below the main wall.

1. Lotto V4 Climb across the lip, then onto the slab.

Felix Block

This block sits just above the left side of the road. You will see it shortly after you head west along the trail.

1. Felix V6 Climb from down low up and across the left-leaning arête on the north face.

Ineditable Boulder ▲

This large boulder is located within the hairpin slopes, up on the left. Hike along the trail that leads west from the parking area and cut off to the left behind talus rocks approximately 150 feet, until you see this tall spire-topped boulder.

1. Edit Worthy V5 Traverse from the far-left side of the south face across to the corner.

2. The Ineditable V6 (xhb) Climb up the right side of the tall south face.

3. Spell Check V3 Climb up the short overhang on the far-right side of the south face.

4. Gray Beard V2 (hb) Climbs up the slab on the north face.

5. Gray Arête V4 Climb up the arête on the left side of the north face.

World of Hurt

You will find these boulders scattered amid the talus slope after you scramble north 150 feet through the talus from Ineditable Boulder.

Darkness Block

This block is located through the talus approximately 150 feet north from Ineditable Boulder.

1. Child of Darkness V9 From down low, climb up the right side of the south face.

Black Caesar Boulder

From the Grotto Wall parking area, hike 0.1 mile up the road to a narrow pass way for cars. On the left you will see this little black wall below a striped slab top.

1. Caesar V6 Climb up the left side of the wall.

2. Black Caesar V4 Climb up the center of the wall.

3. Caesar Salad V3 Climb up the right, shorter side of the wall.

Lincoln Creek Area

Continue up the pass another 0.8 mile from the Grotto Wall Boulders parking area, or 9.8 miles total from Aspen. Turn right (south) onto Lincoln Creek Road and drive downslope to the west about 1 mile, into Lincoln Creek Campground. The boulders and minicliffs are located along the dirt road and campgrounds.

Intruder Boulder

This is a roadside boulder just past the entrance to the campground.

1. Intruders V4 Climb the steep prow on the south face just above the road.

Tract Wall ▼

This is an awesome minicliff with beautiful, river-polished, black-striped granite.

Laybacks, stemming, and crack climbing abound. Continue northwest down the road another 300 feet from Intruder Boulder.

1. Leaning Crack V0 Climb up the crack to the left of the watermark.

2. Stem Gem V2 (hb) Stem up the stair-stepped black watermark.

3. Pissy Crack V6 (hb) Climb up the left arching crack.

Outhouse Wall ▼

This stretch of granite offers excellent mini-cliff climbing and traversing. Hike up to the campground area on the right from the Tract Wall. The wall minicliff is located behind the restroom.

1. TP Traverse V3 Traverse across the wall from left to right.

2. Zorro V1 Climb the Z crack on the wall's left side.

3. The Lump V1 (hb) Climb the tall face just left of the roofed section.

4. Outhouse V2 (hb) Climb up and out the left side of the roofed section.

5. Highwire V4 (hb) Climb up the seams on the far-right side of the wall.

Sunset Boulder

This boulder is located by parking at the intersection of Highway 82 and Lincoln Creek Road. From the parking area hike across the bridge and head left (south). Follow the Roaring Fork River for approximately 175 yards and then head to the right on a faint trail that switchbacks upslope. The Sunset Boulder is on the left side of the trail.

1. Target Practice V4 (hb) Climb the overhanging crack on the south face of the boulder.

The Cube

Continue a short way up the trail to an opening and you will see this large cubed block.

1. Cubed Square V3 (hb) Climb the leaning lines of the east face.

Wild Rock Boulders

Continue up the pass another mile from Lincoln Creek (10.8 miles from Aspen) and park on the right, below the Wild Rock Wall. Hike across the road toward the talus field, skirt around to the left side, and locate the trail that leads to the Wild Rock Wall. The boulders are on the left side of the slope, 100 yards northwest, in a flat before the uphill talus field toward Wild Rock Wall.

First Boulder

This boulder is about 15 feet east of the road and lies before James Brown Boulder.

1. First of Fifth V3 Climb up the overhanging northeast arête.

James Brown Boulder

This large boulder, 50 feet west of First Boulder, sits on the flat close to the talus slope. It is the right boulder of a group of three large boulders that sit next to each other.

1. Funky President V3 (hb) Climb up the northeast arête's right side.

2. Hot Pants V4 Climb up to the triangle on the north face, exiting right.

3. Sex Machine V4 From down low, climb straight up through the triangle to the top.

Middle JB Boulder

This is the center boulder of the three.

1. JBees V4 Climb up the face just left of the tree.

2. Body Count V2 (hb) Climb the gray face just right of *JBees*.

Lefty JB Boulder

This is the left boulder of the three.

1. Moon Tide V1 Climb up the overhanging seam left of the V seam on the face.

2. Chick Climb V2 Climb up the V seam on the face.

3. American Hero V4 (hb) Climb up the corner through the gold and white rock.

Bullfrog Boulders
(Upper Boulderfield)

Continue up the pass another 0.3 mile (11.1 miles from Aspen) to a large parking area in front of the boulderfield. The boulders extend several hundred feet across the flat; you can see them just left of the road. Problems have also been done in the talus slope above. This is a favorite area for locals, and hundreds of problems exist in the convenient boulderfield.

Parking Area
Warm-Up Boulder

This stumpy boulder sits within the parking area and is characterized by a chalked west-side traverse.

1. Middle Earth V4 Climb up the center of the west face.

2. Right On V2 From down low, climb up the holds right of *Middle Earth*.

3. High Road V3 Traverse across the west face's upper lip.

4. Scoopen V6 From down low, climb up the scoop on the left side of the north face.

5. No Camping Here V7 Traverse into Scoopen.

Lightning Bolt Boulder ▼

To locate this large boulder, hike 100 feet north of the parking area. It has a roof and crack on its south face.

1. Lightning Slot V3 Climb up the slot left of the roof on the south face.

2. White Roof V2 Climb up and mantle over the roof.

3. Lightning Bolt Crack V0 Climb the crack to the right of *White Roof*.

Dihedral Rock

From Lightning Bolt Boulder hike approximately 50 feet right (east) to this dihedral rock.

1. Super Dihedral V2 (hb) Climb the crack in the left-facing dihedral on the west face.

Side Block

This block is located just down and right of Dihedral Rock.

1. Mike's Prow V2 From down low, climb up the southwestern prow.

Left Dependent Block

This block is 30 feet right (east) of Side Block. Cruise up behind *Mike's Prow*. It is the left block of two sitting next to each other.

1. The Thing V3 From down low, climb up the north face.

2. Figure It Out V4 Climb the bulge on the face.

3. Tree Arête V3 Climb up the arête on the left side of the face.

4. Tree Slab V2 Climb up the arête right of the tree.

Right Dependent Block ▼

This is the block on the right-hand side.

1. Dependent Arête V2 Climb the right-angling southwest arête.

2. Dependent Traverse V4 Traverse from right to left across the southwest face.

Loner Stone ▲

This leaning chunk is located approximately 100 feet east of the Dependent Blocks.

1. The Loner V4 From down low, climb out the flake system on the north side.

Tower of Power Block ▶

This tall block is just north of Loner Stone, upslope about 20 feet into the talus. It has a leaning, overhanging, black-, white-, and gold-striped southwest face.

1. Bob's Prow V6 (hb) Climb up from down low on the far-right side of the southwest face.

2. BHhb V7 (hb) Climb up the center of the southwest face, right of *Bob's Prow.*

Black and Yellow Block ◄

This block is upslope, within the talus, approximately 75 feet north of Power of Tower Block.

1. Yellow Wall V3 Climb up the middle of the northwest face.

Gray Cube ▼

Continue east 75 feet across the talus from Black and Yellow Block.

1. Gray's Left V1 Climb the left side of the easy face.

2. Gray's Right V0 Climb the right side of the east face.

Pappy Block

This overhanging block is downslope from Gray Cube, within the talus and trailside.

1. El Vere V6 Climb out the east-facing overhang's far-left side.

2. Che It Loud V8 Climb out the center of the east-facing overhang.

3. Pappy V1 Climb out the right side of the east overhang.

Hand Jive Boulder ▼

This huge boulder is 250 feet due east of Loner Stone. The problems are highball, and there is a pine tree on its summit.

1. Triple Decker V4 (hb) Climb up the east arête.

2. Double Decker (hb) Climb up the sloper-whitened northern arête.

Slab Rock ▲

This rock is just downslope from Hand Jive Boulder. You can see it just off the road down east from the Bullfrog Boulders parking area. It has nice crack and corner problems.

1. The Groove V0 Climb up the grooved corner on the left side of the face.

2. Diagonal Crack V1 Climb up the diagonaling crack, right of the groove.

3. Slab Traverse V4 Traverse the south face from left to the right.

4. Left Leaner V1 Climb the left-diagonaling crack on the right side.

Far East Block

This block is on the easternmost side of the boulderfield within the forest, about 300 feet east of Hand Jive Boulder.

1. Roofy V3 Climb out the roof on the east face.

Far East Road Block

This block is just east of Far East Block, but sits closer to the road.

1. Invisible Seam V1 Climb the slight seam on the east face.

2. Tree Overhang V2 Climb out the overhang, right of the tree on the west face.

Left Dynamic Block ▼

This block is located 50 feet northwest of the parking area. It is on the left-hand side of a set of two blocks. There is a Christmas tree in front of it.

1. Bleed V6 From down low, climb up the southwest arête.

2. Need V2 Climbs up the slab on the south face.

Right Dynamic Boulder

This is the rock on the right-hand side.

1. Dynamic Plan V1 Climb up from the good holds on the face.

2. Dynamic Man V7 From down low, climb up the overhang to good holds.

Ramp Boulder

This slabby boulder is 30 feet west of the Right Dynamic Boulder.

1. The Ramp V1 Climb the slab on the south face.

2. Rampart V0 Climb up the middle of the north face.

Warmer Upper Block ◄

This shielded block is located at the far-west side of the boulderfield, out in the flat. Hike about 130 feet due west from the parking area to a block with a pine tree in front of its shielded north face.

1. Upper Arête V0 Climb the classic north-east arête.

2. Slopey Shield V4 Climb up the slopers just right of the arête.

3. The Shield V1 Climb up the center of the north face.

4. Shield Dihedral V0 Climb up the dihedral on the north face.

5. Diagonaling Shield V1 Climb up and left from the far-right side of the north face.

6. Shield Traverse V5 Traverse across the north face from right to left.

55 INDEPENDENCE PASS EAST

See map on page 457.

There are worthwhile secluded blocks and boulders tucked away along a dirt road within this scenic side valley. You can find them as you head down the east side of the pass toward Twin Lakes.

Directions: From the top of Independence Pass, continue east on Highway 82 for several miles to the third hairpin turn. Turn left onto a dirt track and park. Hike north approximately 200 yards down the dirt track/trail until you see the first set of boulders on the left.

If coming in from the east, drive west 12.7 miles from the Twin Lakes Store and park on the dirt road.

Katie's Block ▼

This nice piece of mountain granite has an awesome west face with many good holds for traversing and climbing upon. From the trail the block looks less significant, because the west face is facing upslope, away from the trail. Hike 100 yards up the trail from the parking area and you will see this block on the left, out in the meadow and scrub brush.

1. Katiedid V1 Climb up the left side of the west face.

2. Katiedidn't V2 Climb up the center of the west face.

3. Katie's Kitchen V0 Climb up the right side of the west face.

4. Katie's Traverse V3 Traverse across the west face in either direction.

Brie's Block ▲

This block is located 200 feet north of Katie's Block on the right side of the dirt track and has a steep, shelved southeast face. A large pine tree sits off its northwest end.

1. Brie's Overhang V3 Climb out the over-hanging south face.

2. Beaudiddley V2 Climb up the seam on the left side of the southeast face.

3. Princeton V1 Climb up from the left side of the top shelf on the southeast face.

4. Mountain Dog V0 Climb up the center of the southeast face.

5. Super Dog V2 Climb up the diagonaling crack on the right side of the southeast face.

6. Doodles V3 Traverse from right to left across the southeast face.

CENTRAL DIVIDE SOUTH

BUENA VISTA AREA

The town of Buena Vista sits at the eastern threshold of the Collegiate Peaks and draws many "fourteener" hikers, as well as rafters, campers, and fisherman. It is also a bouldering paradise, as this extensive area has a wealth of bouldering in the foothills surrounding the town, not to mention the boulders located in the moraines below many of the high peaks. Access to the bouldering is gained off of back roads that take you very close to the boulders. The granite boulders and blocks usually have a wide variety of holds, cracks, corners, and arêtes. The rock varies from smooth and polished to sometimes crumbly due to low traffic. A lot of the rock is good and gets better with tracking.

Buena Vista Area Overview

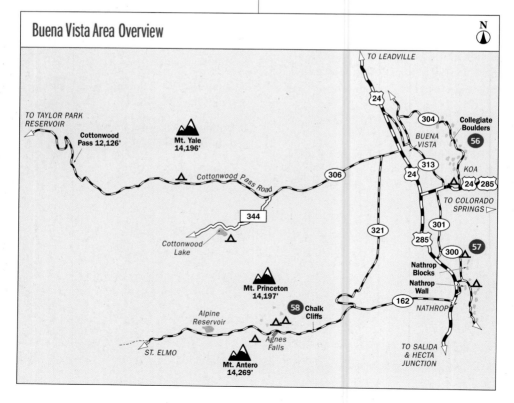

The author enjoying *Berholtz's Arête* (V6) on the Hone Stone, Crested Butte.

Several bouldering areas are located around Buena Vista, as well as Nathrop to the south. The North Town Boulders are north of Buena Vista; the Scenic Boulders are east and southeast. In addition, Buena Vista has all the accommodations you will need— restaurants, hotels, and campgrounds. Don't miss the Coyote Cantina for a fun time. The KOA has been very hospitable as well, with access from its northeast campsites to some of the awesome boulders located on public land.

Directions: Take Highway 24 south from Leadville or west from Colorado Springs directly into the center of Buena Vista. From the Front Range, Highway 285 west is a good bet.

56 COLLEGIATE BOULDERS

See map on page 472.

This is the boulder pack that everyone talks about when they drive down Highway 24 through Buena Vista. The slopes to the east and south of town are extensive boulderfields with every size boulder and block imaginable. Views of the Collegiate Peaks are seen to the west, making this area a majestic setting for bouldering.

Directions: These areas are best accessed from the south via County Road 304. The first area is the Supper's Ready Boulders, which are located on the left (west) side of CR 304 as you come from the south off Highway 24. Behind these boulders (also to the west) are the Ridge Cap Boulders, located on the top of the domed mound. Next are the Railroad Boulders, which are also accessed from CR 304 but found upslope to the east on the right side of the road. CR 304 runs along an old railroad grade, allowing easy access to the slopes above and below.

    To reach these areas from Buena Vista, drive south out of town and go east on Highway 24. Drive about 2 miles (passing the KOA) to a left onto CR 304. Take CR 304 north approximately 1.5 miles and park. Hike west for the Supper's Ready Boulders and Ridge Cap Boulders. The other areas are located up the road and are described from south to north.

Supper's Ready Boulders

These boulders are located just west of CR 304. From Highway 24 drive north on CR 304 approximately 1.5 miles and park on the left side of the road. Hike west on the horse trails, toward the KOA campground, for approximately ten to fifteen minutes. These

rocks are located up the washes, approximately 0.5 mile east of the campground border. Once you are in the washes, the boulders appear and extend to the north and south.

Cell Phone Boulder ▲

This nice boulder is just above the trail to the northeast and has a nice discontinuous crack on its west face.

1. Cellular Savage V1 Climb up the crack on the west face.

2. Katie's Secret World V4 Climb the arête on the left side of the west face.

3. Deceiver Slab V0 Climb the slab on the right side of the west face.

Marriages Boulder ▲

This boulder is just past Cell Phone Boulder.

1. Number 4 V3 Climb the arête on the left side of the southwest face.

2. Who's Next V6 Climb the thin slab right of the arête.

Tinman Rock ▲

Continue north along the washes and boulder bands and you will see this fun rock on the right side of the wash.

1. Tinman's Prow V5 Climb up the scoop then the prow.

Sandbox Area

To find these boulders and blocks, hike northwest out of the Supper's Ready area to another wash and distinguishable trail that leads north. The blocks are trailside and on the slopes.

Sandman Block ▲

This quality block is located trailside, just over a rise, as you hike north along the trail.

1. Sandman Arête V2 Climb the left arête of the south face.

2. Sandbagged V3 Climb up the middle of the south face.

3. Sand Storm V4 Climb over the bulge up the arête on the right side of the south face.

Ridge Cap Boulders

To find these fine boulders continue north from the Sandbox Area. Hike up the trail to a point where it cuts out to the west. You will see the boulders upslope, lining the ridge cap of the prominent dome that rises out west.

Muffin Boulder ◄

You will encounter this boulder when you reach the east end of the ridge cap. It has a thin overhanging seam that splits its southeast face.

1. The Muffin V8–V9 Climb up the thin seam on the southeast face.

Mild Slab

This slabby rock is upslope from Muffin Boulder and is the easternmost rock in a cove of many nice boulders.

1. Mild Slab V0 Climb the middle of the west face.

Helmet Block ▲

This roofed block is just west of Mild Slab.

1. Helmet Traverse V4 Traverse under the roof from right to left.

2. Helmet Roof/Arête V7 Climb up the roof and arête on the west side of the block.

Summit Block ▲

This blocky wall is at the top of the slope at a point where you can see over the rise to the west.

1. Summit Wall V2 Climb up the middle of the north face.

2. Summit Traverse V5 Traverse across the north face from right to left.

Railroad Boulders

These boulders are farther north on CR 304. Drive north and look east for the many fall lines of boulders.

57 NATHROP BLOCKS

See map on page 472.

These are the original gems that were most likely discovered by climbers who were camping in the area during a rafting trip. The spectacular boulders here offer classic problems that have been favorites of Colorado boulderers for years.

Directions: From Buena Vista, head south on Highway 24. At the intersection of Highway 24 and Highway 285, continue due south on Highway 285 toward Nathrop. Drive approximately 3.4 miles to a left on County Road 301. Head east around and over the Arkansas River for about 0.5 mile to a right on County Road 300. Follow CR 300 straight ahead to the south 2.1 miles. On the left side of the road, you will begin to see some very nice boulders. Park on the left side of the road. Most of these boulders have good landings.

Nathrop Block ▼ (aka Buena Vista Boulder)

This block was probably misnamed by a visitor who thought he was in Buena Vista. It is an area gem and is located just off the dirt road (south of Nathrop Cube). It has a steep south face and an awesome overhanging northeast face. The landing is great. Down climb the southwest face.

1. Sunshine Superman V1 Climb up the center of the south face.

2. Southern Sun V0 Climb up the face just left of the southeast arête.

3. Nathrop Arête V2 (hb) Climb up the southeast arête.

4. Light Sentence V3 Climb up from the center of the flat block located on the left half of the west face.

5. Chained Heat V6 Climb up the west overhang just right of the flat block.

6. Chain Reaction V4 Climb up immediately right of *Chained Heat*.

7. Nathnorth V2 Climb up the northwest face.

Nathrop Cube ▼

This block is located a few feet north of Nathrop Block.

1. The Verse V1 Traverse from the left (northeast) face across the north face.

2. Pocket Cube V0 Climb up the pockets on the north face.

3. The Cling V0 Climb up from the under-cling on the south face.

Maiden Block ▲

This boulder is approximately 75 feet south of Nathrop Block.

1. Marrying Maiden V2 Climb up the left side of the northeast face.

2. Pocket Pool V0 Climb the pockets on the right side of the northeast face.

Butler Block ▼

This block is just southeast of Maiden Block. A thick tree stands on the block's left side.

1. Servitude V3 Climb up the pinches on the east face.

2. You Rang V0 Climb up the northwest arête to the slab above.

Raft Block ▲

This lengthy block is located south beyond Butler Block. It is the taller block of two.

1. The Paddle V1 (hb) Climb up the north face to a good hold topout.

Trees Block

Continue down the road 75 yards, past some short boulders, to this block sitting off in the trees to the left.

1. Tree Out V2 Climb up the middle of the west face.

Ruby Mountain Boulders

From the Nathrop Blocks continue south 200 yards down the road (CR 300) along the Arkansas River to a campground and picnic area. This is a stopping point for rafters as well as a launch spot for both kayakers and rafters. Park and hike northeast up into the slopes and you will see many boulders about.

Ruby Boulder ▼

This boulder is up on the slopes northeast from the parking area.

1. Ruby Slipper V1 Climb up the west face of the boulder.

2. Ruby Traverse V5 Traverse the sloped lip, then up the slab on the north side.

Nathrop Wall

This cliff is located across the Arkansas River from the Nathrop Blocks. You can see it just east of Highway 285 as you turn off the highway onto CR 301. Good problems abound along the base of this quality stone, which has a classic traverse on its west face.

Directions: From Highway 285 south of Buena Vista, continue past the Nathrop Blocks turnoff and take a left on County Road 198. Take CR 198 until it fades right and then later fades left just before the railroad. Continue left for 0.6 mile and park at a pull off across the cliff. Hike across the railroad tracks, following the trail to the base of the wall.

1. Talus Dihedral V0 Climb up the dihedral on the far-left side of the wall.

2. Edgehedral V0 Climb up the right-facing corner just left of the overhang.

3. Nathrop Traverse V4 Traverse the wall from the discontinuous dihedral on the right across the wall to the left.

4. Florescence V0 Climb up the colorful wall right of the broken dihedral.

5. Finger Work V2 Climb the pockets up the right side of the wall left of the fence.

6. Big Slot V0 Climb the slot to the right of *Finger Work*.

58 MOUNT PRINCE-TON BOULDERS

See map on page 472.

The road that leads west along Chalk Creek (County Road 162) has a few worthy bouldering areas. Clean granite blocks with good landings characterize these areas. Mount Princeton is seen to the north and Mount Antero to the south.

Directions: From Highway 285 just south of Nathrop, take CR 162 west. Look for the MOUNT PRINCETON sign—this is the same road you take to access the "fourteener." Some hot springs are also accessed via this road. Drive west past the hot springs and past the chalk cliffs on the right. Park on the right just before Agnes Falls. Agnes Falls is a short 0.5-mile hike north. To find Kiley's Boulder, hike this trail about 0.3 mile and look out on the slope to the left. You will see this large granite block out on the flat section.

Kiley's Boulder ▼

This easy-to-access premium-granite boulder is located on the slope left of the trail that leads up to refreshing Agnes Falls. Problems range from moderate to very difficult. Landings are good.

1. Kiley's Arête V4 Climb up the northeast arête of the block.

2. Bob's Ramp V3 Climb up the ramp system in the middle of the north face.

3. Mirror Slab V6 Climb up the right side of the south face.

4. Alie's Route V0 Climb up the left side of the east face.

5. Katie's Route V1 Climb up the middle of the east face.

6. Mackenzie's Route V0 Climb up the left side of the east face.

Hecta Junction Boulders

This is another popular rafter's campground, but it is also a great spot to access the plentiful boulders along the Arkansas River. If you would like to see the bouldering potential along the river, take a rafting trip and prepare to be amazed. Unfortunately the river is deep and wide in many spots, and a lot of the boulders are on the opposite side from the trails. In-depth planning is crucial in accessing some of these areas.

Directions: From Highway 285 south of Nathrop, drive south until you see the HECTA JUNCTION sign. Turn left (east) onto forest road 194 toward Gaping Station Campground. Follow the winding road around, up, and down into the campground, located on the northwest bank of the Arkansas River. Park and follow the trail southwest along the river and you will soon run into these boulders.

River Wash Rock

This is the first boulder you will see as you hike south down the river.

SAN LUIS VALLEY/MONTE VISTA AREA

The quantity and quality of boulders in the valley make this area a bouldering experience that no boulderer should miss. This area is full of distinguished types of rock, such as the welded tuff rhyolite boulders of Penitente Canyon—a unique rock endogenous to the area. Other boulders, such as Elephant Rocks, are of conglomerate sandstone. Some have crystalline and pebbled faces, while others are composed of hardened sandstone, varnished and baked by wind and sunshine. The Fireball Boulders of Eagle Rock, although untraced for the most part, have the most unique rock type in the whole state. Every square inch of their surfaces is covered with pebbles. Other areas offer granite dropping, such as the boulderfields south of the town of Monte Vista—a definite boulderers' paradise. The panoramic view of the Sangre de Cristo Mountains from wide-open spaces adds to the splendor of this secluded environment.

Directions: From Gunnison, go east on Highway 50 to Highway 114, then go south to Saguache. From Interstate 25 in Pueblo, take Highway 50 west to Poncha Springs, then Highway 285 south to Saguache. From Saguache, drive approximately 17 miles south on Highway 285 and then west on County Road G toward La Garita/Penitente Canyon (look for the signs). CR G will fork to become County Road 41 and County Road 38; veer left (south) on CR 38 to access Penitente Canyon, Eagle Rock, Balloon Ranch, Elephant Rocks, and Hidden Gulch, as well as the Breakfast Boulders.

59 PENITENTE CANYON

The quality rhyolite rock in Penitente Canyon has made this area a Colorado classic. The colorful canyon has a wealth of bouldering along the base of the walls, and there are isolated blocks and boulders scattered amid the canyon floors. Take County Road 38 due west to the parking lot at the mouth of the canyon.

Lot Boulders

This boulder gathering is located 50 feet south of the parking lot. Three domed chunks make up the cluster.

Tiered Dome

This is the far-left of the three.

1. Painting V2 Climb up the north face of the rock.

Pocket Dome

This is the middle of the three.

1. The Arête V2 Climb up the northwest arête, utilizing little pockets.

Arête Dome

This is the far-right of the three.

1. Arête Dome V3 (hb) Climb up the arête on the left side of the north face.

2. The Lot V2 (hb) Climb up the center of the north face.

Picnic Boulder

This rounded, crack-split boulder is located up the trail approximately 200 feet past the picnic tables. There are aspen trees around the boulder.

San Luis Valley/Monte Vista Area Overview

N
Penitente Canyon
TO SAGAUACHE
LA GARITA
41
38
G
670
Eagle Rock
Eagle Mountain 10,462'
E39
38
Balloon Ranch Boulders
59
Fireball Boulders
659
660
285
38A
Elephant Rocks
Shaw Springs
112
Sideshow Canyon
33
660
112
Airport
149
160
DEL NORTE
374
SOUTH FORK
160
14
Hidden Gulch
TO
62
Breakfast Boulders
60
13
160
285
360
Beaver Creek Road
MONTE VISTA
15
Boulder City
61
250

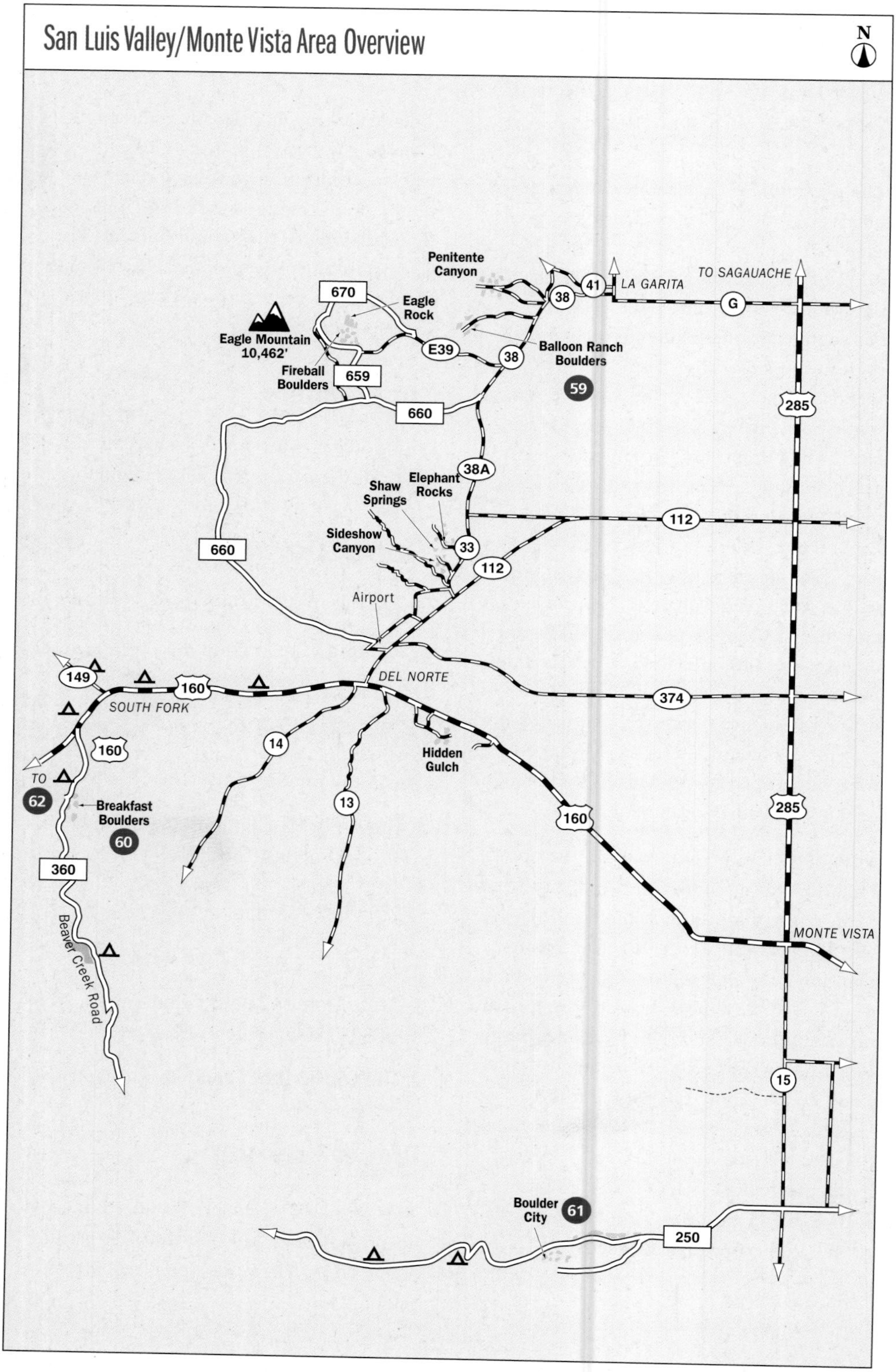

Penitente Canyon

Virgin Painting

To Stokey Boulder

Virgin Block

To Lot Boulders and Parking

1. Round Slab V3 Climb up the slab on the south face.

2. Bulged Slab V0 Climb up the slab just right of *Round Slab*.

Tied Up Boulders

This gathering of rocks is on the left side of the trail that leads to the canyon, in front of the information post.

Triangle Block

This is the far-left block of the gathering.

1. Triangle Crack V0 Climb the crack that makes up the left side of the triangle.

2. Triangle Arête V0 Climb up the arête that makes up the right side of the triangle.

T-Crack Rock

This is the far-right block of the gathering. The crack on the right rises to a horizontal, forming a T.

1. Pocket Face V1 Climb up the left side of the north face.

2. T-Crack V0 Climb up the crack on the right side of the north face.

Trail Rocks

This rock pile is on the left as you hike up the trail, 20 feet beyond the information post.

Easy Slab

This is the easy slab that faces the trail.

1. Easy V0 Climb up the middle of the slab.

Colored Boulder

This colorful boulder is directly behind Easy Slab. Hike upslope.

1. Any Color You Like V1 Climb up the arête on the right side of the overhang.

Virgin Block

This block is up the canyon, down below the famed "Virgin Painting."

1. Virgin No More V1 Climb up the west face from the roof, then up to the left.

2. Pax Slab V0 Climb up the middle of the east face.

3. The Virgin V3 Climb up the northeast face.

Stokey Boulder

This elongated, short boulder is up the trail to the west of Virgin Block, approximately 100 feet to the left of the canyon trail.

1. Cigar V2 Climb up the flake in the center of the south face.

2. The Stokey V1 Climb up the right-side arête of the south face.

Balloon Ranch Boulders

Drive south on CR 38 beyond the Penitente Canyon turnoff, toward Sidewinder Canyon. Look for the SIDEWINDER CANYON sign on the right and take this road west. Drive 2 miles and you will begin to see the boulder-fields; the Balloon Ranch Boulders are ahead approximately 1.5 miles west. The road gets choppy, so be prepared to walk or to use your four-by-four.

Balloon Boulder ▼

This is the prominent rounded boulder with a perfect landing on the front edge of the Balloon Ranch boulderfield. Problems are awesome and clean.

1. Ballooney V1 Climb up the left side of the face.

2. Ball V? Climb up the center of the face.

3. The Balloon V4 Climb up the right side of the west face.

Balloon Dome ▲

This domed boulder is west of Balloon Boulder.

Roof Block

This roofed block sits behind Balloon Boulder to the west.

1. Roof Roof V1 Climb out the center of the roof on the east face.

Fireball Boulders

This rare and unique bouldering area offers a rock type that has unlimited problems and variations. These boulders are covered with crystals and pebbles that range from basketball size to small finger-pinching types. Some of these boulders are as high as 30 feet, while others are one-move summits. Because of the nature of the area, the pebbles can be loose. But once tracked, they become pretty solid.

The boulders appear to have rolled down the hill in a heated volcanic state and collected pebbles and crystals along the way. They came to a rest with the pebbles imbedded on their surface.

Directions: From the Penitente Canyon turnoff, continue approximately 2.8 miles south on CR 38. Turn right on County Road E39, which leads into the Rio Grande National Forest. Follow this road another 2.8 miles, look for the RIO GRANDE sign, and park close to the sign. Hike upslope to the north toward the boulderfield that flows downslope from the Eagle Rock formation.

The Bump

This fun pebbled boulder is seen upslope as you approach the lower end of the boulderfield.

1. Bump Up V0 Climb up the west face.

The Giant

Just up and left of the Bump, this boulder offers good traversing down low.

1. Bearded Traverse V4 Traverse across the west face from right to left.

The Bearded Giant

This boulder is found behind the Giant, up and left of another massive boulder. It has an overhanging underside and a slab that turns steep up top.

1. Giant Traverse V4 Traverse across the west face from left to right.

Paypebble Boulder ▼

This is upslope 150 feet behind and right of the Bearded Giant.

1. Scoop V2 Climb up the scoop on the left side of the west face.

2. Pebbles V2 Climb up left of center.

3. Pebble Mark V1 Climb up the middle of the west face.

4. Pick and Choose V1 Climb up right of center.

5. Paypebble V3 Climb out the bulge on the right side of the west face.

Elephant Rock

This mile-long expanse of boulders strung along the road offers a huge amount of problems with potential for new ones everywhere, especially up the side canyons extending out from the expanse. A few of the areas are mentioned below.

Directions: From the Penitente Canyon turnoff, drive approximately 6.7 miles south on County Road 38 (which turns into County Road 38A then 33) and turn right on Shaw Springs Road. Follow this 0.6 mile and look for the boulderfield downslope from Elephant Rock's southern face.

Shaw Springs

This boulderfield is untouched ground in need of a little traffic. Over time if more people climb on these otherwise useless earth droppings, they may become classic.

Directions: Take the Shaw Springs Road west from CR 33, heading toward the Elephant Rock boulders. Go south on the fourth road to your left. The boulders are seen on the right and left as you head to the cliffs.

Sideshow Canyon

To reach this area, go south on CR 33 past the turn to Elephant Rock and Shaw Springs. About 1 mile past the turn, go right on a road and follow it 0.3 mile into the canyon. The boulders are below a cliff band on the right side of the canyon. It is best to limit bouldering to the lower sections of the walls.

Horizontals Block

This is the far-left block of the gathering.

1. Horizontals V0 Climbs up the left side of the face to the horizontal breaks above.

2. Horizontal Madness V1 Climb up the center of the face.

Open Dihedral Block

1. Open Up V2 (hb) Climb up the bulging face just left of the open book.

2. Open Book V? Climb the open book.

Ultimate Sideshow Boulders

This is another side canyon with plenty of established problems and new ones to be had. To find it, follow the directions for Sideshow Canyon. Drive about 0.2 mile past the Sideshow Canyon boulders and park.

Munge Boulder

Perhaps once mungey before cleaning? This boulder is located 100 feet south of the parking area.

1. Munge V5 From down low, climb up the center of the west face.

2. Little Munge V2 From down low, climb up the right side of the west face.

Freak Show Boulders

From the parking area, hike about 200 feet southwest to the canyon.

1. Explosive Man V3 Climb up the bulge, right of the dihedral on the southwest face.

2. The Grit Spitter V2 (hb) Climb up the slab, just left of the crack.

3. Here Comes Skinny Man V3 (hb) Climb up the center, utilizing pockets on the southwest face.

60 BREAKFAST BOULDERS

See map on page 486.

This area has one really good boulder and then some others. Before the development of other nearby areas, the Breakfast Boulders may have been a safe haven from the spirited kachina winds of the San Luis Valley.

Directions: From South Fork, drive 1.4 miles southwest on Highway 160 and take a left onto Beaver Creek Road. Follow Beaver Creek Road for 2.8 miles, to a left onto the Million Reservoir dirt road. Drive 0.3 mile upslope and park. From the outhouse, hike southwest and then follow the trail south for about five minutes to the boulder.

Breakfast Boulder

This quality granite boulder has many problems.

1. The Big D V5 Climb from the whitened good hold, up the center of the south face.

2. Donkey D V2 Climb up the center of the face from the good rail.

3. Doggy D V3 Climb up the pockets just left of the small tree.

4. Dimensional D V0 Climb up the slab on the southwest face.

5. D's Direct V? Clims the slabby seam on the southwest face.

6. Pilly V1 Climb up to the right of the seam on the southwest face.

61 BOULDER CITY

See map on page 486.

Boulder City is a favorite bouldering area within the state, a true must-visit for any boulderer. There is nothing like driving in an open meadows, coming around a bend, and seeing an expanse of bouldering like you could only dream of. This vast boulder-field is hidden amid the sage and meadow-esque countryside, south of the town of

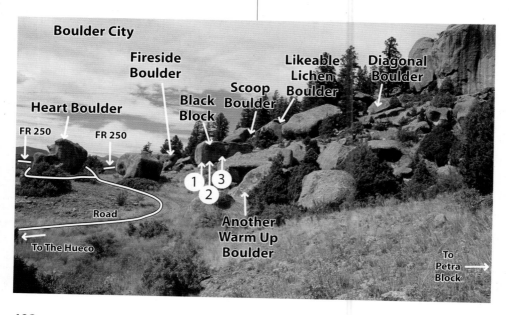

Boulder City

Fireside Boulder

Likeable Lichen Boulder

Diagonal Boulder

Scoop Boulder

Black Block

Heart Boulder

FR 250   FR 250

1 3
2

Road

To The Hueco

Another Warm Up Boulder

To Petra Block

Monte Vista. The numerous granite boulders come in many shapes and sizes, highlighted with a stunning reddish orange glow. Steep faces, classic arêtes, and huecoed and pocketed walls abound throughout this extensive boulderfield.

Directions: From Monte Vista, drive south on Highway 15 out into the open spaces for approximately 12.2 miles, at which point it turns into a dirt road. Turn west onto Forest Road 250. Follow FR 250 approximately 8.3 miles, winding through a small canyon. Take the second road that leads off to the left (south) when you're out of the small rhyolite canyon. This will take you into the heart of the boulderfield.

Heart Boulder Area

Heart Boulder ▼

This huge landmark boulder sits within the first loop on the dirt road. The north face is steep, thin, and crimpy—a challenge to reach its summit. The south side has large huecos with enjoyable moves around them. Park near this boulder and you can access other boulders within the first gathering to the east and north.

1. White Hueco V4 From down low, climb out the whitened hueco on the southeast face.

2. Rebekah V5 (hb) Climb up the black streak on the left side of the north face.

3. Perfect 10 (hb) Climb up the crimps slightly left of center on the steep north face.

4. Perfection V7 Climb across to the right from the underbelly huecos on the left side of the north face and connect to *Perfect 10*.

5. Man in the Moon V3 (hb) Climb the steep micro-edges just right of the center.

Fireside Boulder

Located 30 feet north of Heart Boulder. There is a fire pit close by, which has caused smoke stains.

1. Fire Pit V0 Climb the good-edged face left of the fire pit.

2. Huecoed Pockets V1 Climb up the face just right of the overhang.

3. Kaleidoscope V3 Climb the pockets and arête on the face.

Scoop Boulder

Hike upslope to the north of Heart Boulder to this scooped boulder 150 feet away.

1. Scooper Dooper V3 (hb) Climb up the pockets to the slab on the far-right side of the south-facing scoop.

Likeable Lichen Boulder

This huge boulder is 15 feet east of Scoop Boulder. Exit the north side of the boulder.

1. Likeable Pockets V2 Climb up the slab on the southeast face.

2. Slab Liner V0 Climb up the slab on the east face.

3. Rock Cleaner V3 Climb up the roof on the east face, utilizing the pockets.

Substantial Slab Boulder ▼

This highball-slab boulder is approximately 50 feet upslope to the north of the Likeable Lichen Boulder. Aim for the surrounding big trees.

1. Firball V? Climb the steep west face, utilizing the many pockets.

2. Bunt the Blunt V? (hb) Climb up the prow on the southwest corner via finger holes.

3. Nature Slab V0 (hb) Climb up the airy slab on the left side of the south face.

4. Seemingly Easy V0 (hb) Climb the leaning line behind the big tree.

5. The Slab V0 (hb) Climb the south-facing slab right of the tree.

6. Scary Slab V? (hb) Climb the steep face right of *The Slab* to airy slab above.

7. Slavavert V? Climb up the steep southeast face.

Black Block ◄

This dark block is 50 feet east of Heart Boulder. Several awesome, steep face problems reside on its east side. The landings are flat.

1. Blacky V2 Climb up just right of the southeast arête on the east face.

2. Midnight V1 Climb up a few feet right of *Blacky.*

3. Darkside V? Climb up the sheer face just right of center, left of the hueco.

4. Lightside V2 Climb up the scooped north face.

Another Warm-Up Boulder ▼

This starter boulder is 100 feet east of Black Block.

1. Another One V0 Climb up the left side of the west slab.

2. Another Day V0 Climb up the center of the west slab.

3. New Day V0 Climb up the right side of the west slab.

Shorty Block ▲

This block is near Another Warm-Up Boulder.

1. Shorty V1 Climb up the west face.

Diagonal Boulder

The browned, seam-split boulder is located approximately 200 feet upslope to the east from Another Warm-Up Boulder. Descend across the lichen-covered slab.

1. Low Ball Traverse V3 Traverse across the west face from right to left.

2. Stress V2 Climb up the left side of the west face, before the overhanging section.

3. Whiner V0 Climb up the face right of *Stress.*

Petra Block ▼

This awesome, colorful, cube-shaped block is 100 feet east of Another Warm-Up Boulder. A classic arête resides on its northwest corner.

1. Allesandrina V1 Climb up the classic northwest arête.

2. Hoedown V5 (hb) Climb up the pockets to the right of the northwest arête.

3. Petra V4 Climb up to the pocket in the center of the dark south face.

4. Deflector V3 Climb up the scoop on the right side of the south face.

Road Boulder ▲

This boulder is 30 feet south of Petra Block.

1. Golden Road V6 (hb) Climb up the pocketed west face left of the angling line.

2. Golden Moose V4 (hb) Climb up the west face right of *Golden Road*.

The Hueco Area

This is another extensive area of boulders and blocks down the road from Heart Boulder. Hike or drive 0.3 mile south to this roadside gathering.

The Root Canal ▲

This steep, tooth-shaped boulder is off the roadway to the south, 20 feet in the distance. Descend the roadside route.

1. Triage V2 Climb up the pockets on the west face.

2. Nasty Descent V0 Climb up the flake system on the south face. This is also the descent route.

3. Slab Play V1 Climb up the steep slab on the right side of the south face.

4. Red Face V7 Climb up the far-left side of the east face, right of the southeastern prow, utilizing small pockets to gain the top.

5. Jugs Ahoy V6 Climb up just left of center on the east face, utilizing pockets to big holds up top.

6. Easty V? Climb up the far-right side of the east face, utilizing the arête and pockets.

7. Lolita V4 Climb up from the pocket in the center of the north face.

8. The Pocket V4 Climb up the northwest corner.

Maroon Boulder ▲

This boulder is across the road from the Root Canal.

1. Marooner V1 Climb up the colorful face from a large pocket.

Kia Block

This block is 50 feet north of the Root Canal.

1. Kia V4 Climb up the northwest arête, utilizing the hueco and pockets.

Reverend Boulder

This massive boulder is upslope from the Root Canal. Hike north 300 feet, past large blocks, to this awesome boulder that has airy problems on its northeast face. Descend the left side of the northeast face (V0).

1. Created by God V0 (hb) Climb up the pockets and large in cuts on the far-left side of the northeast face.

2. Loved by All V3 (hb) Climb up the center of the northeast face to pockets.

3. Feared by Satan V5 (hb) Climb from the center and cross to the right, utilizing lay-aways and good holds.

Honeycomb Wall

This honeycombed wall is located 75 feet left of Reverend Boulder.

1. Honeycomb V1 Climb up through the Swiss-cheesed left side of the wall.

Hueco Warm Downs

With the Root Canal as a starting point, hike upslope 200 feet toward the enormous block in front of Reverend Boulder, head slightly to the right, and you will come across this wall full of huecos.

1. Huecos Rancheros V3 Climb up the left side of the face, utilizing pockets.

2. Hueco Benedict V2 Climb up the set of pockets right of *Huecos Rancheros.*

3. Hueco Florentine V2 Climb up the large huecos to single digit pockets right of *Hueco Benedict.*

4. Pockets Bernardo V3 Climb up the set of pockets on the right scooping face, right of the first three problems.

Desirable Block ▼

This awesome-looking block with two black streaks on the left side of its southwest face is downslope from Hueco Warm Downs, 100 feet east of the Root Canal.

1. Desirable Arête V2 Climb up the south-east arête.

2. Desirable Face V0 Climb up the center of the southwest face.

Bishop Boulder

This pointy-top boulder is 75 feet west of the Root Canal and has an overhanging shield on its face.

1. Brown Eye V2 Climb up the west face, utilizing the pod.

Blob Boulder

This blob boulder, with a crack splitting its south face, is 50 feet west of Bishop Boulder.

1. Finger Nail V3 Climb up the crack on the south face.

2. Nails Done V1 Climb up the southeast slab right of the crack.

Another Hueco Boulder

This large, overhanging, huecoed boulder is upslope to the north of Blob Boulder, approximately 100 feet from the Kia Block.

1. White Guilt V4 Climb up the left side of the overhanging west face, utilizing the far-left hueco.

2. Monika V6 (hb) Climb out left from the white hueco to the larger pocket above.

3. The Bathtub V9 Climb out from the low pod up to *Monika*.

Kiddy Block ▲

This block of two close together is 50 feet northwest of Another Hueco Boulder.

1. Kid Rock V0 Climb up the center of the block's north face.

Yasmine's Block

Continue approximately 100 feet north from Another Hueco Boulder and you will see this golden-faced block with arêtes.

1. DYC V3 Climb up the north side's huecoed face.

2. Cliché V4 (hb) Climb up the gold wall on the right side of the north face, left of the classic arête.

3. Yasmine's Arête V5 (hb) Climb up the west-facing classic arête.

4. Excel V0 Climb the pocketed north face.

5. South of the Border V3 Climb up the center of the south face.

62 RIO GRANDE BOULDERS

This huge spread of granite droppings is located along the left and right side of Highway 160, on the east side of Wolf Creek Pass as you head toward South Fork. You can see the granite on the upslope just off the highway, with the majority of the boulders on the left (north) side of the road. There is plenty of camping all along this stretch of highway, west of the town of South Fork. The South Fork of the Rio Grande rages on the south side of the boulderfields.

Directions: From Durango take Highway 160 east toward Pagosa Springs. Continue on Highway 160, past Pagosa Springs, and follow it up Wolf Creek Pass toward South Fork. Drive over the pass, and when you reach the lower highway along the South Fork of the Rio Grande, before reaching the town of South Fork, look for the granite that lines the slopes. Park at any of the day-use areas or campgrounds to access the boulders.

GUNNISON AREA

The bouldering around Gunnison is really quite amazing. How often have us climbers and boulderers cruised past this area only to rush toward the Black Canyon and its majestic wall climbing, or beeline north to Crested Butte's Skyland bouldering area? Well, Gunnison has the Hartman Rocks area just southwest of town. It is a vast land of unique boulder and rock formations that is seemingly endless. One could spend lots of time exploring and finding new gems scattered amid the plentiful boulderfields. There are convenient roads throughout the many areas, creating an easily accessed bouldering experience that should not be missed. Enjoy the panoramic views of the divide.

63 HARTMAN ROCKS

This is a truly classic bouldering area located near the town of Gunnison.

Directions: From the intersection of Highway 50 and Highway 135, go 1.5 miles west on Highway 50 and you will see the HARTMAN ROCKS RECREATION AREA sign. Take a left onto County Road 38 (Gold Basin Road) and follow it as it parallels the airport runways. Continue south approximately 2.4 miles past the runways. Take a right at the HARTMAN ROCKS RECREATION AREA sign to reach the Hurricane Hill Area, the Circle Boulders, the Super Model Area, the Groove Boulders, the White Lightning Area, and Rolly's Area.

To reach Bambi's Boulders and Dominique's Area, don't turn right at the HARTMAN ROCKS RECREATION AREA sign but instead continue on CR 38. See those sections for specific directions.

Hurricane Hill Area

This convenient area offers excellent bouldering close to the car. Turn right off CR 38 onto a dirt road where the HARTMAN ROCKS RECREATION AREA sign points. Head up the steep grade, passing two cattle guards. Just after the second cattle guard, take a right and park in a circular parking area. From here you can access several clusters of boulders. The Circle Boulders are located on the edge of the parking area. The Stash Area is located north down the single track. Hartman's Roof Block is west of the parking area. To reach the Super Model Area, hike downslope to the west onto a road and follow it down and slightly left, skirting a rock formation and continuing around it past a mountain bike sign. Look left and you will see a gathering of pine trees and rocks. This is the Super Model Area. The White Lightning Area is northwest from here.

Circle Boulders

These good warm-up boulders are located within and on the edge of the parking circle.

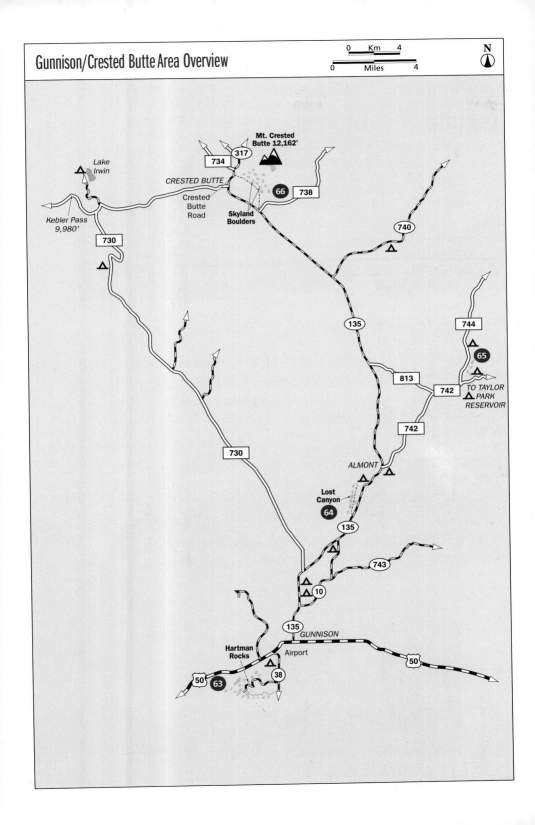

Gunnison/Crested Butte Area Overview

Circle Boulder ▲

This boulder is in the center of the parking circle and offers good warm-up problems on its face,

1. Warm Up V0–V1 Climb a variety of faces on the west face.

Side Boulder ▼

This round boulder is located off the parking area to the northwest.

1. Crack Route V1 Climb the crack up the middle of the south face.

2. Right So V3 Climb the steep slab right of the crack.

Stash Area

This boulderfield is located north of the parking circle and offers many good problems. Hike to the north following the single track for approximately 250 feet.

Super Model Area

The Super Model Area is located by hiking down to the west from the parking area onto a road and following it down and slightly left, skirting a rock formation and continuing around it past a mountain bike sign. Looking left you will see a gathering of pine trees and rocks, the Groove Boulders.

The Groove Boulders

These are the boulders that surround the cluster of pine trees. Three distinct boulders make up this area.

Groove Boulder

This is the easternmost boulder of the three. It has grooves and dikes on its southeast side.

1. Gravy V2 Climb up the west face.

2. Groovy V3 Climb up the pebbles and grooves on the southeast face.

3. The Groove V1 Climb up the dikes and pebbles on the southeast face's right side.

Nameless Boulder

This is the middle boulder of the three. It has a sheer west face.

1. Namelessness V1 Climb up the left side of the west face.

2. Crack Left V? Climb up the center of the west face, left of the crack.

3. Nameless Crack V2 Climb up the right-leaning crack line.

Eric's Boulder

This is the westernmost boulder of the three. It has a low-angle west face.

1. Eric's Vicious Slopers V4 From down low, climb up from the slopers on the east face.

2. West Slab V0 Climb up the center of the west slab.

Super Model Block ▼

This clean, gold- and tan-faced granite block is located west of the smaller boulders surrounding the pine trees. Hike 100 feet due west to this quality chunk.

1. Super Model V5 (hb) Climb up the left side of the north face to the horizontal up top.

2. Model Crack V2 Climb up the leaning crack and flake system in the middle of the north face.

Hartman's Roof Block

This block is about 300 feet west of the parking circle, or north of the Super Model Area. It is characterized by an overhanging roof just off the ground.

1. Hartman's Roof V4 Climb up the roof crack on the boulder.

2. Hartman's Traverse V? Traverse the underbelly from right to left.

White Lightning Area

This fine area is located north of the Super Model Area, or northwest of Hartman's Roof Block. Hike approximately 150 yards northwest from Hartman's Roof Block, through the rock piles. Look for a white-streaked block in the distance from the roof block.

Lightning Block

This block can be seen in the distance northwest of Hartman's Roof Block. It has a distinct white streak on its southeast face.

1. White Lightning V3 (hb) Climb up the center of the southeast face.

Hofnar Block ▼

This overhanging block is to the right and above Lightning Block.

1. Hoof Traverse V? Traverse the underbelly from left to right.

Snail Boulder ▲

This boulder is just right of Hofnar Block and has a short crack on the right.

1. The Snail V1 Climb up the bulging face on the left side of the southeast face.

Rolly's Area

From the parking circle, hike 250 feet south, left of the motocross zone. You can see the backside of Rolly's Block from the parking area.

Rolly's Block ▶

This nice block is split in two by a thin finger crack, and its backside is visible from the parking area.

1. Raleigh's Arête V4 (hb) Climb up the arête on the left side of the south face.

2. ¼″ Master V3 Climb up the crack on the south face.

Rushmore Block ▲

This block is down and around to the south of Rolly's Block and has a scooped-out groove on its southwest face. A face can be seen on the left side of the block.

1. Grand Scoop V2 (hb) Climb up the scooped groove on the right side of the southwest face.

Desert Boulder and Spire ▲

To find these boulders, continue west on the dirt road into the meadow, about 75 yards from Rushmore Block. You can do good but short problems on their north and west sides.

1. Desert West V4 Climb up the center of the west face.

2. Spire North face V1 Climb up the north face of the spire.

Bambi's Boulders

This area has a wealth of good problems on mostly good rock and is easily accessed by driving farther south on Gold Basin Road (CR 38). Drive approximately 2.5 miles from the HARTMAN ROCKS RECREATION AREA sign and turnoff. Drive past a cattle guard and park on the left side. Look for the Bambi trailhead leading west immediately past the cattle guard. Follow the trail along the wired fence line, through an aspen forest, and you will soon see the boulders spread about the slopes. From a small trailside block with a steep face problem on its east side, walk west and you'll see the boulders upslope on the right. The first worthwhile boulder is Mantle Boulder; to reach it, scramble up 50 feet from the trail. To find the other boulders, continue past Mantle Boulder and walk approximately 400 feet west, crossing over slabs and aiming for the upper shelves of rock. This is the main area.

Dominique's Area

To locate this area walk farther west, past the Lilly Boulders. From the boulder carved with LILLY, hike approximately 100 feet west through the wash and then head upslope 150 feet until you reach the prominent blocks.

Mantle Boulder ▲

This is the landmark boulder, which you can see upslope to the west, right of the trail. It has a crack that splits its eastern roof.

1. Hard Mantle V5 Climb up the east face, utilizing face holds and the crack up top.

Lilly Boulders

These boulders surround a boulder that has the name LILLY carved in its side. From Mantle Boulder continue about 175 feet west, past a roofed cliff band with white rock below. Continue until you see the carved-name boulder. Two blocks are upslope beside Lilly Boulder.

Silly Boulder

This is the southernmost boulder of the three, with Lilly being the center boulder.

1. Silly V4 Climb up the west face, finish on the north side.

Dilly Block

This is the northernmost block of the three.

1. Dilly Arête V5 Climb up the leaning south arête.

Handbell Rock ▼

This orange-faced, rounded rock is upslope to the north. It is split by two cracks on its south face.

1. Ding V3 Climb the right side of the south face.

2. Dong V1 Climb up the crack on the left.

3. Ding-Dong V4 Climb up the face and arête between the cracks.

Pinnacle Rock ▲

This rock is about 75 feet west of Handbell Rock.

1. Pinnacled V0 Climb up the left side of the south face.

Dominique Block ▼

1. Whatever Dom Wants V5 Climb up the southwest face, utilizing side pulls to the top.

Dolphin Block ▲

From Lilly's Boulders, locate a single track that heads west. Follow this for 200 yards, toward a prominent block formation in the distance. From the trailhead, head north to the large block that has a crack splitting its southwest face.

1. Porpoise Crack V2 Climb up the crack that splits the southwest face.

64 LOST CANYON

See map on page 503.

This small, sunny cliff of primo Dakota sandstone lends itself to year-round bouldering sessions, as it has quality problems and rock texture. Because it is so close to the road, it has become a great stopping point for the traveling boulderer. The blocky cliff ranges from 8 to 15 feet high and has good landings.

Directions: From Gunnison and the intersection of Highway 50 and Highway 135, drive 7.5 miles north on Highway 135 and you will see this formation upslope on the left side of the road. Park below the sandstone formation on the west side of the road and hike up the trail to the bouldering wall. The trail leads up to the south side of the outcrop.

Pete's Wall ▼

This is a separated section of the wall that you can see from the point where the trail flattens after the steep incline.

1. Pete's Wicked Traverse V5 From the overhang on the far-left side, traverse across the entire face to the right.

2. Extra Stout V2 Climb up the flake to the right of the roof.

3. Average Ale V1 Climb the face several feet right of *Extra Stout,* just right of the right-facing corner in the center of the south face.

The Cave Area ▲

This roofed cave is 75 feet north of Pete's Wall. Problems ascend from the back of the cave from the same point, differing only in the direction you climb out.

1. Atrocity Exhibition V5 Climb out the far-left side of the cave with a long reach to the lip.

2. Unknown Pleasure V4 Climb up and out just right of *Atrocity Exhibition*.

3. The Cave Lap V7 Climb in a rotation around the white rock within the cave.

4. Bob's Dyno Shop V3 This is a dyno problem that utilizes the pockets.

5. Flying High V6 Dyno from the lip to the corner.

The Main Hang ▼

This is an extended section of the main wall with a 200–plus-foot diagonaling traverse. It is located just past the Cave Area.

1. Main Hang Diagonal V? Traverse from right to left, diagonaling ever so upward.

The Web Wall ▲

This lengthy 14-foot section of the Dakota cliff band is located just past the Main Hang.

1. Caught in the Web V4 Traverse the wall from right to left, finish at the slot.

2. Mortimer V1 (hb) Climb the ramp on the far-left side of the south face.

3. Spider Monkey V2 (hb) Climb up the pockets just right of the ramp.

4. The Web V2 (hb) Climb up the left side of the south face just left of a white stripe.

Fat Bottom Wall ▶

This underbelly section of the cliff is located 150 feet north of the Web Wall. It has a prominent prow over the lower roofed section.

1. Rank V5 Climb up small edges to the right of the crack system.

2. Pit Full of Patchouli V4 Climb up the face and prow, to the right of the crack.

3. Fat Bottom Hippie Chicks V3–4 From down low, on the right side of the under-belly, climb up and left to the prow.

4. Stinky V5 Climb from the right side of the underbelly and diagonal across to the prow, finishing up the crack.

Tweaky Wall

This blocky, 15-foot-high cliff is located at the north end of the cliff band. Continue approximately 50 feet north of Fat Bottom Wall.

1. Glory Digger V5 (hb) Climb up the left side of the block, just right of the corner.

2. Celebrated Summer V7 (hb) Climb up right of the corner, finishing to the thin pockets.

3. The Old Timer Arête V0 (hb) Climbs up the browned southeast arête.

The Last Stop

This is at the far-north side of the area, but it is a few feet north of Tweaky Wall.

1. Last Stop V0 Climb up the prow on the south face.

Angler Block

This block is located downslope a short way to the northeast from the northern end of the outcrop.

1. Angler V2 Climb up the right side of the south face.

2. Horsetooth V4 Climb up the middle of the south face.

65 TAYLOR CANYON

See map on page 503.

Known for its multipitch climbs on granite buttresses and great fishing, this canyon also has some nice granite boulders. The main area is located just below Lost Canyon's largest formation, Second Buttress, located near Harmel Resort.

Directions: From Gunnison and Highway 50, take Highway 135 north toward Almont. After 10.2 miles, at Almont, veer right onto Forest Road 742, which leads to Taylor Park Reservoir. Take this road approximately 7.5 miles and then look for the small boulder-field on the left side of the road at the base of the buttresses. The NORTH FORK CAMP-GROUND sign sits in front. Many camp-grounds are located just to the northeast from this point.

The Sugar Cube

This big block sitting at the base of the buttress is characterized by wavy streaks across its south face.

1. Slabs Rule V2 Climb up the sketchy slab on the north face.

2. Average Arête V0 Climb up the flaky arête of the south face.

3. White Grease Streak V0 Climb up the dike on the east face.

4. Out of Bounds V1 Climb up the arête on the right side of the south face.

5. Gloomy V3 Traverse the north face from right to left.

6. Rock Around the Block V5 Traverse around the entire block, eliminating the top.

The UFO

This overhanging block is located a few feet right of the Sugar Cube.

1. The Butter Hole V3 Traverse the face from left to right.

The Slot Block

This gold-faced block sits just 30 feet to the north of the UFO.

1. Snug Slot V4 From a finger lock, climb up the arête on the east face.

2. Something Must Break V4 From down low, climb up from the rock scar.

The Apocalypse Area

This 50-foot traverse wall is at the base of the second buttress. A wooden fence sits in front.

1. Charlie Don't Surf V7 Traverse from the wooden fence to the right, finishing at the slab.

The Pillar

To locate this lengthy spire, hike about 200 feet down North Fork Campground Road. It sits on the left side of the road.

1. Flakes Away V4 (hb) Climb up the slab on the north face.

2. Sampson V7 (hb) Climb up the face to the left of the wide crack, right of the detached flake.

Bonzai Boulder

This boulder is located along the river, down a trail from campsite 8. Hike approximately 0.4 mile to the boulder.

1. Northern One V3 Climb up the north face.

2. Bonzalis V2 Climb up the northwest arête.

3. Samari V6 Climb up the seam on the right side of the north face.

4. Bonzarelli V0 Climbs up the seam right of the tree on the west face.

5. Westward V1 Climb up the slab on the west face.

6. Geronimo V4 Climb up the southwest arête.

7. Bonzai Straight Up V6 Climb up the bulge on the left side of the east face.

8. Bonzai Left V6 Climb up from the left side of the east face up and right, left of the seam.

9. Bonzai Right V5 Climb up the seam on the right side of the east face.

66 CRESTED BUTTE

See map on page 503.

This is one of Colorado's great bouldering areas, with the convenience of the ever-expanding town of Crested Butte just below. Scattered about the west-facing slopes of Mount Crested Butte, these granite gems are some of the best quality the state has to offer. An easily accessed trail winds pleasantly through the aspen groves and meadows, with the boulders appearing in and out of the forest. The number of boulders with excellent problems and landings is astounding.

Directions: From the town of Crested Butte, take Highway 135 approximately 2 miles south and then take a left on Forest Road 738, known locally as Brush Creek Road. Head east to the Skyland Country Club and then take a left at Clubhouse Road. Follow this to the Upper Loop trailhead and park. Hike upslope to the double track that runs to the northwest and continue to the left on the single track. This will lead you northwest to the heart of the boulderfield. You can also access the boulders from the northwest.

5. Berholtz's Arête V6 (hb) Climb up the southeast arête. A direct start goes at V8.

6. Eastward V1 Climb up the scoop to the slab on the east face.

7. Blunt One V5 Climb the northeast prow.

8. Micro Slab V5 Climb up the center of the north slab.

The Shield

This is a huge block with gold and orange colors. It has a pointy left summit. Hike upslope to the east approximately 50 feet from Hone Stone.

1. Clockwork Orange V2 Climb up the left side of the orange rock face on the west side of the block.

2. The Giant V6 (hb) Climb up the face to the right of *Clockwork Orange*.

Zach's Campground

These are the boulders spread throughout the aspen forest east of the Shield. Go explore and have fun.

High Times Block

This 20-foot block is a Colorado gem. It is well endowed with vertical face problems on every side; the east side offers some real classics. Hike about 200 feet south from Hone Stone and you can't miss this perfect bouldering block. Descend the middle of the north face.

1. Machine Head V5 Traverse across the east face from right to left.

2. Left El Skyland V3 (hb) Climb up the classic face on the far-left side of the east face.

Skyland Boulders

Hone Stone ▲

This premier boulder is located in a meadow at the north end of the boulderfield on the west side of the trail. It has a steep, almost river-polished shield on its south face.

1. Bobby's Project V4 Climb up the left side of the southwest slab.

2. Kids Hike V1 Climb up the right side of the southwest slab.

3. Adam's Project V5 Climb up the far-left side of the south face up and onto the slab.

4. Tick Fever V7 (hb) Climb up the center of the shielded south face. A direct start goes at V9.

High Times Block

3. Center El Skyland V4 (hb) Climb up the next classic face a few feet to the right of *Left El Skyland*.

4. The J Crack V5 (hb) Climb up the right-facing corner just right of the center of the east face. Very committing.

5. Right El Skyland V2 (hb) Climb up the classic face and prow on the far-right side of the east face.

6. Casual Comer V1 Climb up the left-facing corner on the north face.

7. Off Ramp V0 Climb up the center of the north face; this is also the descent route.

8. Cheeky Monkey V1 Climb the prow on the west face.

9. Slab Monkey V3 Climb up the slab on the right side of the west face.

Hick Rock ▶

This pointy rock is located within a set of small rocks, 100 feet east of High Times Block.

1. 16 Horsepower V4 Climb up from the far-left side out to the right.

2. Electric Hoedown V5 From down low, climb the prow and arête.

3. Still Feel Gone V4 Climb from the pod up and right through the orange.

The Chunk ▲

This large rounded granite chunk is approximately 50 feet east of Hick Rock. It has an overhanging problem up the chunk.

1. Chunky O V9 Climb up the overhang with tricky side layaways.

Battleship Block ▼

This massive block is just south of Hick Rock, on the left side of the trail. It is surrounded by aspen trees.

1. All Hands on Deck V5 Traverse across the west face from right to left.

2. Anchors Away V2 Climb up the big holds about the wide crack on the south face.

3. Tropic of Capricorn V7 Climb up the right side of the orange, lichen-covered face.

Joint Block ▲

This lengthy 20-foot-tall block is located on the right side of the trail, across from Battleship Block. It has a leaning, overhanging west face.

1. Big 4 V4 (hb) Climb up the northwest arête, staying on the west face for half the climb and exiting to the left onto the north slab.

2. The Long Shot V5 Climb up the left side of the west face, utilizing the arête from down low to a full-on dyno up top.

3. Filth Pig V6 Climb up the southwest arête to the top.

4. Escape Hatch V2 Climb up the right side of the west face, exiting on the south slab.

5. Blunt Boy V1 (hb) Climb up the center of the south face just right of the start of the southwest arête.

6. Mister Twister V2 (hb) Climb up the south face just right of *Blunt Boy*.

The Wedge ▲

This pointy rock is 75 feet east of Battleship Block and Joint Block. There are a few aspen trees nearby.

1. Slab Happy V2 Climb up from the start of the north arête, across to the east arête, then up the slab.

2. Captain EO V3 Climb up the north arête.

Warm-Up Rock ▲

This is the north block of two that are close to one another. This one is on the far-south end of the boulderfield. It has great warm ups.

1. Warm Traverse V2 Traverse the west face from left to right.

2. Mahone V5 Climb up the west face just left of the tree, utilizing the pockets.

3. Hell's Ditch V2 Climb up the left side of the south face through the black stripe.

4. Micro V1 Climb up the south face just right of *Hell's Ditch*.

Spice Rock

This is the south block of the two.

1. Spicy V5 Traverse across the east face to the south face.

The Wave ▼

This beautiful 12-foot block is approximately 200 feet upslope through the aspen trees, east of Warm-Up Rock. There are a few aspen trees up against its west face.

1. Slab Master of the Universe V2 Climb up the left side of the west face just right of an aspen tree.

2. Slabs Kick Ass V2 Climb up the center of the west face.

3. Jagged V0 Traverse the lip of the block from the far right, up and left.

GRAND JUNCTION AREA

Grand Junction has some great bouldering areas. In addition to those described below, there is a boulderfield below the dirt-pile buttes that line the north side of Interstate 70 as you head west from New Castle toward Grand Junction. These boulders are known as the Palisade and Frankenblocks. They have a few problems that offer a good break from the car lag.

Directions: From I-70 heading west there is a FOOD, GAS, LODGING sign just after the Palisade exit sign (exit 42). Look north and you will see the blocks sitting among the dry flats.

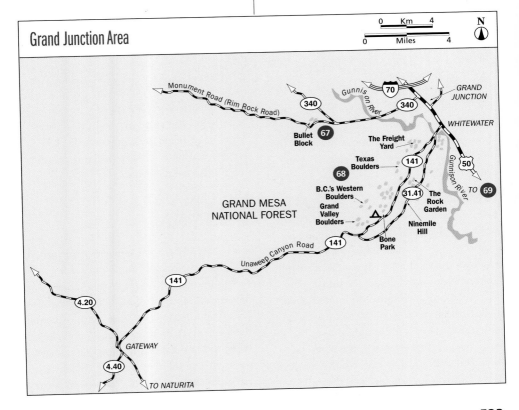

Grand Junction Area

The author on *Varnish Face* (V5), Unaweep Canyon.

67 COLORADO NATIONAL MONUMENT

The bouldering within the monument has had little or no information published about it, but there is a famous block on the outer east side on the north side of Rim Rock Road.

Directions: From just west of the center of Grand Junction, exit I-70 onto Highway 6/50 (exit 26) and follow it back approximately 6 miles southeast. Turn right onto Highway 340 and head approximately 1 mile southwest toward Colorado National Monument to a left onto Monument Road. Follow Monument Road approximately 2 miles to a pullout on the right side of the road. Toward the ridgetop you will see the large Bullet Block. The ridge to the north has a number of good blocks and can be reached by hiking the old road upslope to the corner of the ridge way.

Bullet Block

This solitaire erratic is located within a wash below the ridge on the north side of Monument Road. It is a massive block with good soft sandstone. There are anchors on top for the lengthier lines.

68 UNAWEEP CANYON

This soft Dakota sandstone refuge is loaded with quality boulders and blocks that even the whiniest boulderer will find satisfactory. The areas are easy to access along a 9-mile stretch of Highway 141 just south of Grand Junction. Steep faces, overhanging pocketed walls, and vertical and leaning arêtes characterize this boulderer's getaway. The desert environment makes this a wonderful winter area, and the sandy ground makes for great landings. Camping is also available on some of the more secluded pullouts. Be prepared to find new problems along with the wealth of already established licks. All areas are worth a visit, but B.C.'s Western Boulders and the Grand Valley Boulders have become the most popular due to their excellent quality.

Directions: Take I-70 to Grand Junction and exit south onto Highway 50, toward Whitewater. From Whitewater, turn right (southwest) onto Highway 141 (Unaweep Canyon Road). Follow Highway 141 approximately 1.2 miles and you will reach the first area, known as the Freight Yard, followed by the Bat Cave, the Rock Shop, Texas Boulders, Varnish Area, the Rock Garden, Bone Park, B.C.'s Western Boulders, Grand Valley Boulders, and finally Liquor Store Block. The areas fall within a 7-mile stretch from the Freight Yard to the Liquor Store Block. Specifics are given with each area description.

The Freight Yard

This area is approximately 1.2 miles southwest from the intersection of Highway 50 and Highway 141. At 1.2 miles, head left (south) on a dirt road and park beyond the cement factory. Hike 150 feet south on the road, past a fence and then upslope 100 feet on a boulderer's trail that leads east. Look for a large, extensive, undercut west-facing block at a high point on the western slope.

Superchief Expanse

This large, extensive undercut block sits up at a high point on the western slope. Quality problems are located along its 40-foot expanse, with excellent flat landing zones.

1. Tiers Away V4 From down low, climb out the pockets on the left side of the underbelly, right of the twisted juniper tree on the west face.

2. The Bubble V4 From down low, climb up to the right of *Tiers Away,* starting on the bulbous layaway to the pockets above.

3. Super Supper V5 Climb up the center of the west face, utilizing finger pockets.

4. Super Eliminate V8 Climb up the center of the west face, eliminating the pockets.

5. Supper V5 Climb up the right side of the west face, utilizing the pockets.

The Engine Wall

This small cliff is located downslope west of Superchief Expanse. It has a traverse across its base.

1. West Side Traverse V6 Traverse the base of the west face from left to right, starting slightly left of the big knobs.

The Caboose Wall

This small cliff is just downslope from the Engine Wall and has similar features.

1. West One V6 Traverse the west base from left to right.

2. East One V0 Traverse the east base of the wall.

The Bat Cave

This caved section of the ridge is located 0.1 mile up the road from the Freight Yard. Continue west on Highway 141 for 0.1 mile from the Freight Yard turnoff. Park before the bridge on the right side of the road and hike up and over the fence line. Follow the trail, staying to the left, eventually connecting to a groomed trail that leads up to the ridge-line. You can see the Bat Cave overhang along the trail as it peaks.

1. Bat Traverse V5 Traverse across the overhanging west face from right to left.

2. Chips are Down V6 Climb out the right side of the roof.

Junior Cave Boulder

This bulging boulder is 20 feet to the right of the Bat Cave.

1. Junior V6 Traverse across the west base.

The Slum Block

From the Bat Cave continue along the trail to the next ridge, approximately 150 yards south. Hike downslope to the left on a faint trail that leads toward a few large boulders. The Slum Block is behind this first set of large boulders. The block forms a cove-like area.

1. Slumbuldigulion V7 Traverse across the right side of the coved overhang from right to left.

Texas Boulders

This boulder- and block-filled area, with its landmark massive block in the shape of the Lone Star State, is located another 2 miles up the road from the Bat Cave area. Take a right onto the dirt road just beyond the cattle guard. Drive slightly downslope and park along the creek bed. From the parking area, hike 200 yards northeast up and across until you see the massive block shaped like Texas. The boulders are located around this center-piece. There are bolts at its summit for toproping the tall face routes.

Anchor Block ▲

This lengthy block is located just southwest of the Texas boulder. It has an edge-filled south face. Descend from the east side.

1. Anchor Steam V0 (hb) Climb up the good holds on the left side of the south face.

2. Anchors Away V1 (hb) Climb up the lengthy center of the south face.

3. Conrad V0 (hb) Climb up the right side of the south face.

Horizontal Crack Boulder ▼

This fun boulder is west of Anchor Block.

1. Horizontal Bop V4 Climb up the left side of the east face, utilizing the prow.

2. Horizontals V3 Climb up the pockets on the right side of the east face.

Corridor Block ▲

This block is north of Horizontal Crack Boulder. Walk approximately 100 feet through the narrow squeeze or around to the left. Look for the west-facing block with a prow. This is the far-left side of this extensive block.

1. Corridor Arête V3 (hb) Climb up the northwest arête.

2. Shady West V3 (hb) Climb up to the right of the arête.

3. Corridor Crack V0 (hb) Climb up the crack system to the right of *Shady West*.

4. Sunnyside V0 Climb up the far-right side of the block to the south outside the corridor.

Cancel Christmas Block

From the parking area for Texas Boulders, hike southwest up the dirt road, staying to your right. After about 300 feet, beyond the wood-laden wash, cut upslope to the west for approximately 200 feet and look south for the block at the edge of the open field.

1. Cancel Christmas V6 (hb) Climb up the right side of the pocketed west face.

2. The Grinch V3 (hb) Climb up the lengthy center of the west face.

3. Whoville V3 Climb up the east face left of the center, utilizing the good pockets.

4. Xmas V4 Climb up the pockets in the center of the east face.

5. Vmas V3 Climb up right of center left of the tree, utilizing the pockets.

To Shaft Rock
(5 minutes)

Half Dome
Boulder

To Iron Block
(5 minutes)
and Texas Boulders
(20 minutes)

Varnish Area

To find this area hike down the dirt road to
the west from the Texas Boulders area (past
the Cancel Christmas Block) for about ten to
fifteen minutes. After a meadow you will see
the varnished boulders up on the right, followed by other rocks along the road.

Iron Block ▶

This is on the right side of the road, at the
base of the slope. It looks like an iron.

1. Iron Arête V2 Climb the southwest arête.

Half Dome Boulder ▲

This rounded varnished boulder sits within the first rise in the slope, across and north of the meadow.

1. Regular Route V5 Climb up the middle of the south face.

Shaft Rock ▶

This protruding pinnacle is up the road and west of the meadow. It is a free-standing pil-lar on the right side of the road.

1. Shaft V2 Climb the southwest corner of the pillar.

The Rock Garden

This boulderfield is located on the left (southeast) side of Highway 141. Drive west on Highway 141 from the Texas Boulders turnoff for 1 mile and park on the left-hand pull off just before the smiley face painted on the rock. Hike down the dirt road that cuts back to the east off the main road.

Faces Boulder

This classic boulder is on the right (south) side of the dirt road as you hike from the parking area. It is a lengthy boulder with a classic south face.

1. Two Face V3 (hb) Climb up the center of the south face.

2. Face the Arête V1 Climb up the south-eastern arête.

Cheesy Arête Block ▲

This block is upslope approximately 50 yards south of Faces Boulder.

1. Cheesy Arête Left V3 Climb up the left side of the arête.

2. Big Cheese V5 Climb up the right side of the arête.

3. Cheese V0 Climb up the center of the east slab.

Gash Block

This block is 100 yards south of Faces Boulder. It has a classic layback problem on the left side of its east face. Another large block leans against its cap.

1. Gasher Sends V2 Climb up the layback system on the far-left side of the east face.

Deception Block

This small ramped block is up the road from Faces Boulder. It sits on the right side of the road.

1. Deceiver V4 From down low climb out the overhang on the south face.

Orange Crush Rock

Hike another 200 yards down the dirt road from Deception Block and you will see this illuminating rock on the right. It has a colorful and black-striped north face.

1. The Crush V4 Climb up the black stripe in the center of the north face.

2. Orangina V2 Climb up the pocketed north face just right of the center.

Broken Boulder

Continue beyond Orange Crush Rock to a meadowed area. Look on the left edge of the flat and you will see this big boulder sitting independent of the others. Problems exist on three sides.

1. Broken Arrow V2 (hb) Climb up the far-left side of the south face, right of the arête.

2. Broken Corner V2 (hb) Climb up the center of the south face, utilizing the small corner.

3. Broker V1 (hb) Climb up the far-right side of the south face.

4. The Ramp V0 Climb up the right-side ramp on the east face.

5. Token V2 Climb up the northeast arête.

6. Spoken V3 Climb up the left side of the north face, utilizing the layaways.

7. Joken Arête V2 Climb up the arête on the right side of the north face.

Colored Block

Continue down the road another 150 feet past Broken Boulder. Look on the left side of the road for a beautifully colored block.

1. Colorful Paths V2 Climb up the center of the east face.

2. Coloring V0 Climb up the right side of the east face.

Striped Block

To find this orange-striped block continue farther down the road approximately 200 feet from Colored Block. Look on the left side of the road for this striped block.

1. Candy Striper V1 Climb up just left of center on the east face.

2. Striper V1 Climb up the far-right side of the east face just left of the corner.

3. Burnt Orange V2 Climb up the northeast prow's right side.

4. Stars and Stripes V7 Climb up the center of the crimpy north face.

Pole Block

This stubby block is 100 feet beyond Striped Block. Look for it on the right side of the dirt road.

1. Pogo Stick V1 Climb up the southeast arête's left side.

2. Pole Vault V3 Climb up the southeast arête's right side.

3. White Pole V0 Climb up the center of the east face, slightly left of the white stripe.

Bone Park

To find this prime camping and bouldering spot drive up Highway 141 another 0.7 mile from the Rock Garden. Turn right (north) onto the dirt road and circle and look for the prominent, almost limestone-looking boulder sitting on the right side of the circle. This is Fossil Block, named for its bone fossil on the east face. This is also the parking and camping area for B.C.'s Western Boulders, where you'll find the sought-out Upper Boulderfield.

Fossil Block

The lengthy cubed block is on the right side of the circle, close to the road. Look for the fossil on the east side.

1. Fossil Dihedral V1 Climb up the dihedral system on the south face.

2. Fossil Haul V0 Climb up the center of the east face, utilizing its good holds.

3. Fossil Traverse V5 Traverse around and across the entire block.

Victoria's Secret Boulder

This hidden boulder is approximately 200 feet northwest of Fossil Block. The overhanging northwest face has good problems.

1. Victoria V2 Climb up the left side of the northwest face.

2. Seduction V3 (hb) Climb up from the fire ring on the northwest side.

3. Kinky V5 From down low, climb up the left side of the west overhang.

4. Ted's V3 Climb up and right of *Kinky*.

Plethora Boulder

This block, off the right side of Highway 141, is located 200 feet west of Fossil Block. It has a nice southeast underbelly with good problems.

1. Work It V6 Climb up via a dyno from down low to the lip on the far-left side of the southeast face.

2. Caught in a Zipper V6 Climb up the line just left of the center of the southeast face.

3. Head Way V5 Climb up the right side of the southeast face.

4. Southeast Groove V4 Climb up to the groove from the start of *Head Way.*

5. Underdyno V4 Dyno up from the under-cling pinch slightly right of the arête.

6. Plethora Traverse V5 Traverse across the east face from right to left.

7. The Pud V5 Climb up through holes to the arête.

Gonad Block

This round, steep, and smooth-faced block is just left of Plethora Boulder.

1. By the Balls V0 Climb up the pocket problem just left of the center of the south-east face.

2. Balls of Fire V4 Climb up the seam right of the center on the southeast face.

3. Balls and Chain V5 Traverse across the southeast face from right to left.

B.C.'s Western Boulders

This field of boulders and blocks is located on the west side of the creek. Hike southwest from the Fossil Block parking area, following the cairns along the wash to the creek. Cross the creek and follow the boulderer's trail to the cow trail crossing. Head left 300 feet and you will see Artifact Boulder, capped with a huge roof on its south side.

Artifact Boulder

This roofed boulder is a cow's den, and it stinks.

Big Black Block

Follow the cairned trail another 100 yards west from Artifact Boulder and you will see this isolated block with an intriguing north face.

1. Dark V3 Climb up the face left of the crack line.

2. Dark Crack V0 Climb up the crack on the right side of the face.

3. Grande Arête V0 (hb) Climb up the quality, classic arête on the left side of the north face.

4. Horizontal Black V2 (hb) Climb up the left side of the north face just right of the arête.

Hole in One Boulder ▲

This lengthy rectangular block is upslope from the east side of the road, approximately 0.8 mile from Bone Park. Park on the left side of the road and hike upslope approximately 100 feet to this bright reddish orange block.

1. The Cyclopes V3 (hb) Climb up the right-hand arête and face of the south face, utilizing the unipod.

Brain Boulder

To find this boulder drive southwest on Highway 141 for 2.1 miles from Bone Park. Park on the right and hike 100 feet along the dirt road until you see this brain-looking boulder.

1. Psycho Boy V6 Dyno from the pocket undercling, just right of the center of the southwest face, up for the lip.

Bucket Cave Rock

This massive rock, with an awesome over-hanging northwest face, is located 100 feet downslope to the west of Brain Boulder.

1. Hell in a Bucket V3 Climb the buckets out the left side of the northwest overhang.

2. Bucket Brigade V5 Climb out smaller holds right of *Hell in a Bucket*.

3. Soaped Out Bucket V4 Traverse across the northwest overhang.

4. Bozo Buckets V4 From down low, climb up and right on the south face.

The Black Wave Area

This is an extension of Brain Boulder and is located south of it. Hike 175 yards toward and beyond the distant ridge, keeping to the west side of Highway 141. Look for the bright red block and the dark black block.

Big Red Block

You can see this massive red block with black streaks as you approach from the ridgeline.

1. Big Red V4 (hb) Climb up the black-streaked northwest face, left of the tree.

Black Wave Boulder

This black-faced boulder is 30 feet southwest of Big Red Block.

1. Black Wave V4 Climb up the left side of the east face, from the crack to the tree top.

Blacked Out Boulder

Of all the boulders in this area, this large one is closest to the highway, approximately 60 feet southwest of Black Wave Boulder. It has a plus sign (+) in the center of the east face.

1. Dizzy V1 Climb up the left side of the east face.

2. Spells V2 Climb up the face just left of the center.

3. The Count V3 Climb up just right of the center from the micropinch, up and left.

4. Out of It V1 Climb the right side of the east face, right of the nip.

Grand Valley Boulders

From Bone Park, drive southwest on Highway 141 another 3.1 miles and park in the large pullout on the right side of the road. Look for the GRAND VALLEY OVERLOOK sign. The boulders are just west of the parking area. across the creek. Hike beyond the creek and then take the dirt road approximately 200 feet west. The rock texture is of great quality, and the location is within a reasonable distance from the car.

Chinese Algebra Boulder

This boulder is located along the side of the dirt road and has a thick white streak on the left side of the northeast face.

1. Equate V1 Climb up the left side of the northeast face.

2. Minus V2 Climb the face just left of the thick white streak on the northeast face.

3. Chinese Algebra V6 From down low, climb up the left side of the west face and then mantle off.

4. Plus V3 Climb out the right side of the overhanging west face.

5. Multiple V1 Climb up the brown, far-left side of the south face.

S Crack Block

This lengthy orange block is 100 feet north of Chinese Algebra Boulder. Junipers sit behind and to the right of the block.

1. Playground V0 (hb) Climb up the center slab of the south face.

2. Prowground V2 (hb) Climb up the southeast prow.

3. S Crack V1 (hb) Climb up the S crack on the southeast face.

4. S Seam V3 (hb) Climb up the line to the right of the S crack.

5. S Traverse V1 Traverse across the northeast face, then up.

Box Car Block

This polished block has a caved southeast side. To find the block, hike upslope approximately 100 feet north of Chinese Algebra Boulder. A nice flat slab sits in front of the southeast face.

1. The Slot V6 (hb) Climb up from the cave on the left side of the southeast face, then up to the top.

2. Avoidance V4 (hb) Climb up the face on the far-right side of the cave.

3. Boulder Pad V3 (hb) Climb up the center line of the southeast face from the boulder.

4. Seems Thin V4 (hb) Climb the thin line to the right of *Boulder Pad*.

5. Box Carête V0 Climb up the arête on the right side of the southeast face.

6. Racing the Sun V2 Climb up from the pyramid on the left side of the north face.

Arête Boulder

To find this boulder with an arête, hike upslope 100 feet west of Box Car Block.

1. Left Arête V3 (hb) Climb the left arête of the southeast face.

2. Hueco Way V4 Climb up from the hueco to a lengthy reach for the top.

3. Invisible Sun V6 (hb) Climb up the leaning line, utilizing the crimps.

4. Right Arête V3 Climb up the right arête of the southeast face.

5. Arête Slab V0 Climb up the center of the east face.

Pink Floyd Boulder

This large boulder is located northwest across the meadow from Arête Boulder. From Arête Boulder, hike approximately 300 feet northwest, toward the cliffs, and cross the meadow.

1. The Machine V3 Climb up the thin line on left side of the south face right of the branches.

2. Earthbound Misfit V3 (hb) Climb the pocket in the center of the south face.

3. Summagumma V7 Climb the thin face just right of *Earthbound Misfit*.

4. Comfortably Numb V6 Climb the thin line up the blackened section of the right side of the south face.

5. Pinky V0 Climb up the middle of the east face.

Liquor Store Block

This is another lengthy block located across the road from the Grand Valley Boulders pull off. Hike across the road to the dirt road and hike upslope 200 feet to this block with a horizontal handrail across its north face.

1. Liquor Up V6 Traverse across the north face from left to right.

2. Latina Heat V5 (hb) Climb up the bulging left side of the north face.

3. Beer Run V3 (hb) Climb up the face right of *Latina Heat*.

The Tavern Boulder

This boulder is just right of Liquor Store Block.

1. Tavern V3 Climb up the arête.

69 BLACK CANYON

The bouldering in Black Canyon of the Gunnison National Park is limited along the rim, but it is plentiful down deep into the gorge. If you do happen to be near the Painted Wall Overlook on the south rim of this awesome canyon, you might want to check out these boulders. Four solid granite blocks with cracks, steep faces, and slab problems characterize the bouldering here.

Directions: From Montrose take Highway 50 approximately 10 miles east and go left (north) onto Highway 347. Take Highway 347 about 5.5 miles to the south rim entrance station. A fee is collected here. From the entrance station, drive west another 5.2 miles and park at the Painted Wall Overlook. From the parking area, hike 175 yards west up the road, past a curve in the road. Continue down the trail approximately 150 feet to the granite blocks.

Marmot Blocks

Ivory Block

This is the first block you will see on the left as you approach the blocks. It is the second largest of the four, yet it is wider than the larger Serpentine Block. You can see two other smaller blocks in line to the left of Ivory Block.

1. Tan Line V3 Climb up just left of the center of the north face, utilizing the white holds.

2. Ivory V3 (hb) Climb up the lengthy center of the north face, utilizing the layaways.

3. Neon V2 Climb up the leaning flake on the far-right side of the north face.

4. Fluorescent V1 Climb up the northwest arête.

5. Light Crack V0 Climb up the right-hand crack, on the left side of the south face.

6. Lightning V2 Climb up the face just right of the right crack on the south face.

Paint Bucket Block

This corridor-forming block is just left (east) of Ivory Block. Descend to the northeast.

1. The Brush V0 Climb up the slab on the left side of the northeast face.

2. Easel V1 Climb up the northwest prow up and right from the horizontal break down low.

3. Oils V2 Climb up the southwest arête from the south face.

4. Acrylic V3 Climb up the crack on the left side of the east face.

Linquin Block

This is the left most of the three in a line, just east of Paint Bucket Block and forming another corridor between the two.

1. Canvas V1 Climbs up the small holds on the left side of the west face.

2. Gesso V2 Climbs up the southwestern prow moving left up top.

Serpentine Block

This is the larger, elongated block with a letter V formed by two cracks on its north face. Good problems abound on this choice granite. You can't take sandstone for granite.

1. Left Line V0 Climb up the left line forming the V on the north face.

2. Right Line V0 (hb) Climb up the lengthy right line forming the V.

3. Isadry V2 Climb up the far-right side of the north face just left of the prow.

4. Splitter V0 (hb) Climb up the dihedral crack just right of center on the west face.

5. Snakes V3 Climb up the far-right slab of the west face.

6. Temptation Crack V2 Climb up the steep, southwest line.

7. Stoner V1 Climb the face left of the off-width on the south face.

8. Dragon V1 Climb up the thin face right of the off-width.

9. Sea V0 Climb up the slab right of the center on the south face.

NORWOOD / NATURITA AREA

70 NORWOOD

Most of the bouldering around Norwood is located north of town at the Riverview Boulders and the Sandborn Park Boulders. These areas offer good problems on Dakota sandstone. There is also some bouldering southeast of town along the San Miguel River.

The Cove Boulders

The Cove Boulders are north of Placerville (south of Norwood) along Highway 145. You can see good Dakota sandstone amid the trees just off the road. The Specie Creek Boulder is across the highway from the Cove Boulders.

Directions: From the intersection of Highway 62 and Highway 145 in Placerville, drive approximately 3.5 miles north on Highway 145. Park on the dirt road on the right side of the highway, just past Specie Creek Road. Hike to the boulders seen in the distance.

Cove Cube

This cubed block of Dakota is northwest of the dirt road.

1. Cube Edge V3 Climb up the face and arête on the left side of the west face.

2. Waved Face V4 Climb up the right side of the face.

Riverview Boulders

These Dakota sandstone boulders offer good bouldering and toproping above and below the road.

Directions: From Norwood, go south on Highway 145 and locate the Norwood Bridge. Hang a left onto Forest Road 510 (Sandborn Park Road). You can see the Riverview Boulders on the left side of the dirt road after driving 4 miles from the Norwood Bridge. Hike up the faint road to the boulders.

Sandborn Park Boulders

These Dakota boulders are up the road a mile from the Riverview Boulders (5 miles from the Norwood Bridge) and offer good problems. Park at the cattle guard, where the

Norwood/Naturita Area Overview

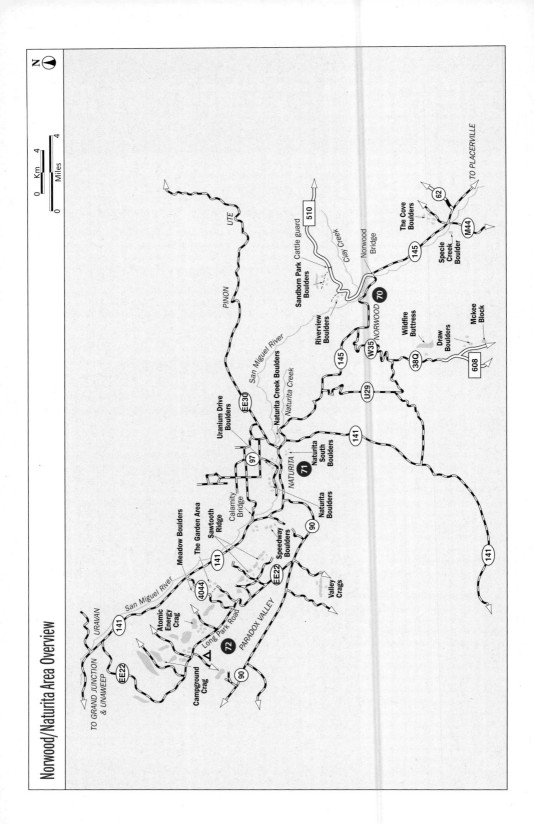

Adam Horan on *The Sickle* (VO), Box Car Block, Durango Area.

road tops out, and hike toward the boulder-laced cliff band in the distance.

McKee Draw Boulders

These Dakota sandstone boulders are located south of Norwood.

Directions: From east of Norwood on Highway 145, go southwest on County Road AA42, then south on County Road W35, to a left on County Road 38Q. This turns into Forest Road 608 at the McKee Draw. After a short way, veer left and you will see the Draw Boulders below the road on the left. The McKee Block is just up next to the road.

McKee Block

This block is next to the road and is distinguished by an overhanging mast on its end.

71 NATURITA

Excellent bouldering surrounds the town of Naturita. The town offers all the accommodations you'll ever need, so stop and enjoy a little bouldering. Four main areas are worthy of note.

The Naturita Creek Boulders are north of Highway 141, where the road takes a turn toward Naturita Creek (east of Naturita).

The Naturita South Boulders are on the slopes south of town. Park at the pullout just east of town and hike up the faint road to a large boulder in the distance.

The Uranium Drive Boulders (where the Uranium Drive-In once stood) are across from the water tower as well as on either side of County Road 97.

And, finally, the Naturita Boulders—the best of the whole crop—are located upslope from Forest Road 26, 1 mile northwest of the town center.

Naturita Boulders

To find this awesome scattering of Dakota sandstone from downtown Naturita, go north on CR 97 and drive a short way to a left onto County Road FF26. Drive 0.5 mile on CR FF26 and park at the pull off. Hike to the north, then west to the varnished boulders.

Speedway Boulders

To find these Dakota sandstone boulders from Naturita, drive northwest on Highway 141. Just past Highway 90, take a left and park on the faint dirt road. The boulders are on the slopes above the west side of the highway. Walk 200 yards up the faint road and then follow the trail into the wash.

Meadow Boulders

This secluded area has good Dakota sandstone boulders along a dirt road. The quality boulders are north of the road. From Naturita take Highway 141 approximately 4.8 miles northwest, past Calamity Bridge and the north end of CR 97, until you see County Road 4044 veering to the west and then south. If you stay on CR 4044, it will connect with County Road EE22 near the Bitter Creek area. Boulders are everywhere you look and four-wheel drive is mandatory.

72 PARADOX VALLEY/ LONG PARK ROAD

This wonderland of rock is another favorite and is well worth several visits. Its landscape is similar in uplift tectonics to the Fort Collins and Carter Lake region. Small cliff bands exposed to the west offer endless boulders and blocks. The vast area has had a lot of exploration but is still full of new and potential challenges. A lifetime of potential exists here. The mild climate of the western slope allows for bouldering at Paradox Valley year-round. This is an isolated place to bring friends and have a good time.

Directions: There are two ways to get here. It is possible to continue south on Highway 141 from Unaweep Canyon (the rival, yet way smaller area). Drive about 90 miles south through the badlands, past the Shamrock Mines, and take a right on an obscure winding road approximately a mile before you get to Uravan. Look for access to County Road EE22, which takes you to the far-northwest side of Long Park Road.

To get here from Naturita, take Highway 141 west to Highway 90. Follow Highway 90 to the southwest eventually curving around to the northwest. Continue northwest along Highway 90 for several miles to a right-hand turn onto County Road EE22, also known as Long Park Road (this turn is about 5.2 miles from the intersection of Highway 141 and Highway 90). The dirt road eventually leads upslope to this wonderland of boulders. Areas along the way include the Lost World, accessed up CR EE22 at 1.7 miles from Highway 90; Adam's Block at 2.2 miles; the Bitter Edge Area at 4.1 miles; the Garden Area at 4.3 miles; and the Atomic Energy Boulders and Campground Boulders at approximately 5.8 miles.

Paradox Valley/Long Park Road

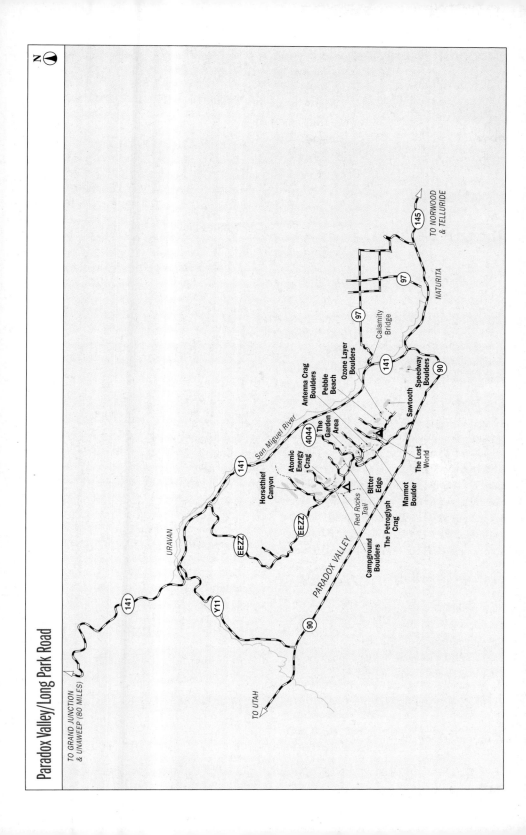

Sawtooth Ridge Area

This is the spiny ridge of rock first seen on the right (northeast) side of CR EE22 as you begin the upgrade road. The Sawtooth itself is thought to be the far-southeast end of the ridge. The other sections of the ridge to the northwest contain the Ozone Layer Boulders, Pebble Beach, and the Lost World at the far-left (northwest) end.

The Lost World

This area is below the Lost World rock formation. This is a rougher rock zone than others up the valley, but the challenges are such that it warrants a visit. A lot of the boulders and blocks are not as well traveled as those in other areas. A whole spread of potential exists here; the upper slopes have really seen little traffic.

Directions: For the Lost World, Pebble Beach, and the Ozone Layer Boulders (all part of the Sawtooth Ridge Area), turn right off Highway 90 about 1.7 miles from Highway 141 and drive the dirt road, staying to the right at a split. The Lost World is on the left. Continue down the road to the southeast and you will see Pebble Beach, followed by the Ozone Layer Boulders. A faint road leads up to the southeast ends of each of the areas.

Camp Boulder

This pullout, camping-area boulder is located on the southeast end of the mesa, east along the ridgeline, just off the road. The south side has fun problems, and the east and west sides are more slabby.

1. The Fee V2 Climb up the center of the south face.

2. Green Greeny V0 Climb up the right side of the south face.

3. East Inn V? Climb up the center of the west face.

4. Beginner's Mind V0 Climb up the center of the east face.

Pebble Block

This pebble-filled block is 100 feet northeast of Camp Boulder. It has a characteristic whiteness.

1. Pebbles Way V0 Climb up the pebbles and pockets on the left side of the west face.

2. Pebble's Hold V1 Climb the good pebbles up the center of the west face.

3. East Pebble V1 Climb up the left side of the east face, utilizing pinches.

Arrow Block

This cube is located 60 feet south of Pebble Block. Look for the graffiti (a downward-facing red arrow) on the south face.

1. The Bow V0 Climb up the pebbles and slabs on the west face.

2. Bomb V3 Climb up the southwest arête.

3. The Beam V2 Climb up the center of the south side.

4. The Wafer V2 Climb up the left side of the east face to the flake above.

5. Smoothie V1 Climb the pebbles up the right side of the east face.

Big Mouth Boulder

This stumpy, hole-filled boulder is approximately 50 feet west of Arrow Block.

1. No Holes Barred V2 From down low, climb up from the left of the big hole to the top of the east face.

2. Middleman V1 Climb up the east face from a point between the two big holes.

Pebble Beach

This area has good quality, pebble-filled boulders and is located just south of the Lost World.

Ozone Layer Boulders

This quality bouldering is found on the next mesa to the southeast of the Lost World and Pebble Beach, the third mesa of the four. Look for the varnished boulders and hike a short 200 feet to the heart of the field. Many sheer to overhanging problems exist.

Cut and Dry Boulder

You will encounter this overhanging boulder as you head east from the parking area.

1. Dry Arête V0 Climb the prow up and right on the southwest face.

2. Feign V3 From down low, climb up the left side of the overhanging east face.

3. Tame V1 Climb the pockets and holes on the right side of the overhanging east face.

4. Cut Arête V0 Climb up the right side of the northeast arête.

5. Same Arête V1 Climb up the southwest arête.

Lacerate Block

This streaked dome block is just right (east) of Cut and Dry Boulder. It has a lengthy, slabby west face.

1. Scary Slab V? (hb) Climb up the center of the west slab.

Waves Boulder

This roofed boulder is upslope to the north of Cut and Dry Boulder. Hike upslope 100 feet to the rippled west face.

1. Retribution V4 Traverse from down low across the horizontal rail on the north overhang.

2. Boogie Board V0 Climb up the left side of the west side.

3. Snorkel V0 Climb through the center of the west side.

Single-Minded Boulder

This rounded, oval-shaped boulder is 30 feet west of Waves Boulder.

1. Juniper V1 Climb up the scoop near the juniper tree on the south face.

2. Lout V2 From down low, climb out the east face's overhanging scoop.

Lip Boulder

Hike upslope to the north from Single-Minded Boulder and you will see this overhanging boulder.

1. White Lipped V4 Traverse across the southwest face from left to right.

Cracked Block

This splitter block is 50 feet southeast of Waves Boulder. Hike to the overhanging splitter off-width on the north face.

1. Ridiculous Man V2 Traverse across the lip, starting at the northeast prow.

2. A Single Moment V2 Dyno to the top of the north face, from the face just right of the wide crack.

Adam's Block ▲

This nice overhanging block of quality sandstone streaked with orange and black is just back from the right side of the road, approximately 2.2 miles from the start at CR EE22 and Highway 90 (0.5 mile from the Lost World turnoff).

1. Tailgate Party V7 Climb up the northwest arête.

2. Cooler V6 Climb up the middle of the west face.

3. Soda V5 Climb up the southwest arête.

Antenna Crag Boulders

This huge bouldering slope is full of potential and has a lot of variety to offer. It is the first mesa, with more to follow.

Marmot Boulder

This large boulder is just off the right side of the road out below the Antenna Crag Boulders. You will find good beginner bouldering and toproping here.

The Bitter Edge/Brain Area

This premier area is covered with solid varnished boulders and blocks, scattered about the slopes below the ridge cap. Drive approximately 4.1 miles from the beginning of CR EE22, up past the Antenna Crag Boulders. Take a right on a faint road and park on the southeast side of the ridgeline. Look up to the ridgeline and you will see the quality varnished stone scattered below. Hike up to the heart.

Steam Shovel Block ▲

This prominent block with a pocketed west face is upslope within the pack.

1. Pick Pocket V2 Climb the pockets on the right side of the west face.

Pumpkin Boulder ▶

This round, pocketed, and huecoed boulder is just right of Steam Shovel Block. A large tree stands behind it.

1. Hueco Reach V3 Climb the face to the huecos in the middle of the west face.

Fire Rock ▲

This rock with a pointy top is farther east within the pack.

1. Fire V1 Climb up the center of the west face.

Fire Cube ▲

This rock is just east of Fire Rock. It has a steep south face with good problems.

1. Retire V4 Climb up the middle of the south face.

Torch Block ▶

Continue up toward the ridgeline and you will see this pillar.

1. Flame Broiled V1 Climb the southwest arête.

2. Sizzle V4 Climb the southeast arête.

Brain Boulder

To find this boulder with wavy brain-gyro-looking ripples, hike up to the ridgeline and locate a corridor just south of Torch Block. Brain Boulder is seen on the west wall of the corridor.

1. The Brain V6 Climb up the bulging face through a heel-hooking hueco to the slopers above.

Bitter South Area

This area is south of the main Bitter Edge Area and offers a softer, pebble-lined rock that is lighter in color and texture. Continue south down the road from Torch Block to the next boulder pack, park, and walk out to the east.

Pierced Boulder ▲

This large, soft sandstone boulder has a hole through its middle. The hole is small and frames a face when you loook through it. Hike through the boulders to the east wash and you will see this boulder.

1. Piercing V5 Climb up the center overhang of the east face. Start in the hole for extra difficulty.

2. Side Mouth V6 Climb out the right side of the east overhang.

Pastel Boulder ▼

This colorful crystalline boulder is west of Pierced Boulder. It offers steep pebble climbing on its west face.

1. Pastel Pebble V2 Climb up the middle of the west face.

2. Holey Moley V2 Climb up to the hole (pod) on the right side of the west face.

The Garden Area

This area has pine groves surrounding its boulders and blocks. The scent on a mild day is a refreshing change from the drier areas to the south. The north-facing boulderfield is loaded with rocks that are full of every hold imaginable, especially the many huecoed faces. Don't miss the Couch. The landings are equally good.

Directions: From the intersection of Highway 90 and County Road EE22, drive 4.3 miles (0.2 mile past the Bitter Edge), past the mine on the left. Take a right onto County Road 4044 and drive 0.3 mile to the hilltop. Park and then hike upslope approximately 250 yards to the north side, up the faded twin tracks. At the base of the north ridge, hike 250 feet east, past a detached block, and look for the Couch. This classic is a huecoed block that sits just off the north ridge.

The Couch

This classic block offers incredible overhanging hueco problems with a perfect landing. Descend from the south side.

1. Bulge in the Couch V3 (hb) Climb up the left-side bulges of the east overhang.

2. Perfect Couch V2 (hb) Climb up left of the overhanging northeast prow, starting in a horizontal break, up to and through the huecos.

3. Couch Potato V2 Climb up right of the northeast prow, utilizing the huecos above.

4. Tan and Gold V4 Climb up the center of the northeast face through the tan and gold rock.

5. Relax Traverse V5 Traverse across the northeast face, utilizing the huecos from right to left.

Camping Boulders

These boulders are on the right (east) side of the road just before the turnoff for the Atomic Energy Boulders and the campground. They are east of the campground.

Bomb Boulder ▼

This boulder is just off the road to the right before you reach the main access road to the heart of the Atomic Energy Boulders.

1. The Bomb V2 Climb up the huecos on the west face.

2. Bombs Away V0 Climb up the ledge system in the middle of the south face.

Dismantle Block ▲

This fine block is east of Bomb Boulder. Good landings abound.

1. Concrete Caves V2 Climb up the middle of the south face.

Love and Peace Block ▶

This block with an arête is north of Dismantle Block and offers a classic steep arête.

1. Love and Peace V4 Climb the northeast arête of the block.

2. Daughters of Zion V5 Climb the steep south face.

There is plenty of potential for new problems, and a lot of recent problems are sought out. Wander the wonderland; pick and choose your line. Look for the quality boulders and blocks with good landings spread about the western slopes of the Atomic Energy Crag. A good place to camp is south of the crag, with awesome bouldering near camp.

Directions: This area is 5.8 miles north from the intersection of Highway 90 and CR EE22. Look for the dirt road on the right-hand side. There is a big boulder sitting across the road on the left. Park off CR EE22 and walk down the road to a fork. The first quality blocks are sitting in between the right and left fork, 250 yards up the road.

Arrowhead ▲

This steep arrowhead-shaped rock is north of Love and Peace Block.

1. Bow V3 Climb up the middle of the north face.

Atomic Energy Boulders

This massive scattering of boulders offers quality rock with mostly good landings.

Between Blocks

These cubed blocks are approximately 500 feet up the dirt road and sit within the fork in the road. The left-hand block is Sugar Cube and the other is Varnished Block.

Sugar Cube

This is the boulder that sits along the left fork, to the left of Varnished Block. It is a lengthy, white, cube-shaped block.

1. Pocket Top V3 Climb up the steep, right side of the north face, utilizing the finger pockets up high.

2. White Wash V2 Climb up the center of the west face right of the right-facing corner.

Atomic Energy Crag

Atomic Energy Boulders

Between Blocks

CR EE22

3. Whitey V1 Climb up the southwest prow.

4. White Trash V3 Climb up the leaning arête on the left side of the south face.

5. Lilly V0 Climb up the slab in the center of the south face.

6. Trailer Trash V1 Climb up the right side of the south face left of the arête.

Varnished Block

This elongated, orange-varnished block sits along the right fork, to the right of Sugar Cube.

1. Burnt Orange V3 Climb up the finger pockets on the right side of the north face.

2. Clock Work V3 Climb up just left of center, left of the thin line on the northwest face.

3. Tootsie Pop V0 Climb up from the roof on the west face.

The Righteous Boulders

These are two independent rocks. Kings Boulder, which is more like a pinnacle, is on the right side of the road. Shield Block, which is more of a block, is on the left side of the road. At Between Blocks, take the right fork and then hike another 150 feet until you see these rocks sitting on both sides of the road, across from each other.

Kings Boulder

This orange-faced, lengthy north-facing boulder is on the right side of the road.

1. Kingline V1 Climb up the big holds on the left side of the north face.

2. Dreamsicle V1 Climb up the center of the north face.

3. Juice V0 Climb up the flake system on the far-right side of the north face.

Shield Block

This cube is on the left side of the road across from Kings Boulder.

1. SW Arête V1 Climb up the southwest arête, from the west side.

2. Shielded V0 Climb up the center of the south face.

3. Finland V2 From down low, climb up the layaway southeast arête.

4. SE Arête V3 Climb up the southeast arête from the east face.

5. Central Pods V? Climb up the center of the east face from the pockets.

6. Leaner V2 Climb up the leaning northwest arête.

Neighborly Block ▼

This block is just east of Shield Block.

1. Howdy V0 Climb up the center of the west face.

TELLURIDE AREA

This famous mountain town is located in the southwest corner of Colorado. Amazing amounts of bouldering exist here, some that is yet to be tapped. The bouldering areas described here are all easy to get to along roads that require very little hiking. The untapped bouldering is found at higher, more obscure elevations, where granite comes clean as a whistle. The Ilium Boulders is a great place to get a pump at a lower elevation.

Directions: Locate Highway 145 in the southwest corner of the state. This highway is Telluride's main access road; it leads southeast through the valley to the town. This is also the way out of town, unless you want to do some extreme four-wheeling over the pass to the east. On the way in from the northwest, stop at the Ilium Boulders before you drive into Telluride. The Mine Boulder, with its pebble and crystalline face, is at the far-west end of town on the way to the falls.

73 ILIUM BOULDERS

These quality sandstone boulders and blocks are a pleasant surprise. Most of the problems are a perfect bouldering height, with very few highballs. Landings are equally as good. This is an almost velvet-like sandstone area dropped into a meadow amid the variety of trees. It is also one of the best kid bouldering areas on the west side. Prepare for fun cracks, faces, overhangs, and slabs.

Directions: On the way into Telluride, going southeast on Highway 145 along the San Miguel River, drive approximately 1 mile past Lime and turn south (just before the long incline toward Telluride) onto a side road (County Road 625) that leads down west and then south. Take this road approximately 1.5 miles past a big boulder and then park on the right. Cross the road and head 300 feet up-slope on a trail that will eventually lead you from the south end of the boulderfield across to the north end. The boulders almost parallel the sloped meadow and the tree line.

Lego Block (Sun Block)

This block is located at the south end of the boulderfield. Its cubed and varnished shape is a welcomed site. Descend to the east face.

1. Blocks V4 Climb up the center of the west face.

2. Snap V2 From down low, climb up the overhanging crack through the southwest prow.

3. Legoland V0 Climb up the center of the south face.

Telluride Area Overview

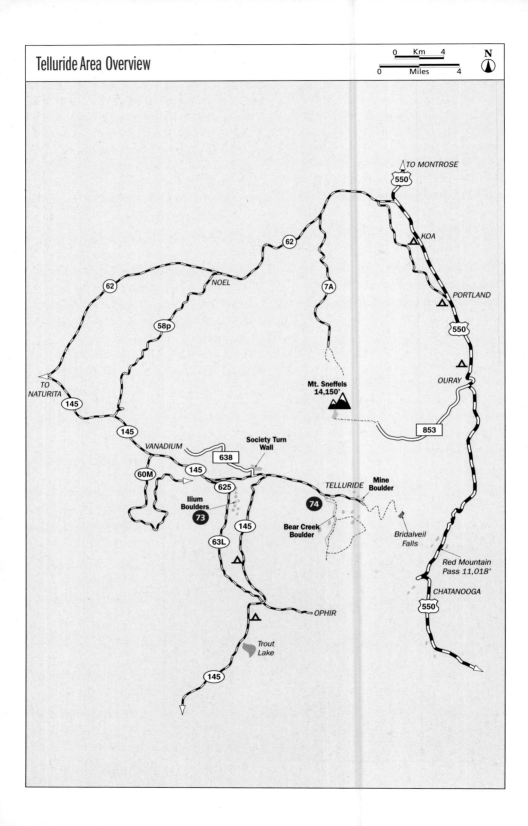

0 Km 4
0 Miles 4

N

TO MONTROSE
550

KOA

PORTLAND

550

62

NOEL

62

58p

7A

TO
NATURITA

145

145

Mt. Sneffels
14,150'

OURAY

853

VANADIUM

Society Turn
Wall

638

60M

145

625

Ilium
Boulders

73

145

63L

TELLURIDE

Mine
Boulder

74

Bear Creek
Boulder

Bridalveil
Falls

Red Mountain
Pass 11,018'

CHATANOOGA

550

OPHIR

Trout
Lake

145

4. Legs Go V3 Traverse the south wall, right to left, across to the west face.

5. Support V0 Climb up the middle of the east face.

6. Cracked V1 Climb up the thin line on the north face.

7. Pressure V1 Climb the thin holds to the right of the seam, left of the trees.

Stack Boulders (Eggs) ▼

These two boulders lean against each other to form one concentrated bouldering area. Hike approximately 100 feet north from Lego Block and you will run into these blocks.

1. File V0 Climb up the middle of the easternmost boulder's west face.

2. Low Down V2 From down low, climb up the southeast arête of the east boulder.

3. Pocket Way V0 Climb from the pockets on the northwest face of the westernmost boulder.

4. Fingers V3 Traverse from the south side to the west side of the westernmost boulder.

5. Bow Arête V0 Climb up the southeastern arête of the west boulder.

Leaning Block ▲

This pillared block is north of Stack Boulders. Hike another 100 feet north along the trail. A trail from the road leads straight up to this block.

1. Pillar Ramp V0 Climb up the ramped southwest corner.

2. Lean Jean V4 Climb up the left side of the south face, utilizing the southwest arête.

6. Sam's V1 Climb the thin line on the left side of the east face.

7. Herb's V5 Traverse from right to left across the east face.

8. Triangles V1 Climb up the northeast prow.

9. Al's V3 From down low, climb up and out the overhang left of the north face crack.

10. Mel's V? Climb up the steep crack on the north face.

The Tank (Premier Boulder) ▲

This large block is approximately 100 feet north of Leaning Block. It has a splitter crack on its south side.

1. Huecoed V0 Climb up the huecos on the left side of the west face left of the corner.

2. Dish V2 Climb the slab on the west face.

3. Squat V3 From down low, climb up the arête on the right side of the west face.

4. Wide Eyed V0 Climb the off-width that splits the south face.

5. Casual V0 Climb the slab on the south face to the right of the off-width.

Sub Block ▼

This orange and black block is located upslope, southeast of the Tank. Hike upslope 100 feet until you reach this lengthy block.

1. Zig Zag V2 Traverse the west face across, up, and across again.

2. Lower V2 From down low, climb up the left side of the south face.

Pocket Block

This pocketed block is approximately 100 feet beyond Sub Block to the southeast.

1. Diagonal Pockets V2 Climb across the pockets and up the west face.

2. East Slab V0 Climb up the center of the east face.

Cube Block ▼

This cube-shaped block is 30 feet north of the Tank.

1. Aero V2 From down low, climb up the southwest face.

2. Aerobic V1 Climb from the south face around and up the southwest face.

3. Cubed Traverse V4 Traverse the entire block; no top holds.

4. North Slab V0 Climb up the center of the north face.

Pylon Block ◄

This pillar block is located 10 feet north of Cube Block. It has a splitter crack up its southwest face.

1. Northette V1 Climb up the left side of the north face, utilizing the arête.

2. No North V2 Climb up the right side of the north face, utilizing the underclings.

3. Pilon Crack V2 Climb the steep southwest-facing splitter crack.

4. Opposition V3 Climb up the south face, avoiding the flake.

5. Flakes a Lot V1 Climb up the flake system on the south face.

Jug Boulder ▼

This large-holds boulder is located just north of Pylon Block.

1. Juggy Traverse V1 Traverse the southeast face.

Gray Slab

This slab is at the far-north end of the Ilium boulderfield.

1. Gray Slab V0 Climb up the center of the west face.

Dueling Arêtes Block ▼

This stumpy block is located downslope, below Gray Slab.

1. Aerial Arêtes V0 Climb up the arêtes.

.74 BRIDALVEIL FALLS AREA/MINE BOULDER

See map on page 556.

This area has good boulders with pebbled walls, including Mine Boulder, just off the road on the way to the Bridalveil Falls trailhead. The panorama is spectacular, and the granite boulders in the distance call for a visit. The many pebbles imbedded in these boulders allow for multiple variations.

Directions: From downtown Telluride, follow the main street east out of town to the gravel road. On the left you will see the Pandora Mill and parking area shortly thereafter. Park and walk up the road, curving around to the left then right. Mine Boulder is hard to miss, as it sits in clear view of the gravel road.

Mine Boulder ▲

1. Black Gold V0 Climb up the thick black stripe in the middle of the southwest face, utilizing and pinching the pebbles.

2. Butch V0 Climb up just right of center on the southwest face, utilizing the pockets and large pebbles.

3. Sundance V0 Climb up the undercling face just left of the southwest corner.

4. Pandora's Box V2 Climb up the left side of the south face, right of the prow.

5. Hightail V4 Climb up the pebbles right of *Pandora's Box.*

6. Hole in the Wall Gang V2 Climb up from the hole, then left, on the south face.

7. The Kid V2 Climb up the pebbled face just right of the hole.

8. Gamblin' Man V2 Climb up the right side of the south face.

9. The Loot V5 Traverse from right to left across the south side.

Bear Creek Boulder

This large boulder is along the hiking trail that follows Bear Creek. In downtown Telluride, park at the end of Pine Street and hike approximately 2 miles south along the Bear Creek Trail. The massive boulder is on the side of the trail.

Wasatch Boulder

This boulder is approximately 2 miles from Bear Creek Boulder. Hike past Bear Creek Boulder up the Wasatch Trail and you will see this boulder.

DURANGO AREA

75 DURANGO

Although best known for its mountain biking, the foothills surrounding the town of Durango offer some good bouldering on solid sandstone. The Turtle Lake Boulders area is conveniently located just off the road and offers great roof, face, and crack problems. The Box Car Block is one of the nicest massive blocks of Dakota sandstone found anywhere in the state.

Box Car Block

This massive, beautifully colored block is located just up and behind the Centura Medical Center. Made of Dakota sandstone, it offers extended classics and traverses on its east side, with a less-lengthy south side. This is a block you might hope to find along the sandy shoreline at Horsetooth Reservoir.

Directions: Heading north on Highway 550 from downtown Durango, turn left at the Centura Medical Center. Park in the lot on the south end of the medical center. Hike along a trail that leads north across the hillside and you will see the massive block in the trees.

1. The Sickle V0 Climb across the flake system up and right on the left side of the south face.

2. Durango Kid V2 (hb) Climb up from the hole in the center of the south face.

3. Durango Durango V2 Traverse from right to left across the south face.

4. By the Highballs V4 (hb) Climb up the steep southeast prow.

5. Captain's Corner V3 (hb) Climb up the prominent, overhanging, right-facing corner on the left side of the east face.

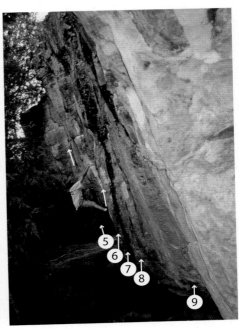

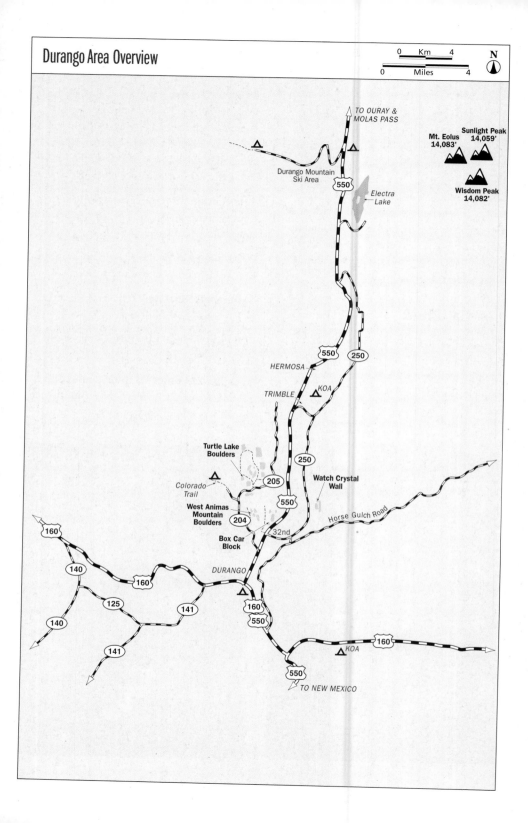

Durango Area Overview

TO OURAY &
MOLAS PASS

Durango Mountain
Ski Area

550

Electra
Lake

Mt. Eolus
14,083'

Sunlight Peak
14,059'

Wisdom Peak
14,082'

550   250

HERMOSA

TRIMBLE   KOA

Turtle Lake
Boulders

205

250

Colorado
Trail

West Animas
Mountain
Boulders

204

Watch Crystal
Wall

550

Box Car
Block

32nd

Horse Gulch Road

160

140

160

DURANGO

125

141

160

550

140

141

KOA

160

550

TO NEW MEXICO

6. Chris's Flake V3 (hb) Climb up the flake system right of *Captain's Corner's* corner on the east face.

7. Rock and Company V3 (hb) Climb up the steep face to the left of the black stripe.

8. Crock and Company V2 (hb) Climb up the sheer face right of the black-striped block.

9. BH Arête V4 Climb up the leaning northeast arête to the dicey top out.

West Animas Mountain Boulders

This extensive area is located on the western slopes of Animas Mountain. A good amount of keen trail hiking is needed to find these somewhat hidden and secluded boulderfields, which are scattered below small cliff bands to the west and northwest of the Animus Mountain summit.

Directions: This area is on the way to the Turtle Lake Boulders. From downtown Durango, drive north to a left on Twenty-fifth Street. Follow this northwest and it will become Junction Creek Road (County Road 204). Drive approximately 1.5 miles and take a right into the subdivision, continuing to the dead end, and park. Locate the trailhead for the west side of Animus Mountain and hike north 2 miles.

Turtle Lake Boulders

These quality sandstone boulders offer an awesome variety of face, crack, arête, and overhanging challenges. They are easy to get

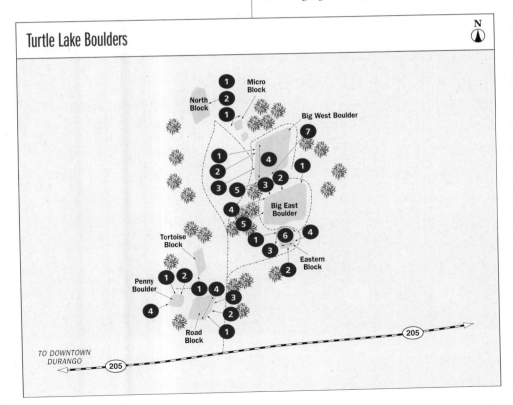

Turtle Lake Boulders

N

to by driving and parking across the road from them.

Directions: Head north out of downtown Durango and turn left on Twenty-fifth Street, which turns into Junction Creek Road (CR 204). Follow this northwest approximately 3 miles and turn right onto County Road 205. Drive past the lakes on the right approximately 1 mile and park at a pull off on the right. The first boulder is just off the road, on the opposite side of the parking area. Hike across the road and up the trail and you will run across the boulders amid the scrub oak thicket.

Road Block ▼

This white block of sandstone, although it looks almost like limestone, is located just off the road a few feet up the trail on the left. You can see more boulders from beyond this block.

1. Tie Dihedral V0 Climb up the southeast dihedral.

2. Pod Cast V2 Climb up the left side of the east face, right of the dihedral, utilizing the pebbles from the hole.

3. Yellow Jacket V2 From down low, climb up the horizontals on the right side of the east face.

4. Terrapin Traverse V3 Traverse the east face from right to left.

5. Pocket Pool V1 Climb up the pockets on the north face.

Penny Boulder

This gold nugget is located 20 feet west of Road Block.

1. Your Thought V1 Climb up the left side of the north face.

2. Ante V1 Climb up the north prow in the center of the north face.

3. Touch of Gray V0 Climb up the slab on the right side of the north face.

4. Diagonals V1 Climb up the left side of the west face.

Tortoise Block

This block is 30 feet north of Road Block. It is surrounded by a few insignificant rocks.

1. The Tortoise V4 From down low, climb up the southwest arête and layback system.

Eastern Block

This stumpy block is located northeast of Road Block. Hike north 30 feet up the trail and go right on a trail that leads east through the thicket. The block is 75 feet due east. A big boulder, Big East, can be seen just north of this small block.

1. Brick Arête V2 From down low, climb up the layaway northwest arête.

2. The Wall V3 Dyno up the center of the south face, utilizing the underclings.

3. Heroes V4 Traverse right to left across the south face.

4. Easy-East V0 Climb up the middle of the east face.

5. No North V0 Climb up the center of the north face.

6. Philosophy Traverse V5 Traverse around the entire block.

Big East Boulder ▼

This huge boulder is just north of Eastern Block and offers good challenges on its faces. An even larger boulder, Big West Boulder, is to the northwest. Descend south. Many other projects exist here along this steep highball wall.

1. Big Up V6 (hb) Climb up the far-left side of the north face.

2. Extension V6 (hb) Climb up the center of the north face.

3. Big and Bad V3 Climb up the right side of the north face, left of the prow.

4. Big Prow V2 (hb) Climb up the northwest prow from the west face.

5. Big Easy V0 Climb up the thin line in the center of the west face.

6. Little Easy V0 Climb up the middle of the south face.

7. Project Ahoy V? Climb up the center of the east face.

Big West Boulder ▼

This is the largest boulder of the lot and has problems on all sides. It is just northwest of Big East Boulder.

1. Upper D V1 (hb) Climb the off-width on the left side of the west face.

2. Grande V3 (hb) Climb up the steep face right of the off-width.

3. Elevation Thin V6 (hb) Climb up the thin-edged face right of *Grande,* right of the center of the west face.

4. Western One V4 Traverse the west face from right to left.

5. Fade Away V4 Climb up the southwest prow.

6. Beckon the Call V8 From down low, climb up the thin overhanging face, right of *Fade Away.*

7. The Wonder V4 Climb up and out the overhanging right side of the overhanging section of the southeast face.

8. Angler V0 (hb) Climb up the slab on the right side of the south face.

9. Heeler Traverse V4 Traverse across the big holds on the left side of the southeast face.

10. Gray Beard V0 (hb) Climb the highball ramp system on the east face.

11. Scooped Again V2 (hb) Climb the scooped section in the center of the east face.

12. Slot Shot V1 (hb) Climb up from the slot just right of the scoop.

13. Downlow V6 From down low, climb up the northeast arête.

14. Holy Moley V2 From down low, climb up from the hole on the far-right side of the north face.

Micro Block

This small block is just northwest of Big West Boulder. Another rock sits between it and Big West Boulder.

1. Micro Huge V2 Traverse the block from the north face across to the left, finishing at the southwest corner.

North Block

This block is northwest of Big West Boulder, or 100 feet due north of Road Block. Hike the path to the northwest from Big West Boulder or take the left path from Road Block. The block is characterized by a varnished northeast side.

1. Pearly Gold V1 Climb up the gold and white southeast face just left of the prow.

2. Golden Year V0 Climb up right of the southeast prow.

3. Right On V0 Climb up just right of center on the northeast face.

INDEX

ABOUT THE AUTHOR

Boulder, Colorado, resident Bob Horan has climbed for over thirty-five years. As a teenager he climbed the Grand and Middle Tetons in Wyoming and El Capitan and Half Dome in Yosemite Valley. He has established hundreds of new routes and boulder problems in the Boulder area and throughout the state, pushing standards with such climbs as the first free ascent of the *Rainbow Wall* (Eldorado Canyon's first 5.13) as well as *Beware the Future* (5.14) in the Flatirons. He believes the skills he developed bouldering allowed him to push free-climbing standards on longer routes. He has also dabbled in competition climbing, placing second in the Masters category at the first annual Horsetooth Hang, third in the Men's Elite division at the first National Climbing Competition in Washington, D.C., and second in the Men's Speed Climbing at the first Continental Climbing Championships. Horan has published numerous photographs and articles in various climbing magazines, and he has authored some of the first bouldering guidebooks ever written. At the University of Colorado in Boulder he graduated magna cum laude in psychology and completed an honors thesis in behavioral neuroscience. His children—now in high school—have enjoyed bouldering with their dad throughout Colorado.